Educating Noah...Travelin'

Second of the Two

Noah

Copyright © 2024
All Rights Reserved
ISBN:
978-1-917116-61-9

Dedication

To my true and fantastic best friend and wife for over 60 years, Lynn, who backed me up and accompanied me on this life's journey!

Acknowledgment

To my true and fantastic best friend, who backed me up and accompanied me on this life's journey.

CONTENTS

Dedication ii
Acknowledgment iii
About the Author x
Preface xiii
2018 Finish The World 2018   01/03-03/15 2018 January 1
January 3rd, the first day 1
Day four, Oranjestad, Aruba 3
On day five, we are at Willemstad, Curacao. 4
Day Six 5
Day seven 6
Day eight St. George, Grenada 7
Day nine, Kingstown, St. Vincent 8
Day 10 9
Day 11, (January 13th) Bridgetown, Barbados 9
Day 12, Scarborough, Trinidad 10
Day 13, Monday 01-15-18 10
Day 14, Tuesday 01-16-18 11
Day 15, January 17th 11
Day 16, January 18th 11
Day 17, Friday the 19th 13
Saturday the 20th of January, Day 18 14
Sunday, day 19, another day at sea 15
Monday, Day 20 15
Tuesday, January 23rd, Day 21, crossing the Atlantic. 17
Wednesday, the 24th of January, Day 22 17
Thursday, January 25th, the 23rd day on the cruise 19
Sunday, the 28th 21
Tuesday, the 30th 26

Wednesday, 31st of January, Sao Tome 26
February 1st, a day at sea. 28
Friday, the second day at sea 29
Saturday, this is the last day at sea before another port, February 3rd.
.... 29
Sunday, February 4th, Walvis Bay, Namibia 30
Monday, February 5th, the second day of Walvis Day 33
Tuesday, February 6th, this is the last day at sea before Cape Town, South Africa. 34
Wednesday 02-07 35
Thursday 02-08-19 37
Friday, 02-09-18, ... 38
Tuesday, Feb 13th 47
Wednesday, February 14, Valentine's Day. 49
Thursday, February 15th, ... 51
Friday, February 16th, 2018 52
Friday, February 23rd, a day at sea, heading west. 59
Monday the 26th, a day at sea. 63
Tuesday, 2/27/18 at sea. 64
Wednesday, February 28th 65
March 1, 2018. Male, Maldives 66
Friday 03-02-18 67
Saturday, March 3rd, Mangalore, India 69
Sunday, March 4th, Cochin, India 71
03-05-18, Monday 74
Tuesday, March 6th 75
Wednesday, March 7th, ... 76
Thursday, March 8th 78
Friday, March 9th 79
Saturday, 9th of March 81
March 14th, we should arrive in Singapore by 10:00, ... 90

Thursday the 15th of March	93
British Isles Holiday, May 2018	97
It is Friday the 25th before the Memorial Day weekend	97
Sunday, beat the 06:00	99
Monday, After Memorial Day weekend	103
Thursday, the 31st of May	106
Day ten	115
Tuesday, 06/05/18	117
Alaska II	125
Monday, the 17th of September	125
Day 2 at sea	126
Day 3, partly cloudy, low 50s, the air is crisp, light breeze.	127
Day 4	129
Day 5, Skagway, Alaska	131
Day 6, at sea, Hubbard Glacier viewing just after noon	133
Friday 13th, Black cats, white cats, walking under ladders…	135
Day 7 Sitka	136
Day 8, Wrangell, Alaska, USA.	137
Day 9 at sea	139
Day 10, Victoria, BC, Canada.	140
Day 10	143
Madrid/Portugal Douro River Cruise	145
Friday	152
Sunday	156
Monday	158
Tuesday	159
Wednesday	162
Friday, October 26th, Pocinho, Portugal	165
Saturday, the final full day on the Douro	166
Sunday bags out at 3:10 A.M.	167

2019 170
Cuba 172
02-02-2019 172
Sunday, February 3rd, Havana, Cuba. 173
Monday, February 4th, Havana 177
Tuesday February 5th, Havana 179
Wednesday, February 6th, a day at sea. 182
Thursday, February 7th, Cienfuegos 183
Friday, February 8th, a day at sea. 186
Saturday, February 9th, Santiago, Cuba. 187
Sunday, February 10th, last day on board. 190
Monday, February 11th, We are headed home. 191
Exploring French Polynesia 195
March 2019 195
Day 1, March 1st 195
Day 2, March 2nd 196
Day 3, Sunday, March 3, Raiatea, the Sacred Island. 198
Day 4 Monday, March 4th, Bora-Bora, the first of two days here . 201
Day 5, Tuesday, March 5th. Our second day at Bora-Bora. 203
Day 6, Wednesday, March 6th, our first day at sea. 204
Day 7 Thursday March 7th, Fakarava, French Polynesia 207
Day 8 Friday, March 8th, a day at sea. 207
Day 10 Sunday, March 10th 212
Day 12, March 12th, the last sea day before Easter Island. 216
Day 13, Wednesday, March 13th. 219
Day 14, Thursday, March 14th 220
Day 15, March 15th 220
Day 16, Saturday the 16th of March 223
Day 17, March 17th 225
Day 18, March 18th, Monday 226

Yellow Knife, Canada ... 238
Tuesday, September 2nd, the day after Labor Day weekend ... 238
Saturday Morning, up at 3:15 ... 243
Israel, Egypt, and the Suez Canal ... 245
Saturday morning, about 2 A.M ... 246
Sunday, October 27, 2019 ... 249
Monday, today was the Masada & Dead Sea tour. Duration: 11.5 hours; long day! ... 251
Tuesday, October 29th ... 253
Saturday, November 2^{nd,} ... 261
Wednesday is the last day at sea before Salalah. ... 268
Friday, a day at sea ... 271
Saturday, this is the last day at sea before our final port. ... 272
Sunday ... 273
2020 ... 280
February 2020 Caribbean Getaway ... 280
Sunning on the decks, bar, and other Friday 02/07/2020. ... 280
Saturday, a new day; I need to learn this ship! ... 281
Day four, LAND…Ocho Rios, Jamaica ... 284
Day 5, Tuesday, February 11th ... 286
Day 8, Costa Maya Mexico ... 290
Day 9 Saturday, February 15th, last day at sea before port tomorrow ... 292
Cruise Lines and Where ... 297
Countries and States visited: ... 298
Countries and Islands: ... 298
Islands: ... 298
FINAL ... 300
2021 ... 315
DAY 2 ... 321
Day 3 ... 322

Road Trip Southwest USA June2021 323
Columbia River Escape 08/08/21-08/16/21 333
McGivern Rhine Adventure 10/06-16 2021 350
2022 364
Stars and Stripes Honor Flight 05/21/2022................................375
Dracula's summer castle 408
Great Lakes Cruise 07/29/22-08/09/22...409
Mississippi River Road Trip August 21, 2022 to August 25, 2022430
2-FER; MAIN STREETS and AMAZING APOSTLE ISLANDS Sept. 26-29th; Oct.2-5th..436
Sunday October2, 2022 another adventure,.................................441
2023 445
July29-August 18,2023 458
Final cruise..486

About the Author

Work History

Retired: Travel the world; Currently driving for ERS, taking seniors to appointments, since December 2020, Bell ringer for Salvation Army for one year, one semester as money coach for Secured Futures; Seven years as volunteer DAV Driver; Driver for Chip's Trucks; flying into Canada and drive pickup trucks back to Chicago area; solicit donations for 6 Cities Veteran's organization. Four-time condominium board member, including president three times, treasurer once;

Synergy (Aide, Companion)	02-13-----01-15
Home and Hospice Advantage (Nurse Manager)	08-09-----12-31-13
Kindred Hospital (CNA, LPN, RN)	08-06………08-09
Brotoloc Health Care Systems (Part-time CNA)	03-06………..08-06
Full-time student MATC (registered Nurse)	08-05………..12-07
Immanuel Presbyterian Church (Property Manager)	05-02………..08-05
Knight's Popcorn Corp. (Owner/manager)	05-91………..06-02
Streicher's Police Equipment (Sales-road)	12-98………..11-01
Milwaukee Public Schools (7th grade teacher)	07-98………..11-98
Clark Oil (Store manager)	06-96………...07-98
E & N Cleaning (Cover-All Franchise)	06-94………...04-97
Jordan Financial (Mortgage Broker)	01-95………...06-96
Krall & Co. (Road sales, hydraulics repair)	10-93………….01-95
Income property (Three family in Cudahy, WI)	04-85………...06-91
Noah P. Borkenhagen Insurance (owner)	10-82………....10-94
UW-Milwaukee (BBA Industrial operations)	09-74………..12-77
Roller Fabrics (mechanic, supervisor, plant engineer)	06-72………...10-82
USAF Vietnam Vet (Airborn Radio SSgt.)	06-68…………..06-72

Other experiences include shot blaster, retail sales, soda jerk, copy machine repair, Nolyn's Vending company owner, short order cook, and radio engineer; and I published my autobiography, "Educating Noah," Eagle Scout in the Boy Scouts of America, the senior warden in the Masons.

Page Blank Intentionally

Preface

Many people say that when they retire, they are going to travel. Einstein was quoted that you start learning after school. My first autobiography outlined my life, including over twenty occupations and a few small businesses. Educating Noah has been discontinued and is no longer in print; the publisher is out of business.

I had no idea how extensive this continuation was until I was preparing to publish. There will be two volumes; this is the first, and to make the concept complete, I am listing the different trips and ventures we did during that book.

Here is a list of those places:

1970's

Road trip to Louisiana and Texas

Bus trip from Mexico City to Acapulco in Mexico

1980's

Road trip to Nevada and Arizona

Caribbean Cruise

Disneyland in Orlando, Florida

A week's stay in Puerto Varerta, Mexico

1990's

Alaskan Cruise

Hong Kong, China

Peru, Ecuador, Panama Canal, Costa Rica, and Bahama Islands cruise

2009

Ireland

Sturgis North Dakoda (Took a Honda Goldwing motorcycle to the biggest Harley Davidson festival)

Paris and Normandy river cruise

Spain, Morrocco, and Canary Island cruise

Route 66 road trip from Chicago to San Diego

Route 1 road trip up the California coast

2012

Transatlantic Cruise includes Puerto Rico, Antigua, Funchal, Portugal, Madeira, Malaga Spain, Barcelona Spain, Genoa Italy, Pisa, Italy, Florence and Rome Italy.

Austria, Germany, and the Czech Republic

Rio, Brazil, and the Amazon

Educating Noah…Travelin'

2018
Finish The World 2018
01/03-03/15 2018
January

January 3rd, the first day

The first day started early. Tiffany showed up exactly on time at 02:45 (yes, 2:45 AM) for the drive down to O'Hare Airport. There was no traffic, the roads were clear, and we arrived early. The baggage check went well, the TSA went smoothly, and the wait was comfortable. We had decided to make this "the splash." It is a small luxury cruise line in Oceania, "the finest cuisine on the sea," and the flights were booked first class.

It was interesting how nice it was to be casually seated amongst the first passengers to load, with wide, comfortable seats with plenty of storage above and a great breakfast. We both fell asleep during the three-plus hour flight to Miami (lost an hour flying East) and awakened to a cheerful "Thank you" handwritten napkin and energy bars at our elbows!

The transfer went well from the airport to the ship. We waited in the café for our rooms to be prepared, and we easily found the room. Lynn was surprised at the size; it was quite small. To give an idea, I had to sit sideways on the toilet so my knees could bend in the bathroom! It is cozy, double bed and porthole, one step up from an inside room.

We ate in the formal dining room with two other couples, one from Scotland and the other from South Africa. The food was outstanding, and the conversation was pleasant. Afterward, we listened to a string quartet in a lounge, but soon felt the rush of the day come back, and both of us decided to crash, although only at 9 P.M. we were done!

Our first day at sea started relatively late, a little before 8 AM! Last night we unpacked all the clothes and stashed the suitcases, the mattresses are very comfortable and seem to have soft centers with stiffer edges to counter the ship roll, so you don't roll out of bed, kind of like sleeping in your mother's arms so to speak, a very nice feel!

Noah

We had made arrangements with Maria, the room steward, to leave two programs every night for us, so at breakfast, we planned our days, and we agreed to meet for lunch at 12:30. We contacted the desk to open our safe (we could not open it the night before) and asked that the small table and drink tray to be removed to get us a little more room in the cabin.

This ship, as mentioned, is the smallest ocean cruise ship we have been on, at only 30,000 tons, 600 ft. long, 96 ft. wide, 10 decks, and 648 passengers with a crew of 400. The passengers are like the previous Holland Cruise; older, we have seen no one under 21 (except crew and entertainers) and most other than crew over 65. The casual dress seems to be "country club"; some even wear sweaters with sleeves tied around the neck. This is very formal and "ritzy," the interior of the ship elegant, with dark paneling with sheers and drapes, woven rugs, muted music in the background, and soft indirect lighting. I found out that the Horizons Lounge holds 160 people and the Insignia Lounge/Theatre 380 people at full capacity; this is how I gauge attendance. There are no photography people on board and no photo gallery; I was not even approached once to buy the drink package! In most other cruises, you are hounded by these folks, especially by the photographers and bartenders, for the first two to three days.

I did attend the Metabolism class put on by the health spa; there were 8 folks in attendance, and the summary is as follows:

It takes 21 days to form a habit; It takes exercise, especially aerobic (O2), to burn fat; To burn 1# of fat, it takes 3500 calories. Your program should consist of 3 days per week for 45 minutes, 3 sets of ten repetitions of upper, mid, and lower body exercises, both push and pull.

I then toured the ship and took a picture of Cuba as we passed and pictures of the lobby and staircase to be able to complement the written descriptions of this ship; it is partly cloudy and 67 degrees.

Lunch, Mexican theme in the café, bean bag toss, and putting were the activities to earn Big "O" points to exchange later for promotional items.

A martini tasting (the original martini was 1 2/2 oz. gin, 1 ½ oz dry vermouth) and a late afternoon trivia for activities (the original Aladdin was Chinese)

We had dinner at the Polo Lounge, a specialty restaurant. Both the specialty restaurants need reservations but are complimentary on this Cruise line (This applies to both specialty restaurants) with two couples from America, unique high-end food. I have a copy of the menu to show. Everything was perfect and tasty!! good conversation;

Evening, Brain Teasers (A group of angels is called a Host), and a show that was well attended by a trio of baritones, we checked out the night "action," about 20 people, one older guy hopping around, a couple of women "expression" dancing, had a drink, then finished off the night, another hour change, tomorrow.

On the second day at sea, we slept in; not much happening today. Basically, a repeat of yesterday: I am skipping the Margarita tasting; we may not take in the solo trumpet/singer show tonight. I went to the gym, worked my arms as much as I could, and walked 13 laps on deck for a nautical mile (a nautical mile is longer than a land mile, 6070 ft. vs. 5289 ft.) It is overcast, light rain, 80 degrees, and 75% humidity…a lazy day.

Baggo, shuffleboard, putting for points, Trivia (a group of ponies is called a string), and brainteaser (the gangs in West Side Story were the Jets and the Sharks) dinner was with two American couples. Did I mention how clean everything is kept? Every restroom has tissue dispensers and waste disposals at the door (you use the paper to open the door). All food is served; you just point, the linens are changed 2X per week, and each cabin is issued a small bottle of disinfectant when we are at the port to carry along.

Day four, Oranjestad, Aruba

We arrive at 10 a.m., all aboard at 10:30 p.m., and the conversion is $1.00 US=1.79 AWG (Aruban Florin). This is the second time here. Last time, we took a tour of an Aloe farm and an ostrich farm. This time, we toured the town on our own and explored a local flea market.

I was back on the ship by noon, worked on tans, played the on-ship activities, and actually won 1st place in trivia (The first Olympic symbol ring is blue, and the connection between nerves is called the synapses). We had dinner; dinner on this ship is not available anywhere before 6:30 P.M., at the café, again surprised, lobster, steak, sushi, parsnip, and truffle soup. Wow, the food on this ship is amazing!

Noah

We walked our nautical mile (actually, I did) and took a picture of the sunset. We were told in town that there was to be a carnival parade at 8 P.M. on the main street, so we went back to town.

We waited and waited and waited. The parade was on "island time"; Lynn left at 9:15, and I waited till 10:00, still no show; all aboard was 10:30; disappointed but onward and upward!

On day five, we are at Willemstad, Curacao.

The US dollar is accepted everywhere here. We have been here before also, a very colorful Dutch colonial styling, and visited an ostrich farm and local sights. This is a larger town divided into four sections. We will explore the town on our own today, like yesterday. It is Sunday, and this is a small ship, so most of the shops are closed. We walked the town, crossed the floating bridge, and then took the ferry back due to the bridge being open for a three-masted schooner. This is the location of the oldest synagogue in the Americas, and due to the size of this deep-water harbor, it is one of the largest oil-handling ports for Venezuela, including one of the largest refineries in the world.

Back to the ship, light lunch, played the three games for points, then attended a lecture on the islands, "Explorers, conquers, and conquest," the main players being the Portuguese, Dutch, British, and French. After the lecture, we met with the lecturer in the foyer and had an interesting conversation on Vikings, the Moors, and American slavery. He said he would have a series of lectures on slavery later on in the cruise; there is so much to learn, how things really came to be, fascinating.

Attended formal tea; I will be drinking Earl Grey and green tea from now on. The crumpets were "delightful," as we agreed with an English passenger who commented, "How civilized this was." ...This is the biggest event on the ship; next to dining, there are 170 place settings set on the Horizon Lounge daily.

Tried to get an outstanding picture of the sun going down, and you can actually see the sun slowly drifting into the sea; the only problem was, as last afternoon, the sun went behind a low cloud bank before being distinguished by the sea!

Dinner, and I will say this again and again, was outstanding, not only by selection but also by quality! One more trivium and a comedian show. By the way, there is only one show, one show time on the ship due to the few passengers.

Day Six

Kralendijk (derived from Coral reef, or coral dike in Dutch) Bonaire, part of the Caribbean Netherlands. Today is our first planned excursion. We met at 9:15 for the Bonaire Highlights and Cultural Explorer excursion. The money is the American dollar. The island caters to tourists, scuba divers, and snorkelers. The surrounding reefs are well-preserved and easily accessible from the shore.

We were packed into a 14-person bus, and off we went. The tour was off the island. We went north first. Most roads are single-lane, in fair shape, and beep before entering corners; it is 84 degrees, humid, with a 10-mph breeze. This is a coral reef island, 46 kilometers long, 43 kilometers wide (a kilometer is 6/10 of a mile), larger than Aruba but with fewer people at only 19,000. This is a Holland-controlled island; most of the beach areas that have houses are worth over $1 million. There are also gated communities with much more expensive houses, $3-5 million each or more. Health care is covered by the government, a small hospital on the island; if surgery is needed, the patient is flown out to Aruba, Columbia, or Houston, Texas, USA. The entire island is designated as a park. Anyone caught littering, it is a $1000.00 fine.

Schooling is included (government-paid for) if a citizen wants to continue to college. It is also included if you test high enough. However, when you graduate or quit, one-half the cost must be paid back by the family to the Holland government. English, Dutch, and Spanish are spoken here, kids wear uniforms to school, and Papiamentu is the native language.

Discovered by the Portuguese in 1492, the rainy season is October to February; they do not have hurricanes due to the high mountains and only 50 miles from Venezuela. This side of the island has large storage tanks for Venezuelan oil, and they have a few modern windmills for electricity (almost constant winds). Everything must be imported (gas is $5.60/gallon, and we pay $2.30/gal at this time). They have some goats and donkeys on the island, and a few small vegetable farms, but the soil is poor at best. Most of the island is scrub and cactus. We passed a fresh/saltwater lake that is too salty for fish but great for brine shrimp, and flamingoes love brine shrimp; we saw a few "pinks "in the distance.

We stopped at a tiny museum, tasted cactus liquor, and were introduced to a Colobus tree. The fruit is inedible; however, the outside of the fruit is used for cups, bowls, and mariachis. We paid fifty cents each to use the bathrooms, took the 10-minute tour of the old house (museum), and then off to the south side of the island.

One different observation: most houses have walls of cactus around the property, and many have barbed wire interwoven between the cactus about 4 feet tall!

There is no unemployment paid. At 67, citizens get a government pension of $700.00/month; many people on the island have 2-3 jobs. The south side of the island is a sea salt production facility. This was one of the only exports of the island, run as a plantation until slavery was abolished. Some of the very small slave houses were kept, and the salt facility was owned by a company in Minnesota, USA.

The finished product, 500,000 tons a year, dries in the sun and then is shipped mainly to Trinidad, Florida, and South Carolina. The water around the facility is heavily salted and pink, a by-product of microorganisms that live on salt. It does take a couple of months to dry the salt for export.

We walked the streets upon returning to town, back on the ship for a late lunch, then Trivia (the farthest south city of Australia is Cambria, between Perth and Sydney.) We took third place (a group of frogs are called an army.)

We were invited to a private cocktail party for Oceania Club Members. It included free drinks and appetizers, so the theatre was full, just an acknowledgment of repeat cruisers. Some had over 600 days of cruising with this line!

We then had reservations for our dinner at the Toscana specialty restaurant: Excellent Italian food... I asked for and have the menu. The couple we sat with were from St. Louis, originally from East Africa; both just retired on December 31st. Nice folks, good conversation.

Day seven

At sea, 80 degrees, partly cloudy light breeze; games, catch up on ledger. I do check the internet daily due to my mother's condition. We have been gone a week now. No news is good news. I also asked for today's dinner menu so we can show the unbelievable selections available; restraint is difficult! So, I now have a menu from the two specialty restaurants and the main dining room to show!

Played the games for points, went to a discussion of future cruises, and got my one hour of sun baking and mile walk in. Today we were accompanied by a flock of brown Boobies (BIRDS!). There are three types of Boobies, brown, red-footed, and blue-footed ones around the Galapagos Islands. It was interesting to see them plunge out of the air deep into the water.

Our trivia team scored another 1st place, our second! How many countries are larger than Australia? (4, Russia, USA, Canada, and Brazil)We also now have a team mascot, BB, a parrot hand puppet I picked up at the ship's store. He brought us good luck!!

Dinner in the café listened to a piano player, then a string quartet, Brainteaser Trivia, another 1st place! How much does a British "stone" weigh in pounds? (14) Watched the final show of Shades of Bublea', a trio of young guys singing the songs of Michael Bublea.'

Day eight St. George, Grenada

It is in the high 70s, and light rain. We are doing this port on our own; we are docked right outside town. This island is known for its beach with multiple shades of blue. That did not happen; the beach was extensive, but the overcast sky and intermittent rain dampened everything. We hired a cab with two ladies from England and toured the island, visited a waterfall, tasted rum and other drinks at a distillery, and walked a stretch of the beach.

All the roads are 1 ½ lanes, and they have a medical doctor school on the island; if you go, you have to spend 5 years on the island to pay the government back. Friendly folk, the cab tour was $25.00/person and two hours plus long, well worth the $10.00 tip I gave the driver for both of us. We were back on ship a bit after 1:00, grabbed lunch, and played some of the games. Both Trivia (In the Bible, which came first, the chicken or the egg...the chicken? He created birds, the original color of Coca Cola...green.)

Caribbean Happy Hour, dancing with the singers and dancers. I was one of the three male guests, and only about ten female guests joined in during the two-hour, double bubble session. The evening ended with Ritch Shydner, comedian. he tended to talk a bit fast, and maybe 75-80 guests came to the show.

Day nine, Kingstown, St. Vincent

The lower 80's, overcast, scattered showers forecast. This is the rainy season, but like yesterday, the rain comes and goes, 10 minutes here, then clear, later 20 minutes. We started out with a drizzle, with nothing to see close to the port, so we decided on a mini tour with two other couples in a small van. As in Grenada, this is a poor island, most if not all the cars are used cars imported from Japan, the roads here are a bit worse than in Granada, but again, only a bit more than one lane shared, and yes, blind and hairpin turns. The first leg of our trip was up to a lookout point; there are cattle on this island, along with goats and sheep. No sidewalks except in town, curbs, or guard rails. The highlight of the day was the Botanical garden. Five minutes before we arrived, the sun came out, and the rain stopped for the day! (TA DAA!)

It was $2.00 for admission and an additional $4 each for a guide, and we found both were well worth it! He described all of the plants and trees, including a rubber tree, a Boom Boom tree (when the seeds hit the ground, they make a "boom" sound), and a Lady tree with blossoms like a hairbrush and eyelashes. It was a beautiful walk; everything was in bloom: white, red, lavender yellow, and, of course, different shades of green.

On the short walk back to the ship, I tried the local beer; it was quite good, then back on to the ship, lunch, sun tanning, and games. I then came back to the room to the diary, then could not find my camera…

I turned the room inside out, went back up to the sun deck, went through all the used towels, nothing; checked with the servers, nothing; went down to lost and found, nothing. Checked at the luggage security, nothing; went out to the shops on the dock, cabby stand, nothing…depressed, I returned to the cabin, then remembered what Lynn said about the rock samples slipping down between the beds.

I reached down between the beds, and yes, there it was…WOW! I was so relieved! Off to games and Trivia. What president was a king…? (Gerald Ford was adopted and changed his name to the adoptive parents.)

It was Cuban night in the cafeteria, so we went there, ate too much, and attended the last production show for this first segment of the cruise. (Lynn's rules!)

Day 10

Castries, St. Lucia, another island known for beaches; hopefully, we can walk the town and explore the beach and the town. It was in the low 80s, and scattered showers. We took a water taxi to town, not much of a wait. It was comfortable and only about a 10-minute bus ride to town. The cab hawkers weren't too bad. We made our way to the craft complex of stalls for vendors, did a couple of aisles, bought a few things, then toured the fruit and vegetable market and walked back to the ship. After a comfortable mile of cool breeze, we walked along the shore and got some pictures of flowering trees and a couple of crabs! Filed and labeled everything. Tomorrow is Barbados, and we will be losing some of our entertainment and some folks that just signed up for the first 10 days, lazy afternoon with sun and cool breeze.

Day 11, (January 13th) Bridgetown, Barbados

The forecast was similar to the last three ports: 80's and scattered showers. This is the end of the cruise for some. Transfers to the airport started at 5:30 a.m., and all those endings were off by 8:00 a.m.!

We were crammed into a minivan for the 1 ½ mile to town, 14 full-sized tourists in a Toyota minivan!! (But it was only $2/each)

On the dock next to the ship was an old sugar elevator with three spouts to fill cargo ships. It was cemented in and shut down, and the gangways were chained and blocked, like Hawaii, another casualty of worldwide labor.

Downtown was not impressive: bigger island, streets with two lanes and sidewalks, the usual high-end jewelry shops, and, like the last three islands, a KFC. We walked a little, then took the beach walk back to the ship. We picked up another soccer shirt, stones, local money, a little artwork, and postcards, then back for another lazy afternoon on the ship…gotta got brown! We had another muster drill with life vests, dinner in the formal dining room, and a pleasant discussion with a couple from Vancouver, Canada.

Day 12, Scarborough, Trinidad

The 80s, scattered showers; two blocks walk to town and the attractions we want to see, especially another botanical garden! I found out that there will be a ship-building contest, so I am starting to gather the materials. This time, it will be a submarine!

There are no showers in sight; it ended up hot and humid, and in the upper 80s, both got attacked at the gate by Cabbies. After being approached three times, I told the rest that the other four were turned down, and he made the 5th. In all, we were approached 7 times to and from the gardens. The gardens were free, maybe an acre; we had to stay on the path, and the grass of the path was uneven and wet (from the night before). We walked a bit, but the heat and humidity became depressive; we walked back to the terminal, exploring the few shops that were open (It is Sunday, shops that do open are open only 10-2), and returned to the ship. The games are back on. I gathered more info for the boat building, worked on tan, napped, and will be up late tonight; tomorrow is a sea day. Taffy sent an update on "ma"; she had a small fall trying to get out of her chair without assistance, no worries, and no problems. I reinforced checking with hospice to ensure a renewal of her coverage at the end of this month for another 3 months due to the continued decline in balance and strength.

Trivia: what is the largest island in the world…(Greenland.)

Day 13, Monday 01-15-18

The overcast, breezy, mid-80s and 3-5 ft waves, this mid-sized ship is rolling, barf bags are out by the elevators, and only a few decks permit going outside. This was another sea day. Playing games, going to the IT room, and he set up shortcuts to get on and off the internet on-board; he also cleaned my computer. He told me something very interesting. He said, "Don't learn; understand. Once you understand, the learning is much easier and sticks more." Another note on the door, checking to see about yellow fever vaccinations for an upcoming port of call. Lynn is in charge, and she accepted the delegation to check with them if our exemption stands.

What was the first English-speaking country to grant women the right to vote? (New Zealand, 1893.) Where is the perfume river? (Vietnam), and finally, which big cat cannot retract its claws? (Cheetah.) The magician was very good, mostly card tricks and sleight of hand.

Day 14, Tuesday 01-16-18

The forecast was scattered thunderstorms at a high of 83 F; it was in the upper 80s, with matching humidity and scattered clouds. Devil's Island, French Guiana, we need to be tendered to the island Devil's Island is one of a three-island cluster that was a small portion of a French penal colony (1852-1946). Many of the more than 80,000 prisoners never returned from the harsh, disease-infested island, much less escape. The 1973 movie Papillion, starring Steve McQueen and Dustin Hoffman, was centered on this island.

We spent about 2 hours on the island, mostly ruins; paths were uneven, cobblestone, staircases without rails, and steep. All signs except for one were in French. Even the clerk in the souvenir shop spoke French, very broken English, and all prices were in euros. I had enough Euros' to pay for the few things we wanted. Everything was up a hill. The entire island is about 1 mile long and ¼ mile wide; the heat was oppressive. Got pictures of flowers, peacocks, and a marmot, but no monkeys. Back on the ship, we were provided the yellow fever exemption. We also received notice that while we are in Brazil, we will be subjected to a 25% tax on purchases on land and while in Brazilian waters on the ship!

It was 60's night at 10:30, and at sea tomorrow, so we danced a bit, actually about 9-10 dances, and had fun with all those on the dance floor. We started with about twenty passengers in the entire room. When we left, there were eight.

Sea sponge, plant or animal…(animal); what was Mrs. Munster's first name? (Lilly). What does a horologist specialize in? (Clocks.)

Day 15, January 17th

Same as other days, partly cloudy, 80's, it is another day at sea. We played the games, listened to the string quartet, and got sun, Caribbean night for dinner. The show was four singers.

Who sang Johnny Angel? (Shelly Fabre), The PGA allows how many golf clubs in a bag? (14, 9 irons, 3 woods, 1 putter, and a pitching wedge).

Day 16, January 18th

Noah

Thunderstorms, hot, humid (this is winter, so we are told that it rains every day, all day; in summer, it only rains every few days, and only for short periods of time). We docked at 10:30 AM in Belem, Brazil, and we were tendered into the docks. On one side of this delta are lush vegetation and primitive docks and shacks. On the other side are skyscrapers and the largest city in the State of Para in the north of Brazil. It is located 60 miles or 100 kilometers inland from the Atlantic Ocean. This was the first European colony on the Amazon, part of the greater Amazon delta, and emptied about 20% of the Amazon River into the ocean. Note that fresh water is lighter than salt water. It sits on top of the salt water for miles into the ocean.

The water is brown; the tender ride to shore was twenty minutes. Our first stop was the open market, food, nuts, vegetables, clothing, spices, and oils. It rained off and on, the market was crowded, and a good 3-4 blocks long, a block wide. I found two interesting items made out of rubber. After the market, a short drive to check out a fort; in front of the fort (actually, the back of the fort, the front is the river!), the streets are lined with mango trees, and yes, one did actually drop near a kid making him jump! Next was a cathedral (nice and dry inside) and very clean and beautiful.

On the way to our last stop, we drove through the old town; the larger older buildings have outside walls covered in Portuguese tiles, the streets are narrow, coils of wires hanging from the poles, this is the 1700s part, lots of Graffiti.

It is raining on and off. The paths in the botanical garden are half underwater, with a few trees in bloom, mostly green and wet, and some cages with animals and birds. I did shoot some flowers, some caged birds, a rodent, and an iguana. We finished the ½ hour walk, wet feet and all, and back to port. We are told "thank you "in Portuguese is (phonetically) "Obregato" to males and "Obregata" to females.

I wanted to get some local Brazilian Real since we would be visiting two more Brazilian ports. The person behind the glass in the exchange office was horrible. First, she wouldn't get off the phone, then got two more calls, then she required me to look at my passport, then she didn't have much but $50 BRRs ($17 US); after about 15 minutes, I ended up with about $38 US worth of BBR's for my $40 US and just left!

The trip back to the ship on one of the ship's tenders was only about 10 minutes. Back on the ship, we changed clothes and had dinner. Lynn went to the show. I diarized and worked on the boat.

One note and I talked about this at dinner with another couple. (He was a former FBI agent.) Throughout the entire tour today, on shore, there was a high presence of police, and there was even a plain closed officer riding with us. At every stop the three tour buses stopped, there were several police cars with officers out, and there were officers outside the church square and at the gates of the botanical gardens, not to mention the docks where we loaded. The "tourists" were protected without us knowing why...

Day 17, Friday the 19th

It is another day at sea, on our way to the second Brazilian city, Fortaleza, down the coast. There were some problems last night; one group on a river excursion got stranded when their boat grounded. It seems that the captain of the excursion boat miscalculated the tide. After several tries of unloading and rebalancing, three other boats came and pulled them off the shoal. They came back to the ship three hours late! (The chef did provide them with food when they returned...he didn't want them to starve to death.)

Then, we had a medical emergency, and one passenger was ferried to the hospital. (He actually died the next day at that port's hospital.) We had to wait for the tide change, which put us nine hours behind schedule, so we wouldn't be able to reach our next port of call until the 20th at 7 p.m. rather than 10 a.m. All the excursions were canceled, and the money was refunded. We are to be in port for only 3 ½ hours at night.

Today is when I get the rules on the shipbuilding (about 60% is done, and I believe I have all the parts I need!) They require that the ship built has a cargo area able to carry 6 full cans of soda, so now I will have to design a sub/cargo ship...just another challenge!

The lecture was on Brazil, and like most of America's history, it starts with the European discoveries. I did ask the lecturer why this was, and he told me it was, in part, due to the printing press use, and since it was initiated in Europe, history was centered on the Europeans!

The story of Brazil is boom and bust. First, it was the Brazil wood trees, then sugar, which was slave-based agriculture, so the Portuguese imported slaves from Africa for the labor (slaves were used throughout the Americas for plantations, and these types of crops, sugar, and cotton the most slave intensive;) when the price of sugar bottomed out, (it is still produced, but now for ethanol), Brazil was the last country to outlaw slavery in 1885, there was the gold rush of 1816, that went bust, then cattle were introduced for beef and leather after the price of leather and beef declined, the last crop was and currently is, coffee. America is the biggest consumer of Brazilian coffee, accounting for 70% of the total production.

We played all the games for "O" points, played both trivia and had a reservation at the Toscana restaurant. We ate "early" at 6:30; after a fifteen-minute wait, the waiter asked if it would be all right if we dined alone, and yes, we did. Worked on the boat, and Lynn went to the show.

What does the FUBU clothing line acronym stand for? (For us by us)What is the Star of India? (Sapphire.)

Saturday the 20th of January, Day 18

The captain confirmed that we would not reach port till 7PM today, so again, sun, games, and eat...

Lynn decided not to go ashore. She stayed for "Dancing in the Streets" on deck since it was before 9 p.m., it was well attended, and about 50 guests were on deck dancing. We docked after 8 p.m., 26 degrees centigrade and muggy. I was the eighth person off the ship at 9 p.m. A tour bus was provided from the ship to the terminal. The terminal was empty, just chairs. Everyone walked through the terminal to another waiting bus to take us downtown. Downtown is right on the beach of the Atlantic; the beach was clean and extensive. At 9:40 at night, the area was well-lit. Over 300 vendors were set up on the beach selling tourist stuff, souvenirs, and arts and crafts, and this was a Saturday night! Here were families, tourists, medium crowd, polite. Anyone in a crosswalk stops traffic here.

It became too late and too dark, but on the way home, we toured the beach. It was very clean; there was a small concert with locals and then an area of small fishing boats resting on the sand with tables set up for selling fresh catch when they came in. I was back on the ship at 10:40. It took longer to come and go than the time I spent in this city to join Lynn and the usual small group (about 20) of late-nighters for karaoke.

Trivia today: who was the third musketeer? (Armin) what was the name of Batman's butler? (Alfred)How many feet is a fathom? (Six feet.)

Sunday, day 19, another day at sea

Today was The Grand Buffet at lunch, set up in the dining room. Like we need more food! I had too much sun, my tan is pretty dark, and my face, legs, and upper torso are. Lynn says this is the darkest I have ever been! I was down and sleeping most of the afternoon. The show was pretty good, the six singers and dancers, the string quartet and the house band.

After the show, we went up to the lounge and danced to "Motown." The ship was rocking a bit, and after 5-6 dances, we were done. The "late night" group is pretty consistent, about 18-20 people. (only half of those dancing)

Monday, Day 20

In Recife, Brazil, mid 80's scattered thunderstorms were the prediction. Recife is known as "Brazil's Venice," with over 40 bridges connecting the islands and eight million residents. We arrived in port at 8:00, all aboard was 4:30, and the 1:30 excursion was for 3 hours on a catamaran, with a visit to a prison converted to an arts and craft market, so we had the morning on the ship. This is the last day before leaving Brazil, so we will have to spend the last of the converted BBS money. Tonight, we start the five-day transatlantic trip. Lynn put out her patches in case we have a bit of a rough ride.

The bus ride to the catamaran was re-routed to avoid a protest march. The guide told us this one was teachers wanting higher pay, but the protests are losing their effectiveness in that there "seems to be one every week." Sound familiar?

The catamaran was basically a pontoon boat; we went along the shoreline and two rivers, old and new bridges, and old and new buildings. They are trying to bring back the downtown, which has slipped into decay. Many buildings are empty, there is a lot of graffiti, and the traffic is terrible. The narrow streets are lined with parked cars and jammed, and half-million-dollar new apartments from 10 years ago are now selling for 40% less.

Most of the fruit grown here is exported, vineyards are becoming recognized for their products, and there are still some remaining linen factories, some sugar cane farms, and, of course, tourism contributes a lot to the economy... The city was established by the Portuguese, then the Dutch for 24 years, and then there was freedom from Europe. The British did not have a cemetery, so when a "Brit" died, the body was sent back to England in a used rum barrel. Most, if not all, of the cemeteries are above ground due to the rock base. The religion was Catholic, but it has become more protestant (about 64%) over the past century; like everywhere else, the churches were connected to politics. There are 112 old Catholic churches here, and the rich would try to outdo one another by building a grander church than the others.

If a daughter or young girl wasn't married, she was forced to become a nun; the problem was that the church had too many nuns! So, the culture evolved. The alcohol of choice here is whiskey and beer; Asti Spumoni is also made here.

The health system is basic, as with most places here in South America; the rich have the best care through their own doctors or money under the table, and the rest have "third-world care." Many come from all over the world for specialty heart and plastic surgery, which is much cheaper than most and with excellent results.

The government is trying to upgrade the educational standards in that the standardized tests show Brazil has one of the lowest-performing students. The brightest are sent to colleges, and it is five years for lawyers and six for doctors. The new goal is to have the children have a degree or a vocation when leaving school.

The diet is mostly seafood (one kilo (2.2 lbs.) of shrimp sells for $10.00 US (equivalent). Many capture crabs, take them home for a couple of weeks, feed them coconut milk to clean out the pollution, and sweeten the meat. There are also quite a few coconut palms; each tree produces about 360 coconuts a year.

Many of the specialties are desserts; the nuns used egg whites to starch their habits, so egg yolks were plentiful. That, with the sugar cane, created very rich desserts! The arts and crafts prison was extensive; we were able to spend the rest of our Brazilian money on some real "treasures"! We returned just in time for the ship to leave. As we left the harbor, an announcement was made that happy hour would begin at six, be extended to two hours, and that the Brazilian tax of 25% would no longer apply; the lounges were full!!

A meal, a beer, and a very hard trivia, and we called it a night. What was the origin of the name "Thomas"? (Twin) What Country has the most post offices per capita? (India.)

Tuesday, January 23rd, Day 21, crossing the Atlantic.

It is bright, windy, and warm; it is a little strange with no land in sight, no birds, just the ship, light, fluffy clouds, a blue ocean, and a sky!

The Atlantic is the second largest ocean, a bit larger than half the size of the Pacific. However, it is the heaviest-traveled ocean. The name was derived from Atlas, one of the Titans of Greek mythologies. It has an average depth of 12,881 ft. (2.44 miles!), with the deepest point in the Puerto Rico trench, which has a bottom of 28,681 feet. (5.43 miles!)

We did the usual "at sea" activities. I attended a cooking demonstration by the head chef and his head cook. They seemed to enjoy sharing their knowledge and worked very well together, with humor and good nature. It was entertaining and informative, and there must have been 70 people attending one of the biggest events. They also provided recipes and ingredients for the three dishes they made: Gnocchi, fish roasted with tomato, fennel, and olives, and Risotto Al Fungi Porcini. He steamed the fish and then tested it with a knife. I asked what he was looking for, and he replied, "The knife should go in easily and come back completely clean, and then the fish is cooked"!

We dined at the Polo Grill and shared a table with two women who travel together. We had a good conversation, played trivia, and called it a night.

How many pecks are in a bushel? (Four); what monarch died in 1902? (Victoria).

Wednesday, the 24th of January, Day 22

On the 2nd day at sea crossing the Atlantic, the waters are calm, it is in the low 80s and breezy, the sun is bright, partly cloudy, and the water is a magnificent blue!

I got up early, walked a nautical mile, checked my e-mail, and documented. I usually have to attempt getting online 6-7 times before

Noah

I get into a search engine. This was on the first try! I wonder how bad it is on other ships with younger people who are all on their devices! It is still amazing how many of these folks are on their iPads, reading or doing games and puzzles!

The lecture today is on "Voyages of Discovery" and "European Colonization". The briefly highlighted facts presented are as follows: The least corrupt governments in the world today are Denmark and New Zealand;

The Portuguese and Spanish "discovered" the Americas, and within 20-30 years, the disease they brought with them wiped out 80% of the American (North, South, Central, and Caribbean) population. They were looking for spices and gold and traded steel when they could find it. They were also on a mission to spread Christianity. They also introduced cane sugar and grew sugar cane to make sugar, molasses, and rum. These processes were very labor intensive, so there was a demand for cheap labor. South African tribes were more than willing to exchange slaves for steel. This formed the Triangle Trade, from Europe to South Africa, to the Caribbean, and then back to Europe.

Sugar was actually from the Muslim merchants who brought it from Asia. It was called "sweet salt." Of all the slaves shipped before the English stopped the slave ships, 30% went to Brazil, most of the balance to Europe, and a very small percentage to North America, with the total estimated number of slaves estimated at 20 million. Of those slaves, 1% died in the ships, and about 33% died the first year in captivity.

The term "Blue Blood" comes from looking at the inside of an arm; if you see blue veins, you are blue blood, and dark-skinned people don't have the contrast. This was just the beginning of racial casting.

I look for flying fish in the ship's wake. The disturbance scares them. While I was on deck waiting my turn at one of the games, I saw groups of these flying fish from 1-3 to 30-40, all blue and silver 8" to 10" in length, skimming over the ocean about a foot above the water for 4- 40 feet; no birds in sight!

Today, we got to play games on deck for Big O points. It was well attended by guests. This included the Officer's challenge on the games. There was shuffleboard, ping pong, water ball, crazy putting, and Baggo, set up on three decks. If you beat an officer of the ship, you got a point. If not…nothing!

I and a number of others have been fighting sinus headaches for 3 days now; hopefully, they will stop before I run out of sinus medication! At the last trivia, one of our players believes in scents and aroma therapy. She provided me a "dab" of peppermint to try, and I placed a bit inside each nostril.

What did the scarecrow say to prove he had a brain? (The triangle ratios, A squared plus B squared = C squared); what was the name of the "Love Boat" … (The Pacific Princess).

Thursday, January 25th, the 23rd day on the cruise

The water is calm, with scattered clouds and a bright, sunny day! Today, we had two drills, one for abandoning ship and another for the ship being under attack by pirates, no one to be on deck, especially deck 5 (the lowest outside deck), and no one in cabins, all in the corridors away from the side of the ship.

I asked for and received another dose of peppermint essential oil. This was the first lunch I had without a pounding sinus headache, and I will be ordering some of this stuff when we get back!!

The game rotations were changed. I worked on that tan and tried to work with Lynn on another cruise, but her priorities were different than mine... trivia, dinner with two couples, good conversation, got the "stare" two or three times from some uptight woman at the other table, we must have been talking too loudly…again!!

I worked on the boat; Lynn went to the "prom"; it is basically the same 20-25 people, and she danced for a half hour to an hour. When at sea, the casino is open, but it never seems that busy, with 3 or 4 slots being played. Occasionally, the roulette wheel and maybe one, sometimes two, blackjack tables have people at them.

What is the traditional 10th wedding anniversary gift? (Tin or aluminum). What is the second biggest food-eating day in America? (The Super Bowl).

Friday, this is the third time, so far, that we have crossed the equator, and today, the "Polliwogs" get converted to "Shellbacks," we planned to attend. It seems to be a different ceremony on each ship; this one did not include a dump into the pool. (maybe due to the age

Noah

of the guests?) There was a procession and costumes, and then those who wanted to be initiated went before Neptune, asked to be a shellback, kissed a fish, and were doused with water. It was a lot of fun.

Games, trivia, and a variety show. What noodle dish is named from the Italian words for "cooking pot"? (Lasagna); in what movie was the term "Greed is good" used? (Wall Street).

Saturday, yes, enough with the counting days! This should be our last day crossing the Atlantic. We have had an exceptionally calm crossing. Another sunny day, light breeze, 80s and sunny, waves less than ½ meter. We lost another hour last night, which makes a total of 5 hours lost on the cruise, and of course, the one flying down to Miami, there will be more to come. Tomorrow, we will be 1/3 done with this cruise. Games and work on the tan again today (I have an Oreo butt).

There is no going out on deck 5. That is the first exposed deck; exits to that deck are closed till January 31st, when we are out of this first pirate area. There are fire hoses set up and charged with water on both sides of that deck (to prevent pirates from coming too close to the ship), and someone from the bridge is observing outside on both sides at all times.

The lecture was mostly information on the next two ports, warnings of yellow fever, skulls, and other possible "upsetting" things that tourists might find offensive or disgusting. The Togo area was responsible for about 20% of the African slave supply for the Portuguese. It was the main thing the Africans had to trade for steel, gunpowder, and weapons, and what was needed in the Americas, mainly South America, for the sugar cane farms that were so labor intensive. Since the disease, the Europeans introduced wiped out 80+ percent of the native population in the Caribbean South and then North America.

Africa is the world's second-largest and second-most-populous continent. It covers 6% of the earth's total surface, a little over 20% of the total land area. As of the census in 2013, Africa has 1.1 billion people, which accounts for 15% of the world's population. It contains 54 recognized countries or states and 9 territories. (There are also two de facto independent states that have limited or no recognition.) The population is the youngest of all the continents, where 50% of

Africans are 19 or younger. Algeria is the largest country by area, Nigeria by population. It is the only continent stretching from the northern temperate to the southern temperate zone. The northern half is primarily desert, with the central and lower areas containing both savanna plains and dense jungle. It is the hottest continent on earth, with 60% of the land consisting of drylands and deserts.

The European trading empires were as follows: First was the Portuguese 1500s to 1580s, then the Spanish in the mid-1600s, and the Dutch followed in the 1670s. The French in the early 1700s, followed by the British in the 1750s. The British banned slave shipments and slave trade in 1801.

Tonight's show was billed as "When Tango Meets Rock." We watched the first dance, which was a typical high-stepping tango, and then the second started with make-up like the Rocky Horror Show and just a small variation of another Brazilian Tango, so we left.

Today's trivia questions. What was the last name of the man who invented the whirlpool bath? (Roy Jacuzzi) What Country has the longest coastline in the world? (Canada).

Sunday, the 28th

The weather is in the low eighties, overcast, and humidity in the 60s; we are in Africa, the city of Lomé, Togo, Africa. The money is the West African Franc (XOF) with a conversion factor of approximately $1.00 US 526 XOF

We docked late. This is one of the busiest ports on the western side of Africa (we are told, "One of the cheapest"). There are cranes and containers everywhere! We docked a half hour later than expected, so when the tours started, it was a frenzy to get bus tickets and then get to the busses. There was a welcoming group, stilt walkers, dancers, and a band, a fun welcome, and yes, I got pictures!

We were warned about yellow fever, so most of us wore long pants, loose shirts, socks, and lots of bug spray. Six buses, loaded to visit the same places, and it is Sunday! None of the crew were permitted to leave the ship at this port. (Many shops and businesses are closed here, too, on Sundays!)

Our first stop was an open Fetish market, Voodoo stuff and ritual needs, skulls, dried birds, hides, and local carvings. There were about ten vendors, basically selling the same semi-preserved remains of animals. A quick tour, then off to the Palace.

The main road was two lanes, one lane each way; however, the tour buses drove mostly in the middle due to the ever-present holes in the asphalt. It was another situation where we had the biggest vehicle, so we drove where we wanted to with a blast of the horn to clear the way.

Then we pulled over, and the bus was overheating! A mechanic appeared, and ten minutes later, the bus was running again. Many immediately complained about no air on the bus, asked to open the windows or leave the bus, and were told no! In this area, the buses traveled in caravans of 3. Each bus had 2 armed guards and a representative from the ship. When our bus pulled over, the other 2 buses in our group did also and stayed with us. (People amaze me as to being so ignorant!)

With the air back on and the bus moving, we stopped at a school complex to check out the schools. They must have received compensation for being there because the school rooms were full of kids; I joined in with several of the classes in singing and waving. The restrooms were all outside; the buildings were benches and open areas with decorative concrete blocks for ventilation and a blackboard in front of the room for instruction. One small teacher's desk, no bookshelves, no decorations, but a lot of smiling kids!

The basic language here is French, but in high school, English is taught as a second language. In 1960, Togo gained their independence. They are slowly becoming more capitalistic and have more freedom. As the guide explained, "You can now say what you think, even about the president. Before, if you said the wrong thing, you would disappear!"

This was the poorest country we have visited to date; it is actually the poorest Country in Africa! Most people live in shacks made of plywood and sheet metal, with very little furnishings, if any, no indoor plumbing, cooking on pottery stoves, and dirt floors. Clothes other than school uniforms are very colorful, including headscarves and hats matching the outfit, along with any materials or spreads. There are 40 different ethnic groups or tribes.

As we traveled to the palace, most vehicles were small motorcycles. I saw up to five people on a motorcycle, 250cc or less, and most taxis are on the back of one of these motorcycles. All but the main roads were dirt, piles of garbage, many vacant buildings without roofs, and in decay.

Healthcare is a combination of herbs, priests, religion, and a few modern hospitals. There is now more of a Western education: grades 1-6 in French, the four mid-grades with both French and English, then the final three in High school, both languages; an option for university if you qualify. The school used to be mainly for boys. The girls were trained at home to be housekeepers and cooks. That is changing now, and girls are receiving a "formal" education also.

The main export is agriculture, coconuts, mangos, sugar cane, beets, and yams. There is a lot of superstition. If you sweep the floor at night, it will offend the gods, and you will end up with smallpox as punishment! The supper is the "meat" meal and the largest meal in this culture. So "rabe" is the wine; Whiskey is given in Voodoo to "wake up the spirit."

Parents first need to approve a spouse, and parents of women must provide a dowry. You go to the government to get a certificate, then you go to church to get a date, then you can get married.

Chocó is the god of war, and Zanbeto is the strong man's guardian god who comes at night to protect the family.

We arrived at the King's house for a welcome ceremony. Many people dressed up and danced to drums, a procession, and a small ceremony where the chief spoke to the group of six bus loads in his native tongue. This was then translated as basically a "welcome to my country speech." They then asked for questions, and the king seemed to understand the questions but replied in his native tongue that had to be translated…A bit of show BIZ? There were benches provided for most of us, and yes, of course, a few thought they had to record the ceremony standing in the front, blocking the view, and those others with point-and-shoot phones and cameras that stood and focused, adjusted, and take a thousand pictures before moving aside for someone else…" stupid" would be a kind statement!

One of our friends asked to borrow $5.00, and the kids saw me give it to her. OOOPS; immediately, 50 kids descended on me with their hands out asking for money…the whole 50-60 yards to the bus! One of our other friends felt a small hand inside his pocket. When he turned, the small boy just smiled and moved on.

Noah

Back on the bus for a twenty-minute ride, challenging cars and motorcycles and maneuvering around potholes, sinkholes, and other vehicles back to the ship. A light lunch, a couple of games, supper, night trivia... We watched the production show "Tuxedo" it was good, we stayed for the whole show.

The letter "d" in Scrabble...how many points? (2) what was the name of the movie that made the phrase "Make my day" popular? (Sudden Impact).

Monday, Cotonou, Benin; we have an excursion to "Ouidah-The City of Voodoo"; we are the first excursion out at 8:30 A.M. That was what we prepared for, but then again...We were up, dressed, and ate, and returned to the cabin to find we were still 2 hours out from our port. It seems that the refueling took a lot more time last night, so our excursion now, which was to start at 8:15, is noon, and we will not be in port until 10 A.M. Anyone who has been in government knows that any deviation in plans screws up everything, and it seems in foreign countries it is worse, and there are no alternative plans by this cruise line!

It is overcast, 80's. Lynn couldn't find her jeans, tore the room apart, and found those; the morning did not start well! This is the busiest eastern Africa port; every other dock in this port is occupied by cargo ships, and containers are everywhere!

As we left the ship a little after noon, the sun was shining, the heat in the mid-80s, and it was hot and bright!

During our excursion, one of the guides told us that there aren't a lot of cruise ships stopping here, and like the last port, we received a lot of stares as we went past, with two security people on each bus, two guides on each bus, and a cruise person on each bus, all four buses kept together and were led by a military vehicle!

The only disheartening thing observed, besides the extent of poverty, was that I saw garbage in the water before we were close enough for the pilot to be dropped off to guide us into port!

The hour-long drive provided some information on this country; however, the microphone was defective, and listening was difficult. This small country has three Capitols: One, the Spiritual, Two, the Political, and Three, and the Historical. The major religions are, in order of popularity, Roman Catholic, Islam, and Voodoo. The major exports are agriculture, pineapples, sorghum, maize, and coconuts.

The traffic was similar to Manila: motorcycles everywhere (you only need a license to drive four or more wheeled vehicles), traffic signals and lanes are just indications… A good portion of the main streets are paved and in good condition.

Cars are descended on by the street vendors at stop lights, selling fruit, nuts, sunglasses, trinkets, and even clothing racks! Unemployment is high, 30%; a typical low wage here is $30/month (the example given was a maid w/o education). The country has 14 different languages, but French and English dominate. School primary is provided by the government. However, the student uniform must be bought by the parents, and due to teacher shortages, there are usually 75-80 students per class. Gasoline is sold alongside the road in glass jars by the liter, with no prices posted. The telephone poles are concrete; there is a lot of trash all over, actually more than I saw in India!

The first stop was the sacred Kpasse Forest. We had another procession, met another king, walked a Voodoo sacred area with statues, old buildings with trees growing in them, buildings with boa constrictors in relief on them, huge trees with bats flying all over, and this was early afternoon! Ceremony dances, we were invited to dance along, and Lynn did. A walk back to the buses included a souvenir stop, and I bought a protection amulet, Lynn a wall hanging, and then off to the "Temple of the Sacred Pythons."

The center of this stop was a hut you walked into that had snakes in a pit, in the corners, and on a ridge halfway up the wall. There were no guard rails, no barriers inside, and yes, you could touch! I was draped three times with three different pythons and posed for pictures out the back, past more souvenir shops, and back on the bus to drive along the slave route. We were there only about forty-five minutes.

On the slave trail back, some tribes even sold their own people into slavery! We stopped at a fort museum showing the poor slave housing and the main building for administration. The inside was sparse, with some tapestries, some old cannons, and gardens. This fort was a symbol of slavery to the people here. When they achieved independence, the Portuguese were told to leave the country in… three days; on leaving, they burned this fort. (It was rebuilt as a memorial to those enslaved in 1989.) The last stop was the "Gate of

No Return," set on the beach, where the slaves were shipped, never to be seen again.

We returned to the ship late. I asked around for local money and was told no one would exchange it for the dollars. I even engaged a vendor with a policeman as a translator, offering more for the conversion, but she still refused.

The heat was smothering; we took showers, grabbed a bite to eat, made the last Trivia, and then called it a day.

Ralph Chester, who was blind since age four, invented what was an option in the 1958 Chrysler? (Cruise Control); what does "MG" stand for in the English sports car? (Morris Garage).

Tuesday, the 30th

The overcast, hot (mid to high 80's), and a day at sea. This was a down day for me. Attended only four activities but had a re-occurring migraine most of the day, so I was sleeping off and on all morning and afternoon. Lynn just did the activities and needlepoint. It's kind of a catch-up day for both of us. The ventriloquist act Serge Massotwas very good. It included some very funny audience participation. Karaoke was a blast! All 18-20-ish folks sang and danced. The shame of it was when asked, the event person said this was more participation than ever before…After all, it starts at 10:30 (drinks are two for one as an incentive). Tomorrow is an island visit, no tour, just a walk-around.

What city hosted the Olympics 3Xs? (London)In what country in Europe do you pay the most for a McDonald's Big Mac? (Switzerland).

Wednesday, 31st of January, Sao Tome

Sao Tome and Principe. This is an island located just above the equator, and relatively small at 50 kilometers by 20 kilometers, that just gained independence from Portugal in 1975. 90% of the food here is imported, 70% of the religion is catholic. This was a holding point for the Portuguese to keep slaves before shipping them to the Americas. The currency, 10,000 STD (Sao Tome Dobra) =0.50 U.S., or .35 EU.

This island boasts 119 species of orchids; we had hoped to get some pictures, but we weren't that lucky. We were to witness a spectacular sunrise, so I got up early, only to be disappointed, just another fiery ball in the mist, so I walked my mile, had breakfast, and picked up Lynn to go on shore. We are being ferried. This port required passports, so we had to go down and pick ours up from the front desk before leaving the ship. Copies will not work here.

I got the tender tickets, but there was an accident on the tenders, so everything was delayed. Finally, on the tender at 9:30, a 10-minute tender to the island showed our passports, then gave them to the ship's pursuer on the dock, and explored the town after a free shuttle. We stopped at a bank, got in line, and after waiting twenty minutes, only four people were serviced. Nothing was in English, all Portuguese, and this was 10 o'clock on a Wednesday. We could not imagine a busy time! We left, three people in line behind us. We just shook our heads!

We found the market, but it was too crowded. It was inside, and already the heat was getting to Lynn. Most everything being sold was for locals, food, fans, hardware, etc. The money, STD, is also the prefix on all the license plates, and talking to one of the tender agents, the $20.00 US would have required a suitcase to handle the bills!

We walked back to the shuttle area, took the shuttle back to the pier, and jumped on the waiting tender. Back in the cabin by 11:30 A.M., showered, and then continued the day.

This was the third of three very poor countries; the only police we saw were at the pier getting on to the shuttle and a few when we got off. This was the more prosperous of the three, but poor is poor! The poorest, by any standard, was that first West African stop, and I'm sorry, those in Appalachia have it much better than 90% of these folks, plus the opportunity most here will never see!

We had afternoon tea today, rather than dinner, because I scheduled a haircut. The hairdresser didn't know how to give a flat top, so she tried. It was OK, but not a flat top... she only charged me for a trim.

What is the second most abundant gas in our atmosphere? (Oxygen); what percentage of our bones is made up of water? (23% we missed this one by 2%, I guessed 25%) What eye color represents 2% percent of the population? (Green); what do Panda bears eat? (Bamboo).

February 1st, a day at sea.

The day started off overcast, low to mid-80s, but the sky cleared, the sun broke out, and I was able to get that hour of baking; I'm getting darker...

The usual activities, some of the information gleaned from the two lectures was the drones are selling quite a bit. You can now get one with a camera for $50.00; the 3D camera did not catch on, even in the phone cameras, but the phone cameras are becoming very competitive, and the quality is starting to rival SLRs! There are very good applications available for under $5.00 to enhance the camera abilities, and with two cameras in many new ones, phones may replace cameras like they did watches!

In the lecture on African Indigenous foods, it seems the first cultivated food in this context was einkorn wheat; this began the conversion from hunters and gatherers to cultivators. Most of this culture came from the Fertile Crescent, that is, the Middle East, with two main rivers, the Tigress and Euphrates.

The Maize variations are actually vegetables, not a grain. Africa produces yams and sweet potatoes to the tune of 90% of the world's production, and they also provide a good portion of the kola nut.

The map she showed indicated that the upper third of the African continent was white, Mediterranean, and Middle Eastern, and the bottom two-thirds was black and pigmy. And we are told African is black??

There are 25,000 variations of the orchid. The most valuable produces the second most expensive spice and has the common name of vanilla orchid; although it is not the most expensive spice, it is the most labor-intensive (It takes months of processing for the final product). The origin of this vanilla orchid is Mexico; the Portuguese brought it over to Africa.

Deck #5 is open again, the fire hoses are put up, and all the doors to that deck are opened again. We are out of the pirate country! (At least for a while!)

We won 1st place at the late trivia. However, some of these trivia folks are getting too serious and complaining about specific questions! If 8 bits make a byte, what is half a byte? (A dibble) What was the name of the Hogworth newspaper in the Harry Potter series? (The

Daily Prophet).

Friday, the second day at sea

On the second of February, we moved our clocks ahead again last night; we are now 8 hours ahead of Chicago. We are off the coast of Angola, with a light breeze, partly cloudy, temperature in the low 80s. The usual games are in the morning, but the times have shifted because today is Fair Day!

The whole deck is set up with different contests for the passengers to win raffle tickets. Lynn and I were able to participate in all but 2 or 3, and the line for the "feed the other guest chocolate and whipped cream blindfolded" was very short... I played with a friend, and both he and I needed a shower and change of clothes after that one! Roll the dice, stuff a pillow into a case the fastest, tie sailor knots, ring the liquor bottle, etc. We must be lucky in love.... We didn't win anything but went to another presentation to win a $250 cruise certificate. We may be looking at three options, and no, we didn't win that either.

Games in the afternoon, I attended a gin tasting. Gin comes from the Dutch, and it seems England does, also. We tried 5 gins, Boodles, Tanqueray 10X, Plymouth, Hendricks (not made like "gin") and Van Gogh. Each of these had a distinctive taste, and we drank each one straight. The best, we agreed, was the Van Gogh... a Dutch brand. (Made in Holland, need to check out their Vodka!)

The best tonic water is Schweppes; in India, tonic water is called "Jesus Bark." Need to try the following: Pimm's #2 with Cranberry juice...Pimm's Rose, a Misty Pimm's...Pimm's pineapple and ginger beer; and a Vodka by Belvedere, it is a rye Vodka.

Evening Trivia, we won first place even without our fourth couple. The afternoon Trivia had 14 teams of 8, over 100 people! At sea now, the activities have over 60 people participating! Every segment of this "180-day around the world tour" drops off some people and adds new people, so the mix does change, and so does the number of people that are active.

Who besides Justin Hoffman was in Midnight Cowboy? (Jon Voight); in 2002, what was added to the Barbie doll? (A belly button).

Saturday, this is the last day at sea before another port, February 3rd.

Noah

We are just off the coast of Namibia, in what is called the skeleton coast. It is only 63 degrees outside, humidity at 78%, wind at 20 knots, waves at almost 3 meters (8 feet), and overcast. On board activities, a chef's culinary show, we played Bingo again, I won a little more than what the cards cost, afternoon games, Lynn went to a practice for the talent show, and I went to a magic workshop.

After trivia, an enrichment seminar on Cape Town, we went to one of the groups' trivia couples, Henry and Tessa's suite for Champaign, before dinner at the Tuscan specialty restaurant. We had a great time with the "team" at Henry's suite. The women loved the bathtub, and there was about 50 % more room both in the bath and room, plus the balcony and sliding doors. Then the group went to the restaurant, and yes, we got "the look" from a couple of tables for being a bit noisy…again!

Caught the last 15 minutes of the show, then up to the dance floor for a disco night. We were two of six there… I danced a few discos, then went down to the cabin. Lynn stayed another 45 minutes to an hour, did some dancing, and mostly just talked to the host and hostess.

What is the only known bird with nostrils at the tip of their beaks? (Kiwi): Name one of the M&M female character colors: (Green and Brown).

Sunday, February 4th, Walvis Bay, Namibia

It is actually in the mid 60's, a light breeze. Some are wearing medium coats! Another Sunday at a port, which means many of the shops and markets will be closed, along with museums and some public buildings.

We were supposed to meet in the theatre, but then things changed, and we were sent up to the lounge, the line for picking up your passports, then going to a face-to-face with the port authorities, went out of the lounge, down the steps to the next lower deck, across the ship, then through the salon, and into the gym.

One thing seems to be evident: all these cruise lines are reactive, not proactive! Like they have never been here before? It took 45 minutes, in a slowly moving line, to be processed, then down to another waiting area for tickets for the tour, then another 20 minutes for the buses to be called! Needless to say, all the tours started at least one hour late. Since we had to wait, I took the opportunity to get some local money. (This was one of two times they actually had a local money changer on board.) I met Lynn by the exit, and it worked well, but I had doubts if she was coming after waiting 15 minutes!

We crammed 16 tourist people into a Toyota van (the stated capacity was 22 w/o anyone standing!), and off we went. The dock is in a working industrial port, with piles of coal on one side and salt on the other. The drive to town was a good 50 minutes.

This is not a busy tourist port. They only see about ten ships a year from November –February. However, it is the deepest natural port on the Western African coast and Namibia's major port. Freight port, plus an abundance of plankton and marine life, attracted Southern right whales and consequently whalers and fishermen; this, of course, brought fishermen from all over the world, decimating the fish population to a point where fishing commercially is now regulated and strictly enforced...

1884-1915 Germany was the dominant European country in this part of West Africa. It was part of the apartheid system; in 1990, it became an independent democratic republic. Their presidents serve 10-year terms; they are on their third president now since winning independence. Once just outside the dock area, the small Walvis Bay community exists at the mouth of the intermittently flowing Kuiseb River, a very modern and upscale community section (beautiful concrete homes nicely decorated and walled, very much like middle-class homes in Arizona, the best we have seen in Africa yet!) the landscape turns to dessert. This dessert area, The Namib, is a "no go" designated area, nothing but dessert! There is a plateau, and then the Sahara begins. Signs on the road indicate "no Hitchhiking" with a line through a hand with a thumb up! The air in the van is open windows, so it is hard to hear the running conversation. The roads are in very good condition, and true two lanes are clearly marked lanes.

Everyone drives on the left side of the road; everyone is expected to work for a living. Our first stop was DUNE 7, a place where you can climb a sand dune and rent a 4X4 or quad bike.

The way people acquired land was by bartering, giving a commodity for the land. We are told that the President's main job now is to unite the people. There are 2.4 million people here, including 15 ethnic groups, speaking eleven different languages, including a clicking language.

Noah

Our first stop included a young man trying to acquaint us with the "clicking" language...It was really hard to copy; many people purchased some of his artwork, as we did.

We were taken to a new development where the new arrivals are placed. This area is called a democratic settlement community. Tiny homes, wood, and corrugated metal, two homes share an outdoor bathroom, and you must get your water from a community water spicket. There is no electricity except for street lights, and everyone cooks with propane.

The main town was Swakopmund, and the immigrant town was adjacent to it. People look for work in the main town; they have a Tuck Shop, which is like a 7/11 here in the States, however much smaller. They must purchase the goods to sell elsewhere and then bring them to their store. Now, 46% are looking for work, and all are expected to work. You are considered an adult at 18. Christianity is the main religion, and there are no Muslims.

We went to the home of a nineteen-year-old woman dressed in typical Kimba garb. She explained that under apartheid, people were kept separate: white, Kimba, black, and others. The old style for Kimba was to dress in leather "garb" from cows. Eventually, they transitioned to typical German Victorian style for women and suits for men. The well-to-do men always wore a hat and used a cane as a sign of their success and for respect. Later, the Kimba made their dresses less Victorian (less puffy) and designed a hat to look like the head of a cow. These types of dresses cannot be purchased in a store but must be specially made, and the colors are magnificent. For these people, your wealth was measured by how many cattle you owned, not how much money you had.

After that, we went to the Happy African Restaurant for a light African lunch. We were greeted by a tall guy on stilts and tons of kids. Lunch was a dough ball that tasted like honey and fried, very good, dried caterpillars (once I tried them, I had at least a half dozen). They tasted like beef jerky! We had sautéed spinach with onions, mashed beans, delicious chicken, and a dried porridge. We washed our hands in a common dishpan just inside the entrance, filled with warm water and soap, and then ate with our hands. We had to purchase our beverages. About $1 US for soda $2 US for a beer, and the beer were quite good!

In came the guy who was no longer on the stilts. He had an instrument made from a calabash gourd, decorated nicely, with a small steel harp placed in it. He played three songs, and we all sang with him and tipped him for the entertainment. The name of this instrument was Mbila (pronounced Mira).

On the way back to the ship, we started to notice that this location had no motorcycles or scooters and saw only one or two bicycles, just cars and vans.

There is a desalting plant here, as well as a roundabout. We also saw an oil rig in the ocean off the coast... There were Para-sailors over the next dunes. Everyone is being creative, trying to make a living. There is an artificial Bird island available for tourists, and that is the home of one of the largest flocks of flamingos in South Africa.

They do mine uranium here (it has some of the world's most important deposits), have a desalination plant for water, and there is a small steel industry, as well as fishing. This is also the center for the guano collection industry.

Back on the ship, I did the wash, supper was simple, no trivia today, the Super Bowl is at 1 A.M. tomorrow morning, and many are planning to watch in the theatre. The dress is "very casual".

I was not up to 'snuff," so after supper, I left Lynn with friends for the "Feeling Groovy" deck party; she danced with crew members, entertainment staff, and other guests, had little time to sit, all her favorite songs and dances. She then went up with the group for karaoke. Wandered in late! The Super Bowl Party started at 1 A.M., but due to time differences, neither of us attended.

Monday, February 5th, the second day of Walvis Day

It is in the upper 60s with a light breeze and overcast. We decided to take the free shuttle to the modern mall, so we ate a quick breakfast, and we were on our way. It was only a 20-minute ride, and the mall was expansive!

It seemed very empty, even for a Monday morning; the corridors were extremely clean, and every store had an abundance of clerks and check-out people. They were a combination of clerk and security. There were no "cheap" stores to be found, and neither were there any souvenir shops, mostly high-end clothing. I have no idea how these stores survive! I wanted to get some additional migraine meds and some cough syrup; I found both, but unlike in the States, there were no ingredients on the labels, and the wording was vague. I did ask a clerk if she had acetaminophen with caffeine, and she did not know what caffeine was...

I was also looking for a cheap watch. I found some in one store and asked a clerk to open the case, and he got another clerk to open the case. I asked, "what were the prices on two watches?" he took them and went into the back; after waiting a few minutes, I told the original clerk I would be looking around the store. After surveying a few aisles, I came back; both clerks were nowhere to be found, and the watches were back in the case, so I left.

I did find a watch in a kid's novelty store. I bought it after signaling to one of the clerks who was stocking that I was ready to buy. (There are always plenty of employees watching, cleaning, or stocking, but promoting sales seems to be un-emphasized!)

Back to the ship, we turned in our passports and exit visas and had lunch. Played a few of the activities and then took the completed ship model down to show the "guy at the desk," Matthew, the product of all the materials he provided me. He was impressed.

Afternoon trivia, dinner at the Toscana with some of our new friends, late trivia, and an early night back to the room.

Where did the name of July come from? (Julius Caesar)What was the name of the mouse in Cinderella? (Gus).

Tuesday, February 6th, this is the last day at sea before Cape Town, South Africa.

At the first activity, we presented the two dancers (Daniel and Hanna) who have been entertaining and running the activities since we left Miami with a wedding gift from the group. We all donated $10-$15 each, and the total was $500.00. I also threw in one of those gold $100.00 bills. You could feel the electricity in the air. They were totally caught by surprise; the organizer, Dave, also worked with the purser to have Champaign and mimosas for everyone in the group! We all felt great, enjoyed the little celebration, and then back to activities.

I won second place in the boat-building contest. There were six boats entered, and five were able to carry the required 6 full cans of soda. I lost to the ten-year-old; his boat was cute, and it did carry six full cans of soda. I did not know he was in the contest; I did not heed W. C. Fields: "Never compete against a kid or a dog."

I cut out the characters and gave them to the people they represented, then took the boat down to reception.

Practice for the talent show tonight. I got drafted to be in the background with props pictures delegated to John's wife, Michelle, and she promised to get a good up-close seat for pictures!

I convinced Lynn to go on two more cruises with this line, deeply discounted, plus a bonus credit for this cruise, two trivia sessions, and the talent show. As I mentioned before, I was drafted to take place in the back of the group for effects-requisitioned props, and everything turned out well. The "talent" included one old dance couple, two comedians, three singers, a tap dance group, a line dance group, and us, seven folks singing a variation of "hello, mudder, hello fadder" adapted to life on the ship.

What was the sorcerer's name in Disney's Fantasia? (Yensid (Disney backwards)) How many of the States in the US touch Canada? (13)

Wednesday 02-07

We should arrive in Cape Town in the early afternoon. Everyone, including the crew, has to leave the ship and go through immigration, with no exception, and no one can return to the ship until everyone has been processed. It is in the low 70s; the prediction was mid-80s in town. We played our last segment of mini-golf; I got three out of four holes in one!

We cashed in our points for more Oceana-branded stuff. Since this was a longer segment, the prices in points doubled; I thought it was kind of cheap to charge so many activity points on branded items when only maybe 15-20% attend the activities…if that!

As we neared the Cape, there was a great photo opportunity. Of course, many took their picture and just blocked everyone else, but I did weasel in for that 20-second shot! We docked a bit after 1:00 PM, and the required immigration of everyone on the ship went exceptionally well. Kudos to Cape Town!

Since our excursion wasn't till 6:45, we took the shuttle bus to the

Noah

V&A Waterfront, a hub of activities including the largest shopping mall I have ever seen (It is only 4 years old and fully occupied). The Mall of America is dwarfed by this one!

The front of the complex is right on the ocean, you can, and we did enjoy a walk in the cool breeze along the shore, then crossed two one-way streets. Traffic stops if anyone is in the crosswalks, and yes, they drive on the left side!

Everything is very clean, the Dutch and English influence. All of the high-end stores have a presence here, including Vinton, Prada, Rolex, Gucci, and high-end European brands, plus stores like Woolworths (but here this company is clothes only) and a store like Walgreens (called "Click" here) except the drug aisle was only half an aisle, the rest was cosmetics and everything but drugs! Lynn was blocking the escalator when she realized she was holding up people. She apologized, and the returned phrase was, "No worries."

We did find some reasonable stores and a post office to mail some postcards. There is a 14% VAT tax applied to all purchases, then back to the bus stop. The ride back to the terminal was about thirty minutes, and now it was rush hour. This is nothing like the previous three stops in Western Africa; everything was in English, and the streets were all in perfect condition with sidewalks. We did notice that all of the houses were gated and fenced with electrified barbed wire on top of the walls. Many of the homes are relatively new, concrete, built into the side of the mountains, and have lifts up to or down to them from parking areas.

Now, a little about South Africa's most visited city, Cape Town;

If you look up, there is Signal Hill. The hill got its name from being a lookout position for the settlement, firing cannons once for every ship approaching that may be a threat. The convention center that was just recently completed is fully booked, and there is currently a two-year waiting list. The word "strand" means beach, and the beach used to be farther inland, but it was filled in to accommodate the growth. The high street is where all the young people hang out, rows and rows of taverns. There are three different types of medical care: the longer you wait depends on your class, and the cue line may be more than a few hours. 1,300,000 Muslims, but we only saw one woman with a head scarf; we also went through a large Jewish community called Sea Point. Cable Mountain is considered the sixth wonder of the modern world; the age is estimated at 300 million years old, much older than our Rockies!

The Stadium was built in 2010 for the World Cup, holding 68,000 people. Off the coast is Robin Island. This was a leper colony turned into a prison island where Nelson Mandela was held for twenty years. He referred to Cable Mountain as the "Mountain of Hope."

Our excursion took off at the assigned time. As with other excursions with this cruise line, there are no holding seats for people with difficulties. The fittest and fastest get the front seats. We did get seats 4 or 5 rows back. The thirty-minute drive basically was up the mountain for a spectacular view of Cape Town and sunset. It was a perfect setting, so the parking lot was overflowing. We arrived ½ hour before sunset, and we were treated to appetizers (puffy buns with cream and salmon, sushi, cheese and crackers, hummus, and more), water, Champaign, and orange juice. Our vantage point was excellent, and the sunset was great, no bugs!

The park and parking lot were inadequate. There was no place for the bus to park, so after sunset, we had to walk a good 15-20 minutes down the road to our bus. However, it presented a great view of Cape Town at night! We were back at the terminal by nine, cleaned up, and another day done. No activities or shows are scheduled tonight.

Thursday 02-08-19

The forecast is the upper 70s with a light breeze. It is our second day in Cape Town, and nothing is scheduled; we decided to explore more of that shopping activity area. This time, we walked to the complex; it actually took about the same time!

The complex was even larger than I described, with a Ferris wheel and numerous other buildings. We found a few stores willing to accept $U.S.; we tried to convert some additional money, but the bank and Wells Fargo turned us down, requiring our passports, not copies! (The ship keeps the passports.) This is after waiting in both places for quite a while. No wonder everyone outside and inside the US hates banks. They are slow and not accommodating at all!!

We did find all sorts of stuff, a large African store, took both money, I gave them everything I had in both African Rands and U.S., and "Isn't this close enough?" worked, and we left with our booty.

We saw five fur seals on a wharf. They are wild, have a sunning pen, and come and go from the pen as they wish into the ocean. I watched one come out of the bay and up the steps to lie down!

We walked back to the ship with our goodies lunch. This was day two at the Cape. We lost a couple hundred people and gained a couple hundred new people. It seems this is common with every segment, so tomorrow, before we take off, we will have another life vest drill.

The afternoon was ours. We worked on tans, enjoyed the hot tub on deck, checked out the salon and health club, and caught up on connections for the materials for the next ship build, re-established internet connections, along with journaling. We went to the movies after dinner and watched Murder on the Orient Express with Johnny Depp, a pretty good movie. We were served soda and popcorn.

Friday, 02-09-18,

It is in the low 60s and overcast, the visibility is poor at best, and today, our excursion is the cable car on Table Mountain. I got in line early for the tour, got the tickets, and was the first out with Lynn. The walk to the terminal was about a block and a half, and yup, passed by a dozen or so people trying to get those front seats on the bus. I went ahead to get a seat, asked if there were any reserved seats, and was told the one saved was for wheelchair folks, so we got seats halfway back. Lynn was not happy!

The twenty-minute ride up to the cable station put us into a cloud, but we did get some more information on the city. Cape Town was the first city to be established in South Africa; the grain silos and company on the oceanfront have been converted into a high-end hotel ($18,000 Rand/night).

Not too much to see from the beginning, and on the way up, just glimpses through the fog. We passed a lot of high-end auto dealerships. This is a rich town, and a two-bedroom apartment can sell for a million rand. (12 Rand to a dollar), Homes here cost about 64,000 Rand per square meter. There are also apartments for lease; "to let" means to rent. Even with the five dams and many reservoirs, there is currently a severe drought, a mandatory limit of 50 liters per person per day imposed on all residents, sinks in the public toilets are turned off, and you are encouraged to use sanitizers rather than soap and water. We passed by a 1652 Dutch fort (still in town); the Dutch, British, French, and Portuguese fought off and on for control of this city and country. Grain and slaves slaves came from all over Africa.

Educating Noah...Travelin'

This group was one of the dumbest. One couple decided to use the facilities without telling the guide, so there was confusion at the cable car loading zone; I mentioned herding cattle and sheep, one other guy mentioned herding cats, and a few agreed.

On the way up the mountain in the cable car, the floor rotated inside so everyone had a chance to see the vista. Of course, today, we just saw a few glimpses of the city below. As we assented, it got colder, and the wind picked up, making it even colder! We were to spend two hours on the mountain, but a few in the group wanted to leave right away due to the cold, the wind, and the lack of any long-range views.

So, we all agreed to an hour. We walked around the mountain top, nothing to see over the edge, ten to twenty feet to "the mist bank," there was really nothing to see. I even took a picture of the group disappearing into the mist! We explored the tiny gift shop. Lynn tried her charge card again, and it worked, so yep, I bought some more stuff. The fog did lift, and it got a bit warmer as we left the mountaintop and descended. Even with the floor rotating, there were people pushing to get photo after photo, as we declined.

The rest of the trip was winding through the city, the bar row, and the beaches. We even stopped for ten minutes to take beach pictures and pictures of the Twelve Apostles Mountains. I was approached by two vendors and tried to turn them away easily. Finally, the first gave up, and the second said, in front of a guy he had just sold a painting to: "I just sold one of these to him for $14 US. I will sell you one for $10!" I said let me take a look. I liked one and picked it up, and handed him $10.00. He then said that it wasn't enough. I said that was what he asked for, and the other guy who had paid more said the same. I told him to give the ten back, and I would leave, or the picture. He gave me the picture and a sour look. I told him it was a cheap lesson, took my painting, and left.

The Dutch section, a school that teaches surfing, the stadium erected for the Olympics, shaped like a bowl and called the "City Ball."

There are a lot of illegal immigrants here from a lot of the other countries in South Africa. In the past, the Blacks were removed from the city, and those sections they lived in were destroyed; after Mandela, the sections were rebuilt, and the blacks were invited back

Noah

in.

We passed a preserved slave auction house, an arch built to commemorate Arch Bishop Desmond Tutu's birthday, and a Dutch section with brightly colorful houses. It was late morning on a Friday, and many of the restaurants had music playing, some with dancers. There are areas with vineyards, a national park on one border, plus a number of botanical gardens.

Instead of supper, we just attended afternoon tea, then another lifeboat and life preserver drill (this should be the last for us); our afternoon trivia was not scheduled; however, the evening one was scheduled. We lost 4 members to South Africa, so we recruited two other couples. The other couple did not show. However, we took 2nd place! The show was a male vocalist; he started singing familiar songs and tried to get audience participation by clapping along to one song and singing along to another, but both ended shortly after it was started. (Little to no enthusiasm; many looked like it was past their bedtime, and probably was!) When he started singing opera, we left and called it a night.

What was Zeus's wife's name? (Rhea)Of the ocean animals, which has the largest eyes? (Giant squid).

Saturday, a day at sea. It is partly cloudy, and the twelve-foot waves last night have calmed down to three-footers. We are now in the Indian Ocean; it is the third largest body of water in the world, 20% of the earth's water surface. We will be going up the eastern coast of Africa, where many small islands dot the continental rims, including the island nations of Madagascar, Comoros, Seychelles, Maldives, Mauritius, Sri Lanka, and Indonesia. The average depth is 3,890 m (12,760 ft), and the deepest Java Trench is over 24,000 feet. Forty percent of the world's oil production comes from the Indian Ocean. Due to the warmth of this ocean, phytoplankton production is low, of course, with some exceptions, and thereby, life in this ocean is limited due to a lack of food for the fish.

The sun is emerging; it climbed to the high 70s, and all the activities have been reinstated. Lynn beat me at all the games. I reminded the chef of the cans I needed for my final ship model and worked on my tan. This afternoon, we will have our first trivia with our new team. This might be interesting! The lecture was on upcoming ports; our excursion is eight hours tomorrow, so I quizzed the lecturer on what to look for afterward. He also recommended a book, Mark Twain's "The Innocents Abroad," and gave me a quote from Twain's I Just Love: "Travel is fatal to prejudice, bigotry, and narrow-mindedness." I will use this whenever anyone asks why we travel so much!

This was another segment, so another dress-up captains party, free drinks/open bar plus appetizers (highly attended as always!), a light dinner, followed by Trivia, and a clean comedian show.

How many official languages are there at the Olympics? (Two, English and French); who was the author of the saying, "Early to bed, early to rise, makes a man healthy, wealthy, and wise? (Benjamin Franklin).

Sunday Port Elizabeth, the third largest port in South Africa and a population of 1.4 million, is also known as "The Bay." Light rain (this is common year-round in the sub-tropic climate) mid-60s. The town was established in the 1820s to house British settlers to strengthen the border region between the Cape Colony and the Xhosa.

The all-day excursion planned today is a tour of a very large game preserve in an open Toyota Land Cruiser.

Lynn had reserved a front seat for us due to her car sickness and my knee on the bus; we had a call the night before confirming this would be done. However, when we got to the bus, it wasn't. Lynn spoke up, and she was moved into the front seat. The guide had to use the jump seat for 1 ½ hours to and from the preserve.

Here is what we were told on the trip out. At the outside of the port, we passed a green mosque right next to the freeway. Since it is considered a Holy place, it will not be moved. In 1948, blacks were removed from the city, and after Apartheid, everything was changed. The official flag is as large as a tennis court and takes 5 minutes to rise.

The new stadium, which is designed and looks like flower pedals, was finished in 2010, cost 2 Billion Rand (divided by 12 for $US), and holds 46,000 people. As in Cape Town, it is used often and booked years in advance.

The cemeteries are divided by religions, mostly Jewish, Christian, and Muslim.

Noah

This is an industrial hub, having factories for V.W., Isuzu, Coca-Cola, and pharmaceutical companies. There is a sulfur factory, so the creek that runs next to it is referred to as "Smelly Creek."

As in Cape Town, the drought is affecting the entire lower half of Africa. The reservoirs are down to 28% full, and so water restrictions are strictly enforced. The city is very clean, with very little graffiti.

The flamingos are a very pale pink, almost white, reflecting the paleness of the shrinking shrimp population. Just off the coast is St. Croix Island, home to 22,000 penguins. (We did not pass or see this). Hump Back whales pass by, and yes, this was not Whale season. When the sardines are running, the dolphins appear (they eat 2000 sardines per pod), and yup, it isn't sardine season either☐!!

In the 40s and 50s, the farmers were shooting the elephants due to them destroying fencing and crops. The area was down to sixteen elephants! The government stepped in and created several preserves to protect the few that were left, and now the population of elephants in the preserves exceeds seven hundred!

There has been a lot of unrest in South Africa and many wars, and the British tried to make peace many times. There are nine providences in South Africa, 80% Christian, with small percentages of Muslim, Jewish, and Black ancestral worship.

Two languages taught in school, English is the second and mandatory. One of the most common phrases is, "Don't worry, we'll make a plan."

In the Black tribes, 18-year-old boys go to the bush to become a man by completing tasks. When all the survival tasks have been successfully completed, the boys are circumcised and covered in white clay; they are men and on their own to make it in the world.

Currently, in this area, unemployment is 26%; in some other areas and provinces, it is as high as 50%. There are public and private preserves. The private preserves are required to have higher fencing, and if there are any dangerous animals, the fences must be electrified. All reserves are inspected daily for disease.

The government does provide some small housing, but real estate on any water's edge can easily cost $2 million Rand.

We finally arrived at the preserve. Kariega, it is massive at 10,000

Educating Noah...Travelin'

Hectares! (1 hectare = 2.47 acres)

We were herded off the two buses to open, high clearance Toyota Land cruisers, fitted with stadium bench seats seating three deep and three across plus passenger seat. These were not made for older folks; 1/2 high steps were welded onto the outside of the vehicle, with one on top of the rear fender to get in.

This was a three-hour tour in the bush, with rough roads, looking for the animals we came to see! And did we see them! We were within 10-15 feet of two male lions, elephants, gazelles, antelopes, impalas, three giraffes, two males and a female, one of the males guarding the female from the other giraffe (he tasted her urine to see if she was in heat, we are told this is common practice in the animal world) and head on, twenty feet with a rhino! Other animals a little further away were wart hogs (they move away quickly), baboons, ostriches, some white storks, hawks, and dark blue birds.

Two-thirds of the way through, we stopped the truck and went into the bush for a bathroom break and had soft drinks and soda. Then, back in the truck for lunch at a lodge. What a lunch they had! Mushroom soup, freshly baked bread, fruit salads, mixed greens, cucumbers, tomatoes, olives, feta cheese salad, potato salad, rice, antelope steaks and gravy, breaded calamari and shrimp, cake, pudding, ice cream, coconut balls, and honey-dipped doughnuts. We were also entertained by a local group of young girls doing native dances and songs!

The drive back was uneventful. The rain had stopped a half hour before we arrived at the reserve and held off throughout the safari. Everything turned out better than we expected.

I had a light dinner, took some great pictures of the best sunset yet, listened to the string quartet, and attended the staff variety show, which was very good. I found out this is one of the places performers end up when they no longer want to entertain on a regular basis. No Trivia today. We finished the night at the lounge. It was Motown night. About 15-16 people showed up, the host hostess danced along with us, one person jumped in for two songs, and another couple for one song; talk about inactive! After six songs, we joined the inactive and wished the host and hostess a good evening.

Monday, East London, South Africa, with a population of 300,000. It is overcast, and the prediction is scattered rain. This is the

Noah

only river ocean port in South Africa. Our excursion is another "early" one; we are on the bus by 8:30, and the front seat is reserved for Lynn. (Finally, after three requests and a strong comment!) As with most excursions, we have to leave the city. This one will take 45 minutes to get to the location.

We experienced the "East London Leap," which is when cars stop and drivers get out of their cars in traffic and go talk to someone on the sidewalk or in another car. The worst street is Oxford Street, which, of course, we were on? So, at least twice, we had to go against traffic (the wrong way) to continue our journey.

Here are some facts and information shared: A number of large companies have facilities here, including Mercedes, Johnson and Johnson, Nestle, and some fabric manufacturers. In Africa, different provinces are the same as a State in the U.S. and a County in Britton. In the villages (Xhosa), wealth is measured in the number of cattle owned. The property (land) is owned by the chief of the tribe, and the houses are owned by the individuals. Men and women are separated, and the government is trying to provide homes for everyone (you qualify if you make less than 3000 Rand per month), the homes again you own, not the land. Since there were a lot of scams, as with all government projects, you must live in that home for 5-8 years before you can sell it. The government homes are round, two-bedroom, toilet and bath with a kitchen and living room. Unemployment here is at 38%. Like everywhere else, there is an underground economy, with women selling fruits and vegetables (pineapples, apples, and oranges) in the city and on the roads.

The coastline is littered with shipwrecks below the surface. This is a favorite spot for surfers all around the world. Humpback whales pass on migration, May through December. Rugby is THE sport, followed closely by cricket. There are also a number of dairy and beef farms. Nelson Mandela approached Richard Branson for help for this community, "Please help," Branson complied by establishing Virgin Active Gyms in the major South African cities to employ Mandela's people.

The schools are run by the communities. Everyone pays into the school budget, teacher salary first, then buildings and supplies. The ratio between teachers and students is 1 to 40; sports are also taught in school; English is the language school taught since it is "the language of economics and business.' AIDS was a problem for quite a while, and the cure was delayed by a major politician telling everyone that the virus could be destroyed by a drink of carrot, beet, and sweet potato juice. Once debunked, the virus has been controlled, but there are still many problems with it. The AIDS epidemic cost a lot of lives, and many kids were brought up by their grandparents.

The Underlying languages are African and Xhosa. Mandela was a Xhosa.

After the entertainment, the men and women were separated to emphasize the different customs of each. The men all gathered in a corral. This is where all business is conducted with a bit of brandy and some homemade beer. The beer is creamy, gold-ish colored, opaque, and strong. We toast one another, drink the shot of Brandy, and then down the beer. (The beer was cooled with ice cubes and actually pretty good and sweet). We were then marched down a hill outside the view of the village; all of us provided staff to manage the small, irregular, narrow path. At the end of the path was a small hut. These huts are made to house up to 20 young men, depending on how many are to pass from child to man.

It is the father who determines when the boy is ready for passage. This happens two times a year, in June and December. The boys stay on the hunt for one week. There is one week of food for them. Then a medicine man comes down on horseback and circumcises the boys, no anesthetic, no pain meds, and leaves for bandages. They are given corn for seven days, no water or anything else. It is common that after 6-7 days, hallucinations begin. On the eighth day, a small bit of food is provided along with a cap full of water. (that would be the cap from a liter soda bottle.) By the way, the whole ordeal involves only a blanket for the boy. It is called a "dog blanket," and basically, those seven days, the boys just lay around in the hut to conserve energy and water within the body.

So, if you do not pass, quit, or use Western medicine, you are considered a boy for life, and you are treated "worse than a dog." ... Some have died.

What to do with the foreskin? Three options:

1. Give to your father.

2. Bury under a bush. (But then you must check /watch it every day to make sure a medicine man doesn't take and curse you.)

3. Eat it

There is no sex with your wife the two years after your child is born, but you can seek a concubine with the permission of the women in the tribe.

In the tribes, to marry, the men (elders) in the family negotiate the "cost" of the woman, family vs. family, over brandy and homemade beer. Criteria are "bulky". Women are worth much more in cattle, and being a virgin is a high selling point deserving more cattle. Married women wear a scarf covering the ears and a long skirt. After the marriage, if the woman is not pregnant within a year, she must live in a hut with other barren women, eating only spinach, cabbage, and millet for 3 months washing in the river. After three months, the husband comes, and she must be happy and conceive. Arranged marriages are now against the law, and it is enforced that girls must be at least 18 to marry.

Once she has had a child, she wears 2 pink aprons and a white cloth over that. Most men now go to the city to work; the women tend to the family, garden, and house.

The typical tribal diet is vegetarian, with one day a week including meat. The lunch they shared with us consisted of lamb stew, spinach, cabbage, millet mush, squash, and beans, with homemade coarse bread and some type of butter. All was quite good!

The restroom was kind of unique. One guy asked if "ladies or men"? The person who had a limited understanding of English cupped his chest to indicate it was for women or showed sitting to indicate having a bowel movement. The guy indicated no, and we were shown to the back of the building to enjoy the scenery as we "took care of business."

Back on the bus, back to the ship by 1P.M., games participation plus figuring out what we noted while riding on the bus.

A light dinner, since that lunch at the village was small but very filling.

After dinner, we listened to the string quartet. There was no trivia tonight, but we played a computer "Guess where we are" game with two other couples for an hour. Lynn went down to watch the song and dance show. I went scavenging for boat supplies and more seasick meds for Lynn.

What was the catchphrase on the cover of Mad Magazine? (What? Me worry?) What is the most used golf club in the golf bag? (The putter).

Tuesday, Feb 13th

I easily got on the internet; Tiffany sent her weekly report, Ma is doing fine, and my ex-son-in-law also visits her weekly. She is becoming more "needy," her time relationship is faltering, and she repeats herself often.

It is cloudy; the forecast is in the upper 70's. We may witness the pilot for the ship in Durban being lowered via helicopter! Our docking is scheduled for 10 A.M., and our tour of the Valley of a Thousand Hills excursion is to start at 12:45.

No helicopter drops, just another pilot boat coming alongside. Durban is much larger than anyone thought; the city is shaped like a "T," North, South, and West. We went west on the bus to our excursion, the typical hour drive to our destination, so here is more information on Durban and South Africa.

Durban has a population of five million people; it was discovered by Vasco De Gama in 1497. This is home to both a Toyota and Mercedes auto plant.

"Buckles" are pickup trucks, "Pavement" is what we call sidewalk, and "Go to the garage" means to gas up the car, "Robot" is a traffic light. There are a lot of illegals, so the population is inaccurate, along with the 25% unemployment. Durban has one of the largest Muslim communities.

The taxi drivers are called "Professional Suicide Drivers," and they are controlled by the South African mafia; they all drive Toyota mini buses, overload them, and attempt three runs every morning. During the day, they all park together and wait for the evening rush, where it is not uncommon for them to drink or do drugs. A large "people's market" stretches for blocks, and most people here shun the Western medicines for local medicine men herbalists. We also passed several shopping malls; these are like cities. The one we passed had 1100 stores, professional offices, and entertainment similar to our Great America, with wave pools and roller coasters.

Beef cattle and beef liver are some of the best in the world. Rents for a two-bedroom apartment run about 5,000 Rand per month. The banks charge high interest; for homes, the rate is 12%, and you need 20% down to buy an apartment, and to buy one, you are looking at a half-million Rand. The water shortage is here also, and if you use more than you are allocated, you are fined. Just outside the city limits are a number of shanty towns.

Durban has a jockey academy for the horse racing industry, the health care is kind of free, you pay according to what you make, most middle-class pay for two insurances, the first to cover most of the bills you incur but cannot afford according to your income, and the other is gap insurance…confused? Those who can afford to subscribe to private doctors and hospitals. There is also a lack of trust in Western medicine and waiting lines for care.

Schools, State schools, 40 kids/class, private schools 20-25/class.

We arrived at the Phezulu Safari Park. We are escorted to a primitive amphitheater, where we have a fantastic view of the valley. We are then treated to an explanation of Zulu traditions and implements. Zulu's were hunters and gatherers and had little possessions. Wealth was in the number of cattle you owned; the huts have termite dirt and cattle dung floor and walls, with thatched roofs. The inside was sealed with a smoky fire. The tribal dances were demonstrated; whoever kicked the highest was revered. Women dress very colorful. Married women wear clothes above the waist and a flat hat. Men wore animal hides, mostly just around the waist.

Marriage celebrations last 3-4 days; women who are hefty are worth much more than skinny women because they can carry more and work more. A good "price" would be 7-8 cows, plus one for the celebration. There was no restriction on the number of wives a man could have. However, each wife had her own hut. (One room bedroom) The family unit ate together in the family hut.

It never rained while we were there. In the mountains, it was cooler, and the humidity was a good 20% lower!

After the show, we were treated to tea or coffee and scones with jam and coddled cream. Then we explored the collection of snakes and alligators, got some nice pictures of some flowers and a wild monkey, and then went back to the ship.

On the way back, some more info: Presidents serve 5-year terms, usually re-elected once; the president can only serve a maximum of two terms. The cell towers are made to look like trees.

They currently have a number of programs, such as affirmative action, promoting women, handicapped, and black employment in real jobs so that they become productive.

Back on the ship, they collected our passports since tomorrow would be our last day in South Africa, and we needed another face-to-face to exit.

The visas required for this trip were not cheap. Besides having to send out passports for specific visas for Brazil and India, the cost of visiting these countries on visas alone was a bit over $1100.00 each, and that was just for a maximum of one or two-day visits!

Tonight was the African dinner buffet, which included ostrich, crocodile, and two kinds of Spring Bach; all were very tasty and grilled…Side dishes were also provided, and all were tasty! Our team won at late trivia, and then we went to the African moonlight party on deck. I lasted three to four dances, and then my left knee started throbbing. Lynn lasted another half hour. Of the 650 guests on board, only about 30 or so of us were on the floor, including the entertainment staff! Sidelines, maybe another 75, ya, like a morgue after 9:30 pm.

What French bread Frenchmen take home at night under their arms? (Baguette) Is Africa larger than the USA, China, or Canada? (Yes)

Wednesday, February 14, Valentine's Day.

This is our last day visiting South Africa, and we are at Richards Bay; the forecast is low 80s and partly cloudy, and our excursion meeting time is 9:15. Duma Zulu Cultural Village is the excursion today. The pier has about 15 vendors on the pier, blankets laid down, and their products all displayed. The bus ride out is, as usual, a little over an hour, so here is some more information on this part of South Africa.

This port is the largest port for the exportation of coal from Africa. Coal saved this region, and it accounts for ½ of Africa's total coal exporting. Employment is still low; this area still has 26% unemployment at this time. There is also an aluminum smelting plant and a paper manufacturing center.

Noah

As we left the city, a few monkeys were pointed out. We are told that they are very clever. Once in a house, they find food, and they also steal stuff. If one gets in the house, it will unlock another window or door that lets in another or more. Most folks now leave a little food out in the back; the monkeys can get aggressive, and it is illegal to shoot or kill them.

There are a lot of Eucalyptus trees. They were brought in for the mines; they are very straight and make excellent supports, and the problem is that these trees consume a lot of water, which adds to the current drought. There are also some surviving sugar cane fields. When it is time to harvest, the fields are burned, and this gets rid of the rats, snakes, and leaves before the harvest. There is still some gold mining, but the mines are much deeper, and there is less gold. The same is true for the diamond mines.

We pass a sign for the town of St. Lucia; it is not uncommon in this town for hippos to roam the streets after dusk to graze on grass and sometimes gardens! As South Africa is modernizing, the highways are not keeping up with the traffic, and the heavy trucks are shortening the lifespan of the too few highways. The railroads are being re-energized, but the government bought newer engines without taking into consideration the height of the bridges, so currently, the new equipment is very limited due to the height. (The trains do not fit under many existing bridges.)

Hub caps are at a premium. They are often stolen unless bolted on. Food stands along the highway provide good, cheap food for the truck drivers; there are also displays of wooden carved trays, bowls, and mats. It is not uncommon to see a truck pulled over and the driver relieving himself.

Zulu literally means: "People from heaven." The "Lobola" or dowry is expected, and again, the number of cows for the women is considered respect for the family. This was a complete village, demonstrations on how shields and spears were made, living huts, eating huts, and outside fireplace; a sample of beer was passed around, no Brandy... Of the 60-plus people on the two busses, only about 10-15 tried the beer passed around in a common bowl. (Yep, I tried it, not bad, but warm)

Again, with the dancing and more enthusiasm with the men, a couple of the six or so women looked like they "had to be there" with little, if any, enthusiasm. A basket was passed around for contributions, and then we were hit up again two more times?? The souvenir shop only took Rand, and the credit card machine did not work. Lynn joined me and two other couples with long faces and told us her story, so I bought Rand off the friends so she could have those "must have" items.

Back on the bus. There is a big problem with poachers. In 2017, poachers killed over 1000 rhinos for their horns. If poachers are seen, they are shot, and dogs are now at the entrances of all the national preserves to smell out any rhino horns. The government is thinking of legalizing the horns to hopefully bring down the value...

We have been to the poor areas in Mexico, China, India, and now Africa. The conditions here are worse than those: unemployment (reported) is as high as 56%, there is no running water, and people in the states have the naivety to compare a small section of Appalachia? It shows how spoiled Americans are and how little a concept of "poor" they have!

All aboard was 3:30 PM. We had dinner at the specialty restaurant, played the Trivia, and went to the clean comic show. Since Cape Horn, we have had reminders, at least two to three times a day, regarding hand sanitation. All the elevator controls are covered with clear plastic due to multiple daily sanitizing by the staff.

Thursday, February 15th,

7:30, we were told we would be two hours or so late to our port today. We finally cleared the port at 10:20 AM. I had no excursions planned; we would just walk the port. The forecast was a high of 96 F., and it was all of that with high humidity. We played the games to get the points, then went back to the room for sunscreen and bug spray.

The local currency is the Mozambique New Metical (MZN) $1=60 MZN. The main exports are coal, cotton, sugar, chromite, steel, copra, and hardwood.

The walk out of the dock was only two blocks; we visited the train station and then walked a few blocks with vendors. Most of the products these vendors were selling were for the locals: school supplies, booth after booth of cell phone vendors, soda and water, fruits, and nuts. Nothing really souvenir-ish, so we headed back. Besides that, the sun got to Lynn. Any souvenirs made of wood or

Noah

cloth are required to be dropped off at the inspection portal just inside the ship to be inspected for spider and critter eggs and will be forwarded to your room.

We were back on the ship a little more than an hour after we left. All we had to show was the rocks I had managed to pick up and an exhausted Lynn. It is HOT; no one is by the pool. The pool water is warm! All activities have been moved indoors. We are only here for a few hours. At 4:00 PM, we leave for Madagascar.

For dinner and regular activities, we skipped the show, solo male singing opera., Lynn went to the line dancing; 4 people showed up for that! I worked on the boat.

What was the original color of the Statue of Liberty? (Copper); what is the disease caused by severe lack of vitamin D? (Rickets).

Friday, February 16th, 2018

Happy Chinese New Year, the year of the dog! A day at sea. Officers vs. guests on games (there were over 100 guests participating in this!) It is partly cloudy, light breeze, in the 80's. I worked on the boat, and a bit on the tan, and Lynn did more needlepoint. There was only one trivia, the Chinese New Year celebration, so the buffet specializing in Chinese excellent, head chef was preparing the chicken dish. This evening was a little different. It was "Friday Night at the Movies," and the movie was "Three Billboards Outside Ebbing, Missouri"; the language was a bit unnecessary (way too many F-bombs!), but the movie was very good. Another day gone, moved the clocks ahead another hour, and we were lulled to sleep with gentle rocking.

What was King Solomon's mother's name? (Bathsheba) What is the national religion of Thailand? (Buddhism).

Saturday, the sky is bright, the water is calm, tomorrow is Madagascar, and there are warnings about a plague epidemic going on there. We are warned to protect ourselves from flea bites and to avoid contact with dead animals. Warning symptoms listed include sudden fever, chills, painful or inflamed lymph nodes, or shortness of breath with coughing or blood-stained sputum...Welcome to Madagascar!

At noon, the captain made an announcement that the stop to Madagascar had been canceled due to currents and a late exit from the last port. This was the second port Canceled… I was not happy, and the day continued downward. I signed up for the margarita tasting. This tasting took place at the bar by the pool deck. The presentation was constantly interrupted by guests wanting water, soda, and virgin drinks (all complimentary), then the tumblers were filled with ice first, and there were only three varieties to taste. So, in reality, we had 3- ½ drinks for $15 plus an 18% tip apiece! On sea days, the activities are one hour spaced. Most, even with 25-30 people, take 15-20 minutes max, then we wait; no flexibility! The straw that broke the camel's back was we had a reservation for a shared table at one of the specialty restaurants. It took 10 minutes to get in, another 15 minutes to see a waiter, and then no one joined us. This is the third time we asked for "shared" and ate alone.

I went down to the desk, asked for an evaluation form, and wrote up three pages.

Now entertainment is movies, those nominated for the Academy Awards… I could do this at home, with better internet!

Anyhow, tomorrow and Monday will be sea days now. On Tuesday, there will be another pirate drill; I guess I will be working on my tan and the boat…Lynn went to the Disco Night.

Old King Cole called for how many fiddlers? (3); what branch of the U.S.A. Armed Forces have the slogan, "It's not just a job. It's an adventure" (The Navy).

Sunday, Another day at sea! I was still pissed; there was a captain and general manager meeting set for 11:00 in one of the specialty restaurants. Lynn also decided to do another load of wash. Played the games and took the dried clothes out of the laundry for Lynn because the dryers are over the washing machines, and she can't check inside when she empties to make sure all the socks are out. (Or so she says)

I was on time for the meeting only to find that the meeting was moved to the theatre in the bow. When I arrived, I found at least 200 plus in attendance. It was like when they offered free booze!

The meeting was controlled, with lots of apologies and finger-pointing to the weather and forecasting. I went up afterward to talk to the events manager and asked why the elephant in the room was not addressed. He asked, "Which elephant?" and I asked what Oceania is going to do to make up for the two missed ports of calls?

Noah

He told me, "They are working on it with the main office." (Absolutely nothing was done.)

Lunch: worked on the boat. It is in the upper 80's outside, both in temperature and humidity, and the clear sky is beautiful but stifling! Only a few outside reading and sunning, actually too hot!

Played the afternoon games, and then I was approached by the general manager, who stated that he got my note. I told him I heard the excuses this morning, just waiting for the head office to make up what we had all lost, that excuses and saying "I'm sorry" doesn't work, didn't work for my kids, and definitely doesn't work for Oceania!

He started with another song and dance. I stopped him and told him I did not hold him or the staff responsible, but problems should not flow in just one direction, and I hope that he, the captain, and Oceania make this up to us in a real way. He said he would do his best. I did try to make him feel better by pointing out the plague raging in Madagascar, and it may be the "way of the world" TO STOP THIS RUN OF BAD LUCK!

Oh, by the way, something is getting worse on the ship: no more table clothes, nothing is "help yourself" in the café, the library is open only for a short while every day, and the sanitation lectures continue. I actually finished "Killing the Rising Sun" By Bill O'Reilly, and now I am reading "The Devil's Garden "by Ralph Peters, given to me by another guest.

We had dinner in the café with another couple and the woman who lost her husband earlier this cruise. I did get the last two nights of sunsets. We took 2nd place in the late quiz, and I am now in the Mensa quizzes daily.

What is Turkey's national flower? (Tulip); who was the 6th James Bond? (Daniel Craig).

Monday, at sea again, it is sunny, hot (90's) and humid. Tan progression is good, with about 30-40 people playing the games. All the entertainers are by the dining halls, making sure everyone disinfects their hands; you have to wait for a table because they are disinfected between usages, and all the public bathrooms are blocked open to prevent cross-contamination with door handles. I asked for some saved cardboard for the ship but was told nothing like that was given out for a while. All rails, railings, and elevators are being wiped down continuously by the crew.

The library has limited hours, all returned books are wiped down, and the card room no longer has cards. The jigsaw puzzle is gone, but the casino and slots are still running...funny how, when it comes to money generation, priorities change.

The solo guitarist was so good; I will be buying his CD! What a great show!

Tuesday, Dar Es Salaam, Tanzania, we were in port and docked by 8 A.M. went down to the desk before leaving, two to three people in line, then one wanted to know all the stops and places of interest in town. I asked for a map and was told she was out of maps; this was 45 minutes after we arrived! The day went down from there; there were two shuttle buses, one to the port gate and another to a Hyatt hotel in the center of town. We selected the one to go to the hotel, another Toyota van, packed, and had to use a jump seat for the 15-minute ride. At the hotel, we talked to others just as confused and finally located a helpful person who provided a map and directions to the craft market. This turned into a pretty big city; the population is over 2.5 million. Tanzania gained its independence in 1961 and has grown geometrically since. There is absolutely no parking, cars and small trucks are parked side by side on the sidewalks, traffic is fast, very mixed, and a blend of pedestrians, bicycles, Tuk Tuk's, cars, trucks, and buses...all in a hurry!

The market we were looking for was to be only 3 blocks away. We started out with a group but soon lost them due to us stopping in the shade a few times (it was already in the upper 80s and humid. We walked and guessed the streets; many have only a few signs when you can find them, and the map was not to scale. After three blocks in the heat, Lynn decided to give up. We went back to the hotel, caught the shuttle bus back to the ship, and were back on board by 10:30.

The ship was pretty empty in the public spaces, with 6-10 people in and around the pool. I got my daily dose of the sun; Lynn went off to make the needlepoint in the air-conditioned lounge. Nothing was gathered at this port, no stones, local money, or souvenirs, another lost port, but at least we were here and set foot on another part of Africa!

Light attendance on the games and trivia in the afternoon and night, horror stories on a few of the excursions included police escorts, traveling at high speeds in the wrong lanes, and going to a beach that required walking out almost a ½ mile to get to swim-able water; so, we didn't have too bad a day… "count your blessings…" again comes to mind.

The pianist's show was very good, they had a camera on her fingers, and yes, they flew!

Wednesday, in Zanzibar, Tanzania, the forecast is 96 degrees sunny, and we are signed up for "The Spice Tour." This is a beautiful port with expansive beaches. We are docked next to hundreds of shipping containers, but there is a fleet of small and medium fishing boats within about two to three blocks away, and the water there seems very shallow. The tide seems to be extensive! Mainland and two major islands make up this Zanzibar Archipelago "Coast of Blacks." The historic center called "Stone Town" is a World Heritage site and is claimed to be the only functioning ancient town in Africa.

The excursion people still are having problems. Either these folks are that stupid or arrogant. Whenever a tour is announced, people rush to pick up a ticket just to sit down again. However, there are more cheaters here who leave as soon as they get the tickets in order to have a front seat on the tour bus. The fastest and fittest get the best seat… (and cheats!)

We have a Toyota bus van; it actually fits our group of 12 pretty well. As we left the port, we were warned not to take pictures of any soldiers or police. If caught, they will confiscate the camera and will not return it. We drove past mango trees lining the road, and we were told there were 17 kinds of mango trees.

The traffic is as bad as in Manila; the roads are very good, but the traffic far exceeds the capacity. Our first stop was a view across the street from Dr. Livingston's house (Dr. Livingston, I presume?). It has been turned into a government administration building, so there are no tours.

The next stop was the ruins of a palace that burned down in the late 1800's. The king had many wives and three outdoor pools. The story was that after having sex, the two people would both be massaged and then enjoy a hot, cool bath inside.

After we toured the ruins, we walked to the oceanfront, where boat building was taking place. It was interesting to see the variety of small boats completed and in different stages of completion. We also viewed tarps spread out on the ground with small fish and sardines set out in the sun to dry.

On the journey to the Umoja spice farm, we saw an elementary school. All the kids were in uniforms, a lot of small stores alongside the road selling everything from plumbing supplies, fans, food, and open-air food vendors.

The soil is rich, according to our guide. Everything planted here grows and grows well, and the color is reddish orange. We went walking throughout the "farm," which had a cacophony of spice and fruit plants, all growing together without any specific groupings. As we walk an uneven, packed dirt path, leaves are gathered and provided to us to break and smell, to identify the spice. Lynn and I did identify a number of them before the group. The spices included cinnamon (it is the bark from the cinnamon tree that is rolled up to give those cinnamon sticks), nutmeg, turmeric, cardamom, and pepper (there are four colors of pepper, and all can be found on the same tree) vanilla, and cloves (the gold of Zanzibar). All cloves grown must be sold to the government. If caught selling to anyone else, you can get up to 50 years in jail.

The heat, even under the canopy of trees, was oppressive. Lynn got weak toward the end, and they provided her a chair to watch one of the guides climb a coconut tree with just a rope made out of vines configured into a figure 8 and put around the ankles. We were then treated to fresh coconut milk and coconut pieces. We were also given a number of woven gifts, hats and ties for the men, tiaras, frog necklaces, and a finger wrist bracelet for the women, all made from leaves. At the end of the tour, we were in a clearing where we were treated to three different strong teas: pineapple, mango, cloves, and lychee.

We bought samples of coffee, spices, and perfumes at a small stand they had set up. I didn't bargain them too hard! There are about 100 people who work this specific farm, and the tours they supply account for a good portion of their income. Everyone on the bus agreed that this was one of the most informative and educational tours, provided by some very nice people!

It was too hot to be outside, so I played the scheduled games and afternoon trivia, logged all the information, and checked E-mails.

Noah

There was nothing really going on tonight, another production show that was seen before and no late trivia, so we listened to the Smile string ensemble and called it a night, reading and showering.

Thursday, we are in the port in Mombasa, Kenya; the prediction is the high eighties both in humidity and temperature, sunny skies, and another town and area to explore. This is the last port on the African continent. We have the first excursion out. We are met by dancers at the port and only a short walk to the buses, and ours is a 14-passenger Toyota again today.

As we work our way through town, the poverty is everywhere, little shops line the streets, traffic is horrible, and there are way too many Tuk Tuk's, cars, trucks, and motorcycles for the streets they have. The houses we can see are one-room houses with no running water, but most do have electricity.

The first stop is the Bombolulu Center. This is a center set up to help handicapped people learn a trade and make a living on their own, very similar to Goodwill in America, actually part of the Fair-Trade organization. We were taken through workshops where we saw jewelry being made, wood recycled into carvings, and handicapped bicycles fabricated. I asked how many people living here and being trained, and I was told there is a worldwide recession, so only a little over 100 are there currently. Most of the workshops had only two or three people working. They are hoping the economy of the world will turn around.

The buildings were very nice, the equipment was there, and there was a childcare center there; a bunch of smiling kids met us, then a tour of an area where huts were displayed, how the interior people live, and how the huts are constructed. We are told that when some get too old and non-productive, they leave the tribe, go out and live in a small hut to pray for rain and crops for the village, and then eventually pass.

There was a native dance show, and we were then shown the souvenir shop of products they made. There was a lot of jewelry, carvings, and clothing, nothing really in larger sizes, and many items made from empty Coke cans and coconut tree wood. The prices here are justified as "Fair Trade" items. What it looks like is they need someone to market this stuff, manage production, and match production to manufacturing! For example, as I left the area where the three-wheel bikes were fabricated, there was a wall with pictures of handicapped people. I asked who they were, and it was explained to me that these were pictures of people who would love to have a bike but could not afford one. I asked why this wasn't part of the presentation, and he could not tell me…Let's see now, 3 buses of 14 people from a cruise ship and not showing this??

So, we bought some more souvenirs and got back on the bus to Haller Park. Haller Park was a stone quarry for a cement company that ran out of stone in one pit. The owner donated the land to Haller, and he developed it into a wildlife park to help save the animals. After donating the land, the previous owner then filled it in, planted trees, and transferred animals from the wild to preserve them. I just have to note here that we have heard time and time again of the generosity of the "rich," providing for people, animals, and habitats, and all I hear from back in the USA of how the rich should be taxed more, how evil they are, and how they should do more for others…It sure seems that many do not know that greed and envy work on all levels, and Americans have absolutely no idea of what opportunities they have if only they used them.

This was the first time we were able to feed giraffes, and we did. We petted a giant tortoise and got pretty close to a number of monkeys, antelope, and crocodiles. Since it was hot, the hippos didn't appear.

The trip back to the ship was faster; there has been a lot of security, seen and unseen, with the excursions in Africa, and this should be our last port. I contributed to some aggressive street vendors to take home a few more trinkets to distribute; it was hot and muggy, and we both needed a shower. There were showers, a little late lunch, games, naps, dinner, the entertainment was dancing with the entertainment team, raffle tickets if you did dance, we didn't win anything, with chances to win prizes only maybe 120 people showed up (It didn't start until 9:30!!) and that finished the day.

Friday, February 23rd, a day at sea, heading west.

It is sunny, hot, and humid; another game is provided called MENZA, 5 questions, very hard puzzles. The people with the internet have a great advantage. Four correct answers get you a point. If all of them are right, you get 3 points. Played all the games and trivia, but no sunbathing; it was too hot, and even the pool water was too warm.

Noah

The lower deck is sealed off again now as a caution for piracy, clean hands are stressed 3-4 times a day, the personal laundry is closed for germs, all tables are sanitized before you can use them, staff, by all the food entrances on duty to make sure everyone uses sanitizer before entering, and all public bathrooms have their doors wedged open.

An additional trivia was added today: we played all the games. The outside ones were either limited or moved indoors. We were invited to "The Grand Voyage Lunch," a special lunch put on by the ship for those on these segments. We, of course, had to dress up, but we shared a table for ten with new friends and had a good time, great conversation, and superior food. The two choices of entrees were ostrich or monkfish, with special appetizers and desserts; wine was also included.

No sunbathing again today; we played all the activities; the entertainment was the guitarist, who again put on a great show. Afterward, he signed the CDs he was promoting, and we had our signed also; we moved our clocks ahead another hour, and that ended the day.

Saturday, another day at sea before reaching Mahe', Seychelles. I checked to see if there was any word on compensating guests about the two ports missing and was told there was no answer yet. The concern is that rumors are there may be another port canceled due to civil unrest, and of course, everyone is kept in the dark; we will see!

It is hot, upper 80s, but the humidity is bearable. We did the morning activities and a lecture on trade in the Indian Ocean, the different trade routes established, and the catering to the needs and wealth of the world. From April to September, the monsoons and winds take a northern tract, and November to February a southern tract, so depending on the month, you may have to wait up to six months to travel by sail the way you want. The Indian Ocean is warm, the eastern coast of Africa and islands off this and India's coast, traders have been joined by tourists, mainly European, Indian, and Chinese, outnumbering Americans and Canadians by a factor of ten! He also showed the currents and the gyres that accompany them. When I visited with him later on in the day for a fuller explanation of the currents, he brought up a world map showing how there are currents just off every coast and a few trans-oceans. He also showed the gyres and circular flows that accompany the currents in different areas. He then mentioned the Sargasso Seas, the floating beds of seaweed, and brought up the newly formed Pacific plastic islands and the Pacific Trash Vortex plastic seas, formed from garbage plastic. What a shame! How little we learned in school, how egocentric, and from what I see, our education is getting less and less competitive. What a shame!

I finished the boat (Took final pictures), hunted down Jackson, the kid who beat me last time, and asked him if he wanted the leftover materials I had. He said yes, we agreed to meet at his room in 15 minutes, and I gave him all the leftovers…he was very appreciative.

I dropped off the stuff, and he was two minutes late, and I made that point. He was all smiles. We talked for a while, and he was most interested in my selling police equipment. Sun tanning, afternoon games, dinner with friends, trivia, and then we participated in "Name that tune" at 10:30. Wow, almost 30 people! The piano player had little enthusiasm, the game lasted a whole 15 minutes, our team took third place of the four teams, and off to bed.

Sunday, Mahe', Seychelles, the forecast is thunderstorms and low 80s; we have an excursion at 8:15. From the talk yesterday, there are no mosquitoes on this island (one of the few inhabited places on earth), so no need for Deet, and there is a large Christian population, so no need to cover shoulders and knees for Lynn.

We are just south of the equator; Mahe' is the largest of the Seychelles chain of one hundred fifteen islands (Only 27Kilometers X 8 Kilometers), one of the few granite ones, versus coral, and with a population of 92,000, the largest and most occupied of the only eight occupied islands. (Want to buy an island?) Male' was settled in the 1700s, was a French possession till 1812, and then a British Colony until it won independence in 1976. The native language is Creole; this is taught in government schools along with French and English, and in the private schools, only French and English with English only in the upper grades. School after high school is a work/education program where you work two days for the government and go to school the other three days. (We saw this with a religious college in Hawaii and a theme park.); Medical degrees are sponsored in Africa and Cuba with a commitment to work here after graduation for a number of years as repayment.

Tourism, agriculture, and tuna fishing where there is an agreement with any country fishing off the shores or in these islands that tuna is the only fish they harvest, and there is a tuna processing plant here. Most of the towns are small and very clean, with no graffiti, and many people from India also live here. Health care is public and private; public is free and includes drugs, but many convert to private care to avoid the wait. Unemployment is 3 percent, and there is no welfare here. The island is 92% Christian.

So here we are, another Christian port on Sunday. We are on another extended Toyota bus. Our guide introduces herself as Yvonne, the driver as Dennis, and goes over the locations we will be visiting, reminding us that again, this is Sunday, on this island, all liquor stores are closed, people go to church, then go home, to spend the afternoon and evening at the beach with family. (What a nice concept!)

Our first stop was a botanical garden. Our guide was quite knowledgeable about all of the beautiful and unique plants, flowers, and trees. There is one fruit or nut that is shaped like a vagina, which was pointed out in a number of places throughout this island.

The government wants everyone to own a home; homes are built, and you are charged a percentage of what you make. After 15-20 years of paying, the house and property are yours. The homes on the waterfront or with great views run 1.5-2 million Rupees (13 Rupees per $1 US). This country has also banned plastic bags.

The main diet is fish; meat is reserved for holidays and special occasions. When French families come to vacation, they want to stay with families to see how life on the island is and prepare their meals...what another great idea!

We had a walking tour of the downtown area; again, it was like a ghost town, with light traffic, few stores open, a beautiful Indian temple, a church holding services, and yes, a few teenagers on benches in a stupor on drugs.

We loaded up the bus and toured the island. A few brief pictures stop of the beaches, all sand, beautiful, and more than 60 of them with palm trees in the background.

The last stop was a resort for a complimentary soft drink and restrooms. If you brought a suit, you were free to use the beach. I walked the beach, and the water was warm! I looked at what a couple of young guys were spearing with wooden sticks...octopus.

There were also tortoises kept here. You could reach over and touch one's head and lower neck. So, of course, I petted and scratched one. He got up and moved closer for more attention, then his buddy came over and wanted "some rubbin'," too. The top of the neck is rougher than underneath, but it was "gift" day, and all three of us enjoyed the connection. (Me and those two tortoises!)

Back on the ship in the early afternoon, I showered, had lunch and a couple games, and then Lynn watched the closing of the Olympics. I filled out the final arrangements required, reviewed photos, and organized and consolidated my notes. I also made an appointment for a haircut, and they promised they could do it right this time.

We were invited over to Rich and Sharon's cabin for cocktails and snacks before dinner. They didn't believe their cabin was bigger than ours, but they only had a porthole. We had a window! Both of them were postmasters before retiring, and then they built and ran an RV park. No kids, both on second marriages, good discussion, we then went up for supper, after that the late trivia and then the string quartet.

Monday the 26th, a day at sea

Some would call it relaxing, but for me, it's just boring! Went to the activities and attended a lecture given by a guy who crossed the Sahara on a camel. He is the founder of an organization to save the double hump wild camels.

The trek was the reverse done in 1907 (Tripoli to Kumara). Three and a half months, 1462 miles by another adventurist using a shifting road established by ancient Arabs to bring slaves to the Mediterranean countries and the Middle East, way before slavery was popular! The saddest part was that to make a profit, you needed 20% of those slaves you started with to survive the trek… (so having 75% die on the trek is still profitable?)

This expedition comprised 5 men, 21 camels, and various guides. You need local guides because the sand dunes are constantly moving, and there are also different types of deserts within the desert, some flat, some with many dunes, some a combination, etc. GPS has limited use due to this.

On the journey, they were joined by a 7-year-old girl whose uncle asked if she could go with them to a town that was three days out (safety in numbers) to sell two camels. They agreed and were amazed at how self-sufficient she was for the time she spent with them! (Imagine that responsible and mature at 7!)

Interesting statements include: in the desert, there is a scorpion about ½ inch long that has a paralyzing sting. If you happen to have a cattle prod along, you shock yourself just above the bite mark to buy time to lance the puncture and suck out the venom; this is also good for poisonous snake bites. A rock in the desert that seems out of place may just indicate a grave underneath. Cattle prods are used by people who work with camels also, just in case you are on a camel safari yourself. Also, when you are sleeping next to your camels for warmth at night, it is a good idea to cover yourself with paraffin to discourage the ticks, and they may not bite as much…

If a camel, cat, or mouse is born with two different colored eyes, they are also born deaf, and finally, for this day, camels love the leaves from the Acacia tree.

It is mid-80s medium clouds. Got my ½ hour on each side baking, and while doing so, I comprised a list of materials to give to Jackson (the kid who beat me last time). I found him playing ping pong with an Asian guy who was very good and learning from him the skills of the sport. I gave him the extensive list, told him we would build the boat together, that it would support him, and told him I needed an answer in two days; he would have to get the materials, and we would build that boat. He took the list and agreed.

Afternoon games, another free cocktail party, trivia, dinner, and a juggling show, that was a one-man show that was exceptional. Move the clock ahead another hour and call it a day!

Tuesday, 2/27/18 at sea

The 5th-floor deck is still sealed off and hosed out since leaving the last port (pirates); there are also some security people on board that I had not seen. The day is sunny, the temperature and humidity are both in the upper 80's, with a light breeze…Hot, Hot, Hot!

We played all the games. I attended a second lecture by the adventurist: camels can't swim, the tribes consider men old after 40, and many of the young men paint their faces and upper bodies white. A number of tribes were displaced since his journey by the government, and the land was turned into sugar cane fields by a Chinese firm. He also questioned a hydroelectric dam due to its effects

Educating Noah...Travelin'

downstream and commented on the windmills for electricity, another person who doesn't want change, confusing.

There was a special brunch in the dining room, and for lunch, the café was offering seafood; yep, eat, eat, eat, and ALL the food was prepared perfectly, all displayed perfectly, and the servers were willing to place as much on your plate as you wish! We didn't want to dress up plus spend an hour eating, especially in this heat, so we did the buffet. In the afternoon, played games, baked for an hour in the sun, and had another $40.00 haircut (funny how prices are high without competition!) However, she did spend almost a half hour on me and did a very good job!

While waiting for the second set of games, I got caught up in a political conversation. One of the guys was very close to members of the Secret Service in Washington, and there was nothing said positive about the Clintons. Another was in oil and explained how much oil found and processed in the U.S. is taxed from the time it leaves the ground, enters the pipeline, passes through the pipeline when it is, exits the pipeline when it is processed, and then distributed, and finally at the pump... all just passed on, just more undisclosed taxes.

Another was politically connected with a few lobbyists in Arkansas, who had input on the Clintons, and the multiple pensions our senators and congressmen have immediately, how only one currently is not a multi-millionaire, and the benefits extended to family, and the money that flows...disgusting both sides, it really is a swamp!

This is our last night at the Italian Specialty restaurant for the cruise. We were seated in the back at a table for four, and then we waited. We were then approached and asked to move to a table in front of the restaurant at a table for seven. We complied and were soon joined by another couple. We chatted and waited and watched for more couples to join us, but it never happened. It looked like a couple were offered to sit with us, but they didn't, so we had the meal with a very nice couple.

Late night trivia, we skipped the show and later found out we missed a good one, so we committed to see her second show. We did go down to the piano bar for "Name that tune." Our team got a perfect score and won 3 Big "O" points each!!

Wednesday, February 28th

Noah

This will be our last day at sea before we finally see another port. It is sunny, low 80s, both in temperature and humidity again. Morning games, another mandatory safety drill, another equator crossing ceremony, both Lynn and I were again converted from polliwogs to shellbacks. (This is my third time, Lynn's first…finally!!)

I attended another lecture, more on those camels. He clarified that his charity is to save a specific two-humped camel. His are not the Batrum two-humped camels that are estimated at over 300,000, but his are the wild double-hump camels in South Africa. He also studied the Batrum camels, and they are one of the few land-based animals that can drink ocean salt water and water with even a higher salt content.

Camels seem to be highly adaptable to the weather, the Gobi Desert with temperatures ranging from -40's C in the winter to + 50's C (thought the deserts were always hot? Think again!) They really do not like rain or being wet.

All camels have exceptional hearing; the wild ones are very skittish. They are very hard to get close to, even photographs.

Afternoon sun baking (down to 20 minutes per side), afternoon games, and the sign-up for the boat contest, the boy signed up again. His team told me they don't start until a day or so before the judge date.

Afternoon and evening trivia and a variety show by the staff finished off the day. We won again first at trivia, and the show was great, one of the best!!

March 1, 2018. Male, Maldives

The 80s and scattered thunderstorms were the predictions. We are to be tendered in, but due to political unrest, all city tours have been Canceled. Our snorkeling is from a boat and leaves at 8:30 A.M., the first of the three-ship-offered snorkeling excursions.

The morning was a beautiful, warm light breeze; the water was beautiful, with different shades of blue indicating depth and reefs. We are again an hour late, all tours moved ahead, everyone sitting around waiting; I will probably complain again, but it doesn't seem to help.

This is a small island in a small island chain; there are a lot of freight ships, pleasure craft, and a very crowded port. We are cramped into a lifeboat, a ten-minute tender ride to a small, crowded harbor. It was a very short walk to the snorkel boat; there were twenty-four in our group, of those two non-swimmers/participants. The ride to the reef was rocky; at times, the boat was steered by the pilot's foot! Ten to fifteen minutes later, we are fitted with masks, snorkels, and fins. Those who wanted safety vests were fitted (Lynn, yes, me, nope!), and then we arrived at the site. We are on the edge of a reef; it drops from 2-3 meters to 15-20 meters, and we are promised a variety of fish and coral. We are warned to stay away from the back of the boat, coral, and fire coral. Two boat people and our guide are ready…Jump in!

Lynn lasted maybe five minutes, asked for help, and claimed she could not swim, so they swam with her back to the boat. The rest of us swam along the reef; we saw many different fish, some odd coral, and I even saw a small 5-6-foot shark!

After a good twenty minutes, they came with the boat to pick us up. I had trouble pulling off one fin, and then my right knee failed, and I had difficulty getting up the ladder, but with a little help from my friends, I was back on board. We then went to another dive site; I didn't trust my knee, so I stayed in the boat with Lynn and three others. This group saw a 4-5-foot eel along with a bunch of colorful fish and coral. We picked them up, headed back to the pier, and caught a ride back to the ship. Lynn was "starving," so there was no shopping for us on this island, and with the warnings of unrest, we thought this was the best choice.

We both took showers to clean the salt water off, lunch, fifteen minutes on both sides of the sun, and afternoon games. Both of us showed signs of being tired, played afternoon games, sun-baked, had dinner, trivia, and bed.

Friday 03-02-18

The morning was overcast, but by 10 A.M., the sky was bright and warm. There is no forecast given on sea days, so we take what we get. However, the hoses are wrapped up again, and deck 5 is now open for guests to use. (No more pirate threat!)

Morning games with the group, now in the upper 80's, attended lectures. There are two kinds of sand storms in the desert: yellow and black sand storms. The sand will get into everything and anything.

The meeting with kitchen and housekeeping officers produced the following information: on this ship, there are 47 housekeepers and 66 kitchen crew, the waiters and housekeepers are trained on the ship, the two specialty restaurants seat 100 each, this ship goes through 1200 eggs/day, 600 bottles of wine, 750# of rice, 200# specialty rice per week for crew and guests.

The fish that was involved in the equator ceremony was given back to the fishes; it was unrefrigerated for too long!

I also asked and got a breakdown of the costs for the visas for this trip, just to show a peek at the buried costs of traveling.

For the two of us, here is the breakdown per Country:

Brazil (USA)	$798.00
Togo (USA)	$158.00
India (USA)	$738.00
Kenya (All Nationalities)	$198.00
Myanmar (All nationalities)	$158.00
Mozambique (All nationalities)	$338.00
Madagascar (All nationalities)	$118.00
Tanzania (USA)	$398.00

If the (USA) is indicated, it means that different countries are charged a different fee. To go to the USA from India as a tourist or student, it costs per couple (since all the above were for Lynn and myself) $320.00 in US dollars (or Rupee equivalent), non-refundable, non-transferable.

While a U.S. passport is visa-free in 72 countries, Denmark and Luxemburg are visa-free in 172 countries, and the United Kingdom, Sweden, and Finland are at 173!

I also needed to make the model ship more intriguing, so I recruited more people.

One of the couples had an instant print camera, and I had her take a picture of everyone on the team, then had another member make little people using those faces. Also, one member made a pier! I also converted it to a humanitarian ship and made it an all-woman crew to get the environment and feminist vote....gotta' win!

The show was a combination of production staff and the juggler. The woman who volunteered to help the juggler was unsteady, so the juggler called up her husband and me to help her. We did the plate-on-stick trick, then the juggler and her husband took her off stage, the juggler telling me to "entertain the folks until I return," so there I was, on stage, with a stick with a plate on it. So, I spun the plate and danced on stage. The juggler snuck behind my back, and then I sat in my seat to watch. Finally, he came out and relieved me to the applause of the audience. I'm not sure they were applauding for me or glad he took over!

Line dancing was at 10:30. I agreed to go to take pictures of Lynn dancing, and the participation was pitiful! It was the person that was the acting instructor, Lynn, and another lady, five people at most on the sidelines; so much for "late" night activity!!

Saturday, March 3rd, Mangalore, India

We actually docked a little early! This was another face-to-face Immigration inspection, with forms to fill out specifically for today. We had another form for tomorrow, and some people were given the wrong form for today. The inspection was conducted in a much more orderly fashion; people weren't on the steps and on two floors, but the turning in vouchers for bus tickets was again clumsy, but it kind of worked, professionally? We were stopped at the exit for one final check of the right form and off the ship. Buses on the right, terminal on the left, jam up of people at the terminal, so we skirted it and headed for the buses, no direction there also, found our bus (no seat saved), and off we went. As we approached the gate, a cow crossed in front of us, one of the two tag-along people left (guard), and we were off to our first attraction, the Belmont house, a restored 18th-century house for us to tour.

"Namastay" is the local Indian language for "welcome to India." as in Calcutta, this city is known by many names, including the following: In Tulu, the primary language of this city it is "Kudla" (meaning junction, the city is at the junction of the Netravali and Guru Pura rivers) in the Konkani language it is "Kodial", and in the Beary language, "Makala" (meaning wood charcoal which used to be produced on the river banks). Finally, it was officially re-named among 12 other cities, including Calcutta to Mangaluru, on November 1, 2014

Noah

This port handles 75% of India's coffee exports and the bulk of the cashew exports. The major products of this city are fishing, agriculture, mined sand, and tourism.

97% of the population is literate, there is only one public hospital in this city, the rest are all private, there is no welfare, no public housing, we are told that "there are jobs for those that want to work" and "you are expected to support your kids if you make them." Most of the roofs are tile to keep the rooms cool in the summer and warm in the winter; weddings are a big thing. A "typical" wedding will have 1500-2000 guests!

Mangalore has been declared the eighth cleanest in India and ranked India's 13th place to do business destination. India has 2000 languages, many change every 18 kilometers, and with languages, the food styles and spices.

The traffic jams are horrible, from 8-9:30 AM and 5:30-8:45 PM "moving parking lots".

Most educated people work 6 days a week, 8 hours a day, for a pay of around $1000 US /month.

The tour of the house was very nice: a large kitchen, a number of bedrooms and a living room, a nice garden and yard, and they were actually grinding spices in the pantry. We were also provided water and cookies as we toured the house.

Back on the bus for a short drive to the food market. This was a vast covered market with small stalls. It was very clean but crowded; the paths were singular, and both ways, so you sidestepped some others sidestepped you. It was relatively quiet. People smiling and doing business and did not mind pictures.

We made our way through the market, walked a couple of blocks past a number of small storefronts, and shared the sidewalk with motorbikes, Tuk Tuk's, and small cars! Toured the downtown area, we had a little extra time, so the guide stopped at the Ideal Ice Cream Company outlet to buy "The best ice cream in the world." A few of us got off and brought back a scoop of different flavors. I bought an Indian nut flavor and Jack fruit. Both were very good, smooth, and creamy! The guide was good enough to convert the money for us!

We still had a small amount of time left, so he took us to the public beach, which, too, was very clean. On the way back, we were shown sand harvesters, where people take low boats out to the center of an inlet, dive down to the bottom, and bring up buckets of sand to sell. Yes, I got pictures!

On the last leg on the way back to the pier, we were shown how men wear their "skirts," and the guide provided us a demonstration of how women wrap themselves in saris.

The gift shop in the terminal had all the souvenirs I promised different people, plus postcards and stamps!

Back on the ship, afternoon games, journaling, and a lazy afternoon, tomorrow is our second port in India before heading for Indonesia.

A one-woman show, Michelle Montuori, a great singer and comedian with flair, was exceptional and finished the night.

Sunday, March 4th, Cochin, India

This is the second and last port in India. Cochin includes 24 islands, and there are ferries to the most populated ones. One of India's largest naval bases is here. The port is very commercial, and it was established by the Portuguese and settled by the British and Dutch. Vasco De Gama actually died and was buried here in 1524.

We actually arrived right on time, another face-to-face with authorities; these folks were even more efficient than the other port! New visas to fill in, sign, and return when we boarded the ship. These were printed correctly, with no extra steps. By the way, these were inspected before we left the ship at the bottom of the gangplank. When we returned to the ship, these forms were deposited in a box so everyone was accounted for before we went anchor.

There is still a problem with the passengers on this ship, luckily, we had a reserved seat on the bus when our bus ticket was called there were only about 12 people in the theatre when we got to the bus, it was almost full, now many more are picking up their bus tickets and leaving the ship before being called to get the best seats on the bus, so now not only are they some of the most inconsiderate, and self-centered, they don't think procedure and rules apply to them!

As we left the ship, there was a money exchange set up by a bank, again was a first, and I thought what a great idea, especially when this was another Sunday port call in an Indian port that is 50% Christian

Noah

(The population of Cochin is about 1.5 million) and many if not all professional buildings and banks are closed.

The tour buses here always have two people, the driver, and a helper, besides the guide and the shipping representative. The driver's helper jumps out to pay tolls, stops traffic if turns are not negotiable, and actually tries to stop traffic if the bus actually has to back up. Remember, this is "chicken" and "camel nose" driving!

Our first stop was the first Christian Church established by the Portuguese, St. Francis, built in 1503. The best part was the gardens, Pepper trees, Jack fruit trees, different banana trees, and flowers. Actually, black pepper was referred to as "Black Gold," and red, white, and black pepper all come from the same tree and must be hand-harvested. Services are in the local language and then repeated in English; it is not uncommon for a church service to last several hours. The Hindus have no special day for worship; it is up to the individual.

Our next stop was the fishing area, where fisherman demonstrated how they lowered and raised their nets from shore and also showed off their fresh catch for the day. There are a lot of vendors at each stop; the most popular items they sell are scarves, carved animals, wooden puzzle boxes, and jewelry. One of the fishermen liked my "O" white cap, so I gave it to him...

The first high-end stop on this cruise was to an Indian store, expensive carvings, high-end clothes, and jewelry. We received the customary soft drink, and there was an abundance of clerks ready to answer any questions or provide help in any way, and yes, they made several sales. (No, not us, but the soda was cold!)

Next was a 1665 Portuguese "palace" that was nothing special, with ancient wall coverings, no touch, no photos, and a guard in every room.

It is getting hot in the '90s, and with high humidity, the bus is air-conditioned...Thank God!! Monsoon season is from June through September.

The last stop before heading back to Port was Jew Street. Both sides of the street were lined with stores, mostly clothes and souvenirs, but there were also spice shops.

We walked past the building housing the largest spice distributor in India; they are online now for most of their products, 20% to the USA, 40% to Japan, and 20% each to Europe and China.

The spice shops we explored had everything; I found a sample variety for Camille, some Arabica coffee for Art, and some peppermint essence for my sinuses. This is one of the women's co-ops where the government provides low-interest loans. The only drawback was that the marked price was the price. I attempted to bargain three times and got the same answer about this being a "women-owned business" and how everyone there was a woman, etc. But I got what I wanted, and the prices were reasonable.

We had a half hour back to the port, so here is some more information gleaned from our guide. The government also works with charities to provide low-interest loans and tax incentives.

We passed by one of the open-air laundries. They were started in the 1720s, subsidized by the government with electricity and water for the washing and cleaning of naval uniforms. The laundry has expanded for the general public and is very reasonable. It also provides jobs in the area.

Dump trucks are family-owned and painted and decorated by that family. It is very colorful, has a variety of accessories, and different statements professing the family faith, a sense of humor, or just making that truck really personal.

You need to be 18 to get a license to drive (learner for a year after that) and 21 to drive commercially, including four years of driving experience. We are told that to drive in India, you need three things: Good Brakes, Good Horn, and Good Luck.

Tuk Tuks are made in Italy by Peugeot; they cost 150,000 Rupees (17 rupees to a dollar currently ($8850 U.S.); they have a top end of about 65 Km/hr (40 mph)

We got back to the ship a little after 1 P.M., ditched the stuff, and by the time we went for lunch, it was after 2, salads and salty fries plus lots of water restored us. Later, afternoon games and a little downtime.

We ate later than usual for dinner, rested a bit more before evening trivia, and then inspected the decorations for the gala Hollywood Awards to be broadcast tonight for the pre-party and on TV and on the big screen starting at 6 A.M. tomorrow. I didn't stay, had no interest at all in Hollywood elite showing off, and couldn't care less about the awards…Lynn can do as she wants!?! We will see.

03-05-18, Monday

Lynn did not get up at 6 A.M. to watch the Academy Awards live. At 2 A.M., I awoke to searing pain in my left ankle. It felt sprained! I hobbled to the bathroom twice during the night and took a couple pain pills, and Lynn was good enough to ace bandage me so I could use that ankle. (That stinkin' gout!!)

Games in the morning, I was shown what the teammate did with the pictures of people and was told on the guess survey taken before the Academy Awards that I was the person who had NO correct answers to the 24 questions! I am now only baking for 20 minutes per side to deepen the tan.

I talked to the concierge about my disappointment with Oceania and the lack of effort of reciprocation; I also wanted to clarify the discounts on refunds for the missed excursions, and I also requested priorities on reimbursements so that all discounts were applied first if there is money left from the $2800.00, I initially deposited in the account. ($2300 was for the gratuities required)

We talked to a number of other folks about Oceania, who were not happy about the missing ports; one couple got a fully obstructed view, and another, which happens to be from India, suggested two ports that only require 48-hour notice that could have been added. We agreed that the perception they are pedaling is not reality. But then again, they are catering to that smaller group of repeats and world cruisers … nothing new!

Worked with the boat team. Amelia will be providing a paragraph on the Bio-modal for the boat, gathering more material for a pier where the husbands and boyfriends will stand to wave goodbye to the boat, and also a case to enable the boat to carry 18-20 cans of soda.

Afternoon trivia, afternoon games, late evening trivia; ankle still pounding, right knee persisting in not cooperating, we called it a night, another hour advance, we will now be 12 ½ hours ahead of home tomorrow. I finished a second book I got from another guest. It was great, about spies and dealing with the Middle East, that with killing the Rising Sun makes two books this cruise! Attempted accessing the internet after 9, 12 tries, and 15 minutes, but no luck. I will try again tomorrow.

Tuesday, March 6th

There is no forecast since this is a day at sea, but outside, it is bright and sunny. Today is another County Fair Day, so we should see about 1/3 of the guests on deck playing or observing the games. There are also two lectures I want to attend. This morning, it seems the pain in the ankle went over to the right ankle. Sinuses again also, plus knee, what a wreck! Migraine meds, peppermint oil, topical rub sunscreen, plenty of water, and off!

There is no internet access this A.M., like last night. It is included in the cruise, but with only limited access, it gets frustrating, especially when all I want to do is check E-mail! The weather is partly cloudy in the mid-90s, but the humidity is in the 6o, so I again baked for just under an hour.

We are in the largest bay in the world, the Bay of Bengal, the northern part of the Indian Ocean, with India on the west, Bangladesh to the north, and Myanmar to the east. This area has many tropical dolphins, sea turtles, marlins, tuna, and sharks. The surface movement of water changes direction with the seasons, with the northeast monsoons giving it a clockwise rotation and the southeast monsoons a counterclockwise rotation. The climate is dominated by the monsoons; the water temperature is stable and warm. The only animal/fish life we saw was a few flying fish!

The 1st lecture was basically about the processes the charities have to go through with governments. The bigger the government, the bigger the hassle, and of course, it is who you know that finally gets things done! Camels are like llama's spit. They actually regurgitate stomach contents to spit when irritated...He showed us the map of the reserve created for the wild camels. He did admit that this was the "politically correct map" and then, with a laser pointer, indicated the expanded "real" area. It seems as though everyone plays the game of correctness. It's funny the difference between reality and perception again!

The fair was another success; 150-200 people participated. I had more tickets than last time, and so did Lynn, but the results were the same...Nada.

The second lecture was on the upcoming port of Myanmar, and I may later repeat some of this information when we go on the tours, but it will be a good reinforcement.

Myanmar was Burma; the population is about 83 million. In December of 1970, the traffic moved from left to right, causing a lot of confusion, where it seems that in India, both sides count??

The religion is mostly Buddhist (about 90%), Muslim (6%) and Christian, and others the balance. Northern Myanmar is a major supplier of Opium; the balance of the country grows and exports rice.

This has been a country in turmoil since the English granted sovereignty; starting in 2012, the representative government began to flourish, and by 2015, the government became a democracy, and the sanctions were lifted by the rest of the world.

To the North-northwest are the Himalayan Mountains, "the roof of the world." On the other side of the Himalayas is the Tibet plateau. This area extending east is very fertile, including Thailand, Cambodia, and Vietnam.

The Buddhist temples are bell-shaped, and we should see many of them. You should walk around them clockwise, with no shoes inside, and cover your knees and shoulders. Contents are usually relics.

Afternoon games, caught up on notes, found supplies for the crew to finish their projects and worked on the boat to finish our part. We now also have a fog horn box.

Dinner listened to the string quartet, won late trivia, and attended a one-man show. A tenor from Australia tried very hard to get audience participation, but it is hard with a tired and ½ dead audience. Maybe, maybe 1/3 even started to clap when asked to clap along. I felt sorry for him! Tried to get on the internet, but I had no luck again. I will try again tomorrow. I may have to go to the internet room and use their computers it will be three days tomorrow.

Wednesday, March 7th,

A day at sea, it was in the 80's, both temperature and humidity, light breeze, calm seas. Normal sea day activities attended all, got the points, baked both sides for almost an hour, and coordinated and cooperated with the boat team to finish our respective projects. I was advised we needed to put a number on the bow and home port on the stern by my navy person. We also needed a nationality, so we made it

Themyscira, the Amazon women's island kingdom, and Majuro, the port of registration.

I also checked the e-mails from the IT room and arranged for our boat to be last in the contest to have its own table and display with the event's manager.

The lecture was on the origin of Boko Haram, which made the headlines when 20 school girls were captured and carried off.

First, a little history was given. Long before the white Portuguese and Spanish brought slaves to the Americas, Arabs and Muslims were enslaving northern, mid, and southern African people into slaves and marketing them to the Mideast and Europe.

These were the same who just conveniently sold the slaves to the whites when the whites established ports on the western coast of Africa.

In 1804, there was the Fulani Jihad against all non-Muslims in the northern half of Africa, including Nigeria.

From 1900-1960, Britain stopped slave trading and the tribal infighting.

It seems that Nigeria is dominated by small tribes, all with different religions and languages, some mountain and some plain, some hunters, others farmers. Education is primary at best, with little middle and high school training/learning. Nigeria gained independence in 1960, and there has been tribal infighting ever since. When Islamic tribes conquered other tribes, forced circumcision was done to the survivors, and since there was such a low requirement for education, those boys who had a little education saw an opportunity for glory and fame by joining the Boca Haran rather than returning to farming.

To this day, the Nigerian Army is also somewhat divided by faith, with some factions sympathetic to the Muslim faith, and makes raids on locations where the intended targets have been warned. The kidnapping and killing persist today, just not reported on. We are told that much is not revealed to the world here.

In many families, the faith they profess in public may not be the faith practiced at home.

We were shown a picture of a mother with a baby on her back and a dome over the baby's head to protect it from the sun. We were told that the condition called a congenital hip, where the hip is not fully formed around the leg bone when the child is born, is somewhat common. The practice of carrying the child with its legs around the mother's body enables the pelvis to finish forming with the leg held in place around the mother. Thereby, the need for a cast and brace never arises, and the child grows up without limitations in walking.

Gout came back shortly after the sunbathing….stupid me, so hydrate, hydrate, and hopefully, it will go away again! The knee, even with the topical pain medication, makes it.

There were more games, dinner, and trivia, and we went to a birthday/hard-to-climb steps now. What a wreck I am becoming!!! At the anniversary party, we were invited to by friends. It was billed as "You Pick the Hits"; there were a good 50 people there. There was also a private party sign-out for the 180-day folks, and it was also billed as an anniversary and birthday celebration. We stayed a good 45 minutes. This wasn't a very inclusive bunch, and we both felt like outsiders, so we packed up and left.

Thursday, March 8th

Tiffany's Birthday; I can't get out on the computer in our room. I took it to the computer lab, checked e-mails, and wished her a happy birthday! It should be the first since we are about 12 hours ahead of Franklin! It is in the upper 90s, with humidity in the 80s and a haze over the water and sky.

Yangon (Rangoon), Myanmar, will be our place tonight and tomorrow, and we leave the next day. We have two excursions planned; some have overnight excursions here. We are told to look for golden stupas, rice fields, ruined temples, and interesting paths. The area of Bagan (formerly Pagan), covering 67 square kilometers, boasts two thousand Buddhist structures.

The gout kept waking me up last night, plus the bathroom runs. The knee was not getting better, so I rubbed in the knee and drank water like a fish all day. We played the games, but then I went back to the room to remove the bandage on the ankle and take a power nap.

Lunch was fish and chips, and we played afternoon games. Both guys and gals on the boat team are working together on what they will wear and what to do to present our boat. It is kind of fun to watch, and

Educating Noah...Travelin'

giving them a loose leash is providing amazing results!

We entered a very wide river mouth at about 3 P.M., and we are expected to dock at 6 P.M. There are several excursions going out tonight. Some are getting nervous already as to the dock time. The outside is very hazy. It was hard to determine whether there was a shore or not, and the river was brown.

The pier is an industrial one, a very small area for bus pick-up. It is guarded, and no one is allowed outside the bus area. We were docked at 6:45 P.M., but it seems this captain docks late or not at all!

We had dinner with friends, trivia, and then went to the liars show. It is a show where four officers define a word, and you are to guess who is telling the truth! It was a fun game. I guessed three out of four and Lynn two out of four. There were people returning from extended trips in India and others with nighttime trips, so even for this ship, the attendance was only about 50 at best!

Friday, March 9th

The sunny 90s (temp and humid) dress for temples, and our excursion is off at 7:45! Our tour was called "Experience local life in Thanlyin."

Thanlyin, also known as Syriam, is the ancient section of the city at the confluence of the Yangon and Bago rivers. It was part of a thriving major port that was heavily damaged in 1756 during the Mon revolt and only partially rebuilt.

The visas were all handled by the ship, not face-to-face. We got our bus number ticket, and at 7:45, our bus number was called. The drive to town is about 45 minutes, so we get filled in by a very interesting and articulate guide. This is a farm region; the fuel costs are low and not taxed, and oil comes from Singapore. This port has a very high tide. Only about 10 cruise ships come here a year due to the shallow river you have to navigate to get here. The gangplank is changed from one deck to another three times during the day. Many people apply a white powder to their face as make-up (both men and women), and the powder also acts as a sunscreen. It's funny how white people want to tan to get darker, and dark people want to look whiter! There are 52 million people in this country, 85% Buddhist, 400 dialects, and 135 tribal groups. The name of Yangon recently replaced the old name of Rangoon to reflect an inclusive country rather than one named after one tribe (Rangoon). This is similar to what India did with the city of Calcutta! (It was Kolkata)

The British planned for 200,000 citizens, and the city outgrew the water and sewer needs quickly at the turn of the century, so every household had its own well. The land is very expensive to own. One acre costs about $4,000 US; banks charge a high rate for property loans, 13%! They drive on the right side of the road. What a difference! Agriculture is the main export. We stopped briefly to pay a toll outside the port, and it was collected by a guy with a basket! There is a lot of garbage dumped on the side of the road, and there is currently an effort to curb both the garbage and plastic waste.

Motorbikes are not allowed in large cities, and it takes 30 years for a teak tree to mature. We are now at our first stop, a horse and buggy ride through town, two people per cart, VERY small, we sit on the side, and this was not made for Americans! Next was a bicycle ride, a tandem seat next to a driver; again, this was designed for locals. Let's just say that many, if not all of us, overflowed the seats, cramped and uncomfortable, with hard wooden seats. A great experience. We were all happy about the experience, happy also it was soon over.

We then stopped at a huge local market. These folks were selling everything from groceries to clothes, the stores/stalls were crowded with merchandise, the people were not pushy, many smiled, many did not understand English, and many did not know the conversion to US dollars. I did find one vendor, bought a few small items, and was able to get change in MMRs. Lynn used the public toilet; there was a local one and an English one; this one was "Happy Buddha sized, 2X! "

After spending 45 minutes at the market, back on the bus for more info on the way back to port in 1988, there was a student revolution, many who could go to Singapore for higher education, and there have been revolutions every ten years!

There are a lot of stray dogs' rib cages showing. Many of the younger men chew leaves (like tobacco) and spit out the red juice it produces; there are red spots on sidewalks, streets, and curbs. The side effects are the same as tobacco, along with the consequences, including mouth cancer.

Beer is cheap, about $1.00 per bottle, and bottled water is 50 cents. The average diet is rice and curry spices three times per day, 7 days a week. Men (Buddhists) must go to the monastery to study twice in their lifetime, usually around the age of 7 and then again at 20, about 2 weeks each time.

Three stages of life are believed by the Buddhists:

1. Young and educate
2. Build family
3. Retire.

The life expectancy is 50 for men and 65 for women.

Back on the ship, we showered, changed, had afternoon games naps, and then we had formal tea instead of supper. Caught up on lingering, watched a movie in the cabin, and elevated my left ankle to relieve some of the gout.

Saturday, 9th of March

We are in single digits as far as days to return home. We are anxious to return, and I need to do IRS returns for Ma and us, start a severe diet, and find out what is going on with the left shoulder and right knee!

A few more items need to be completed for the ship-building contest. Lynn checked with Jackson, the kid, and he was done. The pier is done; the little people with our faces are done also. The materials for the biosphere are gathered. Now, just coordination on the presentation.

Our excursion today, "Taste of Yangon," starts at 8:45 AM, and we will not return until 2 P.M. in the afternoon, which will end our exploration of this port.

There were four busloads on this tour, and we were given a police escort there, during and back to the ship. The hour to and from the three sites we explored is filled in by our guide. I will try not to repeat what the other guide told us, but then again, I would rather hear from a person than from the papers and the heavily filtered news!

Our guide was trained as a lawyer and accomplished all the schooling requirements, but during his OJT, he decided not to pursue that career, claiming corruption and government involvement. So, he became a guide. We passed a corrugated roofed shack he pointed out as a duck farm. When asked, "Why don't they fly away?" he told the guest they were white ducks, house ducks, why leave the place where you are fed?

Winter here is 70 degrees, and people search for jackets. June through October is the rainy season, November through February is the dry winter season, and March through June is the summer.

The army is all-volunteer, and the minimum service is 10 years. There are 5.5 million in Yangon.

The "longyi" is the skirt men and women wear. Men are plaid, women are vibrant colors; 70% do not wear underwear under the skirt. Men are wrapped one way, women another. There are no pockets, no coins, wallets, and phones tucked into the waistband, and there is little to no theft.

This was one of the richest countries in Asia. Then, In 1986, the communists/socialists took over.

The money was devalued by ½ to make everything "more equal," so now this country /state was no longer the richest in the East. The new government told everyone that everything should be the same, that some were too rich, and that everyone should turn in their money for new money at ½ the value. This country does not have good banks, very few mortgages or loans, everyone saves up money to buy, and everyone "banked under the mattress." The money was exchanged for the new currency, and this really affected the "old people" and those who saved their money the most. Then, a year into this new government, it was discovered that there was a lot of new fake money coming over the border, and the new money was devalued to what it is today, $1300 to $1.00 US, $10,000 Bill worth about $8.00 US, a $5,000 bill worth about $4.00 US. The bills now are 75, 90, 200, 500, 1000, and makes it hard to count or make change.

After 4 years, another revolution and a democratic government were installed with the promise never to change the money again. There are now two parts of this government: the legislative and the military.

The divorce rate is only 2%.

We arrived at our first stop, the Shwedagon Pagoda. We had an hour here, and it was barely enough… To walk the complex, you needed to remove shoes and socks and cover your knees, BOTH men and women. A couple guys did not wear long pants, and they were given skirts! A short elevator ride after checking any backpacks and anything larger than a small purse took us to a long, elevated corridor to the complex.

The main spire was the center of the complex, surrounded by various shrines and temples, gold, white, and wood. Buddha's in most extreme ornamentation, the main spire surrounded by small enclaves with Buddha's in each, some with lions, dragons, and elephants, from small to very large in size, on the front, some with elephants, fourteen represented the day, and divided the day in half, so if you were born on Wednesday morning you would pay your respects at that shrine, your name reflects the day and A.M. or P.M. The walking area was tiled. It is hard to describe; it took almost an hour of non-stop walking just to take in the variations and displays: Buddhas with disco lights behind their heads, mirrored lower temples, different colored wood structures, and lots of gold accented by pure white. I must have taken at least 100 pictures, and I don't know if I can justify how grand and glorious it was! This is the "Mecca" for Buddhists; the goal is to visit once in their lifetime.

There were family processions of kids before they were nuns and monks, the girls having their ears pierced, the boys having their heads shaved. Some dressed all in gold, some dressed in gold and white, and many of the family brought baskets of fruit as an offering.

Buddhists try to practice "be good, nice, and don't do bad"; Karma, Do good and good returns. 9 is the lucky number, and there are 108 beads on a Buddhist rosary.

We were all back on the bus in a little over an hour, thankful that the bus had air conditioning! The drive to the next Reclining Buddha was only 10-15 minutes. When he counted the people to make sure no one was left behind, the word for 8 sounded like "shit"; when he heard the Snickers, he counted for us and played with the numbers, especially the ones with the number 8...We all laughed!

This reclining Buddha was formed from one large piece of concrete; it is the second largest Buddha at 75 feet long. (The largest is Chowtouchi at 6 stories high.) This Buddha is white and has long eyelashes, blue eyes, and red lips; he was pretty and massive, and there again were small enclaves around the covered building to pray and offer water.

There was also a row of souvenir shops just outside, along with a kid selling birds for $1.00 each for free. Before letting one go, Lynn asked what happened to the birds at night, and we were told they were freed; it was mostly symbolic.

We stopped for a photo shoot downtown. A young girl was selling postcards, which I had not seen in the last two days. She asked for $3 for what looked like 10, so I did not dicker with her, and then all I had was a five. She had no change, so I told her to keep the change (10 postcards for $5.00 is a good deal). She was very happy when I returned to the bus. I saw it was 10 pairs of postcards...Karma!!

I don't know how long it would have taken us to get back without the police escort for the four buses, as it was, there were a lot of warning horn beeps, some traffic signals ignored, and watching other vehicles, some had the driver's side on the left, some on the right. Most of the imports come from China or Japan, 50% or more of the population have cell phones, there are 33 letters in their alphabet and 8 vowels, their writing is deviations and combinations of circles.

There are few accidents, and there is no auto or health insurance, so for the autos, the vehicle is treated like a baby; for health, most of the doctor's charges and nursing are covered, but not drugs. Many rely on home remedies.

Back on the ship, a little lunch, games, and "so long" to Yangon; two-hour happy hour, band on deck, we left 45 minutes late...it seems that this captain has a problem with schedules and times. (Have I said this before??)

The production show was good; Lynn liked it. After the show, there was dancing in the streets / Motown. Actually, about 25-30 people actually showed up, and the dance floor had a good amount of people on it. The gout returned again, had a rough night, and wrapped and elevated the ankle and foot.

Sunday, March 11th, a day at sea, 80-85 degrees, sunny and humid. Morning games, more "O" points (we now have more than 600!). The games include mini golf, shuffleboard, table tennis, carpet bowling, and Bean-O, Bean bag toss.

The lecture was mostly about our next port, Kuala Lumpur, Malaysia. This port/city is on the Thailand Peninsula, in the strait of Morocco, and has a population of 700,000. The three major exports are electronics, mineral oils, palm oil, and rubber. In 1988, its twin towers were the tallest in the world. Now, it is the fifteenth tallest.

Educating Noah...Travelin'

The one note about the rest of the lecture is how much the population of the world has increased. In the last 40 years, the world's population has increased by 2.5 Billion!

A wine tasting was offered, but I balked at the price...$75.00 plus 18% gratuity!

I asked the head bartender why, and she told me it included 5 premium wine tastings plus two special ones... I thought to myself, "Three-dollar Chuck," how many cases of wine could I buy back home for over 80 bucks! I passed on the tasting. She approached me later and asked again if I was interested or had changed my mind, but I refused again. Later on, in the afternoon, I asked if they had signed up enough people to have the tasting, and she confirmed that 14 people had taken part, and it was a success. We also had a flyer in the daily Current publication offering a deal on wine by the bottle... all bottles are priced at "only" $47.50 each, a minimum of 7 bottles (total $333.00 but no 18% gratuity!) Passed on this too!!!

Afternoon games, NO sun. I cannot afford to trigger that gout again with dehydration! Worked with the boat team to coordinate everyone. We have 5 couples; we are out to win this!

Dinner was with part of the entertainment team, Steve and Trisha Blake, and another couple. A third couple never showed up?? It was a very nice meal, the conversation was informative and fun, and dinner lasted 2 ½ hours. (This was past the evening trivia, which we missed.)

The entertainment was a comic called Steve Stevens; he was very good, very entertaining!

Monday, our last sea day before our next two ports, and leaving for home. SHIP BUILDING SEA TRIALS, at noon. We met the team at the morning games. Everyone was ready, and we were confident. The five guys were in robes and hats, and the women, the crew, had hats and scarves, white blouses, and light shorts.

After the games, Lynn and I went to the room to get the ship, and we took it down to the desk to show the staff. They were impressed. We explained about the biosphere and the water tanks. We were ready and confident.

We met the rest of the crew and mates 45 minutes before the judging. We set up an extra table, showed off the ship, and taped everything down; the wind was enough to cause problems. Then the other boats showed up, some very interesting. There were a total of 7. I had negotiated the last presentation. All the boats floated. They were able to stay afloat with 1-16 full cans of soda, and then it was our turn. We had our own announcer, we had a presentation with all the guys in robes and hats, and we coordinated a fog horn blown with the bridge. Everything went off well, then they put the boat in the water, and it stopped to the side. We had checked before, but for some reason, it no longer floated, listed, listed badly…it was over. It may have been that the water they had just refilled the pool was fresh water and thereby less salty, or it was too windy, whatever, it failed miserably…I severely apologized to the group. We opened the bottle of Champaign we won and drank that, then I thanked everyone again, and we dispersed.

We (Lynn and I) took the robe down to the room, gave back the hats we had borrowed, and went to lunch. I was depressed; I had let the team down, their confidence in me, and my confidence, but life goes on. At the afternoon games, I got a little sympathy, and I congratulated the guy who won second place. I will congratulate the boy, he won third.

During the games, we presented the dancing team with a good wish for their upcoming wedding in Hawaii; we also presented them with another $100.00 gold bill I donated and about $350.00 in cash; they were flabbergasted!

We took pictures of all of us with them and finished the games for the afternoon. Then Lynn went to practice for the talent show (she will be dancing in the line dance segment). I went back to the room to review the preliminary bill, catch up on lingering, and elevate my feet to prevent another gout attack.

I received a phone call, and one of the guests suggested that I play "Papa" bear in a skit to come down and fill in. I arrived and volunteered to play Papa Bear in a Goldilocks skit, and then Lynn was recruited also. It was a Goldilocks story. Jackson, the kid, and another guest were also recruited. We replaced a couple who backed out at the last minute, and so being "troopers," we will do this and perhaps add something to it!

Dinner with Lynn, I was not in the mood to talk to anyone, and we played our last late-night trivia. Lynn went to the singing program. I don't like classical music, so I finished the notes, set up the comments for the end of the cruise, prepared for our Indonesian port tomorrow, and licked my wounds over the boat.

Here is the "spiel" and pitch:

Introducing the NOOPY ship! Touting an all-female crew dedicated to MOTHER EARTH, the ENVIRONMENT, and HUMANITARIAN AID.

The Noopy ship showcases a BIOSPHERE that will ecologically sustain life as we know it.

This technology will be carried to under-developed countries whose populations are in need of animals, plants, food, and, of course, water due to drought and weather pattern changes for a healthy and better future.

Ship Building Information

Name of ship: S.S. Noopy

Crew Members and rank:

Lynn	Captain
Sharon	1St Mate
Amelia	Manager
Gail	Boatswain
Angela	Engineer

Registry of Vessel/Why/Reason:

The island kingdom of Themyscira has a registry in:

MAJURO

1. The market determines the price (This is the second largest registry, exceeded only by the Bahamas)

2. Provides a flag of convenience,

3. Minimum rules and regulations (No US labor laws), taxes, and finally, the Captain has absolute authority.

Type of ship:

        Tanker/Cargo

What is the itinerary?

Noah

1. To empower women (All women crew)

2. Assist mankind throughout the world by supplying potable water to areas in the world suffering from drought, plus providing a small biosphere for the incubation of food and animals for sustenance and education.

Special Features of this vessel:

1. All female crew (with faces)
2. Shallow draft to make the ship more port-friendly
3. Propeller turns, rudder turns, and crane operates,
4. Removable cargo area hot/greenhouse (biosphere)
5. Transfer hose for potable water 27,000 gallons (by scale),
6. Cargo: the ability to get 20 cans of soda.
7. Lifeboat on cranes to lower.
8. Pier with husbands and lovers waving goodbye.

    (With faces)

9. Interactive fog horn

Tuesday, March 13th, Kuala Lumpur (Port Klang), Malaysia

The forecast was the middle 80s with occasional thunderstorms; the money here is called the MYR Malaysian Ringgit...

This was an unscheduled day; just walk around and take a shuttle bus to the town. We did not know that Oceania parks/docks frequently in the freight piers (cheaper??) So many times, we had to take a bus to the terminal and then another after the terminal. It was sunny, in the 80's, and off to the terminal we went. We took the shuttle bus to a shopping center in Port Klang just to look around and head back. The center wasn't opening till 10:00; it was 9:50, and the place was locked up tight.

One of the other couples approached us and told us that a cab driver was offering a trip to Kuala Lumpur if he had two couples for $40.00/ couple, twenty bucks each, showed us the major sites there, and returned us to the mall by 3:30.

Yes! We agreed and hopped into the Toyota, me in front and three

Educating Noah...Travelin'

in the back seat. It's a little close, but not bad! The trip to Kuala Lumpur took almost an hour (about 30 miles, but this was morning traffic). The driver was quite friendly, informative, and open to questions and discussion. The roads were in excellent condition, and everyone had insurance but did not want to use it. At times, there are motorcycle lanes parallel to the highway. Driving is a combination of "chicken" and "camel nose". Again, the English influence and driving on the left side of the road.

The first stop was the Twin Towers. These were the tallest buildings until 15 years ago, but they are still the tallest twin towers in Asia. We entered the shopping complex of 4 stories at the base. All were high-end stores! We found the restrooms that did not charge to get in and then looked for the elevators at the top of the towers. We walked back and forth, could not find, given directions twice with no help, and finally did find someone who told us to turn left at "Good Chee"'; there was a hall to the front of the Gucci store, then another hall to the right then a small sign to go down steps to the elevators for the tower. The room on top is limited, the wait for the elevator is sold in ½ hour increments, and the next increment available was 2:30. And that wouldn't work, so we joined the other couple at the designated time (noon) at the entrance to meet with our driver and off to our next attraction. The driver did give us a little history of this town. He grew up here, and he was amazed at how fast and how much the city had changed. And oh, by the way, people come to the tower at 7 A.M. to get an early elevator ticket. We passed by some great turn-of-the-century buildings, stainless steel modern buildings, Mosques (the community is 50% Muslim), churches, and temples. Our next stop was a "people" market, where the locals went. It was air-conditioned, two stories, very clean, and huge! There were souvenirs, a food court, a place where they had fish clean your feet, clothing, jewelry, carvings, and even a DHL shipping service at the entrance!

Outside was another market, more of the tent style, a little less expensive and crowded. We wandered through that market and also went down the street to see Chinatown. Lynn was overcome by the heat, and we returned to the entrance at the designated time to meet our driver to finish the driving tour and return. The other couple had talked to the driver and asked how much additional it would be to take us back to the ship, and he agreed to an additional $5.00 each; we agreed to that also. They also wanted to pay the driver with cash, so I gave him my $50.00 for us, and he wouldn't take any more for a tip...

(I guess we Americans tend to tip too much? Many times, some countries consider it a tip an insult)

On the way back through the city, we passed the world's largest covered aviary, the K.L. Bird Park; we noticed no graffiti, so he drove us past a culvert where graffiti is allowed, and yes, there was graffiti there... imagine that, respect on both sides! I asked about drugs. If you are caught with illegal drugs, you are sent to rehabilitation for 6 months. If you are caught again, automatic two years in prison. What about the drug dealers? They are executed! We passed some multi-colored housing units, and we are told those two-room houses are given to government workers after 20 years of service, free and clear (you can sell yours after 2 years of occupying it after ownership.) We had to stop for gas, and the driver pulled up to a natural gas dispenser. I asked him how much it cost to convert and why. He told me about $1000.00 US to convert, which is cleaner, cheaper, and more economical. He showed me the input nozzle under the hood and the tank under the car. He told me if natural gas was not available, he could easily switch to regular gas. That is interesting!

He delivered us to the pier as promised by 3:30. We paid him and wished him well and back on the ship.

I did some documentation; Lynn went to line dance practice for the talent show that evening.

In the Goldilocks story, the couple that had volunteered to be Mama and Papa had backed out, so I was recruited, and then I recruited Lynn. It was a "lesson" story; We helped them get over stage fright, another 15 minutes of fame. There were singers, dancers, and musicians playing in the talent show from the crew and officers, a couple comedians, Lynn's Line dance troop, Zorbas dancers, guitar players, and harmonica players from the guest list. One of the best entertainment venues on the ship! So that ended the day.

March 14th, we should arrive in Singapore by 10:00,

This will be hectic. It is forecast to be in the 80s, with humidity to match. We have to put all of our treasures and clothes in three suitcases, two carry-ons and two purses! I went to the computer lab; it took an hour to confirm our booking, and we still would not print our boarding passes. Then it was the pack, weigh, repack, weigh crap, and yes, of course, it got ugly, and the luggage scale broke too!

Educating Noah...Travelin'

We finally got all three checked bags under 50# and went to lunch.

Our excursion was at 1:45 PM, "Singapore with less walking," we were the third couple to leave the theatre, and when we got to the bus, it was almost full. Luckily, we had reserved seats. Two people were about 10 minutes late; we suspected immigration. Very tight here! (Chewing gum is banned)

Singapore is very new, with many new and very attractive buildings, the city is very clean, as clean as Japan, and of course no graffiti! There are more than 60 smaller islets in the area. In the 70's, Singapore imported sand and dirt to increase the land base by 25% and created reservoirs for fresh water. It is the 4th biggest financial center in the world and the 2nd busiest port in the world. Singapore has the third highest per capita income in the world but also one of the highest income inequalities; it is also very high in the international rankings with regard to education, healthcare, and economic competitiveness.

85% live in government housing, and for the age, the apartment houses look well kept, and the reason is that they are purchased by the worker...ownership brings pride.

The harbor will be moved in the next two years due to larger ships needing deeper water. Some of the new cargo ships transport up to 20,000 containers!

Education is compensatory, the population is 5.6 million, 4 million are permanent, the balance is transient labor, and there is no unemployment here. Four official languages are English, Malay, Mandarin, and Tamil, with English always as either a primary or secondary language.

We pass the opera house. It is shaped like durian fruit, and the locals love it. It is an acquired taste, very sweet, and very pungent (stinks). We also passed by the Marina Bay Hotel, a three-column hotel with a disc layer on top that has an infinity pool; 2650 rooms, always full. The cheapest room is $550.00 US per night.

We exited the bus for a closer view of the harbor, walked a pedestrian bridge, viewed the Marina Bay Hotel and a lion water fountain, the opera house close up, and the surrounding gardens; absolutely no litter, graffiti, or bums (now called street people). There was some "art" being erected showing compressed plastic bottles and wasted plastic, raising awareness?

Singapore was founded in 1819 by Sir Stanford Raffles as a trading post for the East India Company; he brought workers from China, India, Sumatra, Indonesia, and Java. In 1824, Singapore became a British Colony, and the British ruled for 145 years till 1941, when the Japanese defeated the British there. They not only killed the soldiers, but they rounded up all people wearing glasses (intelligent and literate), took them down to the beach, and massacred them. The Japanese ruled for 3 years until the end of the war. (WWII) In 1955, Singapore petitioned for independence, and it was granted a few years later. Singapore then joined the Malaysia Union, but that only lasted 4 years, so Singapore became independent again (1965) and became a member of the United Nations.

We drove through Little India, selling carpets and fabrics, The Muslim area, Arab Street, and China Town. These areas have been declared Historical Buildings, so the storefronts must remain the same. There are only retail sales, no private residences in the back or above the shops. There is a problem in that the kids no longer wish to take over the businesses, so many are sold or just start to go out of business, the storefronts vacant.

Ethnically, 75% Chinese, 14% East Malaysian, 9% Indians, and 3% Portuguese. When Singapore became a major port and industrialization happened, there was a moratorium on taxes for the people…5 years!

There is no graffiti, drug dealers are executed, and if you are caught on drugs, 6 months in rehab, a second offense, and two years in prison…sound familiar? Streets are well kept, parks and walks clean, and no litter to be found. Even the crosswalks have signs to keep to the left or right depending on the direction you are going or coming from.

We were both impressed this place is as clean, if not cleaner, than Japan! It is also the newest city, with green spaces and planted boulevards! What a great excursion!

Back on the ship, I finished packing, weighing, and packing again. We ate supper at 6:30, said goodbye to friends, went back to the cabin to make final preparations, and were in bed by 8:30. Set the alarm clock to 2:10 A.M., took our showers, and called it a night.

Thursday the 15th of March

It is going to be a long and stressful day. The alarm was set for 2:10 A.M. I woke up automatically at 2:00, and Lynn was awake also, so we decided to get ready. Breakfast was ordered for 2:30, but it came at 2:35. The bags we left outside our cabin were gone; we ate our breakfast, called for the dishes to be picked up, and left the ship at 2:55 A.M. Our meeting time in the terminal was 3:20 A.M., and we had customs to deal with plus both of us had two bulky carry-ons. We picked out our three suitcases, went through customs, went through security, grouped up, and went out to the bus. We had to wait for a couple that was late, customs? But at 3:40 A.M., we were off on the 30-minute trip to the airport.

There were 4 terminals; we dropped folks off at 1, then 2, and the balance of us got off at 4. We are told that this terminal and the 5th they are building are going to be fully automatic. We found a kiosk, figured out how it worked, printed our luggage tags and boarding passes, and went to the desk to check the luggage. Then security again gets into the security checkpoint line, the scanners, and x-rays, the passport re-checks, then off to find the gate.

The gate was on the other end of the terminal, but we made it with an hour to spare. We were put on the aircraft first due to Lynn's cane, and we easily found our seats. As stated in the beginning, we flew 1st class to Miami and now from Singapore to Hong Kong and Hong Kong to Chicago. Wow, what a difference! It is a self-contained cubicle with a seat that converts into a bed!

The 3 ½ hour flight was a breeze; I think both of us caught a few winks. We had talked to the Cathay Pacific agents at the luggage drop and gate about the 45-minute short transfer time in Hong Kong, so they had a guide for us when we landed; he escorted us through customs and security and then put us on the right path to the gate for home. We actually were there 15 minutes before boarding!

The parents with children and wheelchair people were loaded first when the gate finally opened 20 minutes late. There must have been 25-30 family and handicapped folks! When all were boarded, we were told the plane was past due for a maintenance check, so we sat for an additional 45 minutes before take-off. We did take off at 1:05 P.M.; time in Chicago was 12:05 A.M. today. We are told this will be a 14-hour flight. We will be catching up on the hours we lost on the cruise!

Noah

We had a few bumpy spots, the business class seats reclined fully to make a bed, and both blanket and pillow were provided, along with a small refresh kit including a blindfold, toothpaste and brush, and even mouthwash. The movie selection was extensive, with over 50 movies, games, and TV shows, along with aircraft data as where we were, speed, temperatures, and estimated time of arrival. Both Lynn and I caught a couple Z's. I watched a couple of the movies and listened to music. We arrived in Chicago about the time projected went through TSA Global. Lynn did not notice a large X on top of hers, so when we tried to get out after collecting our bags, she was sent back to have the information rechecked.

We missed our bus by 10 minutes, so we had to wait an additional 40 minutes for the next one, ride home, and we called a cab to take us home from the bus station. I got home at 6:30, and I brought up all the bags. Lynn went to McDonald's for a light meal… We are home, glad to be here, another adventure done!

Educating Noah...Travelin'

We checked with Tiffany, and on the way home, she told us that Ma had been taken to the hospital after falling and hitting her head. I helped carry the luggage up to the rooms in our condo, gulped down the McDonald's we had purchased on the way home, and left for the hospital. I was shown the x-rays, and it seems that Ma had extensive hemorrhaging on the brain. She has refused intubation for transportation to a specialist, and the doctor recommended hospice. I signed the paperwork. She was tired, made little sensical talk, and at 7:30, I left.

Tuesday, I returned signed additional paperwork for the social worker. Ma was talking clearer, and for the pain, they were providing a fentanyl patch and morphine injections.

Wednesday, a pic line was inserted, and a morphine pump was provided; by Thursday, morphine was given at a measured dose, and the pump was removed.

Friday afternoon, I was given three options by the social worker at the hospice:

1. Have ma transported back to the assisted living
2. Stay on hospice and pay the normal hospital rate for the weekend, or continue without hospice and not be charged room and board that weekend.

I called the doctor, asked for the hospice supervisor, and waited. No response. I called the social worker back and told him to release her from hospice so that she could spend the weekend at the hospital.

The next morning, the doctor came to the room. We stepped out into the hall, and he put her back in hospice. I agreed. I talked to hospice and arranged for transportation back to her room in assisted living, had the bed removed, and they finally got her there on Tuesday, where, after discussion with the manager at home, they promptly fired the Ascension Hospice and replaced them with Heartland Hospice, ma was glad to back with her friends and comfortable.

I started visiting Ma two to three times a week, but she was definitely declining. She had lost all vision in one eye; the other was only shades of grey. Tiffany had tried books on tape, but not only had my mother's vision declined, but also her will to live.

Over the next month or so, one decline led to another: she needed to be fed, then a couple days, she wouldn't leave her room, then the bed. I called all of her friends and all of our relations, and they all came to say "goodbye." Ted was here the last four days before she finally got her wish and passed at 12:30 PM 05-03 2018.

I need to thank my cousin Fred, who brought in a "Hi Google" for her to use the phone and the weekly visits from my ex-son-in-law Mike, and of course, Tiffany for watching over her while I was gone; what great family!!

I started to shift into gear as far as the estate, called all of the vendors, BC/BS, ATT, the accidental life policy, once by fax, the second by E-mail, and finally via registered mail with the death certificate. I went back and forth with the lawyer, called The Salvation Army, and then cleaned the room, turning it back to the facility on May 9th, and asked for a refund for the balance of the month's room and board. I documented everything I could. The lawyer went on vacation, and we were leaving just before he got back, so I sent my brother copies of all correspondence with the attorney, along with copies of the will and trust.

Educating Noah…Travelin'

British Isles Holiday, May 2018

I had arranged with my travel agent to call exactly at 4:30 PM the night before to get a choice of seats in the preferred economy class I paid for. All the airlines are different. Besides the up-charge for a premium economy seat, British Air charges an additional $70 dollars to pick your seat up to 24 hours before the flight, and then the choice is free.

The problem is that we had American Airlines using British Air, and the online site would not load. We both tried 10-15 times with no loading, waiting 4-5 minutes per attempt till the site timed out…frustrating!

The next morning, we both tried again, over an hour a piece, with no luck. He tried their air department, Globus couldn't help, and I tried calling British Air. I was basically brushed off again. However, my agent told me to try going through the American Airlines website; after 3 attempts, it directed me to the British Airlines site, and it actually loaded up. I entered the information, got to seat selection, and found our assignments… both were in the middle coral, and we were separated by three rows. I was not happy! Customer service…non-existent!!)

It is Friday the 25th before the Memorial Day weekend

Taffy showed up 5 minutes late, and the parking lot at the bus terminal was full. (Luckily, we had Tiffany drop us off!) We only had to wait 10 minutes for the bus; one guy was waiting outside and had a set of luggage with puppies and dog pictures on the hard case. Both Tiff and Lynn pointed the luggage out, and Tiff even took a picture!!

The bus was an extended bus, and most of the seats were taken. However, we did get seats together at the rear of the bus. Holiday weekend…traffic was horrible, we arrived at O'Hare 30 minutes late, and Lynn was antsy. We found the British Air short line, and they replaced our tickets. We had no opportunity to check in first or change seats and into the TSA line. The line was long, and no TSA pre-check was honored (British Air does not honor trusted travelers), but within a half hour, we were through!

There was a RED Nose promotion for Walgreens; we put in

$40.00 for chances to win a business/ first class upgrade and three seats raffled, but no luck.

Our seats were in the middle of the middle…I was sitting 3 rows back from Lynn; her seat was in the kid's row, with lots of legroom, but there was a possibility for the family with small children. Of course, she lucked out… the gal in front of me was the first with her companion to recline their seats as we left the ground; about 30% did this. The seats were slightly wider, and there was a bit more legroom, but I spent most of the 7-hour flight with my arms crossed in front of me…The folks on the left and right also wanted and hogged the armrests.

The flight had a little turbulence but nothing really notable; the cabin was quiet, and we arrived on time at Heathrow without any important incidents.

Lynn exited the compartment before I did (I thought). I waited outside the plane, at each intersection of the hallway, before the train to go to immigration, and then finally at immigration, where she caught up. She was doing the same thing behind me! We filled out our immigration cards, lined up in a Disney ride line, and preceded a little over an hour to the immigration agents. They took us both at the same time, and we picked up our luggage, found the Globus representative, and were in a cab with three other travelers, all of us going on different tours. The ride to London was a bit longer than usual, busy for a Saturday morning, and we were in our hotel by 11:00 A.M. (6-hour difference in time (back)).

They had a room for us; we crashed for a couple hours and caught up on some sleep. Our first excursion was to London at night.

We were up and dressed by 4, so we decided to walk around. The hotel we stayed at was only two blocks from the Thames River; we passed a small souvenir shop and got all those promised stuff for friends back home. I took pictures of Scotland Yard, Westminster Abby, and the government buildings with Big Ben. We also got pretty close to the large Ferris wheel on the river, called the London Eye. Each of the 32 capsules can hold up to 25 people, and it takes 35 minutes for a complete turn.

On the way back to the hotel, we toured Florence Nightingale Park for some great flower pictures.

Our excursion was a "Taste of London" that included dinner and a river cruise on the Thames. The dinner was at the Old Cock Tavern; the place dates back to 1549 and has the narrowest frontage of any pub in London.

We had a choice of one drink with the meal, soup (tomato basil) or a tossed green salad, beer battered fish and chips, or a Steak Ale Pie and either vanilla cheesecake or chocolate fudge cake. We took one of each and shared; wow...all fantastic, large portions, and perfectly cooked ...everyone enjoyed it, and not many cleaned their plate; it was just too much of a good thing.

Next was the ride on the Thames. The Thames has two tides per day, five hours up and seven hours down, with a total of 20 feet (6 meters) difference. We are told by our guide that 10,000 years ago, it was a branch of the Rhine.

London is 2000 years old and established by the Romans. The name of the river is from the Roman "Tomanas." The greater London community is seven million strong.

From the river, we saw the government buildings, the Ferris wheel, various docks and wharves, the tower of London, a number of bridges, including the London Bridge, and historic buildings along with the new glass buildings in this iconic city.

I went back to the hotel, set the alarm for 6 A.M., took showers, and went off to bed; we were both asleep almost immediately!

Sunday, beat the 06:00

The alarm woke me up, and I got ready for another interesting day. The luggage was out at 06:45, and the breakfast buffet was at 07:00. They had eggs, bacon, ham, fruits, and black pudding...I had to try it. It looked like a sausage patty or hockey puck, and it crumbled easily. However, when eaten, it had a liverish taste (actually, it is made from sheep's blood) and an odd texture; the more you had, the more you liked. I would have it again!

After breakfast, I went back to the room, gathered carry-ons, and checked out. I waited 15 minutes for the group to talk to the security guard and loaded onto the bus.

Off to Stone Hedge, it started out with the sun shining and easy traffic due to it being Sunday. What could go wrong?

Noah

The guide that will be with us is named John, and the driver, Kevin, John didn't look anything like the young woman pictured in the brochure, and he apologized. We had a couple of hours drive to our first destination, so we were treated with information on the buildings we passed getting out of London, then some history and facts about England.

We passed Canterbury Church, the place where Captain Blye was buried (from the Mutiny on the Bounty); the Chelsea Flower show had just ended, the old buildings/ row houses were all that was left from the great London Fire, all the wooded houses burned to the ground. There are over three hundred fish species in the Thames, the streets are lined with London Pines, and they are known to "eat" the pollution of automobiles and buses. We also passed a Brewery, London Pride Beer. It is made to be consumed at room temperature, and John, our guide, would have it no other way. (I did try it; it was not at room temperature, but not cold, it was good!)

The current cost of gas here is about $1.30 pounds per liter; the price back home on Memorial Day weekend is $3.00 per gallon. (This works out to be about $5.60/gallon US)

As with Milwaukee, the local bars and pubs here are closing at a rapid pace; it is now up to 63 pubs a month! Pubs that do not serve food are just about gone now. All the car dealerships are indoors.

In the past 10-15 years, bike lanes have been designated in the roadways, so now the narrow parked-up streets have basically 1 ½ lanes to navigate, adding to the congestion.

The Celtic Mead is a honey drink. When the Welsh get married, the couple traditionally drinks mead the first month or one moon cycle, i.e., the "honeymoon."

Way back thousands of years ago, a major volcano erupted, causing the island to break away from Europe; then the Ice Age came and went, the seas rose, and the land bridge washed away. The Celts came here first, hunted and farmed, and different tribes just fought between themselves until Rome and the Roman Empire invaded in 55 BC. Caesar called this Island Britannica but was not impressed and took his legions back to Italy, where he met his fate. 90 Years later, the Romans once again returned, stayed a short while, and were defeated by the German Saxons. The Vikings also had an interest in invading Ireland and Britain, so the King at that time (Edgar) split the

Educating Noah...Travelin'

country in two: Vikings and Saxons.

The language was a mix of all the upper European languages, Saxon, Welch, Scandinavian, and Latin, turning into the Anglo-Saxon" English."

The drive to Stone Hedge was about two and a half hours. The sky had turned from sunny and blue to grey, then the headlights of the cars coming at us were on, then the rain started, first light, then downpours. This did not look good!

We pulled into the parking area, and the rain magically stopped, and the sky cleared?!? (Karma) The site is estimated to be 5,000 years old, made by the Druids, and a special site aligned with meaning to the sun and planets for the summer solstice; we saw a place similar in Ireland, and the pyramids also referred to special meanings and alignments in Egypt and Mexico.

The druids practiced the sacrifice of a young (13ish) male or female to the Gods. The Romans put a stop to this practice when they first conquered the area. There have been strange sightings in the areas around these sites with reports of crop circles, shooting stars, and the like, and the area is quite extensive, with many burial mounds untouched for centuries.

The complex is several acres, comprising a stone structure, a museum, a restaurant, a theatre, and a reconstruction of several huts representing dwellings in 2500 BC, plus two large parking lots.

We were among the first few buses to arrive, we received our audio recorders, and you could walk the two kilometers to the site or take the supplied buses. We opted for the bus ride; the 5-minute ride was smooth and crowded. The site has paths around a roped-off area. The closest you can get is maybe 10-12 yards. We circled the structure, took pictures, and then got in a queue to return to the commerce area. Explored the extensive gift shop, walked the hut complex, turned in our recorders, and met back at the bus by 12:30.

The three-hour drive to Plymouth included a potty stop at a complex of fast-food restaurants and restrooms, all quite crowded. The highway was in good repair, a "dual carriageway" is four lanes, a pull-over area is called a "lay by," and the average farm is 57 hectares (1 hectare equals 2 ½ square acres). This is a farm country; there are 30 different breeds of sheep.

Noah

Why drive on the left? Way back when the roads were narrow and banked by forest, there were highwaymen coming out of the forests to attack. Most people are right-handed, so the reigns were held in the left hand, and your choice of weapon in your right hand to fend off the "nares-do-wells." It seemed odd the entire trip, the multiple lane round-a-bouts, and some back-ups with stop signs before the round-a-bouts. Pedestrians are minded to share. They do not necessarily have the right of way. It seems many drivers are making up for lost time on the streets, so pedestrians beware...I got a little shaken, looking the "wrong way" before crossing and then seeing a car barreling at me from the left.

We passed by several fields with white cloth on them. This white cloth encourages growth and protection for the sprouts from rabbits; the crops in the area were mainly sugar beets.

We arrived at Plymouth at 3:30. They have an all-season ski hill here, a horse race track (horse racing is big in England), and this is the home of the Royal Navy. There is a lot of history here, the launching of Sir Frances Drake on his world cruises, Sir Walter Raleigh, and Admiral Nelson; the Mayflower and Pilgrims also launched from here to find a new life in America. I took a picture of the gateway dedicated to the pilgrims.

We had an excursion, a harbor cruise scheduled at 4:30, so we explored the town and watched some local boys jump off the docks into the ocean; when asked how the water was, they replied, "quite cold." they all had wet suits on, or several layers of clothes...the drop off the wharf was a good 15 feet.

The Union flag represents England, Scotland, Wales and Ireland.

The British Navy was mostly comprised of prisoners; you had a choice: be hanged or join the Navy. The others were conscripted...The procurers would go into a pub and buy drinks for the lads, and when they became properly drunk, they were enticed outside, hit over the head, and taken to the ship. After a while, the young men caught on, so they watched for those who bought drinks, so then the procurement changed, and a coin was put into the drink; when the drink was emptied, the coin was found, and that indicated which person was to be taken. That was caught on, too, and where the expression "cheers" came to pass, the glass was held up and looked through the bottom to detect any coin deposited.

Sailors were provided a square wooden plate for when they were provided food; it was their plate, and they were promised three meals a day...Thence the saying: "Three squares a day."

Plymouth is a natural harbor at the mouth of the river Thamar. This is home to the largest citadel in Great Britain. The fort that protects the harbor has no two walls that face the same direction. The fort was constructed of four million pounds of rock. This is the largest naval base in Great Britain, and storage tanks hold enough fuel to supply the entire navy for six years! This was where all the wooden warships and English explorer ships were also made and launched.

On the harbor cruise, we saw the dry docks for repairing ships and several warships, including a number of submarines and even a nuclear sub, capable of staying under the sea for a year!

That evening was a welcoming dinner, turkey schnitzel, fish and chips, and Mac and cheese for the main course selection, all very good, plus a drink was included.

On the way back to the room, we met with a friend from one of our previous cruises that Lynn had invited to the hotel. We met with her and her husband, shared a drink, and enjoyed our conversation; what a great ending to a great day!

Monday, After Memorial Day weekend

Here, it is not Memorial Day, but it is a National holiday called Bankers Day, so most people had off.

We had three stops in Cornwall: St. Michaels Mount, a stony, rocky shoreline just up the coast from Penzance where pirates and highwaymen thrived, then on to Land's End, the southern-most tip of Great Britain, and finally, the resort town of St. Ives.

In all these towns, the housing is side-by-side duplexes, very small yards, and few garages. Most of the area is farmland separated by well-trimmed hedges. A lot of green everywhere, and where there are no crops, there are the moors and clumps of forests. Mining for tin was big here, along with some gold, but the mines ran out, and crops and tourism are now the main income.

We spent about an ½ hour at St. Michaels Mount, took pictures and discovered the beach, there is also a monastery there built by 30 monks, the fisherman's legend is that the archangel Michael appeared

Noah

on this rock (I looked but didn't see him that morning), an hour and a half at Land's End, here it was misty again, but we walked through the shops, took pictures of the beaches, and I got a great picture of an owl. Finally, we drove to St. Ives, which is an incredibly hilly town; the bus dropped us off at a lot above the city, and we walked down at least twelve staircases, 1000 steps to the town below, then down winding streets to the beach. The tide was not due in till 5 P.M., and inside the breakwaters, there was no water except for a few puddles. The tide here is a couple of yards high! (Feet and yards are used, along with miles, yet the temperatures are in Celsius, and gas is measured in liters.)

We walked the streets; every other shop was either food (pasties), ice cream, or jewelry and art. We had ice cream cones. I tried the blackberry and coddled cream. Lynn had chocolate orange, both refreshing and GOOD!

We made it back to the streets, walked a bit, and took the bus back up to the parking lot for a pound ($) a piece, well worth the money!

On the way bus ride back to the hotel, two bat bridges were pointed out; these span the road and have no entrance or exit from the top. They are just there to keep the bats flying high enough so they do not get smashed by high trucks (bats are protected here).

Prince Charles is the Duke of Cornwall and owns a good parcel of land here. We arrived back at the hotel a half hour late due to some accident and having to pull over a number of times for other vehicles coming from the other direction on these very narrow, no- shoulder roads.

We had signed up for an optional excursion to Dartmoor, "Tales of Dartmoor Pub," which included a tour of the town, the history of the town, and legions all provided for by a story teller who accompanied us through the town, in a church, and throughout our included meal that also included two drinks. This was my opportunity to have that un-chilled beer. I had both kinds that were on tap, and they were very good!

The storyteller exchanged interesting stories about the prison located there, legends of the moor witches, and personalities. All presented well, a very enjoyable evening, and the food was exceptional. Less than an hour back to the hotel, I caught up on the notes. Tomorrow, we head off to Wales!

Educating Noah...Travelin'

New day, these English breakfasts have quite a selection, and I have noticed that some of our group are now taking the pork and beans... We are on the bus for a little over two hours to reach our first stop, Builth Wells; on the way, we are filled in on two famous people who were born here or trained here, including Tom Woodward (Tom Jones) and Catherine Zeta-Jones.

There were a lot of local coal mines, but the coal was low-grade and created a lot of soot. There were also huge mounds of coal dust; in 1966, record rains turned one of these huge piles into sludge, and the school at the bottom was covered, killing 166 adults and children.

The Welch were the best bowmen in Europe; when captured, the first and second fingers on the right hand were amputated, so when they met with the English or any other invader and got close in battle, the Welch bowmen would first wag their first two fingers at the enemy!

The Welch joined the British to defeat the French.

Edward the first wanted to conquer both Wales and Scotland; he conquered Wales but not Scotland. Wales did not accept defeat by anyone who could not speak their language; Prince Charles was sent to rule. he volunteered to take a year off from college to spend a year in Wales, go to school there, and learn the culture and language, he did, and Wales has been ruled by the eldest son of British Royalty since then. (All of the prince's speeches since then are in both Welch and then in English).

There are distinctions in the isles, North and South Ireland (North Ireland and South Ireland both now recognized as two different countries), North and South Wales, Scotland is also sovereign, and south of Scotland is England. It is an independent and proud people that want their own country.

We spent an hour here at Builth Wells, taking pictures of the mural on the building, visiting small shops, and using the public toilets. On my walk, I discovered some very beautiful flower gardens and a magnificent yellow tree; yes, pictures of all.

Another two hours to Chester, the Welsh are famous for their poetry also. Prince George liked to romance married women; he was also quite stout; a poem was created to mock him...Listen to the words of the Georgie Porgy rhyme.

Mary had a little lamb came from here, along with Alice in Wonderland with the Cheshire cat; the town of Chester was devastated by the plague and war and fell into ruin, the buildings are black and white, the Duke of Westminster revived the city, he was a Norman, so of course he built a castle and Abby, the difference was an Amphitheatre was built outside the walls of the castle, for all to enjoy, it had the capacity of 7000 people!

We were all issued headsets and receivers. The first 45 minutes of the 2 ½ hours here was a guided walking tour of the town, pictures of the buildings, Abby, and clock tower, ending at the top of the old wall overlooking the amphitheater and a Roman park.

The balance of the time we explored the streets on our own, Lynn and I shared a Crepe with tomato, basil, and mozzarella cheese, with juice water for Lynn and a mixed fruit hard cider for me…yum!

Back to the bus and an hour's drive to our final destination for the day, Liverpool, home of the Beetles. We passed by the Mersey River and saw the ferry on the way to the hotel. (Beatle song "Ferry on the Mersey")

A walk around the downtown area, a small snack, and we are done for the day.

Thursday, the 31st of May

The normal routine is 6:45: luggage out, breakfast, then be on the bus by 8A.M.

We are rotating seats, which I like a lot. Everyone moves back two seats counter-clockwise, and everyone is on by 8 A.M. What a great group of 42!!

We have a short trip to The Beatles Story, which is located in a converted warehouse on Albert Dock (Uncle Albert?) The tour took you through the life and times of the Beatles, followed by a large store of Beatles memorabilia. We (Lynn and I) did not care for the Beatles back in the day, so we were in the first few that finished early, turned in our radios, explored the store, and then Lynn went back to the meeting place, I explored the wharf, that extended about two blocks, and the small low chain guide fence was covered the complete length with padlocks. We have seen these all over the world: Russia, France, and Italy.

The next stop was a little over two hours away, and we were filled in with more information and stories.

English money can be used in Scotland, but if you use the ATMs in Scotland, you will get Scottish currency. (The coin is the same; the smallest bill is a $5-pound note.)

There is little, if any, Highway Patrol. In the cities and on the highway, there are cameras, and you will get a citation and points if recorded breaking the law. The minimum age to drive is 17; the main crops are barley and potatoes, and since we left Liverpool, the highways are 3 lanes both ways!

The civil war in the U.S. really hurt Lancaster County; many English had cotton plantations in the U.S.

Lancaster is also known for its stew, consisting of carrots, potatoes, beef, and gravy, known as the Lancaster Hot Pot.

Stan Laurel (Laurel and Hardy) was born near here; when he was growing up, he was the straight man for his father.

As we approached Grasmere, the hedge rows changed from hedges to stone. The barriers are all stone now, hundreds of years old, and called "dry stone" in that no mortar was used. These were all glacial rocks from the last ice age. As previously seen, all the livestock in the fields lie down, including the horses; our guide, John, mentioned this and said this was common and that Americans thought this was odd and unhealthy for the horse…I was told by my dad that if a horse lies down, it is either sick or dying; it must be just American horses?

A Monkey Puzzle tree was pointed out to us. The real name is a Chilean Pine, called the monkey puzzle because the needles prevent monkeys from climbing the tree. It was brought here in the 1700s, and no, there are no monkeys in England, Wales, or Scotland! (Except in the zoos)

In this area, many of the buildings and churches are made the same way as the fence lines, very attractive, and they are 100's of years old, and I have to mention, the rhododendrons are all over the place, huge bushes, many different colors, and most still in bloom!

The two-hour stop for lunch and exploring this small community was a wonderful experience. The shops were quaint, the people very

Noah

inviting, and this is where we picked up Vincent the frog (sculpture) along with a few other must-haves to bring home, Including the world-renowned Grasmere Gingerbread, which the tour guide and Globus provided each of us a tin. (Tastee!!).

On to the next stop, we noticed some of the fields were covered in yellow; it seems this flowering low plant is called yellow grouse.

The English and the Scots were constantly fighting. We were given the history of both Queen Elisabeth the first and Mary Queen of Scots, both rare females in charge of countries; Mary was recognized as queen of Scotland, France, and England by some; Elisabeth finally won and had Mary beheaded. The nursery rhyme Mary, Mary quite contrary, How Your Garden Grows is about this Mary! King James the First united both England and Scotland in 1603.

Our next stop was just after the border of Scotland in the town of Gretna Green, where the blacksmith married young runaway British couples. We were treated to an enactment with a "volunteer" couple and two "volunteer" witnesses from our group; fun, quick, and very interesting. In Scotland, at one time, you could marry at 12 (with parental permission), then that was changed to 16 with or without parental permission; in England, it was 16 with permission and 18 without.

We explored the small complex; the word "Whiskey" has Gaelic origins and means "water of life" after the ceremony.

Then, just an hour's drive to Glasgow, Scotland's largest city. Checked in just after 6 P.M. dinner was included this evening with one drink. I was willing to pay for a starter, asked to have a fine Scottish beer, and was told the tapper was out...I asked if there was any bottled beer from Scotland... nope! I said I was from Milwaukee in the States, and we never run out of Milwaukee beer! Then ordered a Guinness and walked back to the group.

A few notes before continuing on the notes for the rest of the trip. In most of the hotels in Scotland, Wales, and outside the city of London, there is no air conditioning by choice, even in the homes. The windows are cabled so that they can only be opened a few inches, and of course, if by a heavy traffic area, the outside noise is complimentary. So, allergy sufferers and light sleepers, beware...

The beds last night were well-worn, and Lynn woke with a

Educating Noah...Travelin'

backache; these mattresses are just old, the sink also leaked onto the floor, and the elevator was out.

None of the rooms since we arrived, have pens or envelopes and only a few sheets of paper with a pencil for notes.

I paid for the two additional excursions and asked about the headlines in the morning paper, referring to sexism and ageism now being considered hate crimes; the guide agreed with me that this political correctness is going way too far, and we are waiting for it to finally end and come back to reality. I also asked about the health care in England, and as suspected, everyone pays additional insurance to bypass the cues (as I was told by our French guide in France). He also pointed out that the health care system is nothing like it was 10 years ago, that it is a small percentage that abuses the system and is making it hard for everyone else.

In the morning news, the headlines of the major papers are pointed out, and a few comments are made. Health experts are now calling for a 4% increase in healthcare funding linked to the cost of living index.

"Jack-o-bite" here is James. James was the first king to unite Scotland and England. His son Charles closed the Scottish Parliament (the voice of the people) twice, so the Scots were not happy with him as a ruler. Meantime, Oliver Cromwell was engaged to remove the king. He succeeded, but he was a protestant, so he closed all the pubs, everyone had to dress very modestly and drab, he banished Christmas, and closed the catholic churches, no kilts, no bagpipes, and English was required, not Gaelic as a first language; now the Scots were very unhappy, but Cromwell died, 1660.

His son Charles was very flamboyant; he was referred to as the "Merry Monarch." he re-opened the taverns, people could dress as they wished and worship as they liked, and the Scots were happy again.

Glasgow used to be a vibrant ship-building town; it was the base for ships built by the same company as built the Titanic and the Lusitania, but globalism moved contracts to other countries, and this, with the decreased demand for coal, devastated the town. This is the area where the American actor Jackie Stewart came from; many of the 007 movies were shot here, and also Brave Heart, the movie starring Mel Gibson, who played the main character, the real Brave Heart was actually hung, then quartered.

Noah

We were also told the story of the McGregor's and the Campbell's. The McGregor's would not sign allegiance to the King of England, so the King sent the lowland Campbell's to "convince" them to sign. Since all the Kings in Scotland did sign, the McGregor's relented and signed. In the meantime, the McGregor's welcomed the Campbell's, fed them, offered lodging, and showed them hospitality. The leader of the Campbell's opened a letter he was instructed by the King of England on the eve of the meeting with the McGregor's, and the letter instructed him to have his men kill everyone under 70. It was a slaughter; to this day, no Campbell is welcome to the highlands!

The highway patrol and emergency services in this area have also been replaced by traffic cameras and mobile phones, increasing response times but saving money. The main industry in this area is now forestry and chipboard, or what we call particle board, usually all pine, and the land areas are clear-cut and then replanted with new trees.

Loch means "lake". The first we encountered was Loch Lomond, which is the largest of the lochs and is fresh water. There are thirty-one thousand lochs in Scotland; all but a few are fresh water. During the ice age, there was 1 ½ miles of ice above what we know as Scotland!

There are over 60 islands, and at one time, this was where those that had leprosy were kept. When one of the caring monks came to shore, he was required to wear a bell so that all could avoid him and not become ill. There are a lot of hills and mountains in Scotland. Anything over 1000 ft is called a mountain. As we passed a small waterfall across one loch, the cave behind that waterfall was rumored to be the home of Rob Roy McGregor. He was kind of a Robin Hood, a cattle rustler, and known for his ability with a bow and sword. He supposedly had extremely long arms, with hands extending to his knees.

The deer are becoming a problem with over-population, and Scotland is seriously considering re-introducing wolves to manage the herds, similar to what Yellowstone did in the States.

Back to Scottish history; The song "You take the high Road, and I'll take the low road "is a Celtic song (they were very superstitious) and refers to sacrifice, in that the high road is the heavenly path, and the low road is the devil's path, by which souls of those that are returning from battles outside Scotland return to Scotland, and the sacrifice to help a mate.

"Mc" means "son of"; the name Caledonia comes from the Romans. "Bonnie" means beautiful, and the countryside was just that! The clouds had lifted, the sun was out, and everything was green, vibrant green. The loch, the moors, and the forests of pine, with occasional splashes of yellow, pink, or red rhododendron and other flowering plants and bushes. The "Sweet William" flower was named after a flamboyant King; his son was a horrible person, so the Scots also called the same flower "Stinking Bill" after the son they despised. A mix of four or six lanes highways, then back to narrow two-lane roads passing Glen Coe, Fort William, and reaching the "Road to the Isles," where we boarded a ferry and crossed over to the Isle of Skye to see the Scottish landscapes by traveling around the island. Mallaig, the ferry terminal town, is also home to the Harry Potter Hogsworth steam train. I think I got a picture of it!

We stopped for several scenic photographs of castle ruins and, finally, Loch Ness to see if "Nessie" would appear for us. No luck on that!

We arrived a bit before 6 and included dinner at the hotel and the end of a traveling day in Inverness.

Saturday, the 8th day, the second of June, 2018. It was light outside at 11:00 PM; misty this morning, and at 5 A.M., it was light out already. The room was better, a bit cooler, but we were on a main walking street, and last night being a Friday night, lots of young people, very loud and boisterous, till after 11 P.M.

After leaving early, we had a short stop at the battlefield of Culloden. This was the last battlefield on British soil; the dead were buried where they fell and died, and there were small markers in the field, if any.

Our next stop was Pitlochry; it is a small Victorian village with one main street. The walk to the dam and fish later was several blocks. Lynn decided to walk through town, and I was off to the fish ladders! It was an easy 3 block walk. Took a few photos from the dam, and then on the other side were the fish pools, maybe seven or eight, like shiplocks for the salmon to swim up and down. The observation tunnels were closed. I did see one fish, however…We were told before we left the bus that a footbridge was located a few blocks downriver to cross back to the town. I found some beautiful flowers on the way, then across the bridge, made a wrong turn, ended up in a residential cul-de-sac, turned around, headed down another path, ended up by the hospital, turned back again, and found the way back to town, a twenty-minute excursion turned into an hour, on the way back up the main street I did purchase whiskey flavored ice cream, it was mild and did taste very good!

Back on the bus and more information about the educational system in Britain. There are two systems, public and private, primary ages 5-11 years, then you are tested; depending on the testing, you may qualify for high school through age 18 and then be tested again. Depending on how many "A's" you get qualifies you for different colleges, and you can apply for a government loan; four years of college runs $21-25,000 pounds, and after graduation, you must pay the government back.

Oxford University is actually 36 universities, the same as Cambridge. A total of 72 institutions between the two of them.

When Europe and Britain were taken by the black plague (1665), 160,000 people were taken, the streets wreaked with the stench of death, many people when they went out, would carry posies to smell when they breathed, and in the last stages of the plague, just before passing on, the person would continuously sneezing people would say "God bless you" because their time was short!

We pass through Dundee and pass the ship that was the first to visit Antarctica.

St. Andrew is the patron saint of Scotland. The town of St. Andrews is a golf town with a world-renowned golf course. I have a cousin and friend who are big into golf. I got a scorecard each so they can brag. The extensive beach is where they filmed Chariots of Fire. It is also home to St. Williams University, where Prince William studied. At this time, many American girls also applied to study at this university, and one of these American girls married him!

We walked the town and took a side trip into an aquarium, where we walked the exhibits and saw the meerkats, penguins, and sea lions up close. A snack bar provided a light lunch of a scone and salad plus a blackberry soft drink.

An hour's drive to Edinburgh, founded in 1593, this is a city of

Educating Noah...Travelin'

500,000, 1/10th of Scotland's population. Edinburgh Castle sits on top of an extinct volcano, the best defense point! After a massive fire, the town was rebuilt in 1776. The streets are named after princes first names, and the homes here are taxed by the number of windows, so a number of windows were pointed out that were bricked up to avoid additional taxes (besides what some of my liberal friends claim, no one wants to pay more taxes!)

Lister came from her, the antiseptic Listerine. Traveling through the older affluent neighborhoods, the basement level was for the servant's quarters, and the ground floor was for the primary residents; all had shoe scarpers on each side and oil lamps in front of the foyer. If you were out in the park and your oil lamp in front of the building was out, for a few pence, a boy would show you to your house with a torch and refill your lamp. The buildings are eight-ten-plex's, rather dreary on the outside.

Robert Lewis Stevenson lived here, and so did Doyle, the creator of Sherlock Holmes, and Sir Walter Scott (Ivanhoe, Lady of the Lake). Charles Darwin studied at this University and actually failed in his second semester and left!

We checked into the hotel, and many of the folks took their luggage (ME people). The small elevators could only take two couples at a time; everything got jammed up at the elevators!

We signed up for the Scottish evening, so we only had an hour to change, set up the room, and then go back to the bus for a short drive to the hall.

We were greeted by a bagpiper and sat down at three long tables along with 5 other groups. We had a menu with choices of soup or salad, pork, fish, beef or vegetarian, and a dessert. After the soup or salad, haggis was served. It was a mild form, rolled into a ball and deep fried, smaller than a hard ball but larger than a golf ball. I can safely say I was in the minority as to who liked it. It could use mustard or ketchup or some other sauce in that it was a bit dry, a bit salty. I could also use pepper. I ate two but could have eaten more, but ... (Haggis is usually comprised of sheep stomach, diced sheep's liver, lungs, and heart with oatmeal suet and onions.)

For the rest of the meal, I ordered pork belly, and it turned out to be pork steak; Lynn had veal, which was good, plus a pudding dessert. We were then treated to a show of bagpipes, singing, and dancing, very much like Ireland: four to five dancing ladies plus one guy. They encouraged clapping and actually dancing on one song, but I was with Lynn, too far back to be chosen. It seemed everyone enjoyed it, and we had a short trip back to the hotel for another busy and full day. We both slept well that night.

Today is the second day in Edinburgh, Sunday morning, and yes, I had some more of that haggis but added a bit of sharp mustard and mushrooms; it was quite good with a coddled egg on top!

In the morning, we had a sightseeing trip through the city, both the 200-year-old "new town" and "old town." Passed the hotel where J.K. Rollins rented a room to write some of the Harry Potter books, another hotel where the queen stays in town, the cost? $600 pounds per person per night, and that is the only time when the fountain runs (when the queen is in the house...not anyone else!)

We then drove up the very narrow "Royal Miles" to tour the Edinburgh Castle. The tour involved walking up steep hills and observing how castles were built, with the option of viewing the crown jewels, which we passed on. The line was over 100 people deep! Next, we toured the Holyrood Palace (yes, it is spelled right!). There were tapestries from the 15th and 16 centuries! We saw the complete structure, including the bedrooms and many centuries-old paintings; no taking pictures on the inside, but it was grand on the outside.

Royalty: the queen carries her purse or bag to indicate the mood she is in; King George the Third at 450# liked to walk outside the castle with a short kilt and pink argyle socks...

The Royal Yacht Britannica excursion and dinner was the last extra excursion we signed up for, and that started at 3:30 in the afternoon. I got antsy after the tours and asked how to get back to the hotel. I was told to go left, pass two stop lights, turn left again, and I would be half a block from the hotel.

I walked about six blocks, turned just before the second light, and walked down a winding road to the river...oops, I asked two men dressed like bus drivers where the Hilton was; they had no idea but suggested I retrace my steps to the main road (all uphill for 3 blocks) and go toward the bridge.

I did. The bridge was just beyond that second stop light, and yes,

I was a bit disoriented, so I walked past the hotel (on the other side of the street) over the bridge and walked another block; no, that wasn't it! I re-traced back to the bridge and asked another gentleman from a hotel where the Hilton was, and he didn't know either but suggested I go to the other side of the blue bridge. I did, and as I got closer to the other side, I saw "Hilton" on the building facing the river…very similar to the experience with Washington D.C., where the locals only know where they work!

I stopped for a beer at the bar and asked for a local beer. I selected "Bitter and Twisted." I mentioned later on the bus that I ordered a "woman's beer" as a joke on the bus, but the women did not appreciate it!

I met up with Lynn, rested for a half hour, then explored a few shops by the hotel and boarded the bus for the yacht excursion.

The trip to the dock was short; we toured the entire royal yacht, top to bottom, stem to stern, all the royalty quarters, and the crew quarters. The crew sailors were called "yachties'." It was really plush for the royalty; the royal Bentley was also on board for traveling on shore. How creditably spoiled, special studies for the queen, special banquet rooms for entertaining, a complete infirmary and the royal doctor quarters, plush bed chambers for the royalty and guests…wow!

The tour ended in…wait for it…a gift shop! We were ahead of the group, waited for the bus, and were then taken to a local restaurant where we had a good three-course meal; back to the hotel by 8:00 P.M., caught up on my diary, and tomorrow we are off to York.

Day ten

As with most of the days on this venture, it is misty and cool. The bed was firm, the air conditioning worked, and it had a shower stall. It was a great night for one with bad knees and another with short legs!

Breakfast included Haggis; I used Catsup, a little mustard, and a scoop of mushrooms…tastee! (Also, last time, we will be back in England tomorrow.)

Our first stop today was Alnwick Castle, used in the Harry Potter Films, Robin Prince of Thieves, and the Downtown Abby TV series. I took a picture of the outside, and then we went to the gardens. Lots of pictures of roses; they will be in full bloom in a week or so. We also walked in a maze, viewed several fountains, and had a guided tour called the Poison Plant tour. We were warned not to touch, eat, or brush the plants, everything from nightshade to hemlock and many in between. It was pointed out that many in small doses also cure various ailments, as in the tree bark that has acetylsalicylic acid (aspirin). I asked Lynn not to keep on taking those notes for my own safety!

Next was our trip to York and more information on the Isles. Two-bedroom houses go for around $280,000 pounds (a little over $300,000 US), Scotland about $145 pounds, the closer to the city center, the higher the price, London downtown $5-6 Million pounds, Downtown Edinburgh mid 6 figures; detached are much higher, most are side by side duplexes and four plexes with very small yards. Thirty-forty years ago, you could only afford to rent, and the homes were owned by counsels; when the upkeep became too much, and Margaret Thatcher declared that the councils could sell to their tenants, the tenant was offered the rental to buy at a discount, and mortgages were started.

In the last ten years, the banks pulled back on mortgages, and now many kids still living at home due to cost and no availability of loans. In the bathroom was a sign advertising short-term loans for 39.9% interest. I told the tour guide that was usury, and he admitted it was!

As we drove south, we had glimpses of the North Sea, the route the Vikings took to conquer England, and along the highway (yes, a 4 lanes highway, from here down to London)) were lupines of 5 or six colors! It is almost 3 P.M., and the sun is at 12:00. It's going to be another Long day!

The War of Roses was fought here, Royalty in-fighting. It came down to everyone going out to the rose garden, and the Duke of Lancaster said, "Pick a rose, white for York, red for Lancaster." The number picked was a draw...thus the War of Roses...

Humpty Dumpty referred to Richard the Third, which had severe scoliosis and a hump on his back. In battle, when he was pulled from his horse the first time, he cried out, "My kingdom for a horse," so that his men would see him fighting with them. He was then pulled off his horse again and hacked to death, so the tale goes, "Humpty Dumpty sat on a wall (horse) Humpty Dumpty had a great fall, all the king's horsemen and all the king's men couldn't put Humpty Dumpty together again (he was hacked to pieces beyond recognition)

The pub is short for the public house; "Wick" refers to the market. The Queen's car has a flag on the front. When you see the flag, touch "pause" on your remote, and the TV will show where in England she is.

York, England's most medieval city, we had a ½ hour walking tour, then another 1 ½ hours on our own, 10-foot-wide streets, small crowded shops, as with most of Great Briton, the Celts were conquered by the Romans, then the Vikings conquered the Romans, then the Normans took over. The unique thing here is that the Roman walls were just added on to, so original Roman walls exist along with the subsequent buildings by the Normans. The town shows 350 years of growth and buildings.

Back in the day, after 10 P.M., the chamber pots were emptied into the streets, and there was no indoor plumbing. This was an improvement; it once was time. Before emptying that chamber pot, you shouted "Guard Loo" to warn those below on the sidewalk and street the raw sewage did stink up the city-fed cats, dogs, and rats.

Every other shop seemed to be chocolate, candy, or food, very interesting, all cobblestone, and very quaint. After a short drive to the hotel, dinner was included tonight. We enjoyed the three-course, well-prepared dinner, including Yorkshire pudding, which is basically a puff pastry shell about six inches in diameter, volumes up, then sinks in with a small amount of beef and onion gravy in the middle, a very filling appetizer!

Tuesday, 06/05/18

It is the last day on the road to return to London before leaving tomorrow morning for home. We left early this morning; at 7:15, everyone was on the bus, fed, and a tin of shortbread awaited each of us as a gift on our seats. (This was the second gift; we also got a tin each of gingerbread before.) There is a two-hour journey to Stratford-upon-Avon- Avon for a picture of Anne Hathaway's cottage, then to Stratford, the birthplace of William Shakespeare, born 04/23/1564.

On the way…more information. There was a sheriff of Nottingham, and at that time, most of England was forested, so there was a Sherwood Forest also; Robin Hood's actual existence may be legion and myth. However, the sheriff was the county's tax collector, also known as shire (many towns end in shire). Most people went by first names, and when individual taxes were imposed, a second name was required for accounting since no one wanted to pay taxes; two names were used. You can blame the Normans for the first taxes on individuals in England. ("Smith" came from blacksmith, tinsmith, and coppersmith, and "son" came from David's son, John's son, and Adam's son).

Shakespeare was the son of a farmer who was very close to the local powers, so when there was a play or entertainment in town, he was one of those in the front seats. He did not care for school; he had two siblings, but the plague took both of them. He married Anne Hathaway; they had two children and a small farm. He needed to follow his dreams. He told her that he was going to London to be a success and would return when he was a success.

His father helped him to obtain a letter of introduction, and when he presented it at the theatre, he was brought in. He played women's roles.

A new king was crowned, actors and entertainers, the poor, and Jews (the money lenders) were kicked out of town since the king could not pay his debt and wanted to clean up the town; this group was banished to 1 square mile outside the city limits. The actors and company literally moved the theatre across the river (it was frozen and, in the winter) and set up just outside the limits set by the king. He became very successful and well-acclaimed. He then heard that his son was very sick, so he left the theatre and came back home. His son died soon afterward, and he promised his wife he would not leave again, but at his birthday party, he drank too much and died on his birthday, 04/23/1616.

The original home where Shakespeare was born was bought by a priest to preserve, but the street was too busy and noisy, so he had it moved and burned. We toured the home of a neighbor's house that was preserved to provide information on that time in history. There is a beautiful garden attached and a lovely yard where actors put on short skits while the tour of the house is taken inside, and people explain different functions and positioning of furniture. The main level had a fireplace, living area, and kitchen with a table and another fireplace. Above were the bedrooms, the nursery directly above the fireplaces, and the loft for the older boys. We inspected a bed with a rope bottom and were shown the key to tighten the continuous rope, usually tightened once a week. The rope was made of hemp, it sagged mostly in the middle, and hence the rhyme " Sleep tight, don't let the bed bugs bite" (They would be on the floor and bite you in the butt if the ropes were too sagging) Most of the houses had thatched roofs, great homes for mice, so that is where the cats and dogs went looking for meals if it started raining and raining hard, the thatch would become very slippery, thus the saying "It's raining cats and dogs" as they slipped and fell off the roofs.

We also toured a small tannery; the hides were soaked in urine, and the softest leather could take up to three months to soak in a tub, with boys stomping them for hours. At that time, there were no pockets in the pants; a man wore a pouch held to him by his belt, and this was called a pocket. If it was stolen, the thief was called a pickpocket.

Walked through the garden, took more pictures, walked the town, saw a display for a cream tea, saw a sign, and dragged Lynn in to try one; I ordered two but then found out it was a meal, so I just ordered one, it included 4 squares each of tuna, ham, and egg salad sandwiches, two scones, lettuce, tomatoes, a small pie, an éclair, and a lemon drizzle cake...way too much and time was not on our side, we drank the tea, had the balance wrapped for supper, and the bill came to $32 pounds, I had $35, paid and left the balance for tip (here 10% is considered generous) and off we went, made it in time for the bus to leave.

Two hours to the hotel in London, checked in, repacked suitcases, checked about the connection to the airport, finished up on the diary, tried to check in for the flight, and relaxed. We leave the hotel tomorrow morning at 6:45 for the airport.

When Londoners go to the show, they order and pay for their drinks when they arrive and give the bartender their name. At Intermission, they go back to the bar and provide their name, and the drink is taken off the shelf, and lines are avoided.

When talking with the accent, the "h" is gone, thereby a horse is "orse"; the old slang incorporated rhyming; Old Big; Bobbies are their policemen, the "Bobbies" name comes from the first police officer Robert Bill.

Last day was always a challenge; British Air would not let me log on again. The luggage was out at 6:10 and still there when we went down at 6:30 for our pick-up at 6:45; we reported our slow drain at the desk and picked up the hotel-provided boxed breakfast. The driver asked about our luggage, then found someone to pick them up…it was a little over a half-hour drive to the airport, rush hour, few houses had garages, both sides of the once two-way streets were parked with cars, cars take turns to get through. You must go 4-6 blocks out of your way to make left turns, aggressive "camel nose" driving, no bike lanes, no horns (that is not "proper"), but you can sense a quiet animosity.

Arrived at the airport, tipped in US money, and proceeded to the luggage self-check… they rejected us, had to go to the line for assistance, got our tickets, and proceeded to check our luggage; this was self-help also. The couple had problems ahead of us, and the couple next to us had problems with theirs, too. Finally, an attendant came over and re-directed them to another station. He couldn't make it work either. Ours worked fine, and we sent off our bags.

Now, security, we had to show our ticket at the entrance to the line and then again at the entrance to the actual security bins and x-rays. The laptop is out, and it must have enough charge to power up; shoes, belt, watch, and all pockets clear. I set off alarms, took a special x-ray, wanded, and let go. Lynn got stopped; she had those packaged breakfasts, the butter, jam, and juices were taken out, butter and jam returned after inspection, juice...no go. You would think the hotel would know this? A Hilton??

Now we are past security; it only took 45 minutes to get to this point after drop off, found the screens for departures, and yes, no gate assigned for another ½ hour, so we looked for seats to eat what was left of breakfast. The plane was then delayed for an hour and fifteen minutes, of course, and so was the gate assignment.

I found the restrooms and British Air Customer Service to find what seats we had and where, and possibly change seats together. The seats together were offered, but only in business class. She told me the upgrade was about 1/3 of what was offered pre-flight months ago and told me British Air has special last-minute pricing, so I took it! With the upgrade came a gate assignment. We took the tram to the gate area, took a restroom break, and waited.

I am already tired of people walking and talking on their phones, in line taking out their phones, and on planes, talking on their phones…all at normal or heightened voice levels.

We left Heathrow at noon on 06/06/18 and arrived in Chicago at

2:45 P.M.; it is going to be another long day, TSA. Lynn had to go through it again; her fingerprints didn't completely register.

We missed our first bus home by 15 minutes, but we somehow missed Chicago rush hour traffic; Tiffany was there to pick us up at the bus station, and we got back home, car park, and luggage upstairs by 6 P.M., another great adventure!

While traveling, we decided to go with only two meals a day plus a light snack. We adjusted the day; every day, breakfast is provided by the hotel. We had energy bars and just bought a beverage when we stopped for lunch. I try to taste a lot of different drinks and food. At one stop, I had a bottle of Fentiman's Dandelion & Burdock fermented drink...it was outstanding, especially for a "weed" drink!

It took a couple days to get back on schedule; my knee was acting up. I bought a stabilizer, restocked the house, and harassed the attorney and everyone who had not done anything for the estate while I was gone.

I proofed the pictures from our last trip, 650 down to 510; proofed the writeup; sorted all the souvenirs and gifts, all in four days, including that 30-hour Thursday!

I had a discussion with Murphy, our accountant, one with Craig, the stockbroker, and several e-mails to the attorney to finalize and get everything in motion again.

After getting "proper" documents in finishing up the estate from the attorney, then the bank telling me the "proper" documents weren't, I went over and talked to the bank supervisor; we agreed on a solution and combined the balance of my mother's funds to wait for the results of the final claims with the insurance companies. The attorney is done and paid off.

The life insurance company turned us down after 6 weeks, claiming that my mother did not die soon enough after the accident. The Blue Cross Blue Shield also claimed that her policies were fully earned to the end of the month, even though she died on the 3rd.

I contacted the Wisconsin Insurance Commissioner and filled out three grievances: one against the life company and two against the health company. I received a check from the life company a week later.

I also worked with the board at a June meeting and met the new neighbor across the road.

I wrapped up the estate and sent out the final check to my brother. Three months, not bad, the life insurance company reconsidered and paid, Blue Cross/Blue Shield considered everything fully earned, and the insurance commissioner suggested if I wished to pursue, to go to small claims court; for that small amount, the companies know individuals will not pursue, honesty is dead!

We had a few board meetings for the condo association (I am the president). There are a lot of micro-managing and hair-on-fire e-mails from two new members. We will have additional meetings to address everything...

We spent a weekend in Minnesota with Lynn's cousin Bill, his daughter Melissa, and her new husband, with Bill's other son Nathan and his family. Great food, plus a tour of a family farm showing me the inner workings of a set of four robot milking machines.

The cows go in and get milked without a human. Wow! It takes about eight months to train the cows; they are on 24/7, and the cows have themselves milked when it becomes uncomfortable and are rewarded with a rich feed as a treat while they are milked.

I also went to another offered investment class with online trading. I am bored, and I like this kind of stuff, so I signed up for a more in-depth class to determine what trading to learn. It would be great if it was not too expensive. I played phone tag with my "counselor" since we went to cell phones only; it is kind of a pain to keep this phone with me all the time and keep it charged!

I paid for the $100.00 orientation class. It was three days long and included lunch, so I thought it was a deal. I gained a lot of knowledge but was subjected like the others to a hard sell, the basic real course going for $14-15K, and then a specialty course like options, currencies, or just stocks for an additional $10K-12. I believe the phone tag we had was that the sales girl realized I was a hard sell, which is why the sales manager made the arrangements. Of the 12 people in the class, 10 committed, and I was one of the two that didn't. (Odd man out?) However, I did learn quite a bit, and the $100.00 was well spent.

I still drive one day a week for the D.A.V., had the annual testing and documentation, went to Maxwell Street days in Mukwonago; believe it or not, it was a bit boring, a couple cooking classes, and worked on the condominium board.

The board has gotten out of hand. We have a rogue member who does what she wants, works around the property manager, and then blames the manager for problems. We have had six meetings without the manager and one with; she has sent out for quotes contractors without specs to whom she wants and has replaced the plantings Lynn and I put in last year. Another member has it in for management because he wasn't answered soon enough and in the proper format; the other new member feels the manager was not empathetic enough when she talked to her about a leakage problem.

I confronted this and was told "president" was only a title, and my suggestion to have a face-to-face discussion with management was dismissed as old-fashioned and out of touch. This is after one hundred and fifty-plus emails and face-to-face board-only meetings…consistent? Or just spineless.

The other male member of the board took the lane paint stripper when the association bought it 3 years ago, and he repainted the lines then…three years ago…it has sat in his garage since.

The motorcycle club (Chapter G- Goldwing's) had the monthly meeting, and the same 8 people showed up. Four of us no longer had bikes, and I asked why we still met; we only had a dinner ride, a lunch ride, and a meeting a month, no group rides, nothing this year except the winter get-away, and that only had four couples; we have money due to the fundraiser, I suggested a "Good-Bye" Christmas Party dinner and open bar in December, and kill the club or join a different chapter. I am now "the Jerk". They will think about the options.

Time for another trip! Vancouver to Vancouver with Oceana on September 16-27th.

Educating Noah...Travelin'

Alaska II

We had gone to Alaska when we first started traveling to finish the United States, and like Hawaii, we wanted to return to see how much had changed in between our world travels.

Monday, the 17th of September

The new adventure started early; pick-up at our house for the drive to the Milwaukee airport was at 4 A.M. on Monday, the 17th of September.

I thought this would have been a good idea way back when, but I believe using O'Hare out of Chicago would have been an easier flight to and from Vancouver...I never stop learning, or I just don't learn seems to apply. WOW, that was quick!

I was stopped by security. This time, it was my left shoulder, the only major joint that had not been replaced? He let me look at the picture, and the whole left shoulder was orange...a little on the right, and the hips and knees were nothing...Argggghhh!!

The flight to Minneapolis was 48 minutes, an hour and a half wait, and Minneapolis to Vancouver was 3 1/2 hours; with the premium economy, we got to board the plane both times right after 1st Class, and the seats did have more legroom.

The second flight was across from a family of four: mom, dad, and a two and three-year-old. The kid wouldn't stop whining, crying, and fidgeting; the parents were oblivious. On take-off and landing, the parents did not save the kids ...It was a long flight! Two-time changes, so we took only 1 ½ hours!! (We will pay for it on the way back home.)

Vancouver, passport checks and security, the customary ½ hour bus ride to the docks, another security check, health questionnaire, check-in, on the ship, up to the café for lunch, and waiting for the room to be ready.

The room was available, but there was no luggage at 3:00 P.M. We tried the safe; it locked, but then it would not open! Called the desk, maintenance came and fixed it, and we had a mandatory safety drill at 4:15. We all put on our life jackets, our muster point was the main dining room, and we were shown the proper way to put on our jackets, given all the emergency information, and then we were all marched out to the lifeboats for a final briefing.

Lynn and I went back to the cabin, exactly the same as the last one, laid down (we have been up since 3 A.M.!), and waited for our luggage. They arrived; we unpacked and rested till 6:30.

The buffet (we didn't have to dress up too much) was great! Lynn had her lamb chops, mashed potatoes, and veggies; I had the ginger calamari, escargot, and salmon and tuna sushi. Wow! We also shared a small raspberry tart and pistachio and chocolate tart dessert.

We were still groggy and tired, toured the shops, caught the sunset, and went back to the cabin, showers, and bed. I know it was only 8:30, but that was not our time! Ours was 10:30, and we were exhausted!!

Day 2 at sea

Temperature was low 50s F, overcast, cool breeze, and off and on rain. Crazy golf and Baggo toss, then the first lecture on Alaska. Here are some of the notes:

Forty-ninth State, Stewart's Foley. ($7.2 Million or about 2 cents per square mile) The main export was gold, then oil (Alaskan Pipeline passes 88,000 barrels of oil /hour and is responsible for 110,000 jobs) along with the fishing industry, salmon, and crabs, mainly. Russia is only 60 miles away; at times during the gold rush, potatoes were as valuable as gold!

1400 BC, evidence of humans crossing the land bridge, chasing meat, primarily caribou, carbon dated by the "Clovis Point" found in New Mexico, and the migration continued down the west coast through Central America and South America.

Centuries before Columbus and the Vikings, evidence of the Chinese in 1421. Captain Cook mapped the island. A Russian ship Captain by the name of Behring also mapped the area, thus the Behring straights. Alaskan native tribes, the "Aliate," are defined by the languages they speak, and they do vary significantly.

The largest United States park is in Alaska. It is the Tongass National Forest in Ketchikan, our first Port after leaving Vancouver at 17 million acres.

Jade is the gem of Alaska, Gold is the mineral, and the flag is the Big Dipper and Northern Star. It is twice the size of Texas, the U.S.

state with the most coastline and highest mountain, Mt. McKinley.

Lunch with another great variety of food, played "Wacky Words," attended a shopping lecture, and a trivia with six new teammates we didn't place, but tomorrow is another day.

Welcome aboard by the captain, free drinks for all, but it was dress-up time. We went down about 10 minutes late to avoid the line (everyone shows up for free drinks); after shaking hands with the captain and senior officers and chef, we found a table and were waited on right away; canapés were delicious as well as any bar drink when the space in front was empty, or the drink was gone.

We had a couple of drinks, and although we sat at a table for six, no one joined us, so after a while, we retired to the café for a light supper.

This time, they had an open bar not only at the reception but also at the martini bar and the horizon lounge; this made it a lot less crowded and the service much better than we experienced on the last Oceania cruise. It seemed they improved!

After dinner, we went for the late trivia. This team was better, and we took second place. I was beaten, went to the cabin, and Lynn stayed up to attend the show, a violinist who played a wide variety of music. Lynn said he was outstanding. Clocks set back one hour. Tomorrow, we dock at Ketchikan.

Day 3, partly cloudy, low 50s, the air is crisp, light breeze.

We ate a light breakfast and checked out the views from the ship; we docked at 8:00. a Norwegian ship was already here, and there was to be a Princess ship later today. We checked with excursions to see about seating for Lynn, and they told us to be there 20 minutes early and ask for accommodation.

We were off the ship at 8:15 and headed for the stores; our excursion didn't load till 10:50. We walked the streets, went through the various shops, picked up the stones, and after only three shops had something for everyone on the list, then on to a jewelry store for a birthday gift for another person.

We returned to the dock. I ran our treasures up to the room and exchanged the heavier jacket Lynn had brought for a lighter one. We found out that only 10 people were on our excursion, and we had a full-sized bus!

We took off on time, so we were filled in on local stuff on the way to the other dock. We had lucked out; Ketchikan received 50 meters of rain a year and had 50 days of sun. There are over 500 kinds of moss here. This is the salmon capitol of the world, and Ketchikan is actually an island with a population of 8200 during the tourist season; the "regulars" are 4200. cruise ships and tourism have been the main source of income since the brothels closed in the 1950s.

There are more black bears than people on the island, the tide every 6 hours, and the normal rise is 24 feet! (This is the third highest in the world.) This is the home of the world's smallest Walmart. When McDonald's opened, 10,000 hamburgers were sold on the first day; buildings are limited to four stories; this also has more totem poles than anywhere in the world. (Over 200) three native tribes live here also.

Five types of salmon are represented by a hand: thumb Chum, first finger Sockeye, middle finger King, third finger Silver, and the pinky finger Pink salmon. The 20 minutes to the dock went fast: a quick bathroom break, then on to the enclosed 20-passenger boat.

We passed by an eagle and its nest; the bird flew down to the shore to show off! (They can fly up to 35 mph; drowning is the major cause of death. females lay 1-3 eggs, and when their mate passes, the other dies soon after) Then, a colony of brown fur seals on another beach, and on the last stretch to the lodge, a pod of three humpback whales surfaced and blew. I think I got a tail and a blowhole mist...

We arrived at the Silver King Lodge, where there were quite a few chain-saw cut statues; the story goes that a guest liked it there and bargained for a room with statues. I got a few of them, really detailed, great pictures!!

We took a short nature hike into the woods, and we saw a tree that was one of the oldest in the U.S.A., with lots of mosses. We are told that in 8th grade, the class is sent out into the woods with flint and steel, a knife, a sleeping bag, and ground plastic. This is to learn to survive, no fire, you don't cook the food you find, everyone expected to survive by themselves, no cheating, no help!

Lunch was a crab boil. We sat at a round picnic table for eight covered with newspaper, and our meal was dumped in the middle, including crab legs, shrimp, clams, mussels, onion, garlic, three types of small potatoes, corn on the cob, and sausage. We were offered coffee, lemonade, water, or tea, and when we finished just about everything, a homemade cookie... YUMMO!

There was also a small Navy Base for submarines noted on the way back; the water here is very protected and deep, up to 1800 feet at some depths. (They checked the sonar for audibility tests; there were no subs that we could see, and there was a very small base.) The water is a bit over 50 degrees; it takes about 20 minutes to die of hypothermia.

On the way back, we were informed that Ketchikan means "Thundering wings" in the native language, but now "Jewelry stores" are locally spoken.

Since nothing again was really happening till the one show time at 9:30, we decided to go with the dining room, got in line at 6:30, the opening "gate," and requested a group table. We were joined soon after by two other couples, both from the U.S. One couple didn't talk much, the other did talk, she didn't drink, and he didn't eat any seafood...that was the gist of the "engaging" conversation.

The day of fresh air took its toll. Lynn refused to go to the show and the soul dance party afterward, so we retired to our room at 9:00 PM to join the "dead" crowd and went to bed early.

Day 4

The temperature was 50's to 60's (F), light breeze, partly cloudy, "Crisp" comes to mind! Looking out the window, I saw lots of trees, blue water, and some snowcapped mountains.

Lynn had a hard night, up and down, so she slept in. I went to breakfast, caught a couple of shots of the landscape, and wasn't quick enough with the camera for the humpback that lightly breached the water.

Played golf, Baggo, and table tennis, and I went to lecture Lynn on needlepoint.

The lecture was on Glaciers, mountains, and "The Ring of Fire." Glaciers are constantly moving; they may be thousands of years old, but the water inside is no more than 100 years old due to the constant melt and new rain/snow. They cover 10% of the earth's surface and are the largest reservoir of fresh water. Icebergs are just the tips of glaciers falling into the water.

There are 1,000's of glaciers in Alaska. New Zealand has the fastest-shrinking glacier, and Finland is the fastest-growing glacier. The most famous is the Hubbard Glacier, which is almost 600 ft high. Most of the glaciers are smaller now than when first measured. We are coming to the end of another ice age.

Mt. Everest is the tallest land-based mountain, but the largest mountain is the Hawaiian Mona Kea. 1/2 of it is underwater. It is also the largest not only in height but also in circumference.

70% of the earth is covered with water, the Pacific Ocean in some areas is seven miles deep, and scientists are still discovering new life forms. 98% of the capacity for life on this earth is in the oceans.

Volcanoes about 30 erupt on this earth A DAY! Magma is under the volcano; Lava is what comes out. The Ring of Fire is from New Zealand, up through Indonesia, Vietnam, Korea, China, and Russia, across the Aleutians, down the west coast of Alaska, Canada, and South America, almost to the tip of that continent. The plates are always moving along with the continents.

The Aleutian Islands consist of a chain of islands, 14 large and 55 small ones.

The café was full for lunch, we found a seat outside in the sun, and it was quite nice; we docked as we ate, shared a table with another American couple, drifted down to the room for wallets, and went off to explore Juneau.

We walked the streets, mailed our postcards, and visited the shops we were interested in, and many just because of the 20-75% end-of-season sales. Had a lot of fun with the various merchants. All of the employees are looking forward to the end of the season next week, and as before, the people here are independent, friendly, open, and take you for your word, very refreshing!

Returned to the ship, off-loaded our loot, and readied for our excursion at a salmon bake.

The drive to the bake was only 15 minutes, and I was on a school bus! My knees pushed into the back of the seat in front; the seats were very low, and with my shoulders and knees screaming, it was another test to get in and out.

I bought an Alaskan beer. It was quite good, and the meal included coleslaw, beans, corn bread, Caesar salad with salmon, scalloped potatoes, rice, chicken, and salmon with a brown sugar sauce. ALL was superb, all you could eat, and the dessert was a blueberry cake that was surprisingly moist! Everyone enjoyed eating out under various tents. There were guitar-playing singer pole heaters under the tents, and we were warned that if a bear decided to join us, to just put the plate on the ground and slowly back away...

Back on the ship, Lynn was again tired from not being able to stay asleep at night, and fresh air limited our entertainment; she went to bed. I went down to the lounge after returning more paperwork and had the Black Russian drink special. The place was like a ghost town; maybe 10 people went to the lounge, and I was the first one there, with an hour to wait. Some folks finally drifted in, and the band started playing, but bored and tired, and not wanting to wait another ½ hour, I joined Lynn.

Day 5, Skagway, Alaska

Sunny, 50's, light breeze Klondike, Suspension Bridge, and Salmon bake, leaving at 8:50, we actually docked early, before 7:30 A.M.

Skagway is located on the northern finger of the inside passage; until 1970, Skagway did not have a road connection to the inside world; it could only be reached by ferry, railroad, or plane. It is now connected to the Alaskan-Canada or Al-Can Highway. As in most of these towns we are visiting, tourism is the main source of income, and the end of September is the end of that! The average population is 1100; of that, 300-600 are here year-round, and the balance is summer tourist employees. Utah, Montana, and Pennsylvania have active recruiters and trainers, along with word of mouth; most are college students.

We took off from the pier at 9:00 for an hour's drive through the mountains, crossed over to the Canadian border, and into Yukon Territory (we were required to have our passports) to a lodge with a suspension bridge in White Horse, Canada.

On the way there and back, we were told about the different

glaciers, valleys, and continental divide (Yes, I got that picture), which related to us when we saw and transverse the other continental divide in Iceland!

The mountains, glaciers, falls, rivers, and streams were breathtaking. The highway had very little traffic. The first recognized permanent tribe was the Klinket, fur traders. When the glaciers run water, the water is one part water and one part rock dust. As we drive up the mountains, the trees are smaller, the same much younger tree maybe two or three times higher at lower elevations. Most, if not all, are evergreens and 8-10 feet high. The landscape is basically frozen from October through May.

Here are some of the stories: President Harding came to visit and complained constantly about the primitive conditions and weather. He also visited one of the houses of ill repute even though his wife did accompany him. He also was there to open the railroad connection; a glacier was named after him. Since most of the land surrounding Skagway is designated Federal land and forest, lumber actually had to be imported, increasing the cost of building homes by 150%. Even now, groceries come by boat once a week, and this is the last stop, so sometimes what is left is what others do not want, and expiration dates may be within a month. Our guide made it personal. For her and her husband, it costs $700-$1000/month, and milk alone is regularly $7.00/gallon.

There are no doctors, just three nurse practitioners; our driver was pregnant, and to have a baby, you have to go to Juneau, Alaska; there have been no babies born here in 20 years.

The suspension bridge was over a picturesque gorge with mountains and glaciers in the background; about ¾ of the people went across the bridge. On the other side were a typical Klondike cabin, a food storage structure, and a variety of lookout points. This morning, it was 9 degrees C (upper 40s F), and even at 10:30 AM, there was still frost on some of the landings and signs.

We spent an hour at the bridge site, used the facilities, and toured the gift shop, and had our passports stamped. We were back on the bus for almost an hour to Liars Ville, where we had our salmon lunch. This place showed the tent cities of the past, with a seamstress tent, a barber tent, a saloon, an odd house, a panning stream, and gold mining sleuths.

Educating Noah...Travelin'

The meal was almost exactly the same as the other one we had; the set-up with picnic tables and self-serve was also the same, along with the entertainment, except the singer-guitar player was a "he." I asked, and next week, both this place and the suspension bridge lodge close down, and this bus driver returns home in the lower 48.

During the winter, which starts fairly soon, the average snowfall accumulation is 25-35 feet; there are 12-foot markers above the highway to indicate where the edge of the highway is, white for "good" and red for "off the road" in the culvert or down the slope!

In the early days, to cross the Canadian border, you had to have one ton of supplies per person (a year's supply), or the Mounties would not let you enter; many of the glue factories sold old or horses in poor shape to the gold rush prospectors since they had no idea about horses as pack animals. It was hard on the horses, and many died on the way. Many, when crippled, were just left on the passes to die. It was documented that 60 to 70 horse carcasses were found in just a few miles stretch, one of those cruel things about the past!

The trip back to the ship was short. I got off in town to mail some letters and hopefully finish those "must get" gifts for all those folks back home.

After mailing the cards and getting the remainder of the loot, I picked some rose hips, which a woman identified for me, and I also saw a small family of seals in the water along with two white jellyfish.

In the room, Lynn cleaned the rosehips; they were sweet and very seedy, and I washed the stones collected and labeled them. We also sorted all of the loot the past days so that we accounted for everyone promised.

For dinner, another light one, I joined another couple for a cocktail. The Lychee Martini was excellent; there were two trivia sessions, and we actually won a point at one of them. We also watched the production show Four Singers, Broadway.

Day 6, at sea, Hubbard Glacier viewing just after noon

This morning is in the lower 50s, partly cloudy, light breeze. A little information on the glacier: it flows 76 miles; the glacier itself embraces 24 million acres of international wilderness. The British

Noah

Columbia winter range is also here for the Dahl sheep and a population of grizzly and "glacier" bears, which are silver blue in color and bluish-white.

This is actually a surging glacier, where most glaciers move 1-2 inches per day. This one has moved up to 98 feet per day. While most glaciers are shrinking, this one has thickened in the last century, advancing an average of 80 feet per year.

We are looking forward to hearing that groaning and creaking, hopefully some calving. The daybreak was beautiful. I hope the pictures turn out. Plus, I walked a half-nautical mile before meeting Lynn for breakfast. After breakfast, we started with inside golf; I then went to the lecture "Divided by a Common Language." I got there early to confront him on the definition of Ice Age. I told him that I was taught it was the presence of ice caps on the top and bottom, and he said it is more of a relationship between surface land and water.

I told him I didn't want to be political, but isn't global warming natural? And isn't the cause more the increased presence of man? He agreed with that assumption. Also, blaming China for the biggest part of pollution and acceleration isn't really fair, in that most of the industry has moved to China due to cheap labor, and after all, the most spoken language in the world is Mandarin! I asked when this ice age started, and he stated that it was about 8000 years ago, and it is the third or fourth.

As far as the lecture, we have our understanding of others based on our language, culture, and traditions; therefore, never assume your understanding of a gesture or comment is the same as others. (I mention this several times in arguments on the internet with others that education, background, and experience bring different people to different beliefs and views; don't assume the other is stupid or uneducated!)

The largest number of Spanish-speaking people is in South America and the USA. Thereby, the language on Spanish TV reflects this, which is like another dialect in Spain!

Samples of differences:

Adios in Cuba means "Hello?"

The Toyota MR2 sports car was a dud in Spain because "MR2" is slang for "pile of poop."

The Chevy Nova...In Spanish, "Doesn't go."

Ford Pinto...In South America, an insult to a man's "member."

Coors..." diarrhea"

Coca-Cola's "Adds Life campaign" in Thailand was translated to bring the ancestors back from the dead!

Watch your hand signals, thumb to forefinger, means everything from "O.K" to little value, "Butt Hole" or an insult! Cross fingers, palms up, all different meanings.

Friday 13th, Black cats, white cats, walking under ladders...

Finally, there are no bananas on Alaskan boats because, in the past, there were spiders that came with bananas, and some died from spider bites!

We missed the Northern lights last night...Superstition: do not whistle at the lights, or they will catch you up, and if hunting and the first kill under the lights, you are obligated to give the meat to the community.

Off to Bago, then a presentation on Oceania. I'm not really interested, but I had a chance to win $250.00 credit!

Back to the cabin, it was clear, partly cloudy at 7 A.M.; between 8:30 and 11:00, it was overcast and raining. Then, between twelve and two, when we approached, it turned into a drizzle and overcast for pictures of the Hubbard glacier; we were within 50 meters; wow, just simply doesn't describe it. I took quite a few pictures, hopefully, to get the shade of blue, but I missed all of the small pieces that broke off. I did get to hear the thunder sounds from behind and inside the glacier.

Lunch, mini golf again, inside mini shuffleboard (gotta get those ship points!), and then the martini tasting. The bartender is from Romania, very nice. I let a chant begin with a shot of tequila, and she went along with it! We had 4 specialty martinis, all very good, and then she mixed an additional one for us to try, which, of course, was exceptional. Lots of fun, only eight of us, but even though most were a bit "reserved," I got one woman to work with me on toasts and chants...

Made it to Trivia a bit late. We lost again! Dressed up for another captain's reception for guests that have traveled more than once, met another nice couple with free drinks and canopies, then off for dinner at the specialty Italian restaurant, The Toscana (two specialty restaurant reservations are complimentary and included) nice two other couples, both Canadian, good conversation.

Night time trivia…we won 2nd place! Then it was "quitting." Wow, can no longer handle alcohol, no staying up late? We are becoming part of the Walking Dead!

Day 7 Sitka

The overcast 54 degrees, rain, and this is the day for wildlife! This was also designated omelet day; once every cruise, I had a junk omelet. This is an omelet with everything they have in it. Alongside hash with mushrooms and bacon, it is a great breakfast; big, not good for the diet, but Oceania is known for the food!

Our excursion was at 8:50, and the catamaran was docked right next to the ship. The three-hour tour was billed as a wildlife exploration of the bay in Sitka. Sitka is one of the world's best places to view wildlife. The surrounding waters are an important feeding ground for whales, sea otters, sea lions, and other marine life.

Sitka has an island population of 9,000, and the island itself is 100 by 50 miles. Boat kelp is floating in bunches. It is edible; we each tried a kelp jam that was very good. We maneuvered to a bed of this kelp where a "raft" of otters was together. The kelp has roots to the bottom, anchoring the plants and providing warmth and some protection for the otter families. The males are aggressive, females tend to the pups, and at night, they wrap themselves in the kelp so they don't drift out to sea. Otters give birth in water; they forage for food and can hold their breath for 3-5 minutes. They eat ¼ their body weight each day in food; we came pretty close to an otter floating on his back chomping on an octopus!

They have retractable claws that have a foul smell to ward off predators. The otter's hair is thick, 300,000 to 1 million strands of fur per square inch; it is also oily for warmth and waterproofing the otters.

The devil's club plant on the rocks is good for making ointments for pain relief. We were given a sample, and Lynn said its pain-relieving effect was immediate.

Cormorants, seagulls, and black and white duck-looking birds were abundant. The trees were full of "old man's beard" (not only does this dry fast and can be used as a fire starter, but it also can be used in soups); Spruce tips are used to make beer and jam. There were a lot of small islands, everywhere possible that vegetation could grow. It does! We also sighted an eagle with its nest. Eagles have the white feathered head when they reach five years old.

Whales, yup, we found them; the ones we saw were humpbacks. Whales use Hawaii as a bedroom, and Alaska is their kitchen. They feed here and then swim south to breed underwater for 3-30 minutes.

As they surface to exhale and then breathe in, this seemed to happen 3-4 times before they dive with flukes showing sounding for 5-6 minutes. The eye is located on the jaw hinge to see the food going in and the water going out.

We saw 5 to 6 pods of 3-4 whales, never got closer than 100 feet, but they were great to watch, especially when they were about the size of a school bus, sixty-five long by fifteen feet wide, about the same size as the catamaran we were chasing them in!

After three hours, we were unloaded in Sitka, where we could shop or take a free shuttle bus back to the ship for twenty minutes. I walked the town, Lynn took the bus back right away, and after all, it was still raining on and off, the temperature never getting warmer than 55 F.

There is still a small lake (man-made) near the center of town; it was created while the Russians were running the place, and the ice was used as an income source during the winter. The Russians would export the ice to southern communities.

I joined Lynn at 2 P.M. for games, had a brief lunch, another game, then went back to the room to write up the events, and rest, and trivia...we finally took first!

Dinner was great for me, sushi and tapas um, um, ummm; Lynn had Italian and cream of asparagus soup; nothing really happened till the show. The room had been prepared, so there was a little downtime; the show was the American Idol contest with the singers. We were one of the three-judge teams, and we had a lot of fun. We knew all of the contestants!

Day 8, Wrangell, Alaska, USA.

Noah

Off and on rain, in the mid-50s, our excursion starts at 9:50 A.M., and since it is supposed to be on and off rain, I will give highlights of the excursion and just annotate it after we experience it.

The earliest period of occupation was about 8,000 years ago, established by carbon dating of the Petroglyphs found here. This is the only Alaskan community governed by four flags that of the Tlingit Nation, Russia, Britain, and the U.S. Other cultures, such as Japanese and Chinese influences, are here also with the fish canneries and Timber Company. In the Alaskan gold rush, this was the first base providing lodging, supplies, entertainment, and equipment for thousands of miners.

Wrangell was named after a Russian explorer. It was once a Tlingit stronghold, then a Russian outpost, and then, in 1867, it became an American settlement.

We had the school bus tour of Wrangell. It isn't really that big of a town, but the bus was full, and we were the first 30 folks to leave the shipyard!

This is a summation of notes and observances:

Totems are carved from Cedar and usually buried 8-10 feet into the ground. The ones we saw dated back to only the early 1900's. Most describe lessons to be learned. On the totems, the beak is what determines the bird: long is the raven, and short and curved is the eagle. According to legend, the raven was originally white, but since they stole so much, they turned black from the smoke escaping from the teepee fire. We had a native speaker on the bus because our bus driver was "Too White." The native speaker was wearing a hat made from cedar fibers. They sell for, are you ready…$2,000-$7,000 each, not much different from a "San Pan hat." His hat also had an eagle feather on it. Only a native American can possess an eagle feather.

The tribes in Alaska are usually based on Matriarchal.

There are three ways of getting to this island: boat, plane, and birth canal. As in other areas, birth is not advised or "permitted," pregnant moms are sent to Juneau to deliver; only nurse practitioners work here, and they are not equipped to handle complications.

Legend has it that when the great flood happened, a very large bear came to rescue the natives and carried them up to safety in the mountain range tops.

Educating Noah...Travelin'

The last stop was at the beachfront to view reproductions of the Petroglyph Beach, where rock carvings from 8,000 years before the Tlingit tribes were here. Lynn did a rubbing of a replica, and I went in search of the actual ones on the beach and only found one!

Walked the town, donated more to the economy, and went back to the ship; it never did rain. Lunch, ship games, it was warm enough (57 degrees F to play both mini golf and shuffleboard outside), and we tried our hand at Bingo again...another $40.00 down the drain!!

The buffet is "fish" night, which makes me happy; Lynn will find something she did and lamb chops! I had the grilled fish and the grilled salmon and tried the cuttlefish risotto; it was black in color and tasted like risotto but with some mild spice (cuttlefish? The cuttlefish was chopped up the same size as the rice). Lynn wouldn't touch it. I would have it again!

Another trivia and the comic show rounded out the night.

Day 9 at sea

We are now headed back to Vancouver. We had an hour change again last night; we lost the one we gained at the beginning, the one when we flew from Milwaukee to Vancouver. We will not be adding to the countries and Islands we have visited in that Vancouver, British Columbia, and the Yukon Territory are all Canadian, just that we have added to the Canadian provinces we have visited.

Since we were at sea, games, a lecture on Cruise ships, and a cooking demonstration took up the morning.

The lecture was basically a history lesson on cruise ships, starting from the mid-1800s; the ships were heavily government-subsidized for the dual purpose of transporting military as well as civilian guests. They were very costly to run, many using 1,000 tons of fuel oil per day!

An award was instituted for the fastest ship going across the Atlantic only from east to west against the Gulf Stream. The sinking of the ship Lusitania that brought us into the war was very quick; after the torpedo hit, she sank in only 18 minutes!

The nautical knot is 1-minute latitude or 1.15 miles.

The invention of aircraft and subsequent commercial airlines changed everything, trans-Atlantic and trans-Pacific, from days to hours.

The cooking demonstration was put on by the head chef and his Toscana, a special restaurant chef. They worked well together and had a good attitude. The meals they prepared were Steak Tartar, Veal Medallions, Pasta dough, and Risotto Al Fungai Porcini. As they cooked, they bantered back and forth. The presentation was perfect, and we were also able to taste the preparations and give the recipes. The only negative, again, is the guests, some standing in line and having discussions with the chefs while everyone else is actually trying to taste a small sample, the line jumpers, and the double dippers!

More games, lunch, and a lecture on Captain Cook, and here is a brief:

The currents and circular trade winds from Europe run counter-clockwise, with most ships reaching the mouth of the Americas. (Caribbean) At that period of time, the European ships made the crossing in about ten weeks. He had three major voyages; he was killed on his last in Hawaii. (Although he was welcomed before, he came back at the wrong place and at the wrong time.)

He was a very accomplished map maker and mapped much of Australia, New Zealand, Asia, and the western coast of North America, along with Canada and Alaska. He was one of the earliest captains to demand that the sailors eat sauerkraut or other vegetables daily, have the men bathe daily, and air out their bedclothes. Only one man died of scurvy on all three of his voyages. He was a true explorer and did not turn rogue for riches.

Afternoon games, another Martini tasting for me; this bartender started us out with a half shot of gin, then we tasted four ½ martinis and finished with a special martini, her favorite (gin and vermouth).

Dinner was in the Polo Grill specialty restaurant with two other couples. Everyone was American: three scientists and a doctor. Good discussions, time passed quickly.

We watched the last production show of "Tuxedo"; I was done for the day. Lynn went up to the lounge to dance with the crew members. (She had a blast!)

Day 10, Victoria, BC, Canada.

Educating Noah...Travelin'

Located on the southern tip of Vancouver Island off Canada's Pacific Coast. We are scheduled to arrive at 1:00 P.M. This is our last full day on the ship, the second last port, and our last excursion.

Morning games, the last lecture on "Who did discover America?" and cashing in on the points we accumulated during this cruise.

Notes on the lecture: There is evidence of Arabs and Asians in both North and South America from the 4th and 5th Centuries and Polynesia in South America over 100 years before Columbus. Chinese culture, evidence of Chinese influence has been in pictograms found in New Mexico.

Columbus had a total of three adventures to the Americas. He was mostly in the Caribbean and West Indies, plus the upper part of South America, Columbia, Venezuela, Mexico, Panama, and the lower Central American countries.

There has been some evidence that Chinese maps may have helped guide Columbus (a 1763 Chinese map of the world seemed to be copied from one dated 1418). During the Ming Dynasty, the Chinese had ships 400 feet long and as many as 9 masts!

We cashed in all of our points, a sweatshirt, 2-T shirts, a polo shirt, and 2 pairs of socks, not bad for participating in activities!

We had the Butchart Gardens Floral Adventure as the final excursion right after docking in Victoria. This was the worst-managed tour to start, especially with this crowd. We all had to wait in a corral before they let us go to the buses, calling out bus numbers like school kids, and of course, those in front didn't want to give way for those whose buses were called. After pushing through the crowd, there were no reserved seats for those with handicaps either. Our port was Ogden Point, the capital of Vancouver is Victoria, and we had to pass through Victoria to get to the gardens, so we had a good 45 minutes of information there and back.

There are three pods of Orca whales in the bay, you can see America across the bay, and the Trans-Canadian Highway starts here.

The city is very clean, with beautiful homes; the original Esso Gas station company has as its base here a mini Empire State Building. The clock tower in town, built in 1878, had clocks imported from England. This was one of the few places to get prospector supplies for the gold rush.

Noah

Vancouver exported coal and lumber, both no longer major incomes; now it is mining, lumber, fishing, high tech, vineyards, and tourism. The government in Victoria, being the biggest employer since it is the capital, has 18,000 employees.

The land was being bought up and developed so fast that the farms were disappearing, so the government allowed you to claim an "arm" deduction if you produced $4500/year in sales of farm products. When you see a produce stand alongside the road, they are all on the honor system: take what you want and pay the posted price.

The Gardens was built in 1904 by Jenny Butchart. Transforming the family lime quarry completely, and she wanted to look out over a garden vs. a quarry hole. It is one of the world's premier botanical gardens. Uninterrupted blooms from March through October.

There are 75 year-round full–time gardeners, at peak season, 560 employees to take care of the over one million visitors a year.

We spent an easy two hours walking the grounds, flowers of all kinds. It is like a small village atmosphere: a waterwheel, a Japanese Garden, an Italian Garden, and a sunken garden; fountains, porticos, streams, bushes, trees, absolutely jaw-dropping! There were also two restaurants on the premises, two gift shops, and the original estate.

After touring and enjoying the garden, we were on the bus back, and more information.

The island is quite large, 300 miles long and 60 miles wide, making it the largest island in North and South America; the population is 765,000, of which 82,000 live in Victoria. 42 degrees (F) is the average temperature in the winter, and 70 degrees in the summer, with rainfall of 24 inches per year. The low rain and little snow are due to living in the shadow of mountain ranges.

Gas prices are a bit high; 139.9/liter comes to about $5.60 per gallon. Just outside Victoria is Elk Lake; the Canadian rowing team practices here since it never freezes and the water is very calm.

Animals on the island are Black bears and cougars.

The average home is $967,000, $565,000 for condos, $650,000 for a townhouse, and property taxes about $4500/year.

Healthcare, in 1951, was socialized. It is covered with income tax, but that was not enough, so now there is a $70/month British

Columbia medical tax, or family $150.00; there can be extensive waits for tests and surgeries, 3-6 months for tests, 8-10 months for surgery. There is some low-income housing, and if you qualify, you must agree to keep the property looking good.

Besides income tax, there is a Canadian sales tax of 5% and another 21% Provincial sales tax.

Vancouver is on a fault line, with 12,000 minor earthquakes a year, most unfelt. Between 700-1,000 years ago, there was a major quake and a 33% chance of a major earthquake in the next 10 years.

In 1850, Opium was legal; whiskey was not…go figure!

Back on the ship, I studied the distance between Alaska and Russia; the distance was 168 degrees latitude to 169 degrees 8 minutes, 60 minutes to a degree.

I had my last sushi for a while, along with some salmon tartar and calamari rings. Lynn had her last veal for a while. A few showed up for the "just for fun" trivia, and our four-member team won!! What was the planet that was discovered with the telescope? Uranus!

We packed the luggage out by 10 P.M.

Day 10

We ate our last breakfast on the ship and were out of the room by 8:00; at 8:30, we left the ship and found our luggage. As with everything with this Oceania pattern, ours was the last in the group. It seems everyone broke the rules as far as leaving for excursions, for the ports, and when entering or leaving the ship…

The bus ride was the customary ¾ hour to 1 hour to the airport; we had to sit and wait to check in and then waited till 1:30 for our flight to Minneapolis, a two-and-a-half hour wait in Minneapolis for the Milwaukee flight.

Conversion is 1 US to .75 CAD, or our dollar worth about $1.25 in Canada.

There were only about two weeks before leaving for our Doro River Cruise and a three-day extension in Madrid, so no driving for the DAV. I finished up the notes and added to this, ran the pictures through my Picasa editing program, sent them to Shutterfly, and made the album. I sorted all the loot and distributed it to all the interested parties and the Christmas closet.

We had the annual board meeting, my three-year commitment was up, and I did not stay on. The rogue member is, and now the maintenance men and construction contractor refuse to do any work she is involved in; the striping machine was also promised to a new board member, so we may actually have strips in the parking areas again! I wished the manager "Good Luck." One of the new board members is the guy who blames her for not fixing his porch and thinks the rogue member walks on water (she never told the board about his anxiety until after I received an e-mail from him) three months after she got involved, and Kelly, the manager, told me she only discussed the situation with her once. As mentioned before, a board-only meeting every month for six months, and over 150 e-mails…I do not need this!

I confirmed the last payment on the Tahiti cruise and confirmed the upcoming Viking cruise. Viking seemed to miss the $200/person credit to spend on the ship, so I noted this on my stuff to take along.

Luggage was never taken "down". We just emptied, washed our precious clothes, and packed again for our next adventure.

Educating Noah...Travelin'

Madrid/Portugal Douro River Cruise

We started the adventure by checking out the parking lot by the bus station on Sunday the day before. Not a slot was available, so we made alternative plans just in case. Early Monday morning, I called; the dispatcher indicated there were now 3 slots but could not guarantee one would be open at 10, the planned time of our arrival, so option two, we called Tony, the cab driver.

We arrived just before 10:00. Like everything else, cab fares had gone up, and Lynn hadn't tested Uber, so the cab ride there was $30.00 with tip.

We only had a short wait, I asked, and of course, the dispatcher told us there were 2 parking spaces open (groan). As we entered the bus, to our surprise, it was ¾ full! It leaves every hour at ten past the hour, from 4:10 A.M. to 8:10 P.M., seven days a week.

The ride to O'Hare was quick and easy; we were the first to be dropped off at the domestic terminal. We checked our luggage, but since we were going international (passports need to be checked), we couldn't check in online, and I refused to put my passport on an airline application for using phones. I don't take my cell phone on international trips. (This is subject to change!)

The first flight was delayed, once we were on board, for fifty minutes. United has decided to leave the entertainment to the client (I did not know this, and they didn't tell us either). You stare at the back of a seat. There is a clip to put your phone or notebook with plugs. However, you needed to supply the cord also.

This flight was to Newark, New Jersey, an hour and a half flight, which turned into 2 ½ hours (That delay sitting on the runway for almost an hour). We try to plan a three-hour layover to accommodate delays and problems.

The second flight was delayed also, but that was only an additional 20 minutes in the terminal with a gate change. This was a 777, and with both planes, we had paid extra for Economy Plus, giving us an extra 2 inches of legroom. However, the seats were just as bad, the aisles very narrow, and the tiny extra room meant you got bumped by everyone as they passed in the aisle or rubbed by the serving cart. Ten people across 3/4/3, we had the aisle and middle seat. When they closed the door, the window seat was vacant, so we at least could spread out.

Since there was no entertainment, information, newspapers, or magazines, it grew irritating rather quickly. Even with the center seat to spread out into, neither of us was very comfortable, and the middle seat arm would not stay "up." When only maybe 20% had tablets or phones hooked in, it was a six-plus hour flight to Madrid and seemed much, much longer. Since we didn't have earphones, the announcements in Spanish first, then English, were barely recognizable above the jet and air noise; the dinners provided were good, and yogurt and croissant for breakfast tastes; the ride over was bumpy, ½ the time the seatbelt sign was on, and we were "a shaken" Lynn took her pill!

Two good things: there was a 150 MPH tailwind, making the trip ½ hour shorter, and we were up close to the business class (they had large video screens and all the usual channels, movies, and information stations), so our exit was fairly quick! I had asked to upgrade through our travel agent and personally called the airline, but I was only able to get the economy plus upgrade due to the tickets purchased through Viking; an upgrade to business is not allowed, even for the "long" hauls.

We picked up our luggage, and immigration went fairly well. Only about 30 minutes to go through the lines, found our van driver, and off to downtown Madrid.

The half-hour drive gave us a view of the city; it was, of course, rush hour, lots of motorcycles, and the hotel was in the center of town. I did see quite a bit of graffiti, which I thought was very disappointing, especially when the streets and sidewalks were very clean, and I did not see one homeless person. (I am being politically correct in not calling them bums.)

Madrid is 5 hours ahead of New York, so when we checked in, we were told our rooms would not be ready until after 1 P.M., it was 10:30 A.M. They offered to lock up our luggage, we found a couch, had a croissant, and juice with a cappuccino ($15.00 EU! Yes, it is an uppity hotel) I left Lynn for a walk; she was too tired to move.

This is the banking and upscale hotel district, nothing much more

Educating Noah...Travelin'

except downtown traffic. There is a subway, and a lot of the motorcycles park between the street and sidewalk; most of these bikes are under 500cc or scooters. I did see a rental "Byrd's" motorized skateboard with handles used here.

We got the room a bit early, talked to the Viking Representative about the following days, got our stuff, and crashed for 5 hours in a very comfortable bed.

We were up at 5 P.M., and I was not sure if it was A.M. or P.M., so after figuring out the shower and navigating the high European tubs (they prefer baths), we figured out the TV controller, got dressed, and went out for supper. I tried to look for the Viking representative, but she was gone for the day. Went to the desk and asked about the cabs, they charge by the minute, and our restaurant was only 5 minutes away. Madrid is laid out in circles and angles, not so much a grid, and street signs are hard to find, so we usually take transportation to get our city "legs."

A cab was called; the doorman told the cabbie where we were to go and gave the address. He asked for the address when we first asked because he explained there are so many restaurants in the metro area.

The ride was a bit under 5 minutes; I gave him a 10 EU, asked for change, and took the five, letting him keep the coins, and he seemed content; small tips are appreciated here, and big tips are questioned...

As we had read in the brochures, Spanish eat at different times and have different concepts; Americans have breakfast at 8, the desk and other businesses close from 11-2 for midafternoon break, including lunch, and then the restaurants and nightlife start at around 9 P.M.

It was 7:30; we asked and were told the opening was at 9:00 P.M... The people are both pleasant and nicely dressed, and there are a lot of smokers; we did see one bum as we walked around.

We found a prosciutto shop and ordered two sandwiches, a beer, and a white soda. The sandwiches were served with a small tray of olives, the sandwich was a bun with olive oil and prosciutto, the meat was sweet and a little salty, excellent, the beer was amber, and the white soda was seltzer with a twist. We ate outside, like the locals. The guy at the next table decided he wanted to smoke, so without a second thought, he moved to a chair next to his date and away from Lynn, then lit up. Just an example of how nice folks are here.

Noah

Total bill: $14 EU put an extra $1 EU in the bucket with $15 EU. He was happy, we were full, and we decided to walk back to the hotel. On the way back, we went past a number of restaurants, all closed yet (it was a bit past 8), found and walked through a small convenience store, prices about the same as ours except in the EU, so about 1/3 higher.

We walked the eight blocks to the hotel. I asked the desk clerk to break down two fifties; he would only break one, and then I accommodated him by asking just for paper money, two fives and four tens.

Back to the room, checked our schedule out for tomorrow (Wednesday) since we gained hours and that Monday-Tuesday ended tonight, showers, clothes out, clock set, done.

"Accentors" are the elevators, "habitations" are guestrooms

Wednesday, our first great European buffet breakfast! Plentiful is about what you would say, cereals, meats, cheeses, grilled tomatoes, blood sausage, made-to-order eggs, scrambled eggs, hard-boiled eggs, mushrooms, prosciutto, sausages, cheeses, fruits, varieties of juices, toasts, pancakes, waffles, donuts, croissants, toast…you get the idea!

At 8:30, we met in the lobby for the included excursion of Panoramic Madrid, the most expensive city in Spain, as well as the capital. (Toledo was the original capital, but Madrid became the capital in 1561.)

Here, "republic "means "left-wing"; everything here is built up (adding more stories). Since the city has been here for centuries, there is no space to build. Spain is fourth to Japan, Iceland, Portugal, and then Spain in the world in the consumption per person of seafood, mainly fish.

All the streets are lined with parked cars; some areas have wide boulevards neatly kept with lawns, trees, walkways, and grass. We traveled through New Madrid, Old Madrid, and Hapsburg Madrid with the 16th and 17th-century architecture and designs. The newer buildings don't have balconies, not even French balconies. We passed and were on narrow streets, squares, churches, fountains (one to Neptune, another to Cybius, the Goddess of fertility), and the remainders of the old ornate city gates. (The city was walled, the rich inside and poor outside; the gates are all that is left, and they are impressive!)

Prado means meadow, located in the "Triangle of Art," a section of the city where numerous museums are located. This area had a heavy Arabic influence, with many of the street names reflecting the Arabic language. The final part of the tour was the Prado Museum, one of the world's most loved art institutes. We spent over an hour seeing the art of 16th-century Picasso, Goya, Velazquez, Bosch, and others. Many had a 3D effect; gold leaf was the base of some of these masterpieces to make them stand out., Others had a faint sparkle to them, and still others were painted on wood, not canvas at all.

We passed by the botanical gardens, where new species of plants were introduced to Spain. The weather here is usually dry, so the warm, dry heat in the summer is very pleasant, another reason Spain is a winter haven for Europeans.

We were back at the hotel a little after 1:00, rested for an hour, and then took a cab to the tourist area in the Calle Mayor area; half the time to get there was spent waiting in traffic, and since we were charged by the minute, it was a bit frustrating; However, within 45 minutes we had obtained all the Spanish "loot" we had hoped for and returned home. Note, even though I held my breath a few times both on the bus and in the cabs, we came within an inch of hitting another vehicle when some other vehicles took aggressive advantage of the "no hit" rule. Both there and back with delays, the fare was $13-14 EU, and rounding it up to $15 EU seemed to please both cab drivers.

We went back to the hotel, packed our loot, rested, and 6:00 was our Tapas excursion. There were about 30 people signed up for the Tapas experience already, and off we went back (for the third time today) to where the social action is, Old Madrid.

The plan was to experience three Tapas places, about a half mile between them, helping to settle the wine and food. We were seated at large community tables offered white or red wine and various Tapas dishes. (Tapas means small plate, actually, literally, cover or top) A second glass of wine was about 3 EU, which, as the evening went on, was exercised by about ½ of us. If you actually did not want wine, soft drinks, beer, or coffee and tea were also provided.

The Tapas included…to the best of my memory…different at each restaurant included, cold tomato soup, cheeses, sausages, prosciutto, sesame stick straws, deep-fried veggie pancakes, potato tortilla, bean balls, and deep-fried fish bites. As the evening went on, we were encouraged to share different tables with different couples, the conversations becoming louder and more animated as we moved from restaurant to restaurant, in typical Spanish fashion. We left the last bar a bit after 10:00, walked the plaza to the bus, and had a short ride home; full, a bit tipsy, and still not recovered from the transit flight here, we went up to the room and crashed. Others went for a nightcap at the hotel bar, but "cheap Noah" couldn't see $9 EU beers or $16-18 EU for a cocktail. It was just a bit too rich for my blood!

Thursday, Lynn did not sleep well, so I let her sleep in. This morning, we opted for an eight-hour tour of the City of Toledo, Spain's open-air museum, and the original capitol, way back when. I had another great breakfast, and Lynn was still not feeling good when I returned to the room. She reinforced that she had a rough night with little sleep (and she didn't drink any alcohol!), so I went without her; hopefully, they will refund her money. I asked, but no, the excursion was pre-ordered; sorry, no refund.

There were only 17 in the group, so we had a ½ size bus; since Lynn wasn't with us, I took the back seat and had access to both sides of the bus. As with yesterday, everything seemed to favor the south side of Madrid, so again, we went out of the city through the south tunnel. As with traffic before, it is 0-30MPH or 40 quickly, with little or no space between vehicles and close traffic on both sides. It is overcast, the mid-60s, and all the parked cars have mirrors folded in on both the street and curbsides. As we again passed the Neptune fountain, it was called that, and the figure of the Neptune god represented the original spring where the water supply for the city was.

The buildings advertise Hostels now fairly frequently, and there is a definite increase in graffiti. The drive to Toledo is guessed at one hour; the road turned into a highway, two lanes both ways separated by an island of land. All the barriers, walls, and back of advertising signs have graffiti, apartment buildings, and row houses on the outskirts of town, then scrubland, dry, some planted fields, not many trees. A good half hour out, the traffic going into the city is still starting and stopping, and it is 9:45 in the morning!

This group was pretty quiet; ½ of them reclined their seats fully, another ¼ played with their phones, and the rest of us listened to the guide and watched the scenery.

Educating Noah...Travelin'

Toledo is one of the oldest cities in Spain. It was the first city to fall to the Romans in the famous Reconquista; three cultures coexisted here for centuries: Christian, Moorish, and Jewish. It was also home to the great Renaissance painter El Greco.

As we approached the city, we stopped for a picture of the city from across the river; the mansions along the river have mostly been converted to hotels due to the high cost of maintaining them.

We were then dropped off at the lower parking lot and preceded to the escalators, a series of 8 escalators to take us up inside the city. The streets are very narrow, all well-worn cobblestone, and very few flat areas. You are either walking up or down (steeply), and the city is a maze!

You do have to listen since cars, more frequently than thought, use the streets also, with little room between pedestrians and cars; I am talking inches of clearance.

We stopped outside a number of buildings, showing the different century styles, the grand doors with small access doors, peeked through lower windows to see small inside gardens, up and down streets, different little balconies, and different stone walls.

Our first inside stop was Santo Tome's church to examine El Greco's masterpiece, "The Burial of the Count of Orgaz." we were there for a good 20 minutes of explanation of the various features of the artwork was pointed out.

We then proceeded through the Jewish quarter, the Transito Synagogue, the San Cristo de la Luz Mosque, built in 999, and the cloisters of San Juan de Los Reyes, founded by Ferdinand and Isabella, to the stunning Gothic Cathedral that dominates from within, the centerpiece of the town.

Inside, the size is mind-blowing; we have been in many cathedrals and churches, but this one has to be the largest! The choir and organ loft are elevated and centered in the church, the organ pipes are both horizontal and vertical, massive columns, marble, gold, carved wood, anterooms with painted ceilings, a crypt room, several sanctuaries, on and on, we spent over a half hour inside and we moved quite quickly just to see what we could! This has got to be one of the greatest churches of all on this planet!

We were fast approaching lunchtime, and we were given two

hours to eat on our own, shop the main street stores, and find a place to meet at three P.M., with a warning that it is easy to get lost. We then walked another few blocks to the main shopping street, and our guide left.

The shops mostly specialize in hammered gold, knives, and swords, yes swords, big ones, little ones, very fancy to plain, full-sized swords selling for 40EU and up. How do you get them home? There were other varieties of shops, some clothing, some souvenirs, and, of course, a wide variety of food establishments.

I explored a few of the shops; they are proud of the Don Quixote story, the Knights of Templar, hammered gold plaques, plates, and jewelry. I had a small lunch and met up with the group a bit before three; everyone was on time! We wound back to where the escalators took us down to the bus parking area, loaded up, and the drive back to Madrid was quick and uneventful.

I checked on Lynn, and she was feeling better. Our flight out tomorrow is early. Luggage out at 4:50 A.M., lobby at 5:00 for the trip to the airport. It was still just a bit after 5 P.M.; most restaurants don't open till …9! So, we decided to just relax in the room, do the journaling, watch some TV, go to bed early, pack up, and have an early start tomorrow.

Friday

we got up at 4:10 A.M., and neither of us slept well, which must have been the anticipation for today; luggage out at 4:45, and we heard it picked up just before we left the room at 4:50. We checked out, and they had breakfast in a bag for us, but we turned them down, we didn't want to eat in the cab, TSA would have thrown most of it out. The trip was 20 minutes to the airport (no traffic at 5A.M.). There was no line for check-in. We checked in our luggage, took a full scan at their TSA, and went off to find our gate. We were sitting in front of the gate at 5:45; our flight was at 7:25, loading at 6:45. Due to Lynn's cane, we were some of the first to take the steps down to the tarmac (three flights of stairs), then into a waiting bus that was filled to capacity. Out to the plane, last on first off, but we managed to get up the stairs to the plane, found our seats, and when they closed the door, the window seat was empty, so we were able to spread out.

The flight lasted less than an hour; we got our bags, met with Viking, and had a car ride into the hotel. We were the only ones on that flight, and the driver was nice, talkative, and interesting. He lives with his girlfriend in the city; she is a nurse. He was selling natural food supplements, but it wasn't enough to support him, even with the combined income, so he became a driver. He has been on the job for four months. He told us the minimum wage here is $6 EU, about the same as in the states, but the cost of living and taxes are higher.

We checked into the Tivoli hotel, met with the Viking representatives, filled out the paperwork, and they actually provided us a room by 10:30. Wow!!

I walked around to familiarize myself with the neighborhood; it was very much the same: upscale hotels, banks, and high-end stores. I came back to the room, the suitcases were there, Lynn sleeping, and then I crashed into her.

A meeting was set for 6 P.M., so Lynn and I put on some fresh clothes and walked around a bit to find a restaurant for the evening meal. The hotel restaurant was again very pricy, and I needed to find those promised pens, stones, thimbles, magnets, and something for the kids, which we did!

We were back for the scheduled presentation. It was just another sell job on optional tours offered, which bus we were assigned to for tomorrow's included excursion. And we also checked about our optional excursion to the tile factory, and yes, we were on the list. The nice thing about the meeting was the fruity port wine they offered and included, which was excellent!

After the meeting, we went out again to find a restaurant; Lynn wanted meat, and I wanted the fresh seafood Lisbon is known for. After examining a few menus (there are over 10,000 restaurants in Lisbon), we actually stumbled on a back street of restaurants!

I had skewered shrimp and calamari, and Lynn had sausage, chicken, veal, pork, and lamb chop plate.

·Both came with vegetables, potatoes, and olives; what a feast!

We were stuffed, finished most, and then offered a sweet cherry liquor, which I took, very good, and settled up. The cost is around $40 EU, about the same as a meal for one at the hotel.

It was 9:00, and we were both very tired and bloated. We stopped at a few shops and picked up all the rest of the promised loot for

Noah

friends back home and managed to walk the long blocks home.

This hotel has a rain shower head, a square about 16 inches that just drenches you, and it is a walk-in area, really great!

Saturday, we have a tour in the A.M. and the tile factory in the afternoon. Both of us slept well and had another great European breakfast.

The four-hour A.M. bus tour included a stop and photo session of the Belem Tower, looking at the river's mouth and the Atlantic Ocean. This was the last of twenty-three towers, one built every kilometer on the river as part of the fortress to guard the city and was/is regarded the third safest port in the world. Then, a stop to tour the Jeronimo's Monastery (1502), a product of the 14th through 16th centuries, the monks were kicked out due to the wealth they had hoarded. The wealth then became the people's property. We viewed the inside of the church, the Monastery square, and finally, Lisbon's old quarter, with the hilly labyrinth of narrow streets, cafes, and tiny shops, many of the outside walls decorated with azulejo tiles.

What we were told while traveling, "Bondea" means "Good Morning," "Obregata" means "Thank you" to women, and Obregato means "Thank you" to men.

"Largo" is a small public square, "Apasa" is a large public square. There are one hundred public parks in the city and 28 hills; Lisbon is the second oldest city in Europe, Athens being the oldest. 83% are Catholics, of which it is claimed 17% are active. Portugal is the "Sardine Capitol of the World."

The earthquake of 1755 destroyed most of the original buildings; Marques Pampanga is credited with rebuilding the city as it is now. The port is fifteen miles long; the Tagus River is the border of town across the river, which acts as a natural border, connected by a long expansion bridge dubbed "The sister of the Golden Gate Bridge. In the distance is a monument to Christ the Redeemer, similar to the one in Rio de Janeiro, but much smaller, only 180 feet tall, base and statue.

The cross on all of the older Portuguese ships is called the Vera Cruz, which literally means True Cross.

Way back, before the Roman conquest, Portugal was Lusitania, then after the Roman conquest, it became Portugal, meaning "Little garden by the sea."

Educating Noah...Travelin'

We were back by 1:30, rested in the room, ate our granola bars, and the next excursion was to the Tile Museum.

The Tile Museum was much more than we expected: rooms of different tiles from different ages; the museum was previously a monastery, and the rooms were elaborate, with gold-plated walls, paintings, and ornamentation. Paintings that, when you looked closely, were painted on wood planks, made to look like canvas; we were shown the cheater chairs for the nuns that enabled them to stand during the three to four-hour services. A thirteen-hundred-tile Lisbon cityscape made in 1738!

The blue and white ceramic tiles are called azulejos. I thought this was from the Dutch and Holland, but it originated in Portugal!

The two-and-a-half-hour tour included all participants to make their own tile! We were given blank tiles, patterns, charcoal cloth applicators, stains, and brushes and given time to create our own tiles. There were only eight of us in this group; our instructor finished the tiles by framing each one with the color we chose. We will be getting them back after the cruise when they have been fired, and we were promised that we would be pleasantly surprised at the colors and finish.

More stuff we learned on the bus to and from the museum. The Portuguese consider tiles and tile-making part of their culture; many words of the Portuguese language come from Arabic, and the use of tiles in courtyards and outside the dwellings are also from the Arabs and Moors, using tiles on the outside of the building actually keeps the building cooler inside reflecting the sun and heat. All of the sidewalks are hand-made tiles, and each design is unique; Lisbon and Portugal have petitioned UNESCO to declare them a world heritage.

The Moors also brought Lettuce, coriander, and cilantro. In fact, the citizens of Lisbon actually translate to "little lettuces."

The tile museum was enjoyed by all; we compared our different creations and bet one another on which one would turn out the best...we will see!

Back at the hotel, I rested and struck out for dinner. We wanted something different and found a small bar tucked off a street. Lynn had vegetable soup and garlic bread, I had escalloped veal, ham, and potatoes, Lynn had a 7 UP, and I had some weird mixed drink, all excellent. We have not had anything bad yet! The reason we were looking was the prices of food: a cup of soup at the hotel restaurant was $10 EU, our whole meal at the bar for both of us was $25 EU, including drinks, and both of us went away full, another great experience!

Back to the hotel, diary, pack for tomorrow, transfer to the riverboat and bed.

Sunday

Sunday morning, bags inside the room for pickup by 6:50 (very safe city, but they didn't trust luggage outside the rooms? Kinda like Amsterdam, where petty crime is tolerated), had breakfast, checked out of the room, tried to charge me $8 Eu for a bottle of water, and I told them I was supposed to get two complimentary a day and never received on the first or the last day, so he had me sign an affidavit.

We loaded onto one of three buses for the 180-mile trip to Porto, where we were to board the ship. Our guide today is Fatima, the same as the sacred City in Portugal where there are 8 million visitors a year by pilgrims of the catholic faith.

Here is a summation of information we received: 2,000 words from the Arabic language are some of the bases of the Portuguese language, the "Al" prefix is from the Arabic "the"; Portuguese is a "romance language" and based mostly on Latin as are Spanish, French, and Italian. (The Europeans have an advantage over us here since the base is Latin; it's a bit easier to be multi-lingual.)

After an evening of "entertainment," the Portuguese end the night with green cabbage soup and sausage bread.

On the way to Porto, we stopped at the University of Cambia, established in 1290; Portugal has 18 providences. The Vasco De Gama Bridge over the Tagus River is the longest bridge in Europe, and it is one of 17 bridges over this river. The vineyards here can be up to 3000 years old, along with the olive groves. The cork trees need to be harvested every 9-10 years, or the tree will actually die.

85% of the people here own their apartments in the country; the buildings cannot exceed three stories. 10.5 million people in Portugal, 550,000 in Lisbon.

An apartment in Lisbon is $700,000-1 Million. Outside Lisbon, ½ the price of gas is $1.6 EU / liter, 4.4 liters per gallon; when the world recession happened in 2014, unemployment was at 17%, and now it is down to 6%. Portugal provides 2/3rds of the world's cork.

The Portuguese are very proud that 71% of energy is renewable; of that, 58% is wind and wave energy; they realize that this is more expensive. (The government controls the utilities; they really have no choice.)

Brazil, the world's largest producer of coffee, was "discovered" by the Portuguese, and that is why the language there is Portuguese. The Portuguese like their espresso straight, with no sugar or cream.

We had a rest stop toilet break, and there was an area with three women statues. We were told that they represented the same woman, Queen Isabella, who would go out at night to feed the poor. When confronted by the king, she told the king that she was just collecting roses. When he told her to drop her folded-up dress, the bread she was actually carrying was converted to roses, and she was honored as a saint when she died.

Portugal is actually the third highest per person as far as fish consumption, with Japan number one, Iceland number two, and then Portugal. (Three times more than Spain.) The mild climate is favorable for kiwis, vegetables, and other agriculture. Life expectancy: 83 for women, 80 for men, they have a National Health Service, that service put a tax on sugary products, all schools have a canteen for kid's lunches which consist of vegetable soup, meat or fish, and fruit or Jell-O for dessert.

Sixty-five is retirement, salted cod is the National dish, with tripe (cleaned well and flash cooked so it isn't chewy) stew. The meat was for Royalty.

They are moving to delete borders (one world concept); schooling is mandatory through twelfth grade, books are included, and education is free; it costs $1000/year for college, but you must have good grades to be accepted. (No student loans; parents are expected to pay as their responsibility.)

It was the Jesuits and churches that started the schools; we did stop and visit Coimbra, where uniforms were required for both males and females; they all look like Harry Potter's: black pants, white shirt, black jacket, and of course a cape, actually, JK Rowlings send her children here when she lived in Portugal, interesting how reality is intertwined with fiction. At graduation, the grads shred the uniforms except for the cape, which they all keep; some even get buried with them, and once a Coimbra graduate, always a Coimbra grad. The reason for the uniforms is to portray that all students are equal. We were approached by two of them; they sell pencils for their graduation, EU 2 for one 3/ EU5 representing different majors such as medicine, law, accounting, etc. Yes, I bought three to help them out!

Inside the school, there is a lot of gold leaf, ancient books, and very high rich wood bookcases. The books are taken care of by a special cleaning team called "bats" since they keep the insects away from the books; the bookcases go up a good two stories, and secret corner staircases and ladder support for retrieving the books. At one time, this building complex was a palace grounds and buildings.

Lunch was provided: soup or salad, chicken or fish, and dessert, as well as wines, all excellent; we also had a two-man entertainment duo. The wine was monitored so everyone had their fill (glasses never empty), and the food was also well prepared and plentiful. Then, the final one and a half hours to the ship, we checked in, took the luggage to the cabin, we unpacked, and had dinner, again wine included with dinner. The wine got me…it was after 8. I showered and crashed. Lynn went up to the entertainment.

Monday

Our excursion was to the town of Porto. We are actually docked in the town of Gaia, which is 4 times the size of Porto and known for its boat building (for transporting wine on the river) and granite mining. There are 6 bridges connecting the two cities, and the river divides them.

The homes are tall and narrow to avoid as much taxes as possible. (Taxed by the area of the base) The roads, one very narrow lane, it took us over a half hour to go maybe a ½ mile. The traffic was that bad, and all "camel nose" traffic. Most commute via the metro since the traffic is bad, and there is a scarcity of parking when you get where you have to go! We toured a couple churches and the train station; inside the train station, the history of the station is all done in tile in the large central hall. The blue and white tiles were from the Holland influence, the colors from the Chinese influence, the main walls had blue and white depictions, the upper and ceiling areas were more colorful, yes, and I took pictures!

They have a hotel here with a pool shaped like a wine bottle! Then, we were dropped off to stroll the town and ended up at the Sandeman winery.

Their symbol is a dark man in a cape and wide-brimmed hat (Zorro); we toured the winery and were given information on Port wine; some bottles were still aging from 1917, and some casks also had 30, 40, and 50-year vintages! We did sample two; one had a slight honey flavor, and both were very good. The Port wine is naturally sweet and fortified with alcohol.

Back to the ship for lunch, Lynn decided to sit and read in the lounge; I diarized and then strolled along the wharf and side streets. Our cabin did have a narrow balcony, but we were moored next to another ship, so all we saw was a black hull a foot away!

At supper, we joined an American couple (He was originally from England). They were just married two years ago, a second marriage for both; he lost his wife to cancer, and she lost her husband to cancer also. They were very nice people, good conversation.

The entertainment was a dozen young men from that school in Coimbra we visited the day before, complete with black suits and ties, white shirts, and, of course, the capes!

They were very good, played a variety of instruments, had good voices, and were very comfortable with the audience. The interaction was great, the songs were well done, and everyone had a good time for the show that lasted a good ¾ hour!

Tuesday

We set sail, we could see something besides a black hull, and our Veranda was 12ft. X 3ft. includes a small table and two chairs; we will be using it!

The first presentation is on the Douro River and the region. Douro means "gold"; due to the sun reflecting on the water, it looked gold. This river is 900 kilometers long. This part of Portugal is a wine country. Due to the rock formations (schist rock, yeah, it is schist!) and soil minerals, the roots of the grape vines can go down 20-25 meters, and the stone releases water into the soil at night, so irrigation is not needed, the mountains protect the upper vines from wind and humidity. Last century, there was a problem with insects; they could not rid the vines of these pests until they realized that the insects were below the ground, in the roots. It was found that by obtaining vine roots from other regions and countries, the grapes could be resistant, and therefore, many varieties were grafted to these vines to resolve the problem.

In the 12th century, the monks added 77% alcohol to preserve the wine, so all port wine was fortified, with a higher alcohol content than most; in the 17th century, Port wine was exported. Since there was now a variety of wine vines, the blending of the wines became popular; the wine is "checked" before shipping, and the term "Port wine" is only from this region. As the "talk" ended, we entered the locks. There are five locks on the Douro; this is the deepest, and in reality, it is the largest lock in Europe. As we entered, we had very little room on either side of the ship, actually less than a foot!

When we were completely in, the gates closed, and we filled up at about an inch a second! These locks are also connected to dams; this one also produces the most power per year, at 801 GWH/year. The lift? 30 meters or 109 feet. Since we are going away from the ocean, we are being lifted up to the inland part of the river.

I did go up on the top deck; the canopy on the rear deck was lowered for bridge clearance, and after taking a few pictures, we were asked to stay midships due to the clearance of only about 6-7 feet under the bridges.

At 11:00, we had a presentation on cork. Portugal is the world's largest producer of cork. The cork tree groves are in the south of Portugal. The trees are protected; actually, the cork tree is a variety of oak. Cork is harvested every 9 years after the tree matures, which takes about 20 years. Many cork trees are over 100 years old, some even 150 years old. The cork is harvested by special cutters, so the tree is not damaged by cutting too deep. Once the cork is harvested, it is boiled and then dried for 6 months. 90% of cork is used for wine bottles; depending on the wine and cork specified, the cost of the cork, in some cases, exceeds the cost of the wine bottle. The world is not running out of cork!

Cork is recyclable, so the kids ask their parents for the corks from the wine and then take them to school. The school rewards them with candy and then sells the corks to recyclers for funding programs, and everyone is happy! When the cork is recycled, it is smashed, made into a paste, then rolled out and formed into blocks.

Cork is now used to make...ready for this? Surfboards, furniture, shoes, clothes, hats, dresses, ties, purses, wallets, belts, walls, floors, even construction bricks.

Cork is hypo-allergic, no dust is formed when cutting, is waterproof and fireproof; when there is a cloth backing, it can be used to clean as with baby wipes for those kids that have sensitive skin. Cork does not stretch; it can be dyed, colored, pressed into for texture, and can also be embroidered.

We had lunch late on the ship, and then the afternoon included the Mateus Palace and Gardens, a five-hour excursion. If you were a teenager in the 60s (as we were), Mateus wine was the best of the choices to impress your date. It even had a picture of the estate on the label; now we got to see it for real!

We drove through the hills and county-side; the weather was perfect: low 70s, the sun shining, and the hills covered with vineyards and olive trees, all the hills terraced with stone, rich, beautiful, and peaceful. There were only a few people working in the fields now that the grape harvest was done, cutting the wild grasses and burning them to control wildfires and provide fertilizer for the next season.

The beautifully kept, baroque palace, resplendent with furnishings, priceless keepsakes, Chinese porcelain from the 17th Century, church vestments perfectly preserved, and relics were pointed out by staff as we toured the public part of the structure. Attached were surrounding sculptured gardens, pools, and outbuildings.

Back on the bus, then to another winery, granite vats to keep the mash at a cool temperature, casks, bottles, and vats to age these blended port wines, all sweet and fortified, 19-22% alcohol. The ride to and from the winery was a number of hairpin turns on a single-lane road with no guard rails and on a full-sized tour bus.

We met our ship, changed for dinner, and were treated to a Portuguese buffet and even an excellent Portuguese brandy. On the way into the dining room, the chef was dancing a bit, so Lynn took his hand and danced a few steps with him; everyone was in a great mood. What we didn't expect was for the Captain to come over and ask if he could join our table for dinner; of course, we said yes, so for the next hour, we shared stories, asked any question we wanted to, and had a great and informative time!

The activity was "Name that tunes". Our group was only five folks, four women and me. We had to name the tune, artist, decade, and nationality, and if someone in the group got up and danced an extra twenty points! Participants from each team streamed up to the dance floor and danced to the song. It was lively, noisy, and a great time; third place won a toothbrush, second place a small tube of toothpaste, 1st place a bottle of wine. That ended the evening. (We were in fourth place; some teams had 10-12 people.)

Wednesday

Things were just going too well! I was experiencing gastric pains all night, and they only got worse; breakfast was just a yogurt, and I asked the doctor I had met a few nights ago if he had any Zantag antacids. He said he did, and I asked if he could give me a couple tabs (Viking does not have any medical canteen or personnel). We agreed that he would come after breakfast to my room, and off I went to lie down. By 11:00, I was still rolling around in bed. I asked Lynn to wait in the room when she came to check on me, and by 11:30, still no show by our "friend," Lynn went on the hunt for him. I thought a shower would help, but nope, he did appear a little before noon, gave me two tablets, and wished me luck. I took them immediately, and within 15 minutes, the gas was beginning to be released from both ends. Lynn went to lunch, and I noticed my stool was now black, the sign of blood in the intestine, probably another ulcer, but I was feeling better!

I joined Lynn after telling the tour coordinator that I needed to stop by a pharmacy, and she arranged for the tour bus to stop in Castelo Rodrigo while the rest of the group took pictures of the fountain and other older buildings. The drive to Castelo Rodrigo was a bit over an hour. We stayed there for an hour, and then the drive back.

The scenery was breathtaking: vineyards, almond trees, terraced hillside so calm and picturesque. Lots of pictures, we are very close to the Spanish border, so we can see about the same over in Spain!

Even though the grape vines do not need irrigation, the almond trees do. This is an industry in Portugal, but it is dwarfed by 80% wine, 10% cork, and 10 % tourism.

There are also industries training pigeons, food, fertilizer, and cows; here, cowhides are considered contraband, although shoes and leather shoes are also made here.

The castle was in ruin, on a narrow cobble street, shared with an occasional car, and little level, either steeply up or down, and on cobblestone! When the Spanish conquered the area, they burnt down a part of the castle and forbade rebuilding to remind those left not to rebel or go into Spain.

I believe we finished, if not all, most of our shopping, including almonds, coins, almond liquor, and cork items.

On the way back, as promised, we stopped in town; I was able to get my antacid, Iron supplement, and gas remover. It was not cheap; the total bill was EU 36! (Pharmacies are quite different than in the States; you tell the counter person what you want, and they produce it, a drug store, nothing else.)

Back on the ship, I made up a list of complaints for the manager, including not being able to upgrade to business class because we were booked by Viking and a few other various things I wanted to verify, like Lynn missing the one excursion, and no attempt to provide any refund or partial refund.

I had dinner with a couple we had dinner before, checked about the questions I had, and was told there was no reply from Viking due to the time difference. I met Lynn for the music and dance; I was feeling better, no more alcohol, so the captain's party was just ok, little if no snacks... Dinner was excellent, and I was able to eat it all: squash soup, Sea bass with a chickpea, blend, and a tartlet; Lynn had soup, blah, and blah.

10:30 was quitting time. Hopefully, tomorrow will be much better, and we start with an excursion to Spain at 8:30; it is a 9.5-hour tour, so it should be interesting!

Thursday, we woke to the alarm clock, which was very strange; usually, I am up and about ten minutes before! Quick breakfast: we ate with the same couple as last night; these groups of people are all cliques, with only 5-6 of us not in a group, and kind of ignored, kinda weird, like that plane ride, it seems everyone is getting more selfish, losing communication skills and hiding in their little shells!

On the bus for the 9 ½ hour included tour to Salamanca, Spain.

Noah

Three buses loaded and off on time, crossing the Douro and entering Spain. We wound up into the mountains and entered the Iberian flatlands of Spain.

The contrast was interesting; here in Spain, the land was flat, with vegetable crops, livestock, and fruits, whereas Portugal had all terraced mountains with mostly grape vines, some olive trees, very small vegetable gardens, and no livestock. Spain is five times larger than Portugal, both in population and in land mass.

At the rest stop, a little after an hour of traveling, I asked the guide about the absence of speed traps and police. He told me that there are cameras monitoring; if you go too fast, a ticket is sent to you. If you are a bus driver, the ticket goes to the company and then is deducted from your pay. Too many infractions, and you are gone. Just before every town, there is a speed bump.

Iberian black pigs were pointed out (they are the best tasting); Stork nests were also pointed out; they are as large if not larger than the eagle's nests we have back in the States; the locals here trim the branches by the nests to help the storks due to the high winds and possible damage to their wings.

We arrived in Salamanca (Known as La Dorada or the Golden City due to the glow of the sandstone structures) after about 1 ½ hours; the place is very old, founded by the Celtic tribe before the rise of the Roman Empire, and located 250 feet above sea level. It is the home of Europe's oldest universities, founded in 1134.

We walked to the market, were treated to wine, prosciutto, and cheese sandwiches, and then split into groups; of the three busses, only 7 of us selected the abbreviated tour version, leaving me to question the "no reserved seat" policy by Viking for those needing to exit the front of the bus and requiring more time…fastest and most fit get the front of the bus. Seven people out of three bus loads…really!

We walked for an hour through the cobblestone street, inside the cathedral, and down the vendor street, shops, bars, and restaurants. The tuition at public colleges runs about $1000 EU; private about $6,000 EU per year; there are no student loans; the parents are expected to pay for their kids.

Another two hours on our own, then a 20-minute walk for tea time, small sandwiches, cookies, chocolate croissants, fruit, tea, coffee, and water. I took the lead in passing the dishes (some just eating what was in front of them), then another bathroom break, back on the bus, and a 1 ½ hour trip back to the ship.

Orientation on what to expect tomorrow, dinner. I typed up the occasion, only to have the computer shut down without saving anything additional, so I re-typed it all again; Lynn came back, dead crowd, only singing along, so she was back as I finished up.

Friday, October 26th, Pocinho, Portugal

The ship just stayed long enough to drop us off. We had another lengthy excursion, "Favaios Bakery & Lunch at Quinta Avessada." After another ear-popping hour ride on the bus (drive up from the river, no straight roads, you know!), we entered the little village of Favaios. Just a note here: before the dams were built, the river was wild, with currents, eddies, and some very narrow passages, so chapels were built on the top of hills to "give comfort to the sailors."

This is muscatel country, Favaios, from the grapes of vines, the highest elevation in Portugal, a small village of 1000 people, was voted the best in the world muscatel. A member of each family works at one of the two wineries. We were given tours of the first, sampled the wine, then into the village, walking the narrow cobblestone streets to come to a very small bakery (one of 8) specializing in four-corner bread. (Each bakery produces over 1000 loaves a day, and each tastes a little different.)

We are shown how the dough is made and watched the mixing of flour, yeast, salt, water, and love, resting, then into a wood-fired brick oven, and Walla!

All this while we were munching on fresh bread and a bit of wine! The bread truck goes through town like an ice cream truck with a bell, and the balance is sent to the cities; this hard-crusted bread stays fresh for four days.

We then walked through town past the church, to the …ready for this...Bread and Wine Museum is an interesting museum with a beautiful view from the balcony.

Back on the bus for another short ride to the Quinta Da Avessada century-old estate for lunch, local food, and, again, all the wine you care to drink. The food included unlimited cheese, sausage, bread, cod fritters, vegetable soup, beef stew with potatoes, carrots, and cabbage, followed by two dessert tables set up buffet style; yes, we all waddled out to the bus, the ride back was very quiet!

We were picked up in Pinhao and then cruised to Regua. The weather starts out brisk the last few mornings, 8-10 degrees C, warming to 15-16C. Before supper, we are briefed on what is happening on Saturday and when and where we leave the ship on Sunday. (Lucky us, our time is 3:45 A.M.)

Great supper, we now dine with the other folks that are shunned from the clichés,

Liars Club at 9, the chef, the housekeeping manager, and one of the tour guides were very good; our team only got 2 out of five, the winners 4 out of 5; they did have 12 participants vs. our 4, but great fun!

Saturday, the final full day on the Douro.

A three-hour excursion in the morning, another chapel, reached by 686 steps; some pilgrims still climb these steps on their knees (we took the bus!) as penance. In another shrine, in 1834, most of the monks left, religions were on the decline, and churches and chapels were mostly tourist attractions; we are also shown a 300-year-old chestnut tree. A walk around town, a visit to the museum, last stop shops, and then back to the ship. This is the final time for our bus driver, so we all bid him well!

Started to get ready for departure, tip envelopes, pay the final bill, finish the logging, olive oil demonstration, Jimmy Keys show, Vintage port opening ceremony, Captain's farewell program, early to bed, a grueling day starts early tomorrow!

The olive oil information hour was really interesting. I thought that 300-year-old tree was something, plus those sequoias on the west coast, but then again, we are told there are olive trees 3000 years old! Most trees last 300-600 years. There are over 400 varieties, 40 in Portugal.

The average olive tree produces 20 kilograms of olives every year; to produce one liter of olive oil, it takes 5-10 kilograms of olives! We taste-tested two different olive oils. Extra virgin is the most aromatic and healthiest. Tasting olive oil is slower and more comprehensive than wine. You place it in a small brandy snifter, cup it with one hand, swirl it while holding your hand over the top to produce the aroma, then slowly a bit on the tongue, front to back, swish it inside the mouth, and then slowly swallow. That last swallow will be peppery; most of us started to cough and had to clear with a slice of apple, with tears in our eyes.

Lynn was the first to identify the smells of the second and won a bottle of olive oil! We were the only winners, and we learned more!

The Jimmy Keys Live Show was put on by "The international musical comical entertainer Jimmy Keys." Many of the folk on board were in his group, a mix of English, from where he came from and where he now lives in Naples, Florida. Maybe that is the reason for the clichés…

It was a combination of songs. He accompanied himself on the piano, the show went a little long, and he had some of his group dance to a few songs before wrapping up in a little over an hour.

Vintage Port opening Ceremony: Captain farewell, some of the consumption was shared; for the 8 days on the river, 106 guests, we went through 680 bottles of wine, 125 martinis, and 175 rolls of toilet paper. I had two great wines, Graham's Tawny 10 year, and Kir Royal (Crewe de Cagiest sparkling wine) Cassis-Blackcurrant liquor…tastee; a great dinner, then had them call for wake-up at 2:30 A.M.

Sunday bags out at 3:10 A.M

We were on the bus at 3:40 AM, waited for two hours for our flight, flew from Portugal to Frankfort, Germany in 2 ½ hours, passport checked, we had another 2 ½ hour wait, found a vendor who took US dollars, bought a German oversized hot dog and a large pretzel; (Lynn talked about that dog for two days after!) then another flight, 9 ½ hours to Chicago, waited 1 hour for the bus, 1 hour plus ride to the bus station in Milwaukee, Tiff picked us up, and we were home, our time at 9 P.M., there is a five-hour difference, so travel was about 22 hours, But we are back home after another great adventure.

It took the whole week to "re-adjust." the ulcer seemed to have gone, but I attended a lecture on diets and tried an avocado and macadamia nut diet for a couple of days, which brought back the heartburn and gas...another week!

We have no trips to Cuba in February, and I have an appointment with the bone doctor in January for the final left shoulder replacement scheduling (yes, it is time). I talked to my doctor and got some pain medications that hopefully will not cause another ulcer, and so much for wine from now on!

We have attended cooking classes, community events with the seniors, my son-in-law's birthday, and free seminar dinners, and I have tried an unrealistic regime of walking five miles a day (11,000 steps)after two weeks and failing a couple of days. I now have to wear knee support for my right knee, sometimes both; I will take it down to 10,000-11,000 steps /day only during weekdays to hopefully save my knees. Plus, I need to stay away from those darn Christmas cookies!!

I am also starting my 2019-2020 vacation calendars. Have the February and March cruises paid for and done. Still need the air for the October 2019 Israel and Suez Canal cruise. I edited this second book from the start to now…. It took almost a week!

I divested my E-Trade of the companies requiring K-1 forms to simplify my taxes after next year, went over the vacation file to establish the travels next after the shoulder, to only include a river cruise including Poland and Transylvania; an ocean Cruse including Greenland, and one including Bermuda…that should actually finish up the traveling save a mid-winter Caribbean Cruise.

For now, Christmas and Christmas parties.

Noah

2019

There seems to be a goblin; my computer has jumped to different documents, and my phone does not record messages. I again am becoming agitated with my attempts to lose weight, an exercise program that only seems to leave me with sore knees after 1,000s of steps, half sandwiches for meals, and increasing water intake, meaning more runs to the restroom!

It is late January. I met with my broker, set goals for the year's expected distributions, and accomplished the mandatory distributions from the IRAs and taxes paid for this year.

I found and mailed information to my Online Vacations Representative to look into a Vantage River Cruise to Poland, lower Eastern Europe River cruise next June or July (2020). I spoiled Lynn with Business Air when we flew back from Singapore, so now, EVERY trip must have that upgrade…I may have to go back to work soon!

He (Mike Vitow) looked into the offering and advised us to take the July option so that we have the Transylvania extension first, the minimum required for deposit, with the insurance, extension, air, and package. He returned the answer within eight hours, and I gave him the "go" to lock in this next adventure!

I spent half a day at the VA to try setting up my left shoulder replacement and accomplished about half of what I needed to do, but at least I am in the system, and hopefully, in April or May, I will have that left shoulder, my last major joint replaced. I told him about the shoulder indicating on the metal detectors, and he said it is actually common with large arthritic deposits; he has a knee that triggers the detectors also…go figure! The oldest daughter enjoys her new job, but the younger seems to be locked into hers until she retires. We just celebrated her birthday; she is 42!! Really makes me feel even older!!

My routine is going to the gym 3-4 times a week, walking 40 laps (about 11,500 steps), $5.00 Tuesdays at the Movies, and driving for the DAV Fridays.

The DAV Christmas party, the Goldwing Party Christmas party, and the Volunteer party rounded off the parties, and I ate normally, so I gained back any lost weight. (groan) I can't wait for the Cuba excursion at the beginning of February...I am so bored!

The weather took a turn to the cold, and we finally got some more snow, so winter in Wisconsin is back on! A lot of our friends have migrated south, but both of us enjoy the change in seasons, probably until we are no more...

Noah

Cuba
02-02-2019

This was one of Lynn's priorities; we used Azamara Cruise Line because it was to be "Culturally Inclusive."

Tiffany picked us up right on time; the bus was a bit late, but this time, in the morning (4 A.M.), there was not much traffic! We checked out luggage, TSA we breezed through (fastest yet!); the plane was on time. Lynn insisted on business class, so we boarded with group one, had an included breakfast, and arrived in Miami a bit after 12:30…tram to luggage, found ship transport, and waited for luggage.

Luckily, my luggage had a girdle strap, the zipper and lock completely gone, and the luggage opened.

Lynn went with her luggage and our carry-ons to the pick-up point. I went in line for a complaint on open/ damaged luggage; two people before me, people behind the counter …lunch break...one guy left…our transport connection facilitator came by me, held up the bus for the "DMV" slow pace of the claims representative to take the information and provide the claim paperwork. The whole process took a bit over twenty minutes and produced one sheet of paper and a deadline of thirty days to take the case to an American Airlines facility somewhere for them to send out for repair or replace.

The bus driver was nice, but the porters at the dock would not touch my suitcase, so I had to drag it through the embarkation procedure, and we were one of the few last ones on the ship, and here too, s... l…o…w.

We found our cabin, took pictures of the damaged luggage (((they didn't bother), unpacked my suitcase, went to muster, met a few other passengers, went back to the cabin to unpack Lynn's suitcase, and figured out where to be for supper and the rest of the evening.

It was Italian night at the buffet Café, so Lynn made the decision as far as the venue; we started filling out our visas. There were poor directions on that, too, so we changed the dates to our birthdates, not dates we are here, and we hope the cross-offs don't cost us another $75.00 each!

We toured the ship, and everyone seemed to have the "drink package," which is rail drinks, house wines, and beer; they push high-end wines and spirits for an extra charge.

We went to a Cuba lecture; the lecturer was a retired teacher, and the presentation was quite dry, mostly history. Columbus was not highly regarded, and the Spanish and Portuguese brought a lot of African slaves here, so there was a mix of black, brown, and white. Cubans prefer "Cubans"; no hyphened Cubans.

There is a large statue of Christ the Redeemer, like in Rio; this is from the pre-revolutionary time of 1958; the revolution was in 1959. The population of Havana is about 2.1 million, crime is low, we are reminded not to be conspicuous with fancy jewelry and cameras; average wages are $30.00 /month, everything is regulated by the government, ration stamps, only Cuban currency accepted here, (except for special government stores) for purchases, two types, one for tourists CUPS and one for locals CUCs the difference $1.00 US=1 Peso CUP; $1 US= 20 Pesos CUC so watch the change…CUPs have monuments on them, and CUCs have people.

Buildings falling apart, and there is no incentive to fix them since the government owns them, don't eat street food, and water is not safe; 50's cars keep running because they make their own replacement parts. There is a huge underground economy due to the extensive government control.

The dinner was exceptional; the seafood pasta was prepared individually; mine had calamari, clams, shrimp, peas, corn, and pasta tasty! We walked a bit around the ship, skipped the show, and were out for the night by 9:30, a long day and "getting' old"!

Sunday, February 3rd, Havana, Cuba.

Breakfast in the café got my salmon and ½ bagel; I was happy. Lynn had some fruit and a bit of scrambled eggs. After breakfast, I roamed the ship; it was basically the same size and style as the Oceania ship we were on for the finish the world cruise last January and February. Our tour was Easy Panoramic of Havana, starting at 9:30.

As we watched the ship enter the harbor, you could see the deteriorating buildings and lack of traffic. Even though it was Sunday morning. We docked at a wharf that used to accommodate six ships, now only two; the other two structures that accommodated two ships each were gutted, windows gone, roofs gone, fenced, and one guard.

You check out of the ship with a ship card, then, on the pier, immigration, visa, and passport, you go through security, three or four uniformed folk, three stations, only one or two open, but all having personal sitting and watching, hats off too! The currency converting booths, a 10% government charge, then an additional 3% agency fee on American, Euro, and Canadian.

Our bus is #3; we are the first ones on, so we get second-row seats. The rest of the group started straggling in, with lots of canes and lots of difficulty coming into the bus. Our guide is in 20's, has good English, but talks rapidly and high…she is a little difficult to understand.

In 1956, 82 people (Including Fidel Castro) arrived on a boat who were responsible for the revolution (The boat is preserved in a museum here). The government was corrupt; the mafia had casinos and mansions. When the revolution ended, the mafia and rich fled; (actually ordered out) houses were given to servants, and all furnishings and cars were ordered to be left behind. We drove through the once grand neighborhoods, many of the buildings in decay. It was declared that any building greater than so many square feet was to be designated as a hotel or multifamily and taxed as such; no one to own more than one business or location of the business.

The USA Embassy was pointed out; it was relatively small, especially when the Russian Embassy was no less than 10 times the size. Very little is made here except cigars (the good ones use 5 different tobacco leaves) and rum. They use sugar cane; we are told the best Rum is Santiago De Cuba; the Bacardi plant is long gone.

Hemmingway lived here for ten years before relocating to the Florida Keys. The Cuba crocodile is the country's animal, so I got a carving. If you look at Cuba, the west side is the tail, and the right side is the nose and mouth…now use your imagination!! The Royal Palm is the national tree.

Our first stop was Fusterlandia, an area similar to the Gaudi Park in Barcelona, Spain, with lots of mosaic tile work, odd depictions of people and animals, and interesting structures surrounded by souvenir and art shops…half an hour to explore. You can buy art and souvenirs to some extent, but expensive art and books require tax and three forms of documentation to take out of the country. By the way, there are also limits on Cigars (no more than 100) and rum (no more than a liter per person).

The population of Havana, per our guide 2.5 million, price of gas is $7.20 a gallon. Now, when I was a kid, these cars didn't get more than 8-10 miles per gallon....

We drove past the National Aquarium, lots of paint chipped off, weeds on the ground, no one around, and it is Sunday, noonish, and where are the people??

Since 2012, People can finally sell a home; well, not really; they can EXCHANGE homes, cash only, no loans, and only large businesses are eligible to have loans.

No selling of cars till 1961. The Russian Lada was a very popular car here, selling for 25-30000 EU; China also sold cars here, along with French Peugeots, and all the buses are Chinese.

The Daiquiri and the Mojito were invented in Cuba. The islands of Cuba were prisons, now turned into museums. The 90s was the worst for Cuba's economy, plus the embargo was hard on the people.

We drove under the channel to the fort and visited the Christ the Redeemer statue. The locals say to look at the hands. If you house your imagination, the right hand could be holding a cigar, with the let a glass of rum. Next to the statue is the preserved Che Rivera home, nope, no visitation, guarded and fenced, and a sculpture representing the lifting of Cube from Oppression. Our final stop was a fort with a government store selling rum, cigars, and coffee. The deal here is you buy 5 cigars, and you get the sixth free. I had a list of 15 I needed for the guys back home, so yup got that order filled, along with the rum promised! This was a government store, so they also took American or Euros, again after deducting 10% tax and 3% service charge!

The fort was actually designed by an Italian architect; the infrastructure is made of wood and is covered with brick and sandstone.

We were offered a stop at the market to see more of the artists, but the majority, actually everyone on the bus, determined that we just returned to the ship. (This is our first morning of a two-night, three-day stay) so back to the ship. We must always go back through customs, checkpoints, and inspections. We joined a group for trivia, didn't win anything, and then changed for dinner.

This was Super Bowl night, so the entire deck was set up to watch the game on a projector screen, with a buffet meal with snacks on one side and desserts on the other side, and the waiters were very busy.

We met another nice couple, watched the game for a while, and then went off to our Tropicana Cabaret Extravaganza excursion, off-ship, starting at 8:15 PM.

We left the ship around 8 P.M., went through the mandatory inspections, found the coordinator in the bus terminal, and assigned to bus #2. We were joined by another group of four, and then more folks trickled down; soon, we had over thirty and were directed to our bus.

The ride to the Tropicana was along the sea; many of the people were gathered on the sea wall to catch the cool evening breeze; we are told this is a big gathering stretch in that most if not all, houses do not have air conditioning, it is in the 80's both temperature and humidity.

We also passed several city buses packed to the gills, I asked, and at peak times of 7-10 AM and 5-8 PM, the system was overloaded; the guide did indicate that Uber was being discovered and increasingly used.

We arrived at the Tropicana in about 20 minutes; outside, it looked like a Las Vegas casino with long tables with chairs. We are told the show lasts a bit over 1 ½ hours and starts at 9:30; if you want to take pictures, it costs 5 CUC, and you get a receipt. Just before the show, there was complementary Champaign and also a bottle of rum for every 4 persons; we were not told that a can of Coke (Their Coke) was also provided to everyone.

I did ask how many the hall had seating for and was told 1000! There is a main stage, two higher stages, banking, and also two side stages. The seating is very close but manageable.

The Tropicana was started in 1939; this is their 80th year! The show consists of various numbers, bold colors, up to 200 performers, and many costume changes. Some are very skimpy, and others have elaborate headgear, including ones that resemble chandeliers!

The women bend easier than pretzels, and feats of strength and rhythm are plentiful; what a great night. I asked the others at the table about the remaining ¾ bottle of that great Cuban rum, and they said to take it, so we found our bus in the back parking lot. I handed the driver the bottle and told him, "I don't know nothing"; we found seats in the back of the bus, twenty minutes back to the pier, IDs checked, metal detectors, and back on the ship by midnight; a great busy first day in Havana, tomorrow, all we have is a Cuba buffet and ships program in the evening including an on shore ballet. Shower, shave, and bed!

Monday, February 4th, Havana

We slept in till 7:30; breakfast in the café, the formal dining was too much food for us, and you had to wait the "proper" time between courses. Lynn was off to sewing /needlepoint and the morning quiz; the needlepoint person didn't show up. The quiz person gave points just so Lynn got something for being the only one to show up. I got an hour of sun on the deck, only about 5 other people out there, one on his computer, the others reading books. I asked the porter for an extra pen for my pen collectors and then off to see the arts pavilion about a kilometer west of the pier.

It was upper 70s (F) both in temperature and humidity, bright and sunny. On the way, we saw some graffiti on the east wall, some trash, full trash receptacles, old car taxis, horse and carriage rides, and tour buses, some tourists, some locals, those painting or repairing public servants actually working slower than those back home, walkways blocked by other construction workers, so walking in the street was warranted, one bus came within a foot of me at 30 mph. We had checked with the front desk about the pavilion being open, and one of our tour guides said it would be closed for some Cuban holiday.... The desk was wrong and locked up tight...I crossed the main boulevard and took in the neighborhoods as I returned. Buildings are in decay, wash hanging out, and people sitting in chairs outside their houses, smoking and watching the people pass by. I did find a small outdoor market, threw a little money, and bargained with a vendor. Both of us walked away happy. I did get some additional flower shots, then went back to the ship, caught up on my diary, and reviewed some pictures before lunch.

The ship is like a ghost town. Thirty to forty at the buffet for lunch tried to attend ping pong...no one else besides one guy, shuffleboard, just us too...we went down to the desk and started to complain that no one showed up, but then told to look closely at the schedule, just after the event there was either a * or triangle, (in #1 or 2 font) the * denotes prizes awarded (only two events) ones with the small triangle TEN events just kind of set a time for an opportunity to meet?? I would call these place keepers to show some activity with no actual involvement by the staff…rather sad, and of the twenty-plus cruises, the least effort to keep passengers occupied when not on the ship or on excursions.

I baked myself in the sun for another hour, finished up on the dairying, and then we attended the trivia, two back-to-back ones, the same five on our team, and there were actually about six teams this time; the same team won as yesterday….

Tonight is the "Amazing Dinner Buffet," and later is the Amazing Evening Event: Ballet at Teatro Marti. "Amazing" has different meanings; the buffet had just a few additional items, including sushi, and the desserts had an additional section.

There were two groups for the show at the Teatro Marti theatre. I talked to the shore excursion person, and she exchanged our late session with the early one. It was still a mad rush to the buses; many were held up at the metal screening, others at the passport checks, but it worked.

The ride to and from the opera house was about 20 minutes; on the way back, we were driven in a neighborhood where almost 30-40% of the storefronts had items in them, vs. most of the rest of the town where lucky to see 10% open, with the merchandise. We were treated to how wonderful Cuba is to its people by the tour host; the tour company is owned by the government, and the bus is Chinese. The host was very proud of being a Cuban and explained "free" college and "free" healthcare with the exception of drugs, but the drugs are partially subsidized by the government, which "takes care of their people." We drove past the capitol building; it was pointed out that theirs' is larger than the U.S. Capitol in D.C.

On the way to dinner, we passed a cabin. The door opened, and a naked man (he was old and paunchy, according to Lynn) was there. He said "hello" to Lynn and said he was locked out of his cabin, walked down the hallway a few doors down, and disappeared into another cabin…I was up ahead and didn't see a thing, but Lynn says it, so it has to be true!

The show was very good, resembled a lot of the 40's and 50's shows, a combination of flamenco, ballet, contemporary, Spanish and

Educating Noah...Travelin'

Afro-Cuban rhythms, about 30 cast members, a variety of music and dances, the show lasted about an hour. One unique number, the same as with the cabaret show last night, was a dance in flip-flops. The slapping of the rubber on the floor was unique and highly entertaining., That was it for our second day!

Tuesday February 5th, Havana

Our all-day Best of Havana Excursion started at 8 A.M.

We got into the auditorium early to reserve seats on the bus. It was called in. When our bus was called, we were one of the first to leave the auditorium, and off we went. As we approached the garage, we found the line to the bus was almost full. Got on the bus and had no reserved seat, so Lynn sat down in the seat usually taken by the guide...I didn't argue with her, and neither did the guide, so we still had a front seat. Our guide was Israel, one of the best we have ever had!

On our way to our first attraction, we were provided a few more Cuba facts, so here we go...Havana was the first City in America to have a Chinatown, the first aqueduct in the Americas, and the first "sloppy Joe's" were made here. Up until a few years ago, Havana had the longest bar in the world.

The British were here for eleven months, and then the Spanish took over in 1762. Our guide referred to Fidel Castro as "Him #1" and his brother Raoul Him #2, B.C. as before Castro.

Taxes are high, 240%, on everything imported, and basically, everything is imported; the government has to "take care of its people."

Havana was built 12% by the Spanish, from 1900-1959 80%, and from 1959-now 8%. Whenever Cubans travel outside Cuba, they bring home the maximum of goods back with them: home goods, sundries, car parts, toiletries, and clothes. (A tube of toothpaste in Cuba is $4.00 due to the taxes!) Russia, they being back Lada parts!

18.5% of the population is over 60, life expectancy here is 80 for women. There is a shortage of social security funds, so many of the aged depend on family to survive.

When the USSR, with the splitting up and revolution in Russia, was tough on Cuba, they were importing 13 million barrels of oil per year, and the oil plummeted to 4 million barrels. Two million bicycles were imported from China, and bike paths were provided on the streets. I asked, "Where are all those bicycles?" I was told Most Cubans prefer to walk or crowd onto a bus, the bike lanes, or bike paths, and actually, I did not see one regular bike the time we were here, all three days, anywhere!

Traveling through various districts, Revolution Square, where all the rallies were held, all showing various stages of decay, a walking tour of the Colon Cemetery with various graves and monuments pointed out.

When people die, a ten-foot-deep hole is opened, and all the bodies that day are put in (no charge, if cremated, $15.00). Two years later, the remains are exhumed and given to the family. Of course, if your family has a crypt, the remains are placed there. Some are actually constructed as their previous ancestor's home. The white marble box behind the one a bit longer than a femur bone is for the previous family member's bones to make room for the current family member. The more antibiotics the person has before death, we are told we didn't check, the more preserved the remains are!

One half a column means the person died young, and a bird represents betrayal.

Our next stop was Finca Vigia, the estate of Earnest Hemmingway. We are told his fourth wife did not want to put up with the tiny apartment she and he lived in by the shore. He liked it because it was close to his boat. And the bars. He was upset when he came home one day and found everything gone.

The estate was a good ½ hour away; it was told he was furious until he found the seclusion, the pool, the three-bedroom house with garage, and the guest home for $100.00/month. He actually bought the house the following year from the landlord for $18,500. We could not go inside the house but looked in through an open door and windows, various bottles of liquor around, his weight noted on the wall in the bathroom, a lizard and bat preserved in jars, and a Picasso painting. A separate studio tower connected to the veranda, the pool, and the cabana, with his boat preserved under a shelter away from the house. There was also a small gift shop, café, office, and large parking area for bus parking and taxi hawking rides in antique cars.

On the way to the restaurant for lunch, more information: When the Spanish conquered Cuba, most of the trees were taken, leaving only 10% of the forest when they were defeated in the Spanish-American war in 1868.

Fresh water is at a premium (the water has legs). All the houses have cisterns; water is pumped every other day and is rationed, so vessels and tanks are filled on those days.

Another saying is that you cry twice with onions, the first when you buy them, the second when you peel them!

Twenty-six percent of the people are self-employed, making an average of $500/month, and 74% work for others or the government. 3% own a car; the license indicates the status, the "P" suffix is private, and the rest are government-owned or rented from the government. The cost of insurance and licensing is inexpensive.

Very few school buses are only for handicapped kids. If you send the child to a different school outside of your district, it is your responsibility to get them there and back. The island is very safe. The reason why the outside of the houses looks so bad and needs paint is you don't want to "show off" to the neighbors. Our guide assured us that inside, walls and upkeep are quite different than the decay on the outside.

Our guide did make a statement I need to put down; he said that if something is very outstanding, you will see it, "You cannot block the sun with one finger."

After the revolution, the planned construction of miles of Casinos just behind the sea wall was stopped, and the casinos that were started, like most of the rich and their homes, were abandoned. (1959)

Our meal was at a government-owned Cuban restaurant, Don Cangreco. It was small, but there was air conditioning; we sat at tables of six, served a beer or soda, a small bowl of bread slices, a plate with six very small pieces of butter, a seafood salad plate, followed by a whole grilled spinney lobster, a serving plate with rice, and a slice of squash next to the lobster. We were entertained by a trio that, after performing, went to each table for a contribution, and she didn't leave the table without one! Good food, not outstanding, forks actually too big to dig the food out of the shell. The meal was followed by a small piece of cake and a small ball of ice cream.

On the way to our last stop, in the heart of Old Havana, the

Almacenes San Jose, a huge collection of artists and vendors, we are reminded that chicken, rice, grain, cereal, candy, and beef account for a billion dollars a year; "Him" came from wealth, pictures were actually found with "him" being held by Batista at family gatherings, and the Bacardi family actually contributed a large sum of money to his wedding…he betrayed them all, he tried to destroy the past, did not allow gatherings of people outside the revolution rallies, closed churches and banned religious activities. Our guide told us of the Christmas tree his mother put up in the closet every year…. Nothing was where anyone would report to the government. In Cuba, you can be politically incorrect to the people but never about the government. "Him" had 5 children, four boys and one girl. His daughter lives in Miami and is ready for this. She is the head of the LGBTQ community there, just another group her father persecuted.

We spent a half hour at the Art area, came out poorer, but actually almost completed our entire Cuba shopping list!

Back on the ship, I joined our group for trivia. Dinner was Cuban and quite good. I went up to listen to a string trio and watched two couples show off dancing, one couple smooth and polished, the other way too serious and regimented. The production show was good, with two guys and two girls singing and dancing.

The night was finished with Karaoke; we were really surprised as to how many were there. They didn't have "Sweet Caroline," so we did it a Capella with two other guests. We also tried to get a group up for the YMCA, but they didn't have the background for that either. There were lots of people and very few participants.

Wednesday, February 6th, a day at sea.

We are active; Journey Wake-up quiz; Categories: Wii bowling (I won one of the four playings); Triband; Golf putting; Ping Pong; Taboo; General Knowledge Trivia, Music Trivia; Lynn went to Line dancing; I sunbathed for an hour and went to a lecture on Cienfuegos, our next port.

Notes on the lecture: Cienfuegos (Literally means 100 fires) but locally known as La Perla de Sur or Pearl of the South. This is the second Cuban stop and the first on the south side of Cuba. The city is 1/10 the size of Havana by the Bordeaux and New Orleans folk from the U.S.A.

This is a tender port in that the harbor is too shallow for sea ships. There are 15 providences in Cuba, and these are like the states in the U.S.A. The forts on this side of the Island were constructed mainly to protect the city from pirates; Havana was a rendezvous for the Spanish gold galleons.

The plaza in Cienfuegos is a designated UNESCO World Heritage site. A National hero for Cuba is Jose' Marti (1853-1895), who was a poet, writer, and activist, considered an Apostle of Cuba's Independence," regarded about the same as George Washington in the U.S.A. The third Spanish-American war, with the help of the U.S.A., was the final war winning Cuba's independence from Spain; just the influx of gangsters and the Mafia from the U.S. added to the corruption that Batista was known for. The Communist suppression of religion ended in 1990, and since then, three popes have visited Cuba. Seems the folks in America do not realize this is common with communistic socialism (suppression of religions), just another step away from capitalism. The lecture then went on to start talking about the "rich" people and one in particular who bought sick slaves and brought them back to health to sell them for a profit. I countered that this may have been great for the slaves in that many were actually treated like chattel, and if they became sick or could not work, they were eliminated. Just a different view; I confused some, others agreed with him, and a few with me.

Trivia's, one general, the other musical, beat at both, one team actually Aced the musical one (they had a DJ on the team); Asian buffet; listened to the trio...went to the room to kill time, shoulder bothering me, knees too, cranky, I killed the rest of the night in the room. Lynn attended the second set of the trio band, went to the man sing and guitar show, and took in a few songs at Latin Night, a good showing of viewers, no dancers. It seems participation is at a premium on this ship, but at least people show up!

I had commented on the lack of "hosted " events, the scarcity of waiters on deck, and the pre-filling of the excursion buses on a "How are we doing" form; all three departments contacted us and told us they would do better, the entertainment made the most excuses, and least apology or action, stating lack of participation due to extensive excursions.

Thursday, February 7th, Cienfuegos

Noah

We have an excursion at 8:15 to start the day. "Mountains, waterfalls and natural baths of El Nicho".

The approximate time was 6 1/2 hours, and the activity was listed as "strenuous"; both were true! El Nicho is set 2100 feet above sea level, with pristine waterfalls and pools and great photo opportunities. Now the details: it took us almost an hour to get to the base where we left our small van required to pay, a group of eight with one tour guide. The road was 1 ½ lanes, in good to poor condition; here is what we learned on the way there: When someone gets sick, they go to the doctor's house. The clinic is below, and the doctor lives above; they pay 12% of the price of the natural medicine prescriptions and, if required, are sent from there to the hospital.

When the Communists came into power, the graves were exhumed for any riches; all other properties of the rich were also confiscated. When someone says, "There is a Mango," it means they are attractive.

All farmers must give 10% off the top to the government. If not on government land, the government owns 80% of the land, along with any business not owned by the government, but again, the government owns 80-85 % of the businesses also. It was interesting to hear her talk; it seemed that every other sentence had "the government" in it!

Schools all wear uniforms: grade school, primary school, middle school, and high school, and yes, college, too! The Minister of Work decides /places you in a job. If it is not your specialty or desire, it does not matter.

Before you are accepted to college, you are tested on the English language, and this places you as a major.

Farmers not allowed to butcher cattle must transfer to the government and must buy meat at the market for $5.00 C.U.P /pound (about $5. U.S.) for beef.

Ration cards last only 10 days. 5 # brown sugar, 5# rice, 1# beans, 1# meat, 1# flour, small amount of oil for a family of four. Children 1-7 are allowed milk; each person is allowed 7 eggs per month; 1 egg costs 15 CUC (About $0.75 U.S.). When our guide was in high school, they all attended classes in the morning, had lunch, and then were all loaded on buses to work the government fields in the afternoon.

There are usually three bedrooms, a living room, and a kitchen, all very small; horse-drawn carts are used as taxis, and the main industry is tourism, coffee, and ice cream. You can leave work at any time and run errands without getting fired. Teachers make about $700.00 CUC/month (About $700.00 U.S.); no WIFI, but the kids are taught and use computers in school. Ta plank with here was slavery because the Spanish almost whipped out the indigenous people; they imported slaves to work the fields.

Back to the excursion...the walk up to the various falls, pools, and sites was on a narrow, polished stone path, uneven, unlevel, various grades. Many stairs were of different heights and widths, and few had handrails. A number of bridges were simply a plank with a thin railing over a stream bed 10-15 feet below.

There were a few places to stop and rest, a total including the uphill climb and numerous steps a good ¼ mile. About ¾ of the way, Lynn gave out, and since the only way back was to go back the same way, we picked her up about ½ hour later. At some locations, a few younger people were jumping in the crystal-clear pool of water, and yes, I did take a bunch of pictures.

Lunch was included. We sat in a covered area with picnic tables, offered soda or water, and then served coleslaw, sliced guava, bread slices with mayonnaise, white sweet potato, rice and beans, shredded beef, sliced pear-like fruit sliced and in juice for dessert, followed by Cuban coffee.

On the way back to town, we stopped at the Jobero Verde Community Project, had an experience with an interpretive dance group, passed a small craft fair, and then continued on our journey back to town, quite a few horse carts with people in them, actually saw some bicycles in a few little towns. We had a tour of the City Square, twenty minutes of free time to explore the craft stalls, and back to the van for a short drive back to the ship. There was a long line to get to the parking lot through Cuban Customs, then a twenty-minute line to get into the ship (one entrance). Lots of folks on walkers had to clear the ramp for those leaving the ship...another first!

This was White Night; everyone dressed in white, the entire 9th and 10th deck set with tables and outside grilling, three food stations, one huge dessert and crepe station, and the stage was pumping with music. White banners, white table clothes, I danced a few dances with Lynn; she also danced with the head chef and one of the officers. It was loud, and I couldn't hear to converse; Lynn was dancing, so I called it quits after the staff presentation, entailing all the staff parading around for a standing ovation. Another busy day has drawn to a close.

Friday, February 8th, a day at sea.

Wake-up quiz, Pictionary, Wii Archery (I won!), Golf putting tournament, Dingbats (phrases you had to figure out in 12 boxes), Where in the World Trivia, Bean Bag toss competition.

Destination lecture for me, making jewelry for Lynn; Lynn made a bracelet; here are the notes on the lecture, and some information is repeated from previous sources: Santiago is the second largest city in Cuba. This city has a greater African influence; famous people would be Desi Arnaz (From I Love Lucy) and Emilio Bacardi, an early revolutionary Fidel and Che betrayed.

This was the first capital of Cuba, 1522-1589, but Havana became the capital and epicenter due to the gold transfers, slaves brought to the Americas from the Nigeria area, and gold taken back to Spain and Portugal.

The Spanish conquistadores decimated the indigenous people and replaced them with slaves. The difference between a Privateer and a pirate is the privateer was licensed by the Crown.

870 Kilometers from Havana, with the same language throughout the island but different accents; this is the place where Teddy Roosevelt had his "Hour of Glory."

Of the Islands in the Caribbean, Haiti was the first to achieve independence in 1791; Cuba has been destroyed four times; it is in an earthquake zone; Cuba embraced Soviet/communist ways and beliefs, and the break-up of the Soviet Union devastated Cuba.

75% of what Cubans eat is imported; when you see newspapers covering the windows, it is to shield the sun, and they cannot afford drapes, curtains, or shades.

The billboards are all political, usually with pictures of Che (Who was much more acceptable and loved) or Fidel, and Fidel Castro is only referred to as "Fidel" or "him."

Back to ship activities, Darts (I won! Out of six players), Catchphrase game, Trivia, Musical trivia, then we changed for the LE

Club private party Hour de Orvis, and wine (we had to dress up a bit) the only drinks offered were in your package, another odd thing here. Usually, these events are open bar, anything mixed, and doubles if you want.

Dinner was French-themed: Lynn had a seafood stir fry, I had escargot, frog legs, and sardine salad, and dessert was swan-shaped cream puffs and mini crème Brule finger food.

The serenade production show listened to a set by the trio girl band ended the day.

Just a note, there were only one or two café and a company store in Centrifuge. We did not see one KFC, McDonald's, or Walgreens car lot (new or used), only one large grocery store in Havana, and that was only about 2,000 square feet. Rickety horse-drawn carts seem to be the Uber here for most. The guide we had for the day had a master's degree; the one we had in Norway also did. I assume that since salaries and wages are so heavily taxed, the tips make the difference...especially with "over tipping" Americans, where she probably got $25-$40 tips and paid the same or less for the day in salary w/o paying the government; it seems many know how to work around the system around the world!

Saturday, February 9th, Santiago, Cuba.

As in the last port, we have clearance for docking, so there is no tendering in for any of the destinations on this cruise. Weather today, as yesterday, is sunny and in the low 80s (F).

Our last city tour, the Panoramic Santiago City Tour, with lunch. The tour lasted a little over four hours. The guide, Dennis, was a college English instructor with a master's and is looking forward to joining his partner in the United States as soon as he can provide the path. Since we are having a crisis at our southern border, with a huge backlog, we suggested going through Canada, but he told us they require much more documentation, a non-refundable $500.00 fee, and he knows of two people with family and needed jobs they were qualified for, that were turned away, their fees kept. Interesting on what we are told and what actually goes on in the world!

We first went to the main square, where we disembarked and walked the area. We were shown the government house, the main cathedral, and the oldest house with Arabic style exterior. We stopped at a government store for cigars, postcards, and rum, then a statue of their hero. I actually saw two people bow in front of it!... We walked down a busy street just over a lane wide, with a few parked cars and carts, the sidewalk only ½ the width in the U.S., and people standing on the sidewalks talking to people inside the buildings, not moving as we approached, many others sitting in the doorways, and quite a few dogs roaming the streets, lots of cast iron fences and gates. There are many more Cubans in traffic and on the streets than in both previous cities combined!

About two blocks off the square was a building. We entered and sat down to listen to about 20 people entertain us with various Capella renditions of songs, followed by a short question and answer period, and then back to the square and the bus. Next was the San Juan Hill memorial to Teddy Roosevelt and the Rough Riders. Walked the hill, we then toured the city, including another statue of Antonio Macao on horseback surrounded by 23 raised machetes, the outside of the fort, the view of the sea, mountains, and their first shopping mall, established in 2017 (this was a very small mall). Lunch was at a restaurant that caters to tourists and cruise ships. It was quite a lunch, starting with a salad of cabbage, lettuce, beets, tomatoes, carrots, rolls, and mayonnaise, followed by a thin crust pizza, ½ loaded, ½ plain, followed by rice and beans, shredded beef, a pork chop, fried sweet potato, eggplant, squash, followed by a seafood stew; we had no idea of the feast prepared, most of us passed on the sorbet and cookie dessert! We then waddled back to the bus to be taken to the ship, where in the morning, they took back out visas and provided a day visa; here, they collected the day visa.

Now, what was told us on the bus: The busses are always crowded, stake trucks converted with benches for transportation, and there are over 5,000 motorcycles in the area; we saw most of them with two people, and as in India and Africa, these are used as "cabs" also.

There used to be copper mining, but the veins dried up. Of the Americas, Cuba was the second to be discovered. Coffee is grown in the mountains. Education is free to outsiders also, including room (???). Each providence (State) has its own stadium.

We went past a barracks with bullet holes; Fidel did not want colonialism, and Raul, his brother, felt the same about the judicial system. 56% of Santiago is women. The city has biotech, produces nickel mining, a cement factory, tourism, a beer factory, and also a fishing industry. During the colonization of Spain, Spain was the only trading partner.

If someone owns the land, no taxes are extracted by the government, but if the land is leased to others, 10% off the top goes to the government. Cubans travel they can out of the country to get the things they want, and each brings back a maximum of 240#, including shoes, clothes, bed linens, and sundries.

Finally, the streets are named after Cuban patriots; Billboards and graffiti throughout Cuba commemorate the various rebel leaders. On July 26, 1953, Castro and his small army launched an attack on the Cuartel Moncado military barracks. (This was shown to us with the bullet holes in the concrete.) This incident did not go well, but it laid the foundation for the revolution, and at the following show trial, Castro made his famous "History will absolve me" speech. I asked the guide if things were actually much better since the revolution…he replied, "some things."

The ship sailed at 3 P.M. We went to our room and crashed, got up an hour later, filled out the promised postcards, and took them down to the desk to be mailed…of the 20-plus cruises we have been on, it cost $1 per card to stamp and deliver to the post office, here the cards on land cost me 70 cents each, the ship charged $2.50 each for postage and deliver….got you coming and going!!

Two extremely hard trivia: there are now at least 10 groups playing. Of those groups, the first trivia was won with 14 correct, and the second, on the planets, 17 correct. We just can't win on this ship!!

I went back to the room to catch up on the notes and rest a bit more before dinner-themed Indian Cuisine; the Nan bread was perfect, and the lamb and tandoori chicken were outstanding. Here again, the buffet was sparsely attended, and the specialty and big dining room were filled. This seemed to be the more formal and less adventurous crowd. The Chocolate buffet at 8:30 was reminiscent of the midnight chocolate buffets years ago. This one held amidships, six tables set with a large selection of chocolate delicacies, plus a chocolate fountain; Yup, we had a few samples, it was set up so no tables were to eat at, and of course, the few chairs in the room were occupied by "nesters." As usual, you had to thread your way around couples and others who had to discuss the offerings at the displays or question the contents under the various coatings.

A special production, Alicia Hill, who was a previous singer and now assistant cruise director, sang a number of songs, tried to engage the audience, and filled the room with a great variety of songs; she was very entertaining and worked the crowd well!

Motown at the disco; maybe 20 people; the ship was rocking; Lynn had a lot of difficulty dancing along with the other two couples that were on the floor, so after 4-5 songs, we called it a night.

Sunday, February 10th, last day on board.

Tomorrow, we have to be off the ship by 8 A.M. to catch the transfer bus to the airport at 8:15.

The sun is out, there are few clouds, the temperature is early in the upper 70s, and it is muggy. This is one of the few times we have had a balcony that we could walk out on or sit at a table, and I believe I was out there a total of 10 minutes the whole cruise, Lynn much less. Our room is for sleeping and cleaning up…We did not encounter any animals or fish, no dolphins, no flying fish, few if any fishing boats, and even in the ports, maybe one other cruise ship. We did see a few other cruise ships on our last day heading both south and back to Miami, but no fishing or squid boats…odd.

Here is our final day: wake-up quiz; a game called Heads Up; Wii Deal or no Deal; An Origami class, A Game called "Contextual Anagrams; Lynn went to a final Line dancing class, me, a golf putting tournament, Where in the world Trivia; Scattergories; General Knowledge trivia; and a farewell trivia. Between activities, I was able to roast myself for about an hour, twice, Lynn maybe 40 minutes, twice. She can't take the heat and humidity like me (80 temperature and humidity), and we can't go home pale…you know!

We cashed in our participation points for a T-shirt, pen, and a small folder. We set out our clothes for the trip home, settled up our account, and labeled our luggage; since the zippers were completely pulled out of my suitcase, I banded it with tape to get it home.

Greek night for dinner, everything we like Greek, and more was offered, and like India night, a light showing of people, we really don't get it, the food is ½ the travel experience, and the cruise ships really are authentic!

Listen to the Trio of Women, Karaoke at 8:30; my voice is still flat and dull; that is it for me. I sounded horrible, Lynn agreed. The production shows two guys and two gals finishing up the night.

Monday, February 11th, We are headed home.

Easy off the ship, found our luggage, no immigration? We had paid for the bus to the airport, we were dropped off at a loading dock, and there was an express check-in for the bags, the shortest and fastest ever. At the terminal, TSA has abbreviated just ID, coats off, computer in luggage, quick wand, and we were through!

It took us two sky trains to our gate; all in all, we were at the gate by 9:45. Our plane loaded at 11:30, and life was good!

I called the American Claims Department. I need to take the damaged suitcase to the airport in Milwaukee within thirty days of the claim, and they have someone who will fix or repair it. I will drop it off tomorrow after it is untapped and empty.

Flight to O'Hare on time, walked through the terminal for our bags, still no TSA; picked up our luggage, ran to meet our bus back, actually ran, to find out the bus was late, turned out to be 45 minutes late, we called Uber for the ride home from the bus station; Uber driver quiet; due to the snow storm coming in Lynn went out to the grocery store to get milk and bread, I brought up the luggage, another adventure closes. Six P.M. 02/11/2019

One follow-up note: Since our next adventure was just a bit over two weeks away, I made Lynn come along to the airport and circle while I turned in the damaged luggage. The baggage area was desolate; lots of flights were canceled, and when I found the luggage claim desk, no one was to be found. I found a couple airport cops and asked them where to find someone; they told me to go over to the departure desks across the street and they would help. I went over, and there was no line, but the two attendants were not looking up over their computers, so after waiting in front of them, one asked if she could help. I told her no one was at the luggage claim desk and that there were three people waiting for assistance. She sighed and said she would find someone and to return to the desk. There were three guys now, and I told them, "Help is on its way." About ten minutes later, an official-looking woman with a name tag necklace came over, and two of the other guys told her their problem first; she opened a back door and produced their missing luggage. I stepped in, showed her the suitcase, and asked her what was the next step since I needed an answer soon: repair or replace. She told me she didn't usually work in this section, but produced a suitcase from the room and asked if replacing the damaged one with the one she produced would be O.K.? I asked what I should do, and she said to give me the claim paperwork and leave the damaged one, and we were done. I gave her the paperwork and left with a newer suitcase. Found Lynn; she had circled three times, and the deed was done!

Three times, and the deed was done!

My suitcase is packed and ready for the Polynesian adventure. I worked a couple days for the DAV, and Patti would like me to run the dispatch desk while I am recuperating with the new shoulder. I will find out about the end of March. Now, when the rain comes or barometric pressure drops, the migraines come and stay, lost one whole day. I am also preparing for taxes. The estate taxes are finally ready for Murphy (our tax person) took hours on the phone, then a visit to the Social Security office to get the needed paperwork.

Educating Noah...Travelin'

Exploring French Polynesia March 2019

Twenty-four hours starts the third recheck, I noticed no gate for our flight. Checked O'Hare, but there were no Quanta's listed. I went to the website, but after three attempts, no information was needed. I called Quanta's, and they indicated a twenty-minute hold. I tried calling the O'Hare airport, but no numbers. Frustrated, I e-mailed our travel agent, and within 10 minutes, he called and e-mailed me back. It was Quanta's thru American Airlines, terminal 3.

Day 1, March 1st

It is going to be a long day, actually day one and two, due to the extensive travel time.

Now, O'Hare has four terminals: 1, 2, 3, and international 5 (4??). It seems that United and America fly internationally out of their terminals also. The Uber guy came right on time (10:15) for a quick ride to the bus station. Lynn tried to give him a great review, but when she pressed send, it indicated horrible.... we tried to fix it, and I think she did. Of course, you can't call Uber...customer service????

The bus arrived ten minutes late; we got hung up in traffic, hung up at one stop for a last-minute rider, and finally O'Hare about 20 minutes later than scheduled.

We went to a kiosk to get luggage tags and were confronted by an attendant about using one of the 6 open kiosks until I showed her the Business Class ticket. She then returned behind the counter. I presented both passports, entered the flight, and was told to call over an attendant. We were able to break her away from her casual conversation with another attendant to be told she would take us to the counter. We got to the counter, and the terse attendant took the information provided on the tickets; American did not indicate that we were Trusted Travelers, so even when I gave her the TSA number, she would not accept...put in the "regular" line, computer out, no shoes, and yup, lit 'er up. It was the same left shoulder...wanded, found our gate, and waited an hour for the flight. The first flight left at 3:01 on time.

Noah

We flew from Chicago to L.A., the flight of a little over four and a half hours, mostly cloudy, but it did clear a bit as we flew over the Rockies. What a spectacular sight, but no pictures, camera packed away in the carry-on. Of course, there was a time change, so when we got our bearings and started looking for our flight, we set our watches back two hours. It was now six P.M., and our flight did not leave L.A. until 10:55 L.A. time, so we found a comfortable place to wait for the boards that indicated flights and gates to provide the information we needed.

The boards only "go out" three hours ahead, so our flight won't be posted till 8 P.M. We stopped at an American "info" desk, and the agent indicated that all flights that leave this airport are located in the international wing, so we hoofed it, found comfortable chairs and a table and waited. Being "antsy," I watched the board, and it seemed only one flight left at 22:55 to Papeete, but it had the wrong airline and flight, so I walked to the second last gate, a good ½ mile (I counted the steps) and asked the gate people.

I was told that this was a combination flight incorporating all the following…Air Tahiti TN 101, American Airlines AA7227, Quanta's QF3816, Air Calin SB4601, and New Zealand NZ4091. This was the only flight out that night to Papeete, and it actually continued on to New Zealand.

I walked back to Lynn; she wanted a ride due to the ½ mile walk but was told that only those requiring a wheelchair were given rides…so we slowly made our way to the gate. The plane was a Boeing 787-9 Dream lounger with a capacity of 250-290 passengers, and the gate was overflowing an hour before loading. In that Lynn now insists we fly business, we were in the first group to be loaded on buses. The buses took almost ten minutes to get to the plane, and we loaded from a permanent structure on the flight line with ramps and an elevator. Business class is a whole different world; plenty of overhead bin space and seats recline completely into a bed. We both slept a good 5-6 hours, and the breakfast served was very good and plentiful.

Day 2, March 2nd

We arrived in Papeete just before 6 A.M.; we had visas filled out and declaration sheets done, breezed through immigration, and our luggage was out in the first batch!

Educating Noah...Travelin'

At this time, we will have traveled about 23 hours.

The airport is not that large, but it is basically the only commercial one in Polynesia, Tahiti, or Papeete and is the largest of the island chain. Once out of security, it is open air. It was warm, in the lower 80's, and matching humidity. I shopped at the shops and actually got postcards and stamps in a mailbox just outside the shop!

We watched people till about 8 A.M. and then grabbed a cab to go to the Tuk-Tuk electric bike adventure I had signed us up for. We asked around about how much to pay for the ride and were told around $10.00 US to go to the port. I had also checked online with Trip Advisor, and they indicated $30.00 U.S.; the cab driver seemed confused when I gave her the address, but my description of where it was confirmed that she knew where, so off we went.

Fifteen minutes later, we were there! I asked how much in American dollars, and she said, "$22; then she said $20.00 U.S. I gave her $22, she was happy, I was happy, and we checked in.

This is French Polynesia. We were told we were a half hour early, and they would store our bags, but we needed to return at 9, the designated time, for the 3-hour tour.

We walked around and looked into stores selling beautiful bolts of material and a flower market with unbelievably gorgeous arrangements, food, and souvenirs. Checked out a variety of other shops and headed back to the E-Bike for our ride.

We were introduced to our driver, Mattie, a young woman of 25-28 with fairly good English, and off we went. We were taken to a church which was the only building not destroyed during WWII or any of the past typhoons, the flower market, a pearl shop and museum, two botanical gardens, the Chinese embassy, a small park, where there was a prolific breadfruit tree, We asked, and she said "breadfruit is not sweet, it is used like a "filler" similar to potatoes"; a small shopping complex, and back to the shop. We asked if they would help us get our luggage the three blocks to the shipping dock, and they were very helpful in providing a tuk-tuk to carry us and our luggage there. Very nice people, and our guide was energetic, knowledgeable, and had a good sense of humor; we rewarded all with appropriate tips!

We were supposed to wait till 1 P.M. to check in to the ship, but we just acted like 12 P.M. was fine, and yup, it worked.... We checked in, signed up with everything, and headed for the café for a bite and hydration, both of us now soaked with sweat.

Most had to wait for cabins till 3 P.M. to be made up. We were actually able to get in by 2:45; we crashed for an hour, unpacked, participated in the mandatory safety drill, and went back to the room to dress for dinner.

We were both still exhausted, so we went to the café, where they had my sushi and Lynn's lamb chops...nothing formal that night. Back in the room, we set up our schedules for Sunday. "Sacred Island by Le Truck "leaves by 8:30 A.M. I caught up on the diary, we showered, and an early night to bed.

Day 3, Sunday, March 3, Raiatea, the Sacred Island.

We had breakfast. There were too many excellent selections, but the salmon was on top of my list; they do exchange money, so I got $20 worth of the CFP (French Polynesian franc), joined the groups for excursions, and got out 15 minutes ahead.

Waiting for us was a guy called Heiman (pronounced Hey Mau) dressed up in Polynesian gear, an ornate hat, and touting a conch horn he blew to bring attention. We have led a short distance to the "Le Truck," which is basically a flatbed truck with a shell over the bed, plexiglass sliding windows, bench seats along the inside walls, and a center bench running the length.

This was a three-hour tour with three stops; the first was at the mouth of the Faaroa River that feeds into the ocean. We followed that river via truck to where it was not much larger than a stream, a rest stop, where he was also a stand selling and tasting fresh fruit. I bought a coconut for us to drink. We had breadfruit chips, which were basically thinly sliced breadfruit deep fried with a little salt, and a cluster of Rambo ton, a red golf ball-sized fruit covered with soft black spikes you peal to reveal a milky white fruit that is semi-sweet and has large almond seed in the center, interesting, different, and once you get the hang of pealing these, it isn't too bad!

We walked a short distance to the open-air temple comprising seven maraes (smoothed black stone and coral platforms), where sacrifices were made to the god ORO.

There are flowers growing everywhere, gnarled trees, and, of course, coconut trees. I asked about all the holes in the ground and

Educating Noah...Travelin'

was told those are land crab holes; the bigger the hole, the bigger the crab. They feed on coconuts, and people come at night (the crabs are nocturnal) and harvest the crabs. They then feed them fruit and coconut water and pulp, fatten them up, and after 2-3 weeks, they are clean inside and out, and then dinner!

As we left the site for the trip home, we encountered a downpour of rain. We were inside the truck, but the rain was cool and took away the humidity; it stopped 10 minutes before we got off the bus to go back to the ship. (Wow, what timing!)

Here is the information the 80-year-old guy told us: Raiatea, meaning "faraway heaven" and "sky with soft light," was actually first named Havai' after the homeland of ancient Polynesia, and is the second largest Tahitian island; it was the center of religion and culture over a thousand years ago, and the most sacred island of the South Pacific.

This island is home to a rare, unique plant called the "Tiare apetahi," a delicate white flower comprised of 6 or seven petals that open at dawn with a slight crackling sound. Legend has it that it is the sound of the broken heart of a common woman who was not allowed to marry the son of a Tahitian king. This is the one and only place this flower is grown on Earth.

This harbor is called "22Broa" Big Lips...due to the reef, he did not have any formal education. He is convinced that anyone really only needs the skills to survive, fish, cook, and plant. "If you are an employee, you are a slave to your employer." In 1959, a young man was looking for a place to live, and a deal was struck; he could live there if he taught the old man the English language.

Bora-Bora has a small airport, but Tahiti is the only one that can handle big commercial planes. There are no beaches on this island. During WWII, the population of the island was 1600; 6000 soldiers were housed there; kids were of mixed colors and eye color.

"My fortune is in my body. Money really means nothing, especially in the next world. "... he was good, informative, and liked to talk. I also believe a bit of "BS" was mixed in, but it was a running commentary from the time we left the port.

There are 16 doctors total on the island, and most of the shops are run by Chinese (They have all the money"). He was 13, and his first wife was 19 when he married. He has 20 children and 18 grandchildren; if you leave the island, you cannot keep the land. There are building codes now, but he still does not have electricity, uses a wood stove/oven to heat food, and eats his main meal for breakfast, which basically was prepared the night before and cooked overnight.

Most dwellings have corrugated roofs and concrete brick walls, small living areas, and one or two bedrooms. Most yards have fruit trees and gardens. He pointed out taro root plants as we passed. There are no bees on the island, so everything is pollinated by the men (that is a man's job), and the flowers must be pollinated from sunrise till noon; the men can pollinate 3000 per day.

Vanilla is one of the few plants cultivated. It used to be 300 tons a year, but now it is down to 100 tons. Vanilla still sells for about $125.00 U.S. per pound.

As we walked the short distance back to the ship, we browsed a few shops and got back on the ship by 12:30. It was 80's all day, with some relief from the rain and the humidity, but it bounced back quickly…everyone sweating and uncomfortable.

Light lunch, caught up on diary, sat in the sun, mini golf, Bago with the bean bags, tea and a Polynesian show with new friends from Canada, trivia, and sign up for the shipbuilding contest. Back to the room to change, the Captain's reception (free booze), dinner, and a show.

Captain Cocktail Celebration from 5:45 P.M. till 8 P.M. was in three locations...why?? Free booze, name your drink, and it is yours, plus canopies. Waiters and waitresses always circulated with refills on the drinks and different snacks, and yes, all three venues were full of passengers.

We sat with a pleasant but shy German couple for a while and then sat with an Australian couple, and as usual, we have found with Australians and New Zealanders, the conversation never stops!

We had a light supper and played another trivia with a group taking 2nd place this time…Where is the biggest desert in the world? Antarctica: who was the talk show host appearing in the movie "The Color Purple"? Oprah Winfrey.

The day ended with a folkloric show featuring the "Mamas of Raiatea" with dance, music, and even some audience participation. It was very enjoyable, not any skinny young people except two early twenty male dancers.

There were lots of smiles, and about 1/3 of the auditorium was full…it did start at 9:30 P.M., Day 3, in the tank.

Day 4 Monday, March 4th, Bora-Bora, the first of two days here

Our excursion is the first out at 8 A.M.; it is another Le Truck Island tour. This truck actually had plastic seats, side by side, two on each side, and yes, we were some of the last on and got to the island side of the truck…most items pointed out on the ocean side ☹

Over half of the businesses here are run by the Chinese. They were brought here as slaves. There is one main road that circumvents the island; it is about 20 miles long, and this is what we will be doing for the next 2 1/2 hours. The weather is the same as yesterday: low 80s, both humidity (actually, this might be higher) and temperature.

One drug store, no hospital, 10,000 people, education is only up to middle school, must go to another island for high school and higher, many believe the middle school is enough book learning.

There is no real tide; the boats are pulled out of the water at night due to saltwater worms that eat through the hulls. During the war, there was no combat on this island. The U.S. Army built the road that we drove on and a small airstrip. In 1948, the Polynesian Islands were annexed from France.

You see graves in the yards; you are buried on the property you lived at. If you were a good person in the front yard, an O.K. person in the back yard, and a bad person, or "jerk," buried out in the wild.

Many coconut trees are considered "trees of life," providing wood, food, and alcohol; the roots are very shallow, some only a foot below the ground. Eight freighters a week bring supplies and electricity "most expensive in the world." the water is also, and they have a de-saltation plant which co-mingles the mountain and spring water with the de-salted ocean water. They only have one beach.

Most islanders are Christians; however, there are Mormons, Islam, and some old religions. Turtles are considered sacred in the old religions.

We stopped for a demonstration on how rayon material is tie-dyed, and patterns put on cloth, basically dyes from various plants, and forms made from linoleum that when the material is stretched to dry from dying, the forms block the sun and an imprint was left when the cloth dried. A number of the guests were used as models to demonstrate how the one piece of material is used to dress both the men and the women. A number of local products, including jewelry and vanilla, then off for more ocean and volcano views. The water is shallow on this side of the reef, no more than chest high, sandy with lava stones; we did see two sting rays in the water gliding out.

Eighty percent of the industry here is tourism; about 150 ships visit a year. This is getting close to the end of the tourist season, and like Hawaii, many movie stars have or had homes here. (Brandon, Cruz, Bronson)

We stopped for pictures of the different shades of blue in the water. I walked into the ocean, and it was a very pleasant Luke-warm. We found some more crab holes, the guide placed a flower outside a few holes, and a dark brown/black crab came out to feast so we could see what they looked like.

The Hibiscus plant is used here as an antiseptic salve; the Nonie tree has fruit, but the fruit is inedible. However, natives make an alcoholic drink from the fruit. There are no rivers or waterfalls on the island. Rock lifting and canoeing are their major sports.

The first black pearl farm in the Polynesian Islands was started here; the Japanese taught the islanders how to seed and harvest the oysters.

The tour had one final stop called Bloody Mary's, and outside was an extensive list of celebrities that had visited there. I bought a Bloody Mary…nothing special. Also bought a T-shirt with the name on it…. I thought the souvenirs and drinks "wee" priced high, but then again, where else in the world would I get these!

Back on the ship, both of us were wet with sweat; we rested, ate, sunbathed, mini golf, Bago, and Trivia. The room attendant came through with 12 large empty water bottles for my shipbuilding, the front desk let me borrow scissors for two hours, and the activity coordinator, when asked, stated she could not provide tools or supplies, so it was just more of a challenge!

Dinner at the café; there are too many excellent selections;

tomorrow, we are going to try the dining room. We were still feeling the effects of that long travel day, plus the heat and humidity, so we played the night trivia (2nd place☺): where is the United States flag that has never been replaced or taken down? The moon! Who has the most hair follicles: Blonds, brunettes, or redheads? Blonds

Off to bed; catch up tonight.

Day 5, Tuesday, March 5th. Our second day at Bora-Bora.

We were on the first shuttle off the ship. It is only a ten-minute ride, and we are there just to run around town, pick up some scissors and supplies, and get back to the ship before the heat and humidity get us. Forecast today: 80's, sunny, and humid. We were some of the first in the dock shops; I used this to set the stage for bargaining: "1st sale, good luck." ... We found the rings for Lynn and the daughters, paid for three what another passenger paid for one yesterday ☺; found the town store, mini scissors, local coffee, and floss for boat string; the cashier was accommodating, took some FPC and US dollars.

Outside, four guys singing and played instruments; when I asked to take their picture, one got up, handed me his guitar, indicated for Lynn to get up, sat her next to me on bongos, and gave her a flower crown. We played and sang with them while he took our picture...what fun that was, and yes, I donated additional cash! We were back on board an hour and a half after leaving.

Indoor putting, lunch, again, too many great selections. Ate with a couple from Massachusetts and asked them to join us for supper in the dining room at 6:30; they agreed. Went hunting for boat supplies and worked a bit on the boat after getting some commitment from staff on supplies. Up to a half hour on each side to brown me up, Lynn took a swim in the pool.

Baggo, golf putting, and trivia, what was known as the Pharaoh's chicken? A vulture; where is the atlas bone? Spinal column

We joined a couple from New Zealand for two cocktails. It was a great conversation, even though I had left my hearing aids in the room. We joined the other couple for dinner and casual 2 hours of conversation. My bill of fare was an Indian selection, a thick squash-like soup, a chutney, and a crape dessert; Lynn had steak and a vegetable Kimball pureed carrot and spinach in the shape of a large thimble.

The evening show was the first production show. Sing and dance to 60's and 70's songs. Hopefully, we can stay up longer after this. We were sleepin' by 10; we have become part of the old zombie crowd!

Day 6, Wednesday, March 6th, our first day at sea.

We slept in, and there was nothing much real stuff planned: a couple lectures, Lynn's first line dancing class, and the usual activities, plus work on my darkening. I find it interesting that around the world, darker-skinned people put on white makeup and coloring while white or light-skinned people darken their skin in the sun...

Lynn's first activity was Coffee chat and needlepoint; mine was a lecture by a Biologist called "No brain, no heart, has an eye?" The lecture started with an advisory to everyone that the discussion does contain graphic information regarding reproduction and biological matters so as to not be offended. I found this to be way too politically correct, especially to a crowd of people with no one except the entertainers being under 30 and an average age of 65-70...grow up??

The most distant from us in the animal kingdom is the sponge. The most ancient of the sponge family is the Glass sponge; it spins its body out of silica. If you put a sponge in a blender or grate it, place the pieces in a Petri dish, a little nutrient, and you get new sponges. Sponges self-identify the shape of the sponge is governed by the environment, and the sponge can filter 200 liters of water in hours; they like "dirty" water. There is current research on sponge cells killing cancer cells in humans.

"Jellyfish, Corals, Anomies, Oh My!"

The next stop in the evolutionary change is that now animals have a tissue. There are four major groups: Radial symmetrical (like us, cut in half and have two identical halves) and medusa Types, i.e., Jellyfish. They do have nervous systems.

Fire coral in Florida, the poison that creates a rash, can be neutralized with vinegar from urine.

True jellyfish are Scyphozoans or "Moon Jelly," and like all "Jelly," thrive on pollution. The most dangerous/poisonous "Jelly" is the Cabazon, and this "jelly" is almost transparent.

Educating Noah...Travelin'

Jellyfish have eyes with lenses; the Box Jellyfish uses its eye to hunt, then eats its prey, and afterward drifts to the bottom to rest and nap. One hole is used to eat, eliminate, and mate.

Charles Darwin was the first to recognize how volcanoes support coral. Corals are in continuous warfare with other corals for space. They use shade to prevent sun and thereby kill other coral. Coral works the same as plants; most of our seafood starts life in coral, it acts as a shelter, and of course.

While undersea exploring the coral, you will hear many sounds and clicks, and many animals communicate clean up for the nutrients. Through these sounds and clicks, how come there is no cross-breeding with animals? It is called lock and key and is the fastest mutating section of animals.

Between lectures, I checked in with the ship-building guy and complained about the lack of help from the front desk. I was told that everything was to be obtained through room and food staff. I stated I was at a standstill and thought "not my job" was not supportive, and where was I supposed to get the duct or packaging tape, glue, or string. He told me that those who build the ships bring this with them...I said that gives them an advantage that anyone actually trying to abide by the rules a severe disadvantage...did not seem to affect him...what a joke!

In the second lecture, "An Introduction to Polynesia and Easter Island," the auditorium was full.

There were three groups that settled in the islands from Taiwan. Easter Island is part of Peru, Kit Can is ruled by England, and the French Polynesians are governed by the French.

The settling of Easter Island and others nearby, from 2000 BC to 1000 BC in Samoa and New Zealand.

Scouts were sent out to find other islands against the winds and currents, so when ½ the provisions and water were used up, the scout could return home faster and easier. What the scouts were looking for were clouds that seemed to form over land, a change in the ocean swells, and, of course, certain birds. When a new island was discovered, double-hulled canoes that could hold up to 100 people (including many young women to populate the new island), supplies, plants (bananas, coconuts, sweet potatoes, tarot,), the Mahout plant

Noah

for clothing, animals (chickens and rats) and water were sent out to inhabit the new land. The scouts would have determined the availability of fresh water, usually found in extinct volcanoes as reservoirs, a reef supporting a big fish population, and soil.

Easter Island was discovered by the Europeans on Easter Sunday, and with the name "stuck," there are 1000 statues on the island, and 300 alters. One of the major problems the Europeans encountered with the natives was the different definitions of possessions. Seems "sharing" was expanded by natives; much disappeared off the ships and soldiers to be "shared" by the natives. There are even some paintings showing the presentations with a native taking a hat off the ground.

The daily indoor golf putting, outdoor golf putting, Baggo, some more sunbathing, trivia, and another lecture took up the afternoon. This lecture was on the U-2 Reconnaissance (spy) planes.

The lecturer was one of the pilots; he described the suit, the contracting of the development, the problems of flying that high, including a special fuel, an effective escape system, food and waste disposal for the pilot, and secrecy in developing and testing these, still in use planes, along with the SR 71 USAF reconnaissance planes based out of several locations, including Area 51 which is still active in Las Vegas area. The CIA is no longer involved with these planes. (Or so we are told.)

Tonight is our first specialty restaurant, the Polo Grill; we will also go on deck to see if we can see the Milky Way and other star formations not seen in the northern hemisphere. The captain will turn off all the lights on the deck from 9:00 to 9:15 for the best observation.

The restaurant experience was very pleasant. I met two other couples: a banker and his wife, a nurse, and a lawyer with his wife and a librarian. Two and a half hours of great food and conversation. It was a bit cloudy, so no Milky Way was sighted; few stars…clouds, and a full moon not a good combination for star gazing! Dancing under the Stars was at 9:30, band and production cast on deck singing and dancing, maybe 100 passengers, and the temperature was in the 70s, but the humidity was matching here also. We stayed for almost an hour.

Oh, a gathering of owls is a Parliament; the song "Eye of a Tiger" was from which Rocky movie? Rocky 3.

Day 7 Thursday March 7th, Fakarava, French Polynesia

Mostly cloudy, high 80s, high humidity; the morning started out sunny. There isn't much to do on the Island, no taxis or buses. And a small cloud front coming in, but we had to get off the ship! We were in the second group for the tender, fifteen minutes, explored the shops and the dock area, picked stones for the stone people; and there wasn't anything new or reasonable, so we were back on the ship by 10:30.

I picked up a saved damp box from reception, outlined the places cut, and took it to the kitchen for cutting. The cook had to get permission first but then cut the box where indicated. I complained again about the lack of cooperation by staff, front desk …no avail.

Lunch, putting, Baggo, trivia…the place is getting full, there are not enough chairs, teams are not as consistent as on other cruises, and people getting obnoxious and aggressive. We did actually place third. What does BMX represent? Bicycle Motor-crossing: what city did Brigham Young find? Salt Lake City.

We went to "Brazilian Beats" by the show band, 5:30-6:15 during Happy hour…only ½ the songs were Bazillion…Bummer!

Dinner at the café, the food was excellent. Had swordfish, shrimp, and lobster, and Lynn had lamb chops, all cooked to perfection. Late-night trivia, female singer tonight, so we just called it a night tomorrow; move clocks one hour ahead, and we are at sea.

Day 8 Friday, March 8th, a day at sea.

We both slept late. I was up several times with my left shoulder pounding and then a migraine; Lynn slept well, just a lot! Morning Lynn went to stitch and chat; I went to a lecture on volcanoes.

Notes on volcanoes by Gloeta Massie: We are in the Pacific ring of fire, which is extensive, from here to Chile, up the west coast of South America, through Central America, the west coast of the USA all the way to Alaska, across the Bering straits, then down through Russia, Japan, China, Korea, and Vietnam then back to the islands.

We know more about the surface of the moon than we know about the deep sections of our oceans. There are many underwater volcanoes; as the tectonic plates move, the heat needs to be vented, and weak spots are volcanoes. There are six types of volcanoes.

Volcanic ash is full of nutrients; after the ash cools, lichens start feeding, followed by algae; birds supply fertilizer and seeds...

"Nothing goes to waste in nature."

Overcast turned to rain; the rain continued throughout the rest of the day; outside activities were much hampered. I tried at Bingo, but $20.00 was gone; Lynn went to Cardio dance and indoor putting.

Afternoon, lecture on the HMS Bounty, here is a brief summary:

The voyage started out "bad," orders and ship very late to Bligh, who was relatively young at 33, and Christian (23), both previously sailed together with Capt. Cook and I were good friends. The small ship, only 90 ft. long and a crew of 46, was fitted for the transportation of breadfruit, a high protein cheap fruit, for the slavers in the Caribbean. The mission was to obtain breadfruit plantings, then continue on to chart Indonesian and upper Australian waters for shipping lines (Bligh was known for his navigation). The name of the refitted ship was also changed to the HMS Bounty, which was not good for superstitious sailors.

The readiness of the ship was delayed, along with orders to sail until very late in December; the ship actually set sail from England on December 23rd. Bligh was not promoted to Captain even though he was in charge of the ship (according to records, this did not sit well with Bligh). There were no additional officers and no Marines for security.

Soon after setting sail, Bligh promoted Mr. Christian to Master of the Ship. The best time to cross Cape Horn at the bottom of South America is December through March; due to the delay in sailing, the Bounty arrived in April. After several weeks of failure to actually get around, the course was changed to Cape Town, Africa, where Mr. Christian borrowed money from Bligh for charitable causes, and then southern Australia, to finally arrive at Tahiti. There was only one offense that incurred corporal punishment during this voyage so far, and it was only a few days before Tahiti. And it also seemed there was no effort to pay back the loan by Mr. Christian.

The two botanists on board demanded that the ship stay in Tahiti much longer than a few weeks as planned, but almost five months. Mr. Christian and most of the crew stayed on the island enjoying the hospitality of the natives, treated like family, welcomed into the

Educating Noah…Travelin'

households, and relationships developed. Bligh lived on the ship.

Finally, after taking 10 months to get there five months to grow and load the breadfruit, the ship headed west to complete the charting and head home. Many of the crew had new tattoos, and many had adapted to the culture of the natives. After a few days at sea, Bligh berated Mr. Christian in front of the crew as a thief for not paying him back for the loan; Christian decided to leave the ship in a dory, and the crew decided to back Christian and take the ship. Bligh was then put in the dory with 18 loyal crew members and set off with some provisions.

Bligh and the loyal crew went from Tonga to Indonesia in this small boat in 48 days, they were starved and dehydrated, but did quite a distance in a very small boat and very limited provisions, Bligh did return to England two and a half years later.

Mr. Christian and the mutineers with a few still loyal to Bligh but could not leave with him due to the tiny boat, sailed back to Tahiti; stoked up on supplies, then to another Island, where they built a fort, did not assimilate with any people. A remaining small group, left with the ship to Pitcairn Island previously abandoned by the Polynesians, and divided the island into 9 equal shares; the natives they brought with them both men and women were not given any land, which of course led to constant warfare among the men, and the Bounty? It was burned, so the chances of other ships sighting her were eliminated. Pitcairn Island is only two by one mile in size. The remaining descendants are very proud of their heritage.

Normal activities, I went to the Margarita tasting, only three ½ size Margaritas, presentation seemed strained, the group did not congeal as well as other tastings, and of course the price no longer $15, but $20 with less tasting samples…

A Comedy show, a good clean actually funny comedian, Trivia, and dinner at another specialty restaurant Chez Jacque. Very French, including the waiter, Lynn had shredded duck, pumpkin soup, scallop Carpaccio; and crepe for dessert; I had scallops, cold pea soup, cheese appetizer, and apple pie for dessert. The other couple we dined with were Florida (originally from Chicago) former accountant, and 4th grade teacher, were very nice, and interesting.

Final late-night Trivia and another day gone, hopefully tomorrow won't be rainy and overcast.

Noah

Day 9, Saturday 9th; the ship is rolling, overcast, mid 70's, rain on and off all day. Again, last night, we turned our clocks ahead one hour and again we slept past 8!

I went up to the computer center, cleaned up my e-mails, answered the tax questions I could with the tax preparer, and promised the missing information would be coming for both ours and the estate for my mother when we return.

Table tennis had 14 couples signed up, and by twenty after the hour only six had finished. I tried to join Lynn at Trivia, but the team was full, so I opted to go on the hunt for more boat supplies…again, like pulling teeth, and after several locations and people, I came back empty handed.

A late morning cooking demonstration, the head chef and his souse chef did the program, they talked very fast, had heavy French accents, and no tasting…another disappointment.

We shared a table with another couple from Chicago, back to the room…It smelled like sewer gas, and we had to call the front desk to remedy it.

Another lecture "Giant Claws and Sugar Shells", I got there early, and watched, the first row filled up first, the seating capacity of the theatre is 620, then the "end cappers" couples that sit at the end of the rows, of the first 26 people, 7 couples were end cappers, then the rest filed in, old folks with canes trying to get past and then filling in just past the end cappers only to be brushed and stepped on by others trying to get a seat up close.

On the screen, there was a picture of a brown hairy, ugly squat, six-legged clawed mite; on top, the quote: "Are you lonely? Don't be; Demodex is a type of mite that lives on your face…friends forever."

The lecturer walked through the audience ten minutes prior to the talk, engaging people as to what they liked and didn't in the past talks. Very outgoing, friendly, and engaging. Now, here are the notes:

Flat worms, we are up the scale to bi-lateral symmetry, but first, Boobs. She showed a picture of two movie stars, one Brad Pitt with his shirt off, and an attractive brunette with cleavage showing. She states that evolution is selective and works on sexual reproduction, all traits are selective, being heavier for females, makes you more attractive because you are better suited to make babies, and reproduce.

Educating Noah...Travelin'

Once even humans are no longer sexually active, we deteriorate, become less attractive and become more susceptible to diseases and our bodies start breaking down.

Flat worms, the development of the tube, in one end, out the other, butt developed first! The Christmas tree worm is the fanciest and prettiest, to reproduce, most worms just release sperm and eggs into the water, lock and key, they find each other.

"In nature, it is always easier to be a male than a female"!

Anthropoids all have exoskeletons, have a full organ system, and usually the blood is blue. When arthropods age and develop, they molt, replacing the outside shell. The most important food source in the ocean is the krill. Swarms of krill have actually been sited from outer space.

Lobsters, have a green gland and many of the digestive organs, bladder, and labyrinth, intestines, all in the head, teeth are in the stomach. They are cannibalistic, and the male is highly territorial. When a female enters the male territory, he approaches her and fights, if she is stronger than him, she kills him and eats him, if she matches him, he takes her to his labyrinth, when she is ready to mate, she pees all over him, he stops fighting and mates, then she molts for 24 hours...if during this period another female enters the labyrinth, (she knows by the pee a female is molting), she will fight the molting female and eat her when she wins. The male...He is the dead-beat, he did his thing, he is off to establish a new territory and find another female.

Afternoon games, Lynn went to Cardio dance, then another lecture on Pitcairn Island, we will be anchored off the island Sunday for about six hours. Before going to lecture I met with Lynn to see if the sewer gas had been addressed, and no, it hadn't, another call, a maintenance man came, poured some cleaner down the drains, and said he would let the "boss" know about the smell; He did a good job, the smell did not return!

Pitcairn Island is actually a small grouping of islands, with Pitcairn being the only one occupied by the descendants of the Bounty Mutineers, and there are less than fifty people in total.

The island was named after a 15-year-old crew member (John Pitcairn) of the HMS Swallow, who was the first to site the island on

January 15th, 1790. There are many currents that surround the island, the early missionaries destroyed the carvings and any statues left behind by previous Polynesians. By the 1850's the population was at two hundred, but it is common for Polynesians to want to return to the island of their birth, so the population fluctuates. There are three cars total on the island, most commute on quad cycles. The roofs on all the buildings are oversized, this is to help funnel rain water, the only source of fresh water on the island. There is a small health office, no real hospital, no ability to treat major disease of accident.

Currently the grade school has only three children, when they graduate, they will go to New Zealand to a high school boarding school and tech, or college, and may or may not return.

Once a year there is Bounty day, when the island gathers to burn a replica of the Bounty in the sea. A cargo ship stops every month with supplies from New Zealand, if you want to visit the island you can have passage on this ship, it costs $3500/person, it is a 36-hour journey one way, with sparse accommodations. The island does see a cruise ship several times a year, and since there is no dock, a group comes out to the ship to sell souvenirs, carvings, and stamps. The Pitcairn scandal contributes to the 6-cell prison on the island. Many of the young girls and a few boys looked as though they had been abused, and investigation pursued and most if not all the men accused; judges, lawyers were sent and 6 men were convicted and sentenced to 7 years in prison, the last case was 20 years ago.

I checked out the tea time, which is every afternoon from 4-5; the entire Horizons area is set for about 300 people; I counted 30 that day. I am still on the hunt for supplies for the ship; I talked to a number of chefs, waiters, bartenders, and baristas and actually ended up with two small milk cartons!

Dinner, evening Trivia…1st Place! What do you call a rainbow at night? Moon Beam; what pop star's name is spelled out from Presbyterian? Britney Spears.

The evening show was the production cast singing and dancing with the band to a Beatles Mania theme.

My left ankle was swollen completely, making it hard to walk…the return of gout...arghhhhhhh!

Day 10 Sunday, March 10th

Educating Noah...Travelin'

It is again overcast, light rain predicted all day, Pitcairn Island anchorage. A small thirty-foot boat was out to meet the ship at 7:30 A.M., and the Pitcairns boarded and set up in the lounge to sell their wares. The rain came and went, at times pretty heavy, and it did not clear all day; at 2 P.M., they were gone, and we were off into a fog bank with light rain.

The craft market actually opened early, so yep, I met Lynn, and we cruised the 12 to 15 tables, postcards, magnets, wood carvings, handy crafts, and honey. I got away with only two carvings, and Lynn bought something else. Lynn went off to carpet bowling, and I went to the lecture presented by one of the residents of this island. Here is a summation of what he had to say:

This island is the least populous jurisdiction in the world and is on the United Nations committee list of non-self-governing territories with a current population of 38. All the residents live on the north side of the island; humpback whales come from August through December; the supply cargo ships arrive four times a year from New Zealand. The island depends on the European Union for support, currently to pay for the school teacher, the policeman, the doctor, and the magistrate; they are quite concerned with Brexit. The income level is quite low. Most are self-sufficient with gardens, the volcanic soil is rich in nutrients (cabbage, lettuce, bananas, arrowroot, sugar cane) and fishing (line fishing only for residents only), supplies paid for by selling honey, crafts, working for others, and govt. Subsidies. There are no dogs on the island, just cats, chickens, rats, and birds. Power is provided by a diesel generator power on 0500, off at 2200.

Fourteen to sixteen cruise ships visit per year, at Christmas everyone gets together on the island, exchange gifts and then have a large shared meal. They celebrate Bounty Day on the 23rd of January as the day of their ancestors. Power and internet are the most expensive items on the island, there is no tax, and there is some minor crime. (this was kind of hard to believe...38 people. Everyone knows everyone!!)

When the island was first settled by the mutineers; Fletcher was the first sailor killed by the Polynesian men who were part of the party that did not get a share of land. Fighting continued among the men until the Polynesian women killed the Polynesian men ending the killings.

The supplies brought in are the cost in New Zealand plus 35% for shipping charges.

I went to a Hot Stones Therapy seminar at the health club; I was given a sample treatment and told that one treatment is worth five regular massage appointments. I came back to tell Lynn I got her a session for our anniversary; all she had to do was make an appointment, which she immediately did. Games in the afternoon, worked on the ship, mid-afternoon lecture on "Giant Brains and Tentacles; here are the notes:

Up the chain of evolution, mollusks, to clams to snails; Cone snails are the most toxic, 97 different toxins, they eat fish, have a hypodermic needle tongue, and are more responsible for human deaths in the world than sharks!

The Nautilus can have up to 100 tentacles, and can travel in excess of 20 mph. Squids can have from 10-100 tentacles, have the largest eyes of all mollusks. When they mate, thousands get together and "get together" in one big party!

Octopuses can easily change colors and color patterns, have three hearts, a brain that compares to a dog, 8 tentacles, and, a beak, the only hard part of the creature. They are solitary, learn from other octopuses, and hate astro-turf!

When it comes to mating, the male octopus engages the female, they manipulate one another, and then the male injects a sperm sack, goes off and dies. The female goes off, tends to the eggs, this can be from 24 hours to 4 years depending on condition or type, when the young can fend for themselves, she drifts away and dies.

Musical poster trivia…30 questions, plays, movies, and musicals, the winning team had a perfect score! Off to an early Broadway production show, dinner, another trivia…second place. What gives plants the green color? Chlorophyll; What US animal responsible for rabies in the USA? Raccoon. Two US states that end in "Y"; New Jersey, Kentucky.

We went up for the first session of the Rock and Roll Dance Party, then called it quits, advance the clocks again 1 hour, my ankle was also back to normal…hopefully a new day will bring sun!

Day 11, March 11th Monday, another day at sea. Since we lost an hour and our internal clocks were not "informed" we awoke at a bit

Educating Noah…Travelin'

past 8. Opened the curtains…☹ windy, overcast, and raining…again!

Turn on the TV to get a weather update…nothing; no news is good news? There is another mandatory drill at 10:15, no life jackets required, but everyone must check into their muster station.

Breakfast and we agreed to meet at the muster station, I returned the stapler I borrowed, checked on the ship's registration for the boat building contest, and then went to the computer room to see if I could get a forecast for Easter Island. We had heard rumors early on the cruise about many ships could not land on Easter Island due to weather, then others dispelled the rumor, I need to check myself, the forecast for the next 5 days for Easter Island was mid 70's, both humidity and temperature, and partly cloudy, hopefully this cloud bank will lift and we can get out on the deck!

Muster, only one couple didn't show up in our group; there was a presentation offering a $250.00 credit to one participant from Oceania to sign up for another cruise. We skipped morning games, outside off and on, heavy rains and gusty winds all day, so nothing on deck and no sun again!

Biology lecture, she is that good; I include her Facebook and e-mail if any interest: Facebook: Naturalist Gloeta; E-mail: gloetamassie@gmail.com, notes as follows:

We have moved up the biological chain to spiky skinned animals, Starfish, sea urchins, (star fish curled over) and sea cucumbers (curled around). Various curious and beautiful examples of all three were shown on the projection screen.

Starfish don't have brains; have hydro-circular system and tube feet with eyes on the feet. To move, water is taken in and then projected out the feet to propel them and move. They can grow back arms, as long as the center is not damaged.

Sea Urchins are herbivores and eat algae and kelp; they reproduce quickly and are kept in check by otters and other animals.

Sea cucumbers are the vacuum cleaners of the ocean; they actually eat all the "poop" of all the other animals, and produce sand as their excrement!

Afternoon games, and then our first cooking class: "All Things Roman"; where we all had a work space and equipment, watched our instructor then went to our site to do the cooking ourselves. What did we make? Fresh egg pasta, Rosemary Grilled Lamb Chops; Bucatini All 'Amatriciana; Spaghetti Alla Carbonara; Fettuccine Alfredo; and Mousse Di Ricotta. Yes! All of this in two hours! And, WOW! Simple, and extremely good! I can safely say everyone enjoyed the class, the food, and the instructor, well organized, well-paced, and delicious! (We did get the recipes to take home.)

We were full from our meals, so no dinner tonight! Evening Trivia, we took 1st Place! What is a female goose called? Pen: The launch of the first air balloon took place where? Paris.

The evening show was a magician, the show was O.K. but half way through the arthritis, and gout got me, Lynn joined me as I hobbled back to the cabin, my left ankle twice its size, knees and the other ankle along with lower back screaming; shower, pain killers, took some baking soda water to try to nullify the gout, set the clocks ahead again one hour and done! (This wet rainy weather is getting to me!)

Day 12, March 12^{th,} the last sea day before Easter Island.

I opened up the drapes, and it was ready…PARTLY CLOUDY!! There was some blue sky! Mid-70s temperature and humidity, 15-20 mph winds, but the sun!

Lynn was off to her Chat and needlepoint, me to the Biologist presentation, and here are the notes:

Vertebrae's: The first are called Sea Squirts. These organisms are actually born with a spine, but as they mature, they shed it, but they do maintain a mouth and butt!

Fish are next; cold-blooded vertebrates have bone or cartilage skeletons. There are 25,000 species, 41% fresh water, 58% seawater, and less than 1% both. The majority have scales.

If the fish looks like it has been "run over flat" like Ray fish, they are bottom feeders; as they become longer and thinner, the closer to the surface they are found.

How do fish avoid being eaten?

1. Blend in…we are shown slides of fish using colors to blend in, like flounders, sea horses, and other fish.

2. Hide...find coral or caves or holes, or just join thousands of others in a school and not lag or lead in the group.

3. Visual...a universal "no go or stay away" color is yellow. Bright yellow striped fish are poisonous, bees, Yellow Jackets, and Tigers given as examples. Others may have markings indicating an eye somewhere else on the body, or much larger to confuse a predator.

4. Be fast...flying fish can reach a speed of 45 mph!

One note on the puffer fish: it has a toxin that is currently being explored as an extremely effective pain reliever even in cancer, and it is effective immediately.

Reproduction in fish...most fish are promiscuous, broadcast spawning! The most aggressive sperm is successful; she called it "spear warfare."

Pike fish and Sea Horses, the males carry the eggs, when courting sea horses "dance" with each other (one male and one female) in the morning and at night, now it is possible that if the male wonders off, goes "clubbing" and finds a different female, he could excuse himself, step outside, and actually abort his babies, and have a good time with the floozy, the problem though, when he comes home and dances with his mate, she can detect the change in condition, and end the relationship!

We joined in ship games, a cooking demonstration by the senior chef, and his souse chef preparing: sea bass, duck Foie Gras, shrimp, and crepe suzette; I got the recopies for us and daughters.

I caught the nice warm sun to intensify my tan, more games, a lecture on Area 51, and information that was not classified. A few notes:

All the employees since the start in the 50's is transported to the area via aircraft called "Janet Flight's" which continue today, usually from Las Vegas and undisclosed California cities.

The public and "others" were told these flights were for weather observation. Loved ones and others are told cover stories as to where and what employees do. There have been crashes near the base; they remain unreported and cleaned up. The problems with the U-2 were they had a single cockpit, no trainers, and because of the altitude, the pilots had to breathe pure oxygen.

The U-2 was replaced by the A-12 by a firm called Skunk Works, but that aircraft was still radar-detectable. The current SR-71 Blackbird has little to know radar detection due to design and "saw tooth" placement distorting radar signals so they do not return the radar signal.

Soviet MIGs have been acquired along with China aircraft with similar "weather missions" and are currently being disassembled and looked at in this still very active secret base. The location of all satellites is tracked, and whenever Area 51 is within view, nothing is left outside of the hangers that should not be seen.

According to the lecturer, project Blue Book, the Air Force inquiry into UFOs determined, after investigating 12,600 reports, that there were no UFOs. However, this lecturer, who was a pilot at Area 51, did see strange lights along with others that could not be explained.

An Easter Island lecture provided more background on the island, most of the Moai (statues) were tumbled, destroyed, along with the platforms, some theories say it was one warring tribe against the other, others claim that since the life did not get better for the people, they became disenchanted with the "Mana"…The people were cannibalistic, the island was raided and the natives were enslaved, of the 2000 taken only 15 returned, Chili Annexed the island in 1888 to claim the ocean to where it sits in the Pacific.

There is an airstrip, built by the USA, then closed by the socialist leader in Chile eight years later, then extended by the French, and is now the most isolated airport on earth.

Dinner was at the Red Ginger specialty restaurant. It was exceptional. I had sushi, a watermelon and tenderloin salad, and scallops with sea urchin, something I have wanted to try, and it was about the same taste as a scallop, all expertly prepared and presented. The other couple was from America; good conversation, a pleasant experience. I did order sake; when I ordered it on the Celebrity Cruise line, I had about 16 oz. for about $8…here, I got about 6 ounces for $30…..so much for guessing prices!

We finished the evening with a 50's-60's musical Trivia where our team did not place☹; set clocks an hour ahead, tomorrow is the big day…Easter Island! (Hanga Roa).

Day 13, Wednesday, March 13th.

The day was partly cloudy, with a 10-12 mph wind, the sun peeking out; looking out of our veranda, we could see the island. Since we lost another hour last night, we woke tired. The gout not going away for me, but the wetness and arthritis were better. We filled out the visas we needed to take with us, got the excursion tickets out of the safe, had a quick breakfast, and went down to the waiting area. We had tickets for tour #1 and tender 1. It looked like ½ the ship was there waiting. Fifteen minutes after the time we were supposed to disembark, a new person walked up to the stage and announced that the harbor master refused to land our tenders, claiming the harbor was too rough for us to tender in. The captain drove down the coast and re-approached a half hour later, and the result was the same.

As with us missing the island of Madagascar, the captain made the announcement that we would move on...sorry. THE SAME CRAP, NEVER A CONTINGENCY PLAN!

At least the captain did circle the island and did point out 8 of the Moai, even though we were offshore a good 300-400 yards. That was the morning; we left for Peru at about 1 P.M., with promises to get the money paid for excursions returned.

I worked on the boat; it now has a name, "Bunny," and I actually finished it up before going to bed. We attended a couple of trivia, some games, and another lecture by the biologist. Some of the facts she shared:

In the fish world, the bigger and more mature, the females have better eggs. In clown fish, the dominant largest female is the guard, defender, and most aggressive; the 2nd largest is the male, and he guards the eggs.

Sharks predate dinosaurs; they are actually less deadly than lightning strikes, rattlesnakes, bee stings, and toilet bowls!

Sharks have three eyelids, the scales that cover their bodies are from the same material as their teeth, and many sharks will go through 20,000-30,000 teeth in a lifetime! They do not have an air bladder, and their liver is 30% of their body; lateral lines on the body surface enable a shark to "feel" electrical impulses produced by movement as an example, we as humans can feel about 1.5 volts; a shark...1/1,000,000 volt, yes, they know where you are!!

Lastly, the female's skin is 7X thicker than the male skin, needed to sustain the bites from the males when mating! Yikes!!

I was depressed most of the day and tried to keep to myself; both islands I really wanted to encounter were no longer within reach; this would be the last Oceania cruise!

Day 14, Thursday, March 14th

It was partly cloudy, mid to low 70's, another day at sea, actually the seventh day at sea. I was able to finish Bunny, two anchors, and lines, flag, and oars for the tender and confirmed the two other couples as crew. Lynn had the hot stone massage I promised her for our anniversary, games, and trivia.

There was an event where passengers challenged the officers at various games for game points. We were both able to get some sun-baking time in, and we also took in the early clean comedian show. This was the day for our last specialty restaurant included in the cruise, Toscana Restaurant. We shared the table with two other couples, conversation went well; both Lynn and I asked for the pasta and main course to be served in ½ portions; everything was perfectly presented and prepared; they did serve our anniversary cake; we had asked for everything to be pushed up a bit so that we could leave at 8:20, less than a two-hour dinner! We were able to leave at 8:30 and made it late to trivia, but our gang kept our seats open; they were only on question 5 when we got there, and we took 1st place in the session! What is the periodic symbol for arsenic? As; what is the square root of 1444? 38.

We stopped into the late-night Cabaret for a one-woman show singing "Queens of Rock and Roll. It was a good show that ended the day.

Day 15, March 15th

Another day at sea, any day at sea, the weather is not posted. On the TV, there will be a running script giving only current conditions. In stepping outside, windy white-caps, lower 70's.

I went up to the computer room to clean up my e-mails, and the attendant told me it may not work. We were too far out at sea, and until we got close to Peru, it would be hard to get a signal…he was right. It would not load, so I just made a note to check Sunday, the day before disembarkation, to check for e-mails on that last excursion I

Educating Noah...Travelin'

booked in Lima and clean up any e-mails.

Lynn went to the needle point chat; I attended a lecture on radio-controlled pilot-less aircraft.

We actually know so little; the first radio-controlled aircraft was an anti-Zeppelin aircraft in 1917! The biggest problem is landing. In the USA, it was a N-9 Bomb called the Kettering Bug, and launched on a catapult.

During WWII, 15,000 drones were contracted by the US govt.; The company was bought by Northrop in 1952. By the way, one of the workers on the assembly line was a woman named Norma Jeanne Mortenson (Marilyn Monroe), who was photographed by an actor/correspondent Ronald Reagan, from which two destinies were changed.

There have been many different types and evolving UAVs, with names and models like Fire Bee, Lightning Bug, Compass Cookie; Tadiran Mastiff (Israeli); Bumble Bug, Dessert Hawk, Fire Scout, Sentinel, Hunter, Predator, and Reaper.

These aircraft range in size and payloads from the Desert Hawks, which are launched by hand with very limited range, to the Global Hawk, which is about the same size as a Boeing 737!

The current (Known) Predator has a 48-foot wingspan and can fly up to 30 hours, easily from California to Australia!

Finally, it was time for the ship design and building contest. Lynn met me in the room and first, as promised, showed Bunny to the front desk! We showed her off, then took her up to the pool deck and were able to put her undercover on a table. Mamie and Henry came dressed for the part. She was "packing" as a security officer. Henry had a small chef hat, and he did not bring samples!! Here is a rundown on Bunny:

Crew: Noah Borkenhagen, Captain; Lynn Borkenhagen, 1st mate; Mark Pollet, First Officer; Jane Pollet, Engineer; Henry Mark Chef; and Mamie Mark Security.

Registry: Majuro, Marshall Islands...The reason, the same as all other Oceania ships, is also to avoid excess regulations and taxation ramifications.

Type of sailing vessel: Catamaran

Proposed Itinerary: Polynesian Islands; Ports and harbors. During

Noah

tourist season: Cater to scuba, snuba, and snorkel excursions with glass bottom boat capabilities; during non-tourist season, transport supplies and provide emergency medical evacuations due to the shallow draft of the ship.

Building Expenses incurred and Proposed Annual Maintenance Expense: Tears and Begging: We encountered the least help on this ship than any other, finally able to borrow scissors for a few hours; after multiple requests finally obtained a roll of packaging tape and regular tape, we used bottle opener for wine as a knife, bought a small scissors on the last island to put her together.

Special features: The sail was shaped like a Polynesian style with an up-sweeping lower boom, a propeller and rudder that turned, convertibility from tourist to cargo, a lifeboat with paddles, an enclosed wheelhouse with wheel, two anchors with rope, and a ladder to provide access when not fitted for cargo.

A total of 4 boats appeared with wind speeds of 19-26 MPH, open deck warnings on the ship, cloudy, 72 degrees, and good pool action. Despite conditions, we were asked to transport 6 cans of soda from forward to back the length of the pool and return. We also were to power our ships.

I volunteered to go first, but due to my knees and legs, I climbed back into the pool and kicked it all the way down and back. We had collapsed the sail, and there was no difficulty with the task; we were not given the opportunity to transport 12 cans, but yes, we passed.

The second ship made it all the way, pushed from the outside; the third ship first dumped the cargo, then fell part; the fourth ship, a cargo ship, well-constructed, actually had duct tape (they claim they got it from reception) and was tested in their tub?) It was well constructed, well made, and easily passed. It was close, but both Bunny and the cargo ship took first place! We all got Oceania baseball hats!

The "rain on the parade"? I found that the parameters set were not adhered to; we were to explain where our ships were registered and why, which was not asked of all ships, just one. We were not able to provide the pros and cons of our ships to the judging officers and show any special features or considerations to the officers or the crowd. We were told, "The bigger, the better." Bunny was twice the size of any of the competitors in height, width, and length; this of all the trials and judgments was the hardest, and the reward, the least; they made it as hard as possible to get the tools and materials more than any of all the past ships, again, another Oceania downfall.

We signed up for games in the interior in the afternoon, and now over 40 couples playing, so the lines to sign up start 15-20 minutes before the event; always the same couples in line first, aisles are blocked, viewing of others playing walled off by the same people.

I went to a magic up-front show; the magician showed a few tricks we could share. I also managed to score a little trick card pack!

Up on deck, one small section of the sun did come out, then disappeared behind the clouds, the lounges on the top deck all taken down, a few on the lower deck remained under the deck, 1/3 of them occupied by the same people who spend most every sea day reading, in the shelter of the deck above… BORING!!!

They also show movies in the theatre, and they have TV in the rooms, so I guess that those that don't do anything at home feel at home? And how much a day did this cruise cost to explore the South Pacific?

Dinner, another trivia, 2nd place, what fruit is called the Persian apple? Peach, who was the proverbial victim in the game of Clue? Mrs. Smith.

The shows were just singers, Lynn was tired, my gout was subsiding but still there, and the baking soda water was doing its job, so back to the cabin, bed by 10!

Day 16, Saturday the 16th of March

It was partly sunny, with low 70s mid-60s humidity and windy 20-25 mph winds. I filled out the declaration for customs in Peru, obtained the ship credits/ ledger to ensure the charges were correct, and started the preparation for discharge on Monday. I thought it would be interesting for those who have not cruised or a reminder for us as to the high-end selection offered by these floating high-end restaurants. With a few credits for previous cruises, we were given three reservations at three different specialty restaurants this cruise; none open before 6:30 P.M. There is usually a small line at the opening, but the restaurants are usually full by 7:30.

The morning was dominated by "Marina's Country Fair," where various departments provide games for tickets, which are turned in for the possibility of winning a prize, ranging from Champaign to towels or bathrobes. The games include naming the flag, ring toss over bottles of alcohol, identifying food by shape, identifying the officers, knocking cups off a ping pong table, identifying wine hints of flavor, tying knots, and passing a washer on a wooden handle through a mounted wire without making an electrical connection. Even though the two of us had gathered quite a few tickets,…no winners!

The wind picked up, the temperature dropped, and after 15 minutes of sun, the rain came, so I and about 20 other people left the outside decks to join the rest of the passengers and crew inside for the remainder of the day.

Afternoon games, and another biologist discussion on "Llama, I lichen you lost!"

Her discussions usually start out with a reference to another animal species, then the main species, and usually, at the end, a "tickler" for the next talk.

This day, she started with guinea pigs, described how many families in Peru keep them in little houses outside, and yes, they eat them; she described that they were very boney, and the taste I had when we were there last time did not have the "bone" problem. However, it did taste a bit like rabbit or squirrel.

The camel's origin is in North America; some evolved into llamas and alpacas, and the ones migrating to Africa stayed camels. North American originals became extinct, which may have been the result of the last climate change.

There is currently research being conducted on the Nanobodies the llamas have that have the ability to cross the blood-brain barrier and maybe a cure for Alzheimer's; experimentation on mice is presently being conducted.

Llamas and alpacas are herd-based animals, dominant male with 8-10 females' the male establishes two territories, one for grazing and the other for sleeping.

Offspring are treated differently; at 4 months, the males are kicked out of the herd by the father; the females are kicked out of the herd by the mothers just before rut season.

Sloths, there are two-toed and three-toed. They used to be about twice the size of a current human being and have the slowest metabolism rate, requiring only 200-400 calories per day. Their body temperature can range from 80-100 degrees (F), they have three stomachs, and from eating to eliminating food, it takes 60 days!

Once a week, the sloth leaves its tree to defecate on the ground in a hole it digs and then covers up; then returns to the tree; the sloth grows algae on its body, which supplements its diet when it eats the algae. The enemy of the sloth is the Harpies' eagle!

I also attended a lecture on "How to prevent your stroke." His contention is that high blood pressure is completely preventable, highly recommends the Mediterranean diet.

It takes walking 35 miles to lose one pound; it is what goes in that needs to be monitored. We need antioxidants, limit meat to three times a week, reduce egg yolks, reduce dairy products, and lower your weight to recommended guidelines.

When asked how much longer we would live, he replied, "My concern is not how long one lives. It is the quality of life."

He recommended that we have the Rennin/Aldosterone level and B-12 levels checked next annual check-up. After the show, they paraded the entire ship staff; I believe a third were cooks and chefs!

We had dinner in the main dining room with our trivia team, all eight of us; one couple arranged everything, we walked past the line, and arrangements were made to speed up the delivery so we would be out in only two hours for our final trivia game that night. The conversation was enjoyable, and the food, of course, was exceptional. It was a nice cross-section, one couple from New Zealand, the other from Hawaii and us, and the final couple from the Midwest USA.

Second place at trivia: How old was Michael Jackson when the Jackson Five had 4 hits in a row? 11; What do sailors cross to change from a pollywog to a shellback? Equator

We attended the band show on Abba and then called it a night!

Day 17, March 17th

It was partly cloudy. The program said daybreak was at 8:00, but it was bright at 7. This is the last day on the ship; we will be leaving tomorrow morning a bit after 8. The "Rethink the Crepe" cooking class was at 10 AM, so we decided to skip breakfast.

The ship's internet is working again, but the printer is down. I cleared up the junk e-mails and then proceeded to the culinary station for the class. There were about 20 participants, and it was the same head chef instructor, Annie Copps; she was concise and had everything set up at the various workstations with the help of a crew of three assistants. An upfront demonstration of the first steps or dish, then we went back to our workstations, two to a station, to duplicate what the chef had explained. There was a problem with supplies, so instead of just crepes, we had steak Diane, a salad and dressing, and a chocolate mousse dessert.

We first made the dessert, and after preparing, we all gathered around the chef to see the salad and dressing while the crew cleaned our stations, put our mousse in the oven, and set up for the next course; this continued throughout the two hours, and we ate our results...there were no complaints, using chef's tips and knowledge was enlightening, and why just so much of this or that makes such a difference, I would highly recommend any of these courses, because this was art!

With the two-hour extremely interesting class, we were set for food until our final supper after 6:30.

I got another, probably a final dose of sun...yeah, I'm brown for a while. I expanded on my critique of the cruise, and Oceania tried to get it printed, but the printer was still "down." I talked to the computer guy, and it seems he gets the lack of support others get from the main office; what a shame!

We played final games; one last trivia...what was the first American product introduced into the Soviet Union? Pepsi

We cashed in our points; Lynn got in line ½ hour early; she was 6th; we got the following: 2 shirts, a visor, 2 purse hooks, and two needlepoint kits; this was for a total of 220 points, so we gained 0-3 points per participation in events.

Attended the final farewell variety show; about 500 attended of the 900 plus on board, and it was a good cross-section of the entertainment. Dinner at the café, then pack, luggage out by 9 P.M. weighed and ready finished the day.

Day 18, March 18th, Monday

We are scheduled to leave the ship between 8:00 and 8:20 AM.

Educating Noah...Travelin'

We have to pick up our passports on the way off the ship, pick up our luggage, proceed through customs with our filled-out declarations, and go to the terminal to find our "Private Cooking Class with a Local Family in Lima." The morning on the ship went great; we said goodbye to some new friends, had our last ship breakfast, headed down to the room, picked up our carry-ons, and went off to the auditorium. No wait to pick up our passports, and we only waited 20 minutes for our group to be called to exit the ship.

Our luggage was sorted under a tent right next to the ship; we were told that vendors and cabs could not enter the port, so we asked and found the bus to the terminal/front gate. It was a 20-minute ride, and the terminal/front gate was just that, a one-block cul-de-sac, where the bus dumped everyone without shelter, bathrooms, or benches, bus after bus dumping people off, and being "hawked" by cab drivers. Now, before we were dumped off the bus, we were again warned about pick-pockets and set a price for a cab before getting in!

After waiting a good 45 minutes, I asked one of the drivers if he would call the number for me, and I would pay him $5.00 for the call. After the second attempt, Viator stated that the family would pick me up at 9:30-9:45. I thanked them and gave the phone and $5 to the driver with my thanks.

10:00 Lynn needed to use the restroom. One of the ship personnel helping to empty the buses worked with a bus driver to let her use the bus toilet...very nice. After another 15 minutes, Lynn wasn't looking good; the heat was getting to her, the upper 80s with matching humidity. I called again, but this time, they denied that arrangements had been made and that I would have to take a cab, "It is just 40 minutes away." I told him to cancel it, and he said it was the same day, and we could not, so the guy who had let me use his phone got the job. We loaded into the cab and had the driver call to get the address. We were told the cost would be $30.00.

We saw a good part of Callao and the sister city Lima in the 50-minute drive to the house. We were met by the owner; it turned out to be a bed and breakfast owned by a brother, Johnny, and sister, Amelia.

We dropped off our suitcases and carry-on in the area under the open staircase, used the bathroom, introduced ourselves, and talked a bit. Then, a cab was called, and we went with Johnny to the farmers market.

Noah

This was quite an extensive market, "fresh from the farm and sea," per Johnny; we explored the different vendors as we picked up fish, chicken, vegetables, and spices. The chicken was quartered in front of us, fish filleted, and any fruit or vegetable we did not recognize was identified for us. He paid for the ingredients for our meal, and we piled into another cab and went back home.

We cleaned up, put on chefs' hats and aprons, and started working with Amelia; Johnny's main job was to translate. We started by showing her how she started the chicken in a hot pan, then the fish stirred with a little water to clean, and then put it in the freezer. We were given cutting boards and knives to start chopping the vegetables, onions, peppers, and cilantro, cleaned the potatoes, and shucked the peas.

The meal, after all, was from scratch. She showed us how to crème a sauce for the rice taste in the various pots to see if too hot or salty. Then it was time for Pisco Sours: three shots of Pisco, one shot each of lime juice and sugar cane syrup, and ½ egg white per drink, in a shaker full of ice. Oh, yes, Lynn and I both loved it!!

One note: to tell if the Pisco liqueur is good, you shake the bottle roundly. If bubbles form, it is cheap. If a tornado forms in the bottle, it is good.

Dinner was served on two plates, one a large ceviche salad, then a large plate with a quarter of chicken beans, rice, corn, and sauce to taste. He did also bring out a sauce with spices. We could not finish our plates; everything was perfect. Of course, Johnny, Amelia, and the helper joined. (All three of them were ½ our size, and they all finished their plates; go figure!)

We rested for a while, then we got directions to the shopping mall, four blocks away…we needed to walk off that meal!

The mall turned out to be beneath the street at the oceanfront. It consisted of typical high-end tourist' shops, so we just basically window shopped, briefly met with a couple we knew on the ship (small world), and then headed back home.

When we returned, I had a beer, bought some coffee for a friend, and our host made arrangements for a cab to the airport hotel, where we had a room waiting.

Another 50-minute cab ride, $30 bucks with tip, and delivered right in front of the door. This hotel is within a couple 100 feet of the air terminal. We checked in and paid our money…they put in a $50.00 amenities fee and that was to be refunded after the room was checked. (They did refund the $50 when we checked out)

It was 5 P.M., we found our room, crashed for a couple hours, took showers, and waited, and our flight was scheduled for 1:30 A.M.

We left the hotel at 10 P.M., 3 ½ hours ahead of take-off, but this is an unfamiliar foreign airport; always "difficulties." We found the appropriate kiosk to check in. It would not take my passport, it would not take the flight code, so we got in line. The Disney line wasn't open, and nothing before 3 hours of the flight, at 10:35 it opened.

We were called up, and she had problems, also. I handed her the itinerary with flights and codes…she tried twice, then excused herself with our passports in hand and drifted down to another agent, where together they spent another ten minutes figuring things out. She finally returned and put two luggage tags on, one in large letters indicating the USA. She then proceeded to tell us we would have to transfer our luggage to Mexico City when we landed.

Went through security, wanded, had to take off my shoes (the guy in front of me didn't), and had to take out my computer (No signs), but I got through. We proceeded to immigration, waited in line, and then halfway through, we were told to go to another line. Seems that only two of the 16 officers were able to process Americans and Canadians off a cruise ship. It took these two guys twice as long to process as the regular ones, another 20 minutes! At 11:45, we found our gate and claimed a seat; our flight was now 1:40; we hoped everything would work out from there!

We actually took off at 1:40; the flight was about 6 hours with strong tailwinds. We landed in Mexico City, Mexico; we had to fill out our immigration cards, we had to go through immigration, physically transfer luggage after it was all scanned and reviewed by the Mexican government, walk that through to another conveyor, and then find our gate, which when finally posted was changed 15 minutes later to the other side of the terminal…welcome to Mexico!

The flight to Chicago from Mexico City was a bit above 5 hours; my trusted traveler got X'ed out, so I had to go through an abbreviated line. However, most coming to America had to go through at least 30 minutes of waiting in line for immigration with passport checks and

Noah

screenings!

A bus ride and catching the bus went very well. Uber showed up quickly, and we were home by 5:30. Tiffany called and said she had a boiled dinner for us for supper!

We brought up luggage; it had been 33 hours since both of us had more than a few bits or spurts of sleep, and we were in bed by 7:30; another adventure was done!

Noah

    The next major event was my left shoulder replacement. I worked the system, called in, followed all the rules, and had it done on April 10th! Now, the week before, Lynn tried some foot supports and threw out her back; remedy per her, 6-8 weeks of chiropractic work, she is using a stroller around the house.

Educating Noah...Travelin'

I moved into my room two weeks after the follow-up appointment; the bandage is now gone, stitches dissolve under glue now, no more pulling stitches! Four more weeks of sling before OT gets me ...it is going to be a very boring spring!

Lynn got progressively worse. It got to a point where she could not sit any longer. We got the CAT scan and MRI, and she was to have the operation. Got authorization from Medicare on June 10th, 7 A.M.

I fired the Chiropractor and am negotiating the charges since she didn't seem to notice that Lynn was not improving but actually getting worse... I am also going stir-crazy. I called up an old friend of Perry, my brother-in-law, and got the info to call a used truck dealer in Illinois looking for people to drive back cars bought in Canada. I called "Chip" and arranged a date; the interview and hiring took 10 minutes!! All I need to do now is wait for the call...hopefully, OT will not keep me long!

End of June, Lynn had her operation, incision 2 ½ inches about that far above the butt crack. The doctor removed about a ¼ inch of vertebra and relieved the pressure on the nerve. Lynn spent the night picking her up the next morning, and she couldn't believe the immediate difference. She walked the next day after the recovery. Stitches out next week. I changed her dressing every night and waterproofed the old one before the shower.

I made a run for Chip! Started at 3AM, took a taxi to the airport, flew to O'Hare in Chicago, transferred to another plane, and flew to Winnipeg, Ontario, took a cab to the sale lot, picked up the truck, and headed back. The truck was low on fuel. I checked the tires (low tire pressure light on) and tried to check the oil, but the dipstick was stuck...However, the gauges indicated no problem, so when I filled up, I bought a quart of oil, just in case. Customs couldn't find my boss, so I sat there for ½ hour until they finally found me and gave me permission and a passport to cross back into the USA. Had to fill up 5 more times (It gets only 6-7 miles per gallon) and did have to add that quart of oil. Checked tires each time and grabbed some food at the stations; no dome lights, so directions were no good. I got lost in Illinois, stopped at five different gas stations, and had no maps anywhere. No one except one person knew where Grayslake was, even though it was within 20 miles! Finally arrived (838 miles), it was just before 4 A.M.; put the paperwork under the seat, keys in the gas door, called the cab, and back home by a little after 5 AM. I slept till

10:30, called Chip to see if there were any problems, and let him know that I would be available in two weeks for any more runs.

I was tired of working the desk at DAV, especially when I was mainly just backup, so I went to employee health, pushed to get released to drive, went up to Ortho, talked to the nurses (I know most of them now), had a letter/order written, and they had the doctor sign, took back to health, and they cleared me to drive again, done!

It is now the beginning of August, and both of us are well on the road to recovery; mine is supposed to be 5-6 months, Lynn's 4-5 months! Argggghhh bored out of my mind. We are again sharing house duties (she's helping again). OT released me on July 9th. and I finally finished the estate taxes, a nightmare with this trust… I believe trusts are just another method for lawyers and accountants to make money! I've been driving once a week for the DAV again. I am also now with the 6 Cities Veterans Group. We will be offering a free bus trip for veterans to the capitol for a day's tour of a veteran museum, the capitol, and a museum. I am in the set-up stage and spent a Saturday morning begging to get support from people.

I made another "Chip" run from Halifax, N.S., to Chicago. My first flight was delayed, but I worked with the staff and got on another flight. The second flight was also delayed three hours…that should have been an omen…arrived in Halifax the next morning at 0200. Got a room up and took a cab to the yard, arriving at 0900 sharp. Had to have the truck towed from the lot for a battery, then broke down again on the highway and had it towed again to another repair shop where the new drained wrecked battery was replaced along with the alternator.

My phone and GPS do not work in Canada!! I vowed to fix that when I got home; I went through a very heavy fog bank and two extremely hard cloud bursts with, at best, wipers. Disoriented by vague maps four times, given wrong directions once, and finally arrived at Chip's 0230 Thursday AM (I started there at 1300 Monday), drove home, and off to bed. Friday and Saturday found and ordered a phone and GPS that will work in Canada!

I have also set up and confirmed the next adventures, confirmed flights, and transfers. With what we have coming up is October 25-November 10, Israel and the Suez Canal, all excursions booked and paid; February 7th-16th, 2020, a Caribbean cruise with Norwegian; July

Educating Noah...Travelin'

8th-23rd 2020, Eastern Europe with Transylvania extension; and August 28th-Sepember 8th, a Great Lakes Cruise. So, with the exercise, I haven't been just goofing off all this time!

Bored, ready for another adventure, I called up Chip and asked for a "short" assignment; I was told to show up at the sales lot in Grayslake, Ill. at 0700 on Tuesday, August 13th, the airline tickets and rail boarding pass were sent Monday, via e-mail. I got there a bit before 7, and another driver came shortly after. He was picked up first to go to O'Hare. My cab came shortly after and off to Milwaukee.

Milwaukee to Minneapolis, Minneapolis to Edmonton, Canada. I arrived a little after two in the afternoon. The guy next to me was there first and decided both armrests for him and him alone, and he was up and down with various electronic which train station, so I showed him the ticket, another ½ hour's cab drive to the train station, and I was dropped off...the station doesn't open till 5 P.M. lucky it was sunny and warm, only a bit over two hours to wait!

One other guy was there, so we struck up a conversation. He was cross-country biking. He had his bike in a box and was going back to his home in New York. Good conversation, we shared stories, and at 4:30 joined by a woman to share her story. Time went by quickly. The station was opened at five; we were then told our train was delayed by four, yes, FOUR hours...

The train arrived at 11:10, we boarded, and we were off by 11:45 P.M. The seating was not comfortable, but I think I fell asleep a few hours later. We arrived at my stop, Wainwright, at 5:30 A.M.

I was the only passenger getting off there; the station was closed, and this downtown of 1,500 people was a ghost town at this hour. I asked the conductor about a cab, he found me one and told me he would be at the station in 10-15 minutes, the train then took off.

I saw a Dodge van approaching the station, opened the back door, and asked if he was in the cab; he confirmed. I gave him the address of the motel my boss had reserved, and ten minutes later, we were there. He had no meter and would not take credit cards, so I asked. He said $7.00 Canadian, so I gave him $10 US. He was happy, I was there, and off he went.

The motel was cluttered with work trucks, no answer to my knocks, no answer to my ringing of the bell. The phone call was a

Noah

recording saying to leave a message, and they opened at 8 A.M.

I walked over to a combination restaurant gas station that opened at 6 A.M. I asked the waitress if I could "kill" an hour or so if I ordered breakfast, and she let me in early; when the coffee was ready, she served me up. I tried to call a cab, got another answering service, had a senior breakfast, over tipped her. She called the same guy I had before, and he drove me to the base where I was to pick up the truck. Within 20 minutes, I was driving off the base and heading back to Chicago. I drove and drove, filling up with gas two times, wanting to at least cross the border, and did so by 4:30 in the afternoon. I wasn't too tired, plugged on till 8:30, and then found a motel and called it a day.

The next morning, I left at 5 A.M. and filled up again, and by 11:30 filled up again in St. Cloud, Minnesota, just west of Minneapolis -St. Paul., hopefully, one last time, and the truck would not start, I bought a can of starting fluid, opened the hood, and then, just then, found that I had been putting gas in a diesel engine, the cap to the gas was black, no outside diesel markings...I was screwed.

On the last trip, my guardian angel was at work, and there was a disabled bus being worked on at the edge of the property. I walked over, talked to the mechanic, and he agreed to come over to me after he finished ...about an hour or so ... I notified the attendant that the truck would not start, raised the hood, and waited. The mechanic finished up, came over, said I needed a tow, called a tow truck, and left.

Fifteen minutes later, the tow truck showed up, took me to a garage, and the draining and repair started. I called my boss, and told him what happened, he thought the engine was destroyed. I told him the mechanic didn't think so, and I told him I would call only with bad news.

The owner and his wife left at 4, and the mechanic stayed to get me out. I worked with him and assisted all I could. He was dirty from head to toe, and he said he would be going for his second year at diesel school to get his certification. He also works part-time, so I knew he was dedicated, skillful, and honest; the gas was drained, the fuel filters replaced, 10 gallons of diesel fuel put in, and she fired up. The mechanic took it for a test run and told me where a filling station was. I told him I appreciated his staying to get me out, gave him a $20 tip, and told him to have a drink with me this weekend!

I marked the cap and door diesel and left, filled up the truck, and went off again...arrived in Grayslake at 1:10 A.M. Friday, picked up my car, and drove home...another adventure done. I will spend a couple of nights with that guardian angel at the bar when I finally pass; drinks on me!!

I drove for the DAV that day, and I told Patti my story. She said I could leave after my first two runs. I did one additional one, and there were only 4 people left to go home, so she left me out early. It was sushi Friday. Had my fish, went home, and slept the afternoon away...

Noah

Yellow Knife, Canada

It was time for another adventure.

Tuesday, September 2nd, the day after Labor Day weekend

I was tired of this shoulder recovery, getting depressed, and antsy as to doing SOMETHING!!

I called Chip, the used truck guy, and he asked if I had a regular phone for Canada. I told him I still had the world phone and my regular phone, that I had this figured out, he still wanted me to have a regular phone, …I don't need 3 phones, I told him to terminate me, he said "O.K." I wished him luck in his endeavors. He did as well for me, and then, again, I am unemployed.

I had left the following Friday open with the D.A.V., so I had a whole week not accounted for. I had to get out!!

I had entertained driving the Pan American Highway, as discussed earlier, read a book on two guys who did it and decided not to try, but I still had one more drive-able territory in Canada I had not visited, and looking at a map, Yellowknife, in Canada's Northwest Territory glared at me! It really didn't seem too far, maybe 3 to 4 days of driving, and since Lynn had commitments, I would be able to "push it" with longer drive days, so I made the commitment.

I went online, notified the credit card company of the trip, and noticed that the Amazon Chase card had no conversion fees, so I took both cards along; my regular Chase card was giving 5% back on gas purchases…

Packed a cooler bag with two Snapple teas and a couple of energy bars, an extra change of underwear, a pair of regular pants, a long-sleeve shirt, and a light jacket, kissed the wife goodbye, and off I went.

One note here: I usually plan a route and take a can of spare tire, an emergency tool bag, a medical kit, and a blanket …oops left them in the garage…also took my travel wallet, so no proof of insurance, medical cards, this was really spur of the moment!

I did have both GPS with me for the Canada trip, $150 in cash. I left the garage at 8:30 A.M. Tuesday, September 3rd, 2019, and headed

Educating Noah…Travelin'

for Fargo, North Dakota, to see where I would stop for the night.

About two hours into the trip, an indicator light came on, so I pulled into a gas station, filled up with gas, and bought some oil. I opened the hood and put in a half quart of oil. Since the dipstick seemed to indicate the oil was almost full, and the oil did not feel hot… I relented and looked up the gauge light in the manual (yes, some guys actually look in the manuals) since I had a long way to go. This was a transmission oil light…I had been regulating my speed with the cruise control, so I made a mental note to stop that and hopefully resolve the problem.

Drive, drive, and drive. Minneapolis was horrible, a lot of road construction, and at two-ish in the afternoon, moving at 15-20 mph. The GPS took me around and down the mess and then actually asked me to turn at a non-existent exit, so I plugged in the other newer GPS. It took me back a bit, then I continued the journey; I was a bit pissed and lost at least a ½ hour in time and gas…this was the second problem, the first day, but on I went. I passed Fargo after 6 P.M.; I was tired. I like to start early in the morning and figured I would find a cheap motel, crash for 6-8 hours, and start early A.M. to avoid traffic.

I saw a sign for an Econo Lodge in Valley City, North Dakota, pulled off the road, and told the desk clerk, "I need a sink, shower, toilet, and a bed. Have AAA and ARP. What is the cheapest you have, and I will be leaving very early, what do I do with the key". He said I have a room; I will take your word for the AAA discount, and just leave the keys in the room when you leave. I handed over the credit card, signed and initialed the paperwork, and took the key. I got into the room, called the wife, got the AAA and ARP numbers, told her I was fine and loved her, drank a Snapple iced tea, had an energy bar, showered, shaved, ½ hour of TV, and went off to bed.

Tuesday, I kind of slept in, but after dressing and making sure I knew where my passport was, I was back on the road by 4:30 A.M., with the GPS set for Portal, North Dakota, my entrance to Canada.

I was crossing the border by 9:30 A.M. The site was also under renovation, with only one checkpoint open, combining trucks and cars, but it wasn't too bad…

The maximum speed limit on open roads in Canada is 110 km/hr. Which translates to 68 mph. Most hold at that speed exactly…I used

Noah

my GPS, which automatically changed or reflected my speed in km/hr.

I started to get that dreaded feeling on how far I was planning to go; my next major city, Edmonton, which was way above Montana on the atlas, would arrive after 6 PM…Argggghhh! This is farm country, fields as far as you can see. Wheat, oats, hay, and barley, it looks a lot like North Dakota, with oil wells dotted here and there also. I did notice a lot of the personal vehicles are pick-up trucks rather than crossovers, plus a lot of single and double semi's… semi's going 100km/hr. (60 mph), so lots of in and out driving.

I last about 4 hours on the road, fill up with gas, and use the restroom at each stop. I eat and drink very little so that I can last that long, given my age and conditions. I pushed it past Edmonton to get to a place closer to the Yellowknife "run" and pulled over in Whitecourt at a Super 8 for some sleep.

Wednesday, turned in the key and left the motel at 3:30 AM, hoping to cross into the Northwest territory before noon. These are now all two-lane roads. It is dark, no lights on the side of the road, some sections do not have a fog line or center line, and the traffic is basically non-existent, with 10-15 trucks or cars either coming or going an hour! Promised gas stations are closed or out of business, so now, when I get down to half a tank of gas, I start looking!!

The radio reception, both AM and FM, is fading and from one or two stations to none AM or FM; all here is forest, the road, and me…luckily, I was confident the car would not break down; the tires were fairly new, and I had a few tapes to listen to! Very few towns, just forests on both sides, in front and behind!

I pulled over to the side of the road to take a picture of the "Welcome to the Northwest Territory" sign at 11:50 AM. (I met that goal!) The last gas station passed was out of business; the tank was 1/3 full, and I started to worry. The last four hours, I was also scanning for a motel for the return trip, but no luck with that either…

At 2:53, I pulled into a gas station I had been praying for the last hour; I put in 58.13 liters. I have a 15-gallon tank, and of course, the price was high, $1.45/Liter; currently, at home, we pay about $2.50/gallon! I asked about how far to Yellowknife, and they told me about four hours. Yup, discouraging…also what was with all the tiny flies attacking everyone at the two pumps…sun flies... finally go away when winter comes.

Two bridges to cross and lots of "watch out for Moose" signs; it is a changing time here, the forests that line the road. I saw a buffalo and black bear, both walking alongside the roadway (at different places), a nice-sized beaver house in one of the many ponds, and lots of crows. Little traffic, as mentioned before, the roads have fog lines, and there is a center line, little to no shoulders, and the foliage is an explosion of colors, shades of reds, oranges, greens, browns, and black. Beautiful and unspoiled...WOW.

About an hour and a half out of Yellowknife, the asphalt road turned into another challenge, rolling, bumpy, washboard at times, with swales and dips without much warning.

I arrived (yeah!) at 4:30 PM, looked for something to take a picture of to prove I was there, and settled for a picture of the courthouse with the city name on it and a totem pole. I thought to save a little money and filled up again here; it was only(?) $1.32/liter.

Now, to return, I am still not too tired, don't want to stop now, and hope I don't regret the long upcoming drive.

I did stop at that lone gas station again. It was almost 8 PM, and I saw a bison burger I wanted. It seems everything in Canada is more expensive than in the States, and their dollar is worth .75 of the US dollar! The bison burger was $10.00!!

Driving back, the road was not lit; the moon was only a quarter moon and traffic, again, was extremely light. By 11:30, I started seeing buildings framing semis I came upon (there were no buildings) and imagining something from the sides. I pulled over at a rest stop and tried to sleep in the back. It didn't work too well; no blanket and it was not "friendly" to me, but I got an hour of sleep before that nagging "get back on the road" voice inside got me. Drove another three hours, eyes itching, fingers, and left hand "freezing," so I pulled over again for another hour, this time in the driver's seat reclined...not much better!

After one more hour of sleep, I drove to the town of High Level; approaching the town, I hit a heavy fog bank. it lasted a few seconds, but nothing could be seen, no center line, fog lines, road...NOTHING...scary, but then I was through it, filled up on gas, and bought coffee.

Noah

On the way out of town, I hit another fog bank; this was worse! I stopped the car and could not see the road! I rolled down the window, started backing up, and turned the car to the side to finally make out the fog line on the wrong side of the road, put on the flashers, and sat!

A semi came up from behind, slowly passed me, and then stopped. The driver got out and came back to me and asked, "If I was OK??" I said, "Yes, I just couldn't see," he said that is why he stopped. He couldn't either. I asked him if he had a phone and to call the local cops to get a path out. He came back to me and told me there was a truck off the road ahead and that a wrecker was on the way, and we could follow that! I agreed and thanked him.

Five to ten minutes passed when a wrecker showed up from behind and slowly went past me and the semi. We both fired up and slowly followed him about a half-mile when the fog bank lightened up enough to see the fog lines. We left the tow truck a few miles down the road. The semi in the ditch did not have any casualties, plus two cop cars were there also. It was a slower pace until sunrise; lucky, there was not much traffic. Did I mention the sunrises are spectacular!! The entire sky filled with red and orange…WOW!!

I got revived with the sunrise; every gas stop now includes a coffee or Starbucks triple shot drink. Looking at the Atlas and judging the time of arrival, I picked Saskatoon as my rest and final motel stop.

Traffic picks up as I drive south, especially around the towns, which all have gas stations now, so the quarter tank rule is re-applied. The forests are giving way to farm fields, and the mornings are 12C or 40 degrees Fahrenheit, kinda' of cool for a shirt and shorts, but it keeps me awake! Passed a number of trains, all having 100 plus oil tanker cars, half of the radio stations are in French, all the English people use words like "aut" for "out," "abaut" for "about," billboards claiming understaffed hospitals, an ad for Blue Cross supplemental health insurance, the "normal" touted unemployment of 5-7%. In the gas stations here, they still sell road maps!

When I reached Saskatoon, I pulled into a nice motel; when I got in line to check in, I noticed a lot of kids…Looked around and found that this motel had a waterpark attached…nope, I left, saw a Comfort Inn across the highway, asked at the desk for the cheapest room, rattled off the discounts, and got a single bedroom on the second floor. What surprised me was that there was no elevator! I asked about leaving early, and I was told to stop at the desk on the way out.

Showered, shaved, set up for the morning, called the desk for a 3 AM phone call, and was told they were having phone system problems and could not do this for me; the clock in the room refused to set an alarm time...watched TV for a half hour, asleep by 8!

Saturday Morning, up at 3:15

(my internal clock usually works well!) Turned in my keys, got a receipt for the stay, asked how far to Portal, he didn't know, looked it up on Google, and told me about six hours...off I went!

I arrived at Portal just before 9AM and stopped at the duty-free store to spend the last of my Canadian money. There were two lanes to get back to the USA, and I was back in the good ole USA!

I drove straight through from there did picked up two small sandwiches and pretzels, along with coffee and caffeine drinks. Going through Minnesota wasn't quite as bad as before; crossing the Wisconsin border gave me the feeling of "seeing the barn," so it was "finish this thing" time. My last fill-up was just before Madison, and I arrived home at 12:15 AM Sunday.

Total Miles 4992, Average 998 miles per day, 86 hours driving time behind the wheel, 24 hours of sleep, 5 days of travel

I had my semi-annual appointment with the VA, and I got two additional referrals, one to a dietician and another to a psychiatrist (yikes!). I talked to the dietician, and he asked if I remembered seeing him 6 years ago.... I was 310 pounds then, I weighed in at 277, told

him I would restart my weight loss program, and he gave me a website to record meals and help.

We got a surprise notice of our annual condominium meeting and a proposed $8500.00 assessment, plus an increase in our HOA monthly dues. Needless to say, there was a huge attendance, the board and new management company knew we were prepared to vote against the recommendations, and the meeting was prolonged to where there were only a few minutes for new business. Long story short, we had enough votes to fire the board, five new members were installed, including me …again; and now I have more to do!!

Educating Noah...Travelin'

Israel, Egypt, and the Suez Canal

It has been five months since my last and final replacement, which makes it all six now, and finally, we are off again! Lynn's back operation, although successful, leaves her difficulty walking distances, so at her request, I contacted Swiss Airlines to have a wheelchair accessible. Within a day, they confirmed the provision of a chair at all locations! We have found the non-domestic airlines much more accommodating, comfortable, and friendly than the U.S. ones.

We were to take an Uber to the bus station; our adventure was longer than two weeks, so free parking was not available. The forecast for the day is sunny and in the 50s. We fly from O'Hare to Switzerland, Zurich to Athens, Greece, where we board the Silver Seas Silver Spirit. It is a sixteen-day voyage, Thursday 10-25-19-Monday 11-11-19.

Our Uber was to arrive 9:30-9:40... nothing!!! No phone to call, oops, sorry??? Luckily, I was talking to a neighbor, and he offered to take us to the bus terminal. I had planned an ½ hour buffer, and we arrived ten minutes before the bus came. We were first on the ½ full bus. I sat in the back, and then I heard a loud thud... a wheelchair-bound guy tipped over in the back of the bus while off-loading. The lift had caught on the seat belt swivel housing, and there was a 2-inch drop, which tipped the chair over. I assisted the driver along with his companion to get the guy off the floor and into a seat, collapsed and stowed the chair, and then went back to my seat, and we were off.

Early morning traffic is done by 10, so the other stops and road construction presented no problem. We arrived at terminal 5, the international terminal, there was no line at the Swiss counter, I had printed up the luggage tags and boarding passes when I checked in last night, and the wheel chair showed up just as the baggage was weighed and checked in. Since I weigh each bag at least twice before leaving home, there is no question or hassle.

Having the wheelchair, we passed the lines at TSA in a special aisle, and all they detected was my left knee; Lynn, however, I got a full pat down. She had a sequined decorated blouse...so they patted her and felt her up, and off we went; we "must" fly business now

(Lynn's Rule), so we were dropped off at the lounge at 12:30 to wait for our flight at 2:45..boarding at 2:10, the gate was just next to the lounge. The lounge offered snacks and fixings for salads, sandwiches, coffees, soda, beer, and mixed drinks…all included! (Yes, I know, I paid well for this in business class!!!)

Our first flight from Chicago to Zurich was uneventful; they didn't have the sea bass, but the tenderloin was great; both of us felt it was better than some restaurants! The flight was about 9 ½ hours; a wheelchair was waiting for us, and we were through customs and in the next lounge within twenty minutes! Here, too, were refreshments, even an omelet chef…

I got antsy and had the desk check for the wheelchair to pick us up; they assured me one was coming, and sure enough, we were taken to our final gate ten minutes before boarding. This flight was only 2 ½ hours, Zurich to Athens (Piraeus) and again a meal!

We were met at the plane, she was wheeled down to baggage claim, and believe it or not, ours were in the first ten bags on the conveyor. With bags in tow, we left the area and found the transfer awaiting us. Silver Seas arranged a Black Car, so we were escorted out of the terminal and into the back seat of a Mercedes and taken from the airport to the dock. After about the usual 45 minutes, traffic was crowded, and "camel-nose" lane changes, close quarters, and motorcycles riding between lanes.

At the docks, we first transferred our luggage to the porter, then a line for the first check-in, then a line for the one metal detector, then a line for the one customs agent/passport agent, then off to the ship; there was some confusion, walk or bus, so we went on the bus…wrong, the bus went to all the OTHER ships except Silver Seas.

So, we went the entire circuit, got off when we returned to the same exit, and then walked to the ship, up to the 5th deck, and FINAL check-in to be escorted to our room. It was about twenty-two hours since we left home, and neither of us slept well on the plane; we put a note on the door, put the luggage in the room, and crashed!

Saturday morning, about 2 A.M

We awoke, got up, unpacked, then went back to bed, rested till 5, and got dressed in fresh clothes after a great shower. We toured the ship to find out where everything was and were first to get breakfast.

Educating Noah...Travelin'

Met one of the male dance escorts, Steve, wandering the halls like us, had breakfast with him, and had a good conversation. We went to the desk to get all of our questions answered and requested two itineraries be provided each morning. Finished the ship tour. This ship is laid out differently than many others, and it is one of the smaller ships with 608 passengers and 412 crew.

We skipped the complimentary bridge tour, had a tour of the spa, then, our first program event was regarding the various upcoming excursions.

I had gone through all the excursions at home and listed the ones I liked. Lynn concurred, and I reserved the ones we agreed on, so this would just be reinforcement and hopefully point out what I missed.

The second program was actually a continuation of the first, just the tours after Israel; I took notes to reinforce the tour when we take them. Haifa/Israel is part of the land bridge connecting Africa to the European continent.

This is the 70th anniversary of the creation of Israel, where Palestine was divided between the Palestine Arabs and Jews; the influx of Jews in this area due to the Second World War was greater than 250,000, and the British stopped the immigration, refusing any further migration. Israel was established by NATO and is a representative democracy. $1.00 US =3.50 shekels, and it is illegal to exchange dollars for shekels privately.

Lynn went off to a "Free Ladies Pamper Party", which of course turned out to be a sell presentation for lotions and creams. I sat in the sun, had a Mojito, and went to the ship building orientation. There was only one other guy there, but the officer in charge stated there usually are more signing up after a few days into the cruise...I signed up. We are not supposed to use our room staff to acquire materials, and on this cruise, no water bottles in sight! Another challenge!!

An enrichment lecture was next. It actually picked apart the days of Christ, giving the bible some depth from a historian's point of view; here are the notes:

The western wall of Harrods's temple that still remains is the holiest place for the Jewish faith, called the Wailing Wall.

Galilee is where Jesus spends his first thirty years of life. The Romans ruled the country, what the goal of the Roman's was to just keep the peace, and collect taxes.

It was Harrod the Great that rebuilt Jerusalem that was destroyed by the Babylonians. The Jewish were represented by the religious authority which consisted of priests, an aristocracy and the temple authority.

Nazareth is in the Northern part of Israel, occupied now mostly by Christians and Muslims, few Jews. This is where Jesus grew up, assumed as a carpenter under his foster dad's guidance. At the age of 30, Jesus became a wandering preacher, prompted by his interaction with John the Baptist who preached that the "world was coming to an end, and everyone needed to be baptized."

Jesus spent three years with the message that "the Kingdom was coming" and it seems that miracles were not unusual at this time. To celebrate Passover, Jesus left Nazareth to go to Jerusalem with his disciples.

1. He entered Jerusalem on a donkey (prophesy) and went to the temple.

2. He was horrified by the money changers and merchants overcharging for the sacrifice of animals and high commissions, so much so that he started a riot within the temple.

3. He then went to the top of Mount Olive to celebrate Passover with his disciples. (The Last Supper)

4. He then took a walk through the Garden of Gethsemane.

The governor did not want to go as far as killing him at first, but let it up to the local authority, and he, Pontius Pilot declared the death sentence. Hanging on a cross was a particularly cruel execution, and just hanging there would take two to three days. After a few hours, the guards would break the legs so support was gone, and death was expedited by asphyxiation. But Christ however, was dead before they were to break his legs.

Both of us were tired after this lecture, so we went back to our cabin and napped.

Up again to go to our first Trivia session. We soon had a total of 8 players on our team, six Brit's and us two Americans. We finished with a 17/20 score, which actually put us in fourth place, winners 18 ½, 18, and 17 ½, better luck next time! We called this team "8 is enough".

Captains Welcome Cocktail party, formal dress, drinks, and appetizers; we were joined by a couple from Canada, good conversation; then we were approached by Steve (the dance partner) and his roommate Dan (the other dance partner) to join them for supper.

The show at 10 P.M. was "Lyrically Yours," six singers and dancers doing 70's music and songs; great fun, good audience participation (a good 200-230 total), and that ended the day! The theater has a capacity of about 300…, which doesn't say much for the 600 guests! (Only one show on these smaller ships.) Oh, by the way, The food was as good as Oceania; I had salmon and bagel for breakfast, sushi for lunch, and a light but tasty Asian dinner. Lynn had what she wanted every meal also; wine and cocktails are included on this cruise, so by 11, we were tired, well fed, and feelin' no pain, tomorrow …Israel!

Sunday, October 27, 2019

I was up at 5, caught up on my journal. WIFI is included on this voyage; just setting it up is different with each cruise line, but trial and error plus bullheadedness finally worked out! G-Mail wanted to verify by phone, but Tracphone doesn't work well out of the country, so there was no e-mail on board or at the airports…for some reason, it did not recognize this computer? (Must be the provider) I let Lynn sleep in till 7; we should be on a regular schedule in a day or two as far as "normal" hours. Our port is Haifa (Tel Aviv), Israel. Our excursion is called Harrod's Dream-Caesarea Maritime.

All guests on the cruise must go through a face to face immigration inspection in the terminal building, and issued a landing card that we are to keep on our person in all the Israelian ports along with our passports; we are to return our passports on the 29th before 1:30 PM at the latest, are the instructions!

We were let off a bit after 9 A.M., no problem, except we had to show our passports and entry ticket a total of four times to get out of the terminal!

Once out, we found our bus and waited for the balance of 16 people on this 30-passenger bus. Our first stop was an outlook of Haifa and the Haifa Bay, the golden dome of the Haifa Baha'i shrine and

Acre, in the distance.

Haifa is the third largest city in Israel, with 290,000 people: 70% Jewish, 25% Arab Muslim, and the balance Christian or "other," including the Bahia. This is also the world center of the Bahia religion, with no alcohol, vegetarian-only religion. (This religion was started in the 1800s in Persia, based on science, education, and equality.)

The view of the town and harbor was clear, including the gardens and temple. The Carmelite religion also is centered here.

All the buildings are built into the rolling hills, the buildings are entered in the middle of the building, and elevators are rare, you either walk up or down to your floor.

Israel is now 71 years old, with Independence in 1948. Tel Aviv the financial center, and the most modern of cities; In Israel the education is "free" and the health care is very similar to Canada's, Military service is mandatory for 3 years for boys, after high school graduation, girls 1 year.

Israel is 60 % dessert, the West Bank is the west shore of the Jordan River, they export crops, and knowledge. Most families have three or more kids, which is exceptional for an educated population. Israel does export banana plants, to South America and the Philippians, and starting to cultivate grapes and wine production.

It was a 1 ½ drive to Harrods's Dream, Caesarea, an ancient port once the Capitol of this region, and once a major port. From this place, it is a half day horseback ride to Jerusalem; there was a sign and replica of the stone chair reserved for Pontius Pilot. The ruins are extensive; enough is left to show a hippodrome, extensive bath houses, tile work, gates, fountains, and temples. We did extensive walking to see the various foundations, the workings of the heated bath houses and pools, the aqueducts.

Throughout Israel, there are, and were water shortages, and the moats that were around any of the past structures were never filled with water.

There is only one golf course in the entire country of Israel, and that course is located in Haifa. Most people here live in apartments.

Back on the ship, we rested for a bit, then down for the 4:45 trivia. Only one other couple from our group was back from excursions so

Educating Noah...Travelin'

our team was four short, yet we took 3rd place!

We found the mini-golf activity, out of 10 people I took 1st place, Lynn 3rd, and we were the last to show; now we have some of those treasured points! I am not a good golfer, just lucky ...one hole in one and two birdies...go figure.

I checked two locations that were to save milk cartons for the ship building contest...nothing...but they promised to remember to save...again.

Lynn wanted to try one of the restaurants, we asked to sit with a group, a table for eight had two places left, however, I was told I needed to wear a jacket to enter, so back to the room, put on my sport coat over the same clothes and we were seated.

Great conversation, one lady was a politician, so there was no lack of words!! This was the first time in a long time, caviar was offered as an appetizer, it was recommended by the politician (go figure!) and it was very good, high grade!!

After dinner we had a little time before the harpist performance at ten, so we walked the ship. I felt sorry for the Harpist, he was excellent and put on a great show, but there were only about 30 people who came...this is another ghost ship after 10 P.M.... we joined the ghosts after the performance, tomorrow our excursion takes off at 8:00 A.M.

Monday, today was the Masada & Dead Sea tour. Duration: 11.5 hours; long day!

We are up at 7; grabbed a bite for breakfast, off the ship, customs stopped us, empty everything, I still buzzed the detector, she couldn't find the guy with the wand so she shrugged and let me through...

We were there at the requested time, first on the bus, and then waited; a group came out at eight, all with swimming gear and towels. As they got on I told them that swimming in the dead sea had been called off due to a shark sighting; when I saw the concern on one of the females, I quickly stated that the shark was actually dead (no fish or mammals in the dead sea) the guy behind her chuckled and they continued back to their seats. There were only 18 of us on a full-sized bus; however, we were delayed 15 minutes waiting for a couple that never showed.

Our first destination is through the desert, down past the Dead Sea,

Noah

to an ancient fort (Masada) 70 B.C. to early the A.D. period.

Coming out of the port, the traffic lights allow only 2-3 trucks or vehicles before changing, there is a lot of trash alongside the road, and there are few if any vehicles older than 5-6 years old, everyone jockeying for a place, motorcycles driving between lanes and vehicles, graffiti on the walls and barriers.

On the way we received some Jewish culture facts to share. Currently the unemployment is about 7%; seafood must have scales to be Kosher or eaten, no shrimp, crab, lobster, all per the bible as a guide, no pig or hog products, no dairy with meat. The first king of Israel was Saul, he was not considered a "good" king, and he was replaced by King David, who united all twelve of the Jewish tribes in Jerusalem which was their capitol, 1000 B.C. The current population of Israel is about 9 million, of the Jews, approximately 25% are strict Jews; they are well educated 50% have professional degrees, average family has 2.8 children. 60% of Israel is dessert, and that is where only 8% live; many are Muslims, being the more nomadic people. It is currently 28 degrees C (82 F). During the summer, temperatures may reach 122-degree F.

In the last 70 years, Israel has planted over 300,000 trees; they actually developed a canopy system to grow banana trees that conserves water, produces strong, healthy plants, and exports to the tropics.

Dead Sea is the lowest point on earth, 400 meters (1200-1300 feet) below sea level, the water is high in minerals and salt (33%), there are no known animals in the sea. The sea is disappearing, it loses 1 meter per year in depth.

After almost two hours of driving through the dessert we reach our first destination, Masada. This was a mountain fort, on top of a mountain, with a synagogue, extensive living quarters, baths, guest houses, cisterns, defending walls and a three-tiered palace. This fort was built by Harrod the Great; you need to take a cable car up, and they pack you in, 65/car…yep, sardine time for four to five minutes.

Once at the top, there is a circular path through the complex, we all have whisperers on so the commentary is easily heard and understood. The vistas are breathtaking; you can see the Dead Sea from on top, including miles of dessert vistas and runs by the mountains where the water was directed to the cisterns. Our guide shared a story about his grandmother and her experience with the Holocaust.

After an hour of touring, the line to get back in a cable car was only 15 minutes long. We were given a half hour to shop the extensive gift shop, and yes, we did; I found the 17% VAT tax to be irritating, along with the difficulty of getting the return paperwork! (There was no place to turn in, so I had to eat the tax.)

It was only a short ride to the Dead Sea; we had an extensive eastern food buffet and access to a hotel beach. The food was excellent, and after eating, the hotel provided a towel and soap to explore the hotel beach. Lynn and I went down to the water, and took turns to wade in (Yes, that was a must!) The water was clear and warm; a bit too many small stones made it difficult to walk, so neither of us stayed in very long, just enough to feel the water (it feels the same as ocean water) and take our pictures. After that brief but necessary experience, we washed our feet, turned in our towels and sat in the lobby for the others to finish. The weather was a bit hot, very little breeze, and too many flies!

It was getting late, and our guide said that if we took the planned route home we would not arrive till after 7:30 P.M. They voted, and we missed the Qumran Caves where the Dead Sea Scrolls were discovered, (we were told you could not see the caves from the parking lot) and also missed the views of Jericho. Just another disappointment! I guess dressing and having supper on time is priority??

We changed, had dinner in the cafe, it was Italian, went to the room to type, then off to the Liars Club. We joined two other couples, guessed 3/5 right, and took home 2nd place!! (It did help that Lynn remembered two of the answers from previous Liar Club games.)

Another day gone; set the alarm for 6:00, we need to be on the bus by 7:30 A.M.

Tuesday, October 29th

I was up at 5:15 with my built-in alarm; I got Lynn up at 6:00; we had a nice breakfast and were on the bus just before 7:20. Today's excursion explores Tel Aviv & Jaffa. We have been anchored in Ashdod, which is the port of Jerusalem; it was nothing like Jerusalem 2019 years ago, and this is a working port, all trucks and cranes!

Noah

We started out being the last bus out and going to Jaffa first. Jaffa is the oldest part of Israel; the history is about 4000 years old; the history includes -2400 years occupied by the Canaanites; -900 The Iron Age or the Israelite Period, -800 years the period of Jonah and the Whale, -600 Sidon Control, -200 Monerans ruled, -100 Romans ruled, 0 Vespasian's ruled, 400 Christians ruled, 600 The Arab Conquest, 1000 The Crusades, 1200 Sultan Bay bars, 1500 the Ottoman Empire, 1900 the British Armed forces. Jaffa is the largest Israel Port, 1918-1948, occupied by both Arabs and Jews;

The east to west roads is even numbered, north to south are odd, only one toll road, if you don't subscribe you pay double the charge. A lot of horn blowing, impatience seems to rule, conversation is loud, signs all in Hebrew, and some have English under the Hebrew, some Arabic and Hebrew.

Water pipes are color coded; the purple pipes are recycled water for crops, and black and white pipes are drinking water (potable).

There are ten different Christian churches in Jaffa, along with several mosques and synagogues; a comment was made that St. Francis was the first social worker. The Franciscans Order was started here, their symbol is one naked arm, one clothed crossed, representing Christ and man linked together.

When Napoleon tried to conquer the city, the first few French soldiers were captured and hacked apart, and their heads stuck on poles, this irritated the French so much that when they destroyed the walls, they killed every man woman and child on site. When Napoleon left, he commanded all the wounded, lame, or otherwise handicapped, to go into the lower areas and instructed the doctors to poison the men so that the rest were not hindered in the return of the French army to France.

We had a tour of the museum where we watched a short historical movie, there was also a display of antiquities, and I found one very interesting. It was a display of Caltrops. Caltrops are four shafts about 3 inches long of iron forming stars, they were made to pierce the hooves of the Calvary horses to cripple the horses and bring down the mounted soldiers.

It started to rain, so a vote was taken, the flea market promised was skipped, we did see a little more of the town and a clock tower.

Educating Noah…Travelin'

All homes here are made of concrete, no wood. Our guide gave us a lesson in building styles with pointing out examples as we passed. There are a lot of skyscrapers in Tel Aviv, the transition from old to knew is quite apparent.

We then drove through the rain to Tel Aviv, which is very modern, and is the center of banking and technology. We drove passed the old American Embassy, and the square where Prime Minister Itzhak Rabin was assassinated in 1994.

We were back to the ship a half hour before sailing, final passport check was abbreviated; we turned in our passports on ship, and headed for lunch. After lunch was catch-up typing time and a bit of rest, set sail was at 1:45 and we bid farewell to Israel.

Lynn went to a talk on Broadway shows and productions.

Worldwide, the U.S. has the best shows and productions; they are also the most expensive. Rogers and Hammerstein were not sure they could be a success, but it turns out they were one of the best teams. The discussion was highlighted with movie clips, songs, and snips of examples including South Pacific, the Wizard of Oz, etc.

I hunted around for more boat materials, and then we went down for Trivia; the entire team showed up again, and we had 17/20; third place was 17.5/20!

Back to the room to change (no shorts after 6 on this ship, plus I had to wear a jacket tonight), three formal nights, (tie and jacket, 6 informal nights, jackets no ties required, the remaining 5 nights casual, but long pants required!) Attended a one-man singer show, we were invited to join two women for supper on deck. It was a hot stone dinner; you order a salad, entree, and dessert. After the salad, you are given a flat hot stone to cook your own meat or fish, Lynn had steak, and I had fish, when ½ cooked, you pour a bit of oil on the meat or fish, and turn it over, salt and pepper as needed. It turned out great! Good conversation, excellent meat cuts and filets.

Karaoke was at 10, the songs I wanted were not on the list, and the songs were alphabetical so hard to find when you can only kinda sing in one artist's range (if you know what I mean), I left at 11, Lynn stayed for the 70's music, by the time she got back to the cabin, I was showered and Z'n.

Wednesday, a day at sea, we slept in till 7; I went on deck to get

Noah

some shots of the Suez Canal as we made our way down. It seems to be a fairly narrow passage, more like a river, and narrow at that!

We had breakfast on the rear deck…oops, below the fly line, so swatting flies during the meal kept us irritated. I went off to check with my suppliers, for the boat, got a paper box from reception, and asked our butler to be on the look-out for a few more boxes and some empty water bottles.

The lecture was on Egypt, "From Nasser to the Arab Spring".

The creation of Israel in Palestine was not accepted well with the Arab community. The day after creation, the Arabs invaded, this included Syria, Iraq, Jordan and Egypt. Israel was victorious, however 2/3 of the Arabs in the area left Palestine for refugee camps. Palestine demanded unrealistic compensation for the refugees.

King Furuk was a corrupt Egyptian king, he was replaced in 1952 by Nasser, and the Egyptian government became a republic. Nasser was a Nationalist; he wanted a United Arab State. Egypt is 85% dessert (Sahara) and it needs the Nile to flood yearly.

In the 1880's the British controlled the Suez Canal, Nasser wanted to nationalize the canal, but the British, French, and Israel moved against him.

Cairo has over 1000 mosques, with a strong fundamental Islamic population. There was an Anti-Western sentiment, condemnation of the West, and Christians. Violent Jihad was called against all non-Muslim believers, there was even a duty Jihad against moderate Muslim leaders, originating in Egypt.

In 1967 Nasser closed the gulf of Akbar, Israel fought again and won, Syria attacked from the north at the same time, at the Golan Heights; Israel again won.

Peace was negotiated at Camp David between Egypt, Jordan and Israel with Jimmy Carter but it was flawed.

Sadat was assonated by the Muslim Brotherhood; a few of them included his own generals.

In Egypt, there is an enormous gap between the rich and poor, 12-15% of the population is Orthodox Christian, and Coptic Christian churches are still being attacked. The Sinai Peninsula is currently still a "no-go zone" for Westerners.

Educating Noah...Travelin'

Lynn went to the pool area to read in the sun, I attended an update on the ship building contest, gathered additional boat materials and joined Lynn on the pool deck for some sun time also, yes, we do sit around like many of the others, we soaked in a good 45 minutes of sun before lunch.

The afternoon lecture was on the Suez Canal and Aqaba;

It will take our ship about 12-13 hours to make the transit; Built in the 19th century and is about 100 miles long connecting the Mediterranean to the Red Sea. 1878 BC records indicate a river joining the Nile to the Red Sea. Napoleon was responsible for the upgrading to a navigable connection. In 1858 the canal was maintained by the Maritime Suez Canal Company. In 1956, Nasser nationalized the Canal to Egypt.

It took from 1859-1869 30,000 people at a cost of 400 million Francs. There is a 66-foot draft, it is one way most of the way, there is a lake approximately ½ ways for ships to wait their turn up or down, and last year 18,000 ships utilized it. There are no locks; the Red Sea and Mediterranean are equalized by the lake in the middle of the canal.

Jordan is the crossroads of Asia, Africa, and Europe. It is about the same size as the state of Indiana in the U.S. 98% Arab, Sunni Muslim with a population of 9.7 million. The government is set up with the King on the top, three branches below, Prime minister, Senate and assembly, Judicial. The king is the 23rd descendent of Mohammed.

Team Trivia...third place; mini golf; "nada" for me 1 point for Lynn; dinner with a very nice English couple; and the comedy show put on by the cruise director Nolan Dean was very entertaining, and he has very nice voice for the vocals he sung with the comedies!

Thursday, October 31st Halloween; sunrise 5:57, sunset 5:03 this side of the equator and it is warm...

Enrichment Lecture was on Cleopatra: Separating the Myth from Reality.

Cleopatra was actually Greek, a Macedonian, and the one actual coin that depicted her showed a prominent Greek nose that was a bit hooked on the end. She had married her brother to rule, had two affairs (according to four accounts) including Alexander the Great in the 4th century B.C.; she was the last of the Pharaoh's and she ruled with her

Noah

brother during the Roman Civil War going on between Julius Caesar and Pompey.

Since her brother was older, he was the primary Pharaoh. To introduce herself to Julius Caesar, she wrapped herself up and was presented to Julius Caesar in court. She at the time was 21 Julius was 52; they became lovers, and soon after, her brother "disappeared", and she became the sole Pharaoh of Egypt.

She had a son by Caesar named Caesarean; Caesar was a dictator, but Rome was a Republic, when Caesar was assonated Cleopatra went to the funeral, but then returned to Egypt and her throne.

Mark Anthony and Octavian replaced Caesar, Mark Anthony was a handsome "man of action", and Cleopatra chose him to side with. Mark Anthony with Cleopatra's navy attacked Persia, the Parthenon Empire, but was defeated within three months.

Meanwhile, Octavian became stronger, and demanded the Mark Anthony to be put to death. The story goes that Mark Anthony was mortally wounded, he wanted to die in Cleopatra's presence, and he did sail to Egypt and yes died there shortly after.

Cleopatra, herself, "so the story is told" snuggled up to an Asp, hidden in a basket of figs, brought to her. Most believe this is the romanticized story, that she actually used the much less painful Hemlock to end her life.

Her and Caesar's son was then killed by Octavian, and he then continued to rule the Roman Empire with Egypt as "Augustus".

We played table tennis, I won a first round, Lynn lost her's, but of the 9 people that showed up, we were by far the amateurs, and it was way out of our amateur league with these folks. We watched and then left to have lunch.

On the way we stopped at the on-board sandal maker from Preludio Sandals, Carlos the craftsman had a display and workshop set up on deck during sea days. We took a picture; his sandals start at…$200.00 U.S. for the plain ones!! Yup, pictures are all we got.

The afternoon lecture was a port talk on Safaga (Luxor), talked about what currency is used, most shops accept pounds and dollars and all accept credit cards. We are to watch the dickering, start at ½ the price asked, tips no more than 10%.

Educating Noah...Travelin'

In 1926 Palestine and Jordan became independent from English rule; Petra, actually, was "the lost city", means "rock" and only 5% of Petra has been excavated; much of the area has been destroyed by tectonic shifts over the centuries.

We are told that in Sagafa, the port, the decedents of pirates just became cab drivers ☺

Trivia, we took third place; 6:30, a concert by Francisco Yglesias on his Paraguayan Harp was very entertaining and well attended;

Dinner was on deck 9 at the Hot Stones restaurant again. Very much enjoyed, great food!

At 10:00 was the Halloween party on the pool deck. I brought dog and cat noses just in case, we did get compliments, the disc jockey played songs, the entertainers danced, and we danced with them! FUN!

After a few dances, there was a presentation of "DEATH BY CHOCOLATE" where the pastry chefs displayed a delicious array of desserts with a Halloween and chocolate theme. We had a good sampling and called it a night.

Friday, November 1st, sunny, and we went on different paths. I had an all-day excursion, Lynn had a "pamper day" on board with massage.

We had decided that the Petra excursion would be too much walking for Lynn, and it turned out that she would not have made it!

Start time was 7:30 so I ate breakfast alone, then off the ship. Visas were handled by the ship, but we needed to carry our passports while in Jordan. The bus ride to and from Petra was a little over two hours each way. There is little but desert and mountains, we were given a little history on the way.

Petra is located between the Red and Dead Seas; two hours north of Eilat, and four hours south of Amman. There are 800 tombs, boulevards, and temples, all previously hidden and relatively inaccessible, hidden by high cliffs, and steep valleys. These structures were credited to the Nabateans. Dating to the 7th century B.C... A wealthy empire from Damascus to the Sinai, and most of the tombs were carved during the 1st Century A.D.

We stopped for a view and toilet a little over an hour into the trip, desolate mountains, valleys and sand, every so often some garbage strewn on the side of the road, two or three small towns, poor, old tires, junk car parts, the average wage is 550-600 dinars/month, average family size is five.

We arrived a bit after 10:30, organized inside a gate, and took off. A number of folks were unable to walk far, and were promised a cart ride, but when we came to the place that offered the rides, we were told by our guide that they would have to wait an hour for the rides to start, so the five or six of them were left and the group took off.

One lady was having difficulty walking on the uneven rocky valley; I assisted her and ended up assisting her entire walk, and day. The guide actually set a brisk pace with ½ the group and until the very end of the valley sent the assistant back for us. The total distance to the temple site was mostly downhill, 2 ½ miles! A lot farther than most thought or described. At the site was the temple carved out of the face of a mountain, some vendors, a couple people offering camel rides and a few open tombs.

Since we were the last to catch up with the group, we looked around and Louise and I told the guide we would head back in order to keep up with the group. Yup, 2 ½ miles on a slow incline, rocky, and passed by closely by carts of people, sometimes without warning, and the horses trotting past a rather brisk rate!

We got back to the area where the carts were to pick up the part of the group that didn't want to walk (round trip was $75.00/person) and no one showed. So, we went to the first gathering spot and waited...no one. We were told lunch was included, but not where, so we went up to the parking lot, the bus had moved to another parking lot, and then we found the bus, no driver! Talked to other drivers they called our driver and told us 5 minutes; after 15 minutes more we headed back to the gate, found a few of the people from the ship (there were 12 buses from the ship) and they indicated that the groups were eating at a restaurant in town a few blocks past the gate.

We found the restaurant, asked a leader of another group to contact our guide, and quickly gulped down some food and water. Our guide met us as we left the restaurant, blamed us for not knowing where to go, and took no responsibility for not looking for us the past two hours. Both of us were "steaming" to say the least, plus tired and worn out, 5 plus miles of walking in the heat not to mention the couple hundred extra yards finding the bus and the restaurant! The trip back to the ship was uneventful, no tip for that clown! I joined Lynn at the trivia location, played mini golf activity, filed a complaint with the excursion staff, and dressed for dinner.

By the time we were done with dinner it was after 9, tomorrow was another, even longer excursion, so we packed it in. Lynn's massage turned into a deep tissue massage, so she was aching also, my knees, ankles and hips were "singin' the blues" loud and clear!

Saturday, November 2nd,

It was 90 degrees F, clear, and HOT!

All day excursions, Port of Safaga, Egypt, another early start, pick up passports, off the ship, customs, and then found our assigned bus. The driver turns us away, we find a ship tour representative, she tells the driver this is our bus, as we again showed the guide our assigned paper and we are let on the bus… not a good start!

As we began our 4-hour bus ride, we were told a lot about Egypt.

Alexandria was the capitol until Cairo was built, and then Cairo became the capitol and expanded to be much larger than Alexandria. There are many ports in Egypt mostly on the north and eastern border.

The Nile is a reverse river flowing south to north; 94% of Egypt is in Africa, 6% is in Asia.

Sahara in Arabic is "desert"; in the ancient religion, RA was the SUN god, and was the boss of the gods. Amman ruled the underworld, Orais ruled heaven. Resurrection was important, living after death in heaven or hell eternally, most if not all burials, was on the west bank of the Nile. The scenes painted and carved in the tombs all tell stories; the book of the dead is the same for all people.

Tombs are dug into the side of the mountains; the first thing done was to mummify the body, by removing all liquid. Brains removed through the nose.

Since they were unclear as to the time it took to travel to heaven, food and water were left in the tomb for the journey. There are three types of tombs: the bench which has two floors; the pyramid; and the last was a rock tomb.

There are 62 tombs in the Valley of the Kings, from 1800 B.C. to

Noah

900 B.C.

Arabic has been spoken in Egypt since the 10th century, after 2 1/2 hours the second bus driver switched to behind the wheel, (since the driving time was greater than 8 hours) each bus had an armed guard in a suit, wearing an automatic pistol under his suit coat, and we were informed that there would be a charge of $19.00 U.S. for cameras used in and around the tombs, which the guide collected when the drivers switched.

The closer we get to Luxor, we start seeing green, first shrubs, then trees, Egypt only receives an average of 7 inches of rain, so the Nile flooding every year is critical. There is the upper and lower Nile where north is lower, and south is upper. Egypt was two countries and united as one later when the Arabs took over in the 7th Century, and with them came the Arabic language and religion, replacing the gothic language and ancient god beliefs.

The trip there and back involved 12-15 checkpoints each way, and EVERY intersection had speed bumps where the bus slowed to almost zero to go over the bumps. Military service is required of all males, 2 years after high school, only 1 year for those graduating from college. The unemployment is high in the 7-10% range; most homes are not finished so that they cannot be taxed completely as in many other countries.

There are both public and private education through college, the remark was made "Heaven help you if you get a publically educated doctor" since the public higher education system is rift with dishonesty and bribery.

Our first stop was the Luxor temple, a large complex of statuary, carvings, and chapels. The original was constructed during the New Kingdom, and as new rulers governed, more was added. We walked the grounds, took lots of pictures (the pictures were free to take here) used the toilet facilities, then off to eat a buffet lunch at a hotel.

After lunch we re-boarded the bus to cross the Nile to the west bank and Valley of the Kings. Here is where we got our camera tickets along with entry tickets; BOTH were checked at the entrance of EACH of the tombs we toured, constructed in a period of 500 years from 16th to 11th century B.C.

The group toured three, Ramses IV, V, and III (of 63 so far

Educating Noah...Travelin'

discovered) of the tombs, Ramses III late 1300B.C. was the oldest, and seemed to have the most original color in the wall carvings and corridor ceilings!

I took what pictures I could, all of the depictions told a story, actually multiple stories each different depicting the lives and beliefs of the occupant laid to rest. It was unknown how long it would take for the soul to go to its final resting place, so each tomb was stocked with food and water for the journey, which may have contributed to the bacteria and "curse" for those tomb raiders.

The men during these periods were clean shaven; they are depicted with a square gold goatee that was to represent royalty.

The tomb of Tutankhamen was available for an extra cost, it is famous because he was only 18 when he died, and his tomb was not discovered by the grave robbers. P.S. It is said that many of the grave robbers were some of the men involved in the construction of the tombs.

We had two more brief, photo stops, the remains of Queen Hatshepsut temple; an afternoon tea break for drink and potty, then a final photo stop at the Colossi of Memnon, a number of statues in a farmer's field. It was hot, and a lot of pesky flies, the vendors were obnoxious and pesky, showing items for $1, and then re-niggling once they had your money changing that $1 to $40, the constant speed bump at every intersection and again the 15-200? Checkpoints added to the aggravation of the four-hour ride home to the port.

The re-entry was abbreviated, on the ship, back to the cabin, showers and bed!

Sunday, a day at sea, we will be joining the dead today and just kinda move through the ship, sit around, lay in the sun, etc.

10:15 Safe haven drill; the pirate drill, everyone out of their cabins, off the outside decks, and away from the windows; crew and passengers complied and listened to the short lecture over the PA. This was very similar to our drills going around South Africa with Oceania.

11:00 Scattergories game, our team of 4 came in fourth, with no prize☹

Noon to noon forty, we laid in the sun, it took a while to find a chair that wasn't "reserved", about twelve others were sunning themselves, about ten in the pool, the rest?? We were not even approached by staff with water or drinks, when we got up though, those folks under the deck in the shade were being served…must have been too hot for the attendants and waiters.

Lunch was a treat; it was at one of the two reserve seat restaurants, "free" at lunch. A Japanese restaurant serving sashimi and sushi, Lynn even had 4 pieces! I tried the smoked eel, sea urchin (served on a small cucumber slice with caviar on top…tastee), and a variety of other sushi, I asked for and also received a decanter of Saki; all food prepared by a chef in the center of a very small room, that could only seat 20-24 people.

Enrichment speech on "The political Importance of the Musical"; She went through a number of musicals with excerpts of each, showing and highlighting the words and history behind the stories musicals and songs including Porgy and Bess, Blowing in the Wind, Evita, Age of Aquarius, Cabaret, Money, Showboat and Anne.

Lynn went to the line dancing class.

I found the shore excursion office open, and talked to the manager regarding not getting back to me and the fiasco in Petra; she seemed interested and promised to look into it.

Bingo (it was free), three games, lost, Trivia, not even 4th place, I skipped golf, and Lynn didn't place there either.

It was another STUPID formal night, we went down to a close restaurant, ate at 7:20 only ½ the restaurant was full when we left, and I went to the room worked on the boat and crashed. Lynn went to the show at 10, It promised "Grand Opera classics", she came home early the theatre was too cold.

Monday, yet another day at sea. We both slept in late, almost 8, but then again, the clocks were turned ahead an hour last night.

The lecture was "The Wild West-or; How dare you call me a cowboy!

Her first comment was that "cowboy" was a derogatory term; "ranch hand" was preferred. At least 25% of ranch hands were Mexican or Black, which wasn't depicted in the westerns. Trail food was edible, at best; Spaghetti westerns got their name from being directed by Italian's. Boots were/are pointed so when dismounting they would not get caught in the stirrups, there were very few actual bank robberies, shoot outs, or armed encounters with the Indians, Geronimo was educated, he led attacks because the U.S. Calvary killed his family.

Riding drag meant you were behind the herd; it was usually assigned as punishment or least seniority, involved kerchief over face and chaps.

Advice: Never treat your horse better than your wife, unless you like sleeping in the barn!

Next we went to the "Selfies Scavenger Hunt"; we teamed up with another couple, there were four teams of 3-4 people, we finished last, our I Phone guy was not good at taking photos, and they were slower than us to find the photos we needed to take, plus he easily got confused as to camera angle to get us all (4?) in the picture.....Grrrrr However, we did get participation points for trying...

Light lunch, I developed heartburn, and for most of the afternoon suffered, I finally bought some Zantax which worked!

Afternoon lecture: The Roots of Islamist Extremism";

Islam is undergoing a civil war, 85% are Sunni Muslims, 15% are Shia Muslims; Mohamed died in 632 A.D. He was/is considered the last prophet of God. The two factions have a basic difference in the succession after Mohamed's death, The Sunni believe it was Abu Bakar then Omar, and finally Uthman, the Shia believe it was blood transfer, Ali, followed by Hussein.

Sunni's do not believe in Shrines; both believe that once any land or country turns Islam, it must always be Muslim. In the past both sects got along until the Ayatollah took power in Iran.

Iran is Shia Muslim and has three sects:

Fives, Yemen; Sevens, Egypt; and Twelve's, Iran

Hierarchy: twelve legitimate caliphs; the twelfth is believed to be still in hiding.

The Holy Quran divides people into two groups: 1. the faithful, good, white, or 2. the unfaithful, evil, bad, black.

Wahhabi Islam is the sect of Sunni's where all the terrorists come from; Saudi Arabia is trying to partner with the US and Israel to combat Iraq and Iran. Syria is a Sunni majority country.

Bingo…" free" you win points, neither of us won, Team Trivia; everyone showed up, we failed miserably; golf putting, more folks, nope, no points for either of us!

Dinner, yes, I put on a coat! We asked to be seated at a table with others, we were seated at a table for 6; After 15 minutes we were offered a table for two; after we sat at our new table, a group of four walked in and asked if we wanted to join them, so back to the table for 6.

The two were entertainers, and two guys; the conversation was lively, enjoyed and shared by all.

The show was an Australian soloist singing various popular songs; this ended another day at sea.

Tuesday…at sea again, windy, warm, we are rounding the tip of Saudi Arabia today and heading east.

I started to catch up on my journaling, worked a bit on the boat, and Lynn went to the lecture "Roger's and Hammerstein-The Dream Team".

The correct spelling is above; many times, it is represented as "Hammersteen". Many immigrants to the US were very talented musicians. Roger's original musical partner, Larry Hart, died, and that is the reason for the now famous duo. "Showboat" was their first real success after many failures, and this was followed by "Oklahoma" which broke all previous records, "Carousel" was a hit the next was "a stinking failure". "South Pacific" had many hit songs, not only returned them to the top, it ran for five years, and made millions. "King and I" both picked Yul Brenner to lead. "My fair Lady" followed.

Rogers became ill with cancer, he became depressed, and started writing concert music, then Oscar became ill, but did recover and together on a rebound, they wrote and produced "The Sound of Music".

Soon after Oscar died, many tried to work with Rogers, but to no avail, and so, the end of a great team!

Lynn joined me in the lounge for Scattergories, a now good 20 teams of 2, 3, and 4. We are given a letter, and are asked to write down a one word answer DIFFERENT than anyone else. Sometimes common words win, sometimes uncommon words win, anyone matches, and your team is out! Out of 20 questions, we had 8 unmatched...yeah...no points!

We had lunch on the deck; I worked on the boat and worked on my notes, then joined Lynn on the deck for a half hour of direct sun.

The afternoon lecture was on what to expect in Salalah, our next port.

This country is about the size of New Mexico in the States, it has an arid climate, six months out of a year, and the hottest place on earth up to 120 degrees F. It was settled 9650 years ago, since the first Stone Age, main export for many years was frankincense.

We are told we are expected to haggle, \$1US=0.39 RO(Real's); we are asked to not discuss politics or religion, they are easily offended, no showing of affection in public, no pictures of government buildings, military, police or people without their permission. We are also asked to expose as little skin as possible, bring plenty of water, their water is not safe. It is 10 miles to town from the commercial port with a cost of 12-20 Real's (\$36-60 U.S.) depending on your bargaining skills and if the cab will take \$U.S. We are scheduled to walk the town; our transportation has been arranged.

Job from the bible was buried 20 miles from here, but we are going to skip that attraction.

We watched the water volleyball contest, Team Trivia, we won 1st with 18 1/2 out of 20 points; (Finally!) I gave one of the team our complimentary bottle of Champaign, she provided me with a bunch of people cut outs for our ship. (42!)

Golf putting was next; 19 people showed up, and I took 2nd place! Lynn washed out.

Back to the room, got ready for dinner, it will be the hot stone restaurant on deck 9, Lynn Loves that place! We will eat there one more time just to take pictures!

Lynn back to the cabin to rest, I wanted to check out the Connoisseur's Corner that offered premium cigars. Even before we visited Cuba, I wanted to try a premium cigar, and was told Davidoff was the best. When we went to Cuba, I tried several Cuban brands and

Noah

found them very smooth and enjoyable; here I selected a Davidoff Grand Cru Cello #3. I was charged $16.00 for the cigar and also received a complementary Hennessey Very Special Cognac which was an excellent match; I found the cigar to have a nice draw, but both the Cuban brands to be smoother and more flavorful.

Met Lynn for the show, a production featuring music of the 30's and 40's swing; not my kind of music, but I liked the enthusiasm.

Wednesday is the last day at sea before Salalah.

The forecast is hot but less windy than yesterday. The enrichment lecture "Iran: From Shah to the Ayatollahs, brought Iran from 1937 to the present. The Shah attempted to modernize Iran and told women they were no longer to wear the hijab. This was not taken well by many of the older women, along with the adapting of Western dress and standards. The Shah actually backed Hitler, so at the end of the war, he turned the Kingdom over to his son and moved to Mexico in exile.

The gap between the rich and poor continued to widen, and by 1979 a revolution produced the Ayatollah Ali Khamenei; He was put into office on promises to establish an Islamic Republic.

As with most politicians, when installed what he did was very different of what he promised. He decreed that he would be the Supreme Leader…" Faqih"; this gave him the right to overrule all other branches of government as an absolute authority; the current leader has been in office for 30 years! The names of these folks are very close; the main point in the end was that it is Iran and Iraq vs. Saudi Arabia, Israel, and the USA.

Off to play Scattergories; there are now 16 teams of 2-6 in a team. We didn't place again, best team had 15/20, 2nd 12/20, 3rd 11/20…we had 10/20 Argggghhh.

Lunch, and then I went off to finish the ship…it was time; I am enclosing a copy of description with pictures!

Ship and sailor superstitions: no throwing pebbles or stones into the water…SWELLS: No whistling on board…GALES AND STRONG WINDS: No bananas on board…SLIP ON PEELS, DEADLY SPIDERS CONCIELED INSIDE; No women on board…EXCEPT NAKED ONES ON THE FRONT OF THE SHIP!!

Bingo at 4, yesterday I gave her the tissue paper $100 bills, today I gave her three yellow pieces of paper cut out like diamonds, next will be chocolate...hopefully I will win at Bingo! She played along and shared what the bribe was...

Trivia at 4:45, third place! It was too late for golf putting; the session lasted too long.

I had a number of phone calls. The first was a credit for the Petra excursion I complained about. I asked, and they told me they also credited the woman I was assisting! (Louise), Tendai (our butler) came through with the chocolate. I bribed the assistant cruise director-bingo caller next session and a confirmation on the reservation for the Silver Note restaurant!

I also finished "Florence" the ship, portholes, and flag being the final touches along with 42 crewmembers on deck.

The dinner at Silver Note was well worth the effort. Lynn had cold beef and caviar, lobster on mashed potatoes, and strawberry soup, and I had a variety of sea offerings, the tuna special, and a chocolate volcano. All had deceptive names, and all were outstanding, well-prepared, and perfectly complimented; the couple next to us was from England, and the conversation was very pleasant.

It was another Karaoke night, and Lynn sang "The Gambler." I still could not find a song I wanted to do, and however, I will keep "The Gambler" and "Hotel California" as options next time!

Thursday, Salalah, Oman, we arrived at 9 A.M.; we are signed up for just transportation to the city and back. We have been warned a number of times to dress very conservatory; women: no mini-skirts, shorts, sleeveless or low-cut blouses; men...just must not go shirtless... "How equal".

We plan only to walk the souk or shops, looking to return to the ship before normal closing times of 1-4 P.M. I am looking for frankincense and myrrh...

As we left the ship we were issued visitor cards which were checked on the bus both leaving and re-entering the port, by a guard walking up and down the bus aisle; the ride to town was about twenty minutes and the guide and driver took the scenic through town both there and back to give us a little extra "look, see".

Noah

Information on the country: The main exports are gypsum, limestone, oil, and gas. Yemen is only 2 hours east of this port. Oman has a population of 4.5 million, and the total area is 300,000 square kilometers, with beaches to the south and mountains to the north.

Boys AND girls go to school now, before just boys, women also work now; in Muslim, the belief is in Allah, prophets and peace. Prayer is five time a day, women pray at home or if they go to the masque, they have separate area to pray in the mosque. A man is allowed up to four wives, but he must treat them equally; the man gives the woman a dowry before he marries her. No women were seen on the streets before and after the souk visit.

The signs are in Arabic and English, not much traffic for 9-11 AM during the week, homes are only two stories high, businesses and apartment buildings can be taller; they have a de-saltation plant for fresh water, the souk we visited is over 100 years old, a lot of frankincense, the lighter colored is best, but both frankincense and myrrh is burned, neither of us were impressed with the smell, so we passed. Most of the shops carried fragrances, scarves, and tourist stuff, maybe fifty shops, most exactly the same stuff, and the vendors were not as aggressive as in Jordan or Egypt. Conversion rate $1 US= 0.38 OMR...usually other currencies are less than US dollar, however, I no longer exchange since that India Rupee fiasco, most if not all vendor's take $1U.S.!

We bought a few trinkets, back to the bus, back to the ship, turned in visas and checked back in to the ship. Back to the room for repackaging our loot, change back to shorts, and catch up on log.

On deck for some sun, then everything caught up to us, and we napped a few hours it has matching temp and humidity in the high 80's!

In golf, I was tied in third. Trivia, I showed up late, but they wanted me to answer two questions; one was the "Lethal Weapon" series name. Yeah, I knew that, but I got confused about the drink question and answered "Old Fashion" rather than the correct "Manhattan." I felt bad; we lost a place by one point, so I had a Manhattan to reinforce the memory!

Dinner in the Italian restaurant, shared a table with another couple from Texas and a single from the Bahamas; the single liked to talk, and dominated the conversation, but everyone was pleasant and contributed.

The show was a one-man piano and guitar player that interjected jokes between songs, easy going, entertaining, and clean.

Friday, a day at sea

It was low to mid-80s, and another stinkin' "Formal" night dress day. Today is the big boat judging contest; it's time for "Florence" to shine.

We had a leisurely breakfast and lounged about on the deck, another clear, hot, humid day. We were looking for where the ships were to be displayed, and at 9:15, the first one showed up. It was a little smaller than Florence, and they were filling her hull with ice. Had two masts with sails and looked pretty good. We complimented them and went down to the cabin; Tendai, our butler, helped open the door and wished us luck.

Our first stop was on deck 5 the reception desk, where we had promised to show the finished product...they loved her! Up to the pool deck and we grabbed a table to set her up and wait.

There were five total entrants; one was shrouded in a garbage bag for a grand entrance! All the boats sailed, all the boats floated with the cargo of six cans of soda, the cruise director saved Florence for last; she went over very well, and received about twice the vocal votes as any other, actually about the same as the rest combined!!

I received the 100 points and a lot of handshakes. Posed with her and the team, then disassembled her and left her for a final resting place. Mini golf, no points for either of us, off to lunch, sushi and a salad, 45 minutes in the sun, then rest in the room before more games.

Mini golf, nada for both of us, Bingo I gave "Kat" the assistant cruise director a candy bar, making it money, diamonds, and candy and still no winning at Bingo, however the reaction from the crowd was worth it for both of us!!

Trivia only 14/20 ☹

The show was early at 6:30; "Blues Brothers, soul sister" and farewell by captain and crew. Best show, lots of enthusiasm, the theatre was packed, standing room only; dinner was on the deck again,

Lynn likes it best, plus I needed the pictures of the hot stones.

9:45 started the "Dancing under the Stars" program on the open deck; about 50 (total) people showed up, along with the two male escorts. Both took a turn dancing with Lynn and Slim Pickens, and they needed to be evaluated for future cruises. We wrapped it up after 10:30. Tomorrow is the last day at sea, and both of us are becoming those "old ½ dead folks"!!

Saturday, this is the last day at sea before our final port.

We received the disembark information last night, and before the show, I checked the expenses and which credit card they have to settle up. It was pancake time for breakfast, ordered them and they were blueberry and came on a hot plate…tastee, Lynn had just some fruit and a doughnut.

This is a slow day, always when the next day is disembarking…many take the entire day to pack and review their bills to dispute charges, plus last-minute booking of another cruise on the particular cruise line to get any discounts offered.

We had over an hour before the talk on Dubai, so we both took in our ½ hour of sun; not too many people on deck, when you eat at 7-9 at night, are half dead, and many don't eat breakfast till 8-9:30…

Dubai, of the United Arab Emirates, only recently skyrocketed to the major port and aircraft hub of today, from one of the poorest countries to one of the top five oil producers. The United Arab Emirates consists of seven countries and three million people; their flag is green, red, white, and black. And has one of the highest standards of living in the world.

The beginnings found to date back to 5000 B.C.; 367 of their money equals $1.00 U.S.; we are told:

<u>Never use a yellow ATM machine that is for local banks only and will eat your card! Also, negotiate the price with the cab, including currency, before getting in, and check the meter to make sure it starts at zero!!</u>

Stores in Islamic countries and many in Latin countries have Siesta time when they open from 10-1 and then 4-8; they also always bargain, starting at ½ the asking price. Downtown is four kilometers to town from the port, and the airport is six kilometers from the port. Here, as in many other industrial ports, cabs are not permitted past the entrance gate.

Two major attractions are Burj Al Arab, which is now the 7th largest building in the world and is shaped like a sail, and Burj Khalifa Towers, 2722 feet high.

Arabic is the official language, Islam the religion, although other religions are respected here; always agree on a price before money changes hands, and watch your photos of people!

Final Scattergories: 7/20 is not the best showing. Lunch was themed on the 9th deck, "American Diner," a U.S. Musical Road Trip featuring classic burgers, hot dogs, milkshakes, and beer; a total of 50-60 people showed up… We also attended a final enrichment lecture, "Gonna make a sentimental journey," movie clips of 40's and 50's musicals; not really something we are into, but we were there…

Started packing, final team Trivia 13 1/2 /20 no prizes; point redemption followed, and we turned in our points for little flashlights, money clips, and pens.

After the final dinner on the ship, I sat next to a very nice Australian couple. Then we were going to walk the deck, but they were already washing it down, and high wind caution signs kept us inside. We leave the ship tomorrow at 8:30 A.M. for our final excursion, then go to the airport and fly home.

Sunday

It's going to be a rough 24-plus hour; our bags were out and tagged last night as required by 10; we had breakfast and came back to the room for our carry-ons. We did see our attendant and wished him well (even though this was a "tips included" cruise, we left a tip for him and our Butler on the desk). We waited maybe 10 minutes in the lounge, and our tags were called to leave the ship. I reviewed the statement left for me in the morning and agreed with it, and it will be billed to my credit card.

Customs went very well, but when we got to the staging area, there was no Lynn suitcase!

I left her with the carry-ons and checked the other entire tagged luggage. nope…We were to leave early due to the tour we had, but

Noah

without luggage, we and two other couples were not budging. Finally, the entire luggage was off the ship; we identified the missing luggage by <u>our</u> personal tags. The white staging tags were missing on all three of the "missing" tagged suitcases. On the bus, I told him, "Swiss Airlines, Terminal 1," and off we went.

It was a ½ hour drive to our first stop, so here is some of the information we got on Dubai.

80 % of the people living here came from somewhere else; all religions are celebrated and tolerated. Christmas is Christmas, Ramadan is Ramadan, Passover is Passover, etc.. Like in Singapore, there is no tolerance for drugs, automatic two years in prison, traffic is camera monitored, and $200 fines if violated. Only 5% is agriculture.

The first stop was their most famous Mosque, with only outside pictures. In front were cylinders where carpets were kept for prayers outside the mosque. I had my picture taken trying to enter the women's entrance on the side; it was discreet. (The women's entrance) nothing like the grand front entrance for the men. You would have to apply for tickets to get in, and it would also cost you a good undisclosed price.

The second stop was the beach and the most expensive hotel (2-18K/night), Burj Al Arab 7 star! The tallest hotel here has 154 floors! There were water taxis on the inside of the harbor, and some were small gondola-sized river boats giving tours.

Saw and took a picture of an air-conditioned bus stop, stopped and toured a museum in the old town, where the restaurant offered camel burgers and camel milk, and fourth, stopped and toured the gold and spice souk, over 200 shops. I did buy some Arabic coffee, some tea, and a spice to clear my head when I have sinus problems. It started to rain, so we all headed back to the bus for the 45-minute trip to the airport.

There are 3.3 million people in Dubai and 9.7 million in the state; there are no homeless, no trash or litter, and no graffiti.

There are 65 malls; in 1966, oil was discovered. There are 120 varieties of grapes grown here; camel milk has 0 fat; a one-bedroom home runs about $80,000; a 3-bedroom home $200,000. Plenty of stores had a variety of Islamic women's wear in styles and colors we have never seen.

Tourism is BIG here; there are lots of specialty doctors and clinics, we see a lot of high-end cars, real estate is booming along with the oil, and there is even an indoor ski slope!

We are told this is the safest country in the world, and all roads are camera-monitored.

Most of the meat is imported from Australia.

At the airport, our first stop was Terminal 3; Lynn saw them unloading our luggage and started yelling that we were going to Terminal 1, and Steve, our dancing partner friend, reinforced the putting of the luggage back on the bus.

Terminal one was the second stop. I had to go to the other side of the bus to find our luggage, and into the terminal we went. It was 2:30 in the afternoon, our plane was scheduled for 2:45 A.M. Tuesday, and so we had to wait till check-in somewhere in the terminal. It was crowded, jockeying for a seat, and 9-10 hours to wait!

We took turns guarding the luggage as the others walked around, potty breaks, food, etc. There was not a lot of seating, so one aggressive gal took my seat; we moved. I told Lynn that "bullies" are both males and females. Found another spot, and then two guys broke into a fight behind us, broken up quickly by all kinds of security. And finally, at 10:45 P.M., the gate opened, and we checked in our luggage.

Since Lynn was in a wheelchair, we were pushed through the security lines with priority, not only computer but watch off, a full COMPLETE pat down, and I do mean complete; my carry-on was also inspected, my hands and carry-on wiped for residue, then we were taken to the lounge: snacks, wine, beer, and comfortable seating.

The flight was a bit over seven hours to Zurich, Switzerland. I slept through most of it, and Lynn had problems sleeping…she didn't have the two beers I had at the lounge, which helped a lot!

The landing went well, again a thorough pat down and off to the business lounge for another seven hours waiting for the last eleven-hour flight to Chicago.

There was nothing exciting about the flight to Chicago, although due to the recent snow, it took us ½ hour to taxi to our gate. Both Lynn and I had to go through additional security because the stupid TSA machine could not get our fingerprints again!

We were out for the bus at 5:10; International terminal pick-up is at 20 past every hour from 4:20 A.M. to 9:20 P.M. Or so the schedule states, and nope, no bus, both of us in light clothes, mid-20s and windy...

The 6:20 bus was on time, but the driver had no idea about the other bus???; and just opened the bottom luggage doors and told the group to put in the luggage on their own, the 80+-year-old woman who was waiting with us included. I objected; he didn't seem to care, and I wasn't close enough when she got there to help.

We were back at the bus station in Milwaukee. Taffy's taxi picked us up, and her boyfriend actually helped carry the luggage up to the condo. Another adventure closes; both of us are evaluating further travel after our next three planned cruises! Now, the jet lag 3-4-day adjustment begins.

Both of us agreed that this was not a favorite adventure; neither of us was a big drinker, the dinner jackets for supper seemed pretentious, and the excessive time to travel to the different excursion sites got old. It was interesting to see how many people not of the Jewish faith live in Israel, how tolerant Dubai is regarding religions, and how intolerant Singapore is regarding drug use. I am still surprised by how many people travel w/o compression socks and how many need to have a backpack both on excursions and as a carry-on, with no regard as to who they brush with them on the bus, in aisles, or on sites. One last thing is the number of people married to their phones, needing WIFI on buses, taking longer than most for selfies at different locations, or eating with the phone playing next to them, even with others at the table...

Educating Noah…Travelin'

It took almost the entire two weeks to recover; it's the Christmas season. Had Thanksgiving with Tiffany, her boyfriend Nat, and Cruz; we ordered the fixin's from Sendicks; it cost about the same as going out, so next year, who knows...

I am looking at volunteering in a financial program. Had to send background info to both the company and MPS, and then I had to be screened. The first information session is in January.

I had a deal with my grandson to pick him up during Christmas break on my way to the gym, but then he got his grades…I e-mailed him strike 1, C's, D's, and F's. When he told me it would be good, he lied to me. The worst thing he could do is cancel pick-up and drive lessons; he needs to take responsibility!

Noah

2020

It's a new year; working extra days at the DAV, went to the first class on Money Coaching, and will soon be leaving for our annual Caribbean vacation. The grandson let us know the finals did not turn out as he wanted. I guess he will learn that studying on break an extra hour is really expecting too much.

Our youngest daughter, Camille, let us know at her birthday dinner that their dog died. They have replaced him with a rescue dog that had three previous adoptions in the last 2 months and asked that we do not meet Silas until they have him acclimated to his new home.

I am gaining weight, losing drive, and getting depressed, will have to work on all three after this new adventure.

February 2020 Caribbean Getaway

Sunning on the decks, bar, and other Friday 02/07/2020.

The alarm was set for 3:00 AM; I woke up at 2:55, turned off the alarm, and took to the bathroom. After freshening up, I noticed Lynn had risen also: I opened the shades, set the thermostat down, put out breakfast, and finished our morning checklist. We had double-checked Tuesday about slots/parking availability and again assured we would have a spot.

Left at 3:50, it was 23 degrees F and partly cloudy; we arrived at the bus terminal at 4:15, got our parking slip, the bus arrived, and we were off. The bus was ¾ full, the trip down was fast, little traffic, and the roads were clear.

We checked our bags, got Lynn a wheelchair escort, TSA went well (only my left shoulder showed up), and we were at our gate by 6:30. Originally our flight was for 7:45, now the flight was 10:30, PLENTY of time …. Since Lynn insists on business class, that is the way we roll, in America you still have to be a member of an airline club to use their lounge, so we had to sit at the gate with others…

Gate change, from Gate 1 to Gate 20; we slowly walked to the other end of the terminal, plunked down our new location, and relocated the restrooms. If I am not walking (to get my steps in), we check the board every half hour or so to ensure we are at the right gate; the announcements are garbled at best!

The flight was on the new time, the seats were actually comfortable, and the two-hour-ish flight was uneventful. We landed a bit before expected, so we had to wait for our gate. We found NCL transfer soon after we promptly retrieved our luggage.

The ride as usual was about thirty minutes from airport to port, then we sat…twenty minutes on the bus we had our luggage unloaded, then around the terminal and got in line, a very long line… Eventually the line was moved inside…it took a little over THREE HOURS to clear customs and get registered in, (Due to the world-wide corona virus, all passports were thoroughly checked for travel to or from China the past 6 weeks) it was after 5 P.M. when we got on ship, no welcome cocktail, we found our inside tiny room.

No steward to be found, I left Lynn in the room to go to the desk and have the bed separated for that needed additional space. Had a cocktail, met up with Lynn, found the buffet café full of tired, pissed-off people with O.K. food, returned to the room …not changed over to twins yet, walked the ship, had a beer, listened to some music in the atrium, and went back to the room to find it just being finished up. It was 8:40 PM we went to bed….both of us were exhausted, and we will unpack tomorrow.

Saturday, a new day; I need to learn this ship!

We had two programs as requested. We unpacked the luggage and hung everything up, set up our schedules, and went off to breakfast. The buffet was not as crowded, most of the passengers actually looked where they were going, and breakfast was much better.

We toured the ship, played good morning trivia, and have yet to get a team together. Located the elevator banks, and walked outside, it is clear sunny and mid 60's.

Lunch was Greek specialty; good selection, people piling their plates high and then going for seconds; food was varied, and good, including dessert, not as crowded, and most were actually not blocking food areas, and actually watching where they were going.

Lynn had her Valentine's massage, an Asian bamboo roller

Noah

massage. I toured the ship, then found the "Deal or no Deal" desk to buy two cards for the game at 2 P.M.

I found two chairs, the cards cost $30.00 each and sat and licked my wounds (still seems like a lot of money for one game, waiting for two P.M. and Lynn. Two O'clock came, Lynn was still gone, the game started, and on the screen came "NOAH B" ...THE MC LOOKS AROUND, SEE MY HAND, AND I AM THE CONTESTANT!!

I walk up, and she places me behind a microphone and asks where I am from. I tell her, and the game begins. I was to pick one of 16 numbers on the screen. I picked 15 she asked why that number was. I told her that was the number that called out to me!

I then had to pick four different numbers. All ranged from 30 to $150.00; then I was offered $115... I turned to the crowd for help...got a majority of thumbs down, so I did, too!

Then I had to pick another three numbers, after they were exposed, I was asked again, I hammed it up with the crowd, the offer was $230.00 and I took it! They turned over the last numbers, and I was asked if I wanted my number or the offer...I stood firm, my number was $1.00 so I won BIG!

Then, when I sat down, Lynn joined us. She didn't believe me at first, but when others congratulated me, she believed me!

Later we played Destination Trivia, we took second place but no prize, and we had 14 correct out of 15!!

Lynn went to line dancing, she watched, it was inside and crowded, I started the journaling before it got to be too much to remember.

Dinner was at the O'Sheehan's Bar and Grill; I had the fish and chips, Lynn had the shepherd's pie, both were very good. We ended the evening listening to a four- piece soul band, and watched the not so newly-wed game with three couples; one couple married 3 days, another 15 years and the third, 68 years. Cost of first dates, bra sizes, and sizes of male members were described. Lots of laughs, fun for all, we were still not fully recovered so off to the room to finish the days journalism, hot showers and off to bed, hours ahead one hour, tomorrow is another day at sea.

Sunday, Feb 9th a much warmer day at sea. Bright sun, upper 70's

Educating Noah…Travelin'

but windy, 15-20 knots. We did notice no religious services offered, or chapel room, but every day there were Friends of Bill W., LBGT, and Solo travelers meets….

Morning trivia, walked the deck, make-up boat drill, signed up for tender transfer on Tuesday, and watched a Sushi demo…no samples???, checked out port of call t-shirt event, walked the deck some more and had lunch outside.

Afternoon Trivia, poolside hits with the band, Chinese Herbal Remedies lecture, easy afternoon. The lecture was just another "sell" for herbal meds and acupuncture, more "Ying and Yang, and tongue analysis;

Lynn got the "runs" and found a bathroom, I waited for her: she didn't return, so I watched a Patron tequila tasting, watched a woman making faces and passed her drink to her husband who also "made the face" since Lynn never showed up , I started to leave , and the woman said something, I couldn't hear, I went up to her and advised her to take some salt and lime, she declined and they offered me the last shot of the premier Patron which I accepted and drank…It was VERY SMOOTH… Thanked them both and then left to check on Lynn.

She was in the cabin, resting…I asked what she wanted, and since it was later in the afternoon, she asked for a ham sandwich… I went up to the cafeteria found some prosciutto and a lettuce and a bun, and brought them back with some orange water to settle her down, and left.

I had seen a cigar room, asked who to ask, went to the bar outside, ordered a cigar and Rob Roy and joined the cigar folk. They promptly provided a light and we sat and talked. The guy (big guy with tattoos head to foot) in the corner liked to talk, said some of his lineage was 40% native Aztec; and complained about the young folk today not having the same work ethic us "older" folk, seemed to have, and the conversation was lively from there.

His wife joined in, she runs a cupcake business and said her most popular was cannoli! Imagine that, a Spanish cupcake company selling cannoli's!!

I finished the drink and cigar, checked on Lynn, then on to find something else to do, this was our last sea day, we received a note that our transfer at the end of the cruise was cancelled due to our leaving before 11 AM and that we would have to find our own transportation to the airport when we disembark, so just another challenge on the last day!!

I went out to find some cookies for dessert for Lynn, one of the bakers said he would help me out, and provided a plate with six cookies covered in plastic wrap…she was happy!!

I then went out, just to wrap up the night, purchased a movie for Lynn to watch in the room, and off to have a bit to eat and see some entertainment. I saw the never–ending line for people still trying to sign up for internet…250 minutes for $125.00, 100 minutes for $75, or $14.80/day…we locked our phones in the safe, we will take them out and charge them before we leave…yes. We actually enjoy being away from the internet and phones!

After the show and another $15.00 Margareta and snack (included) I headed back to the room; set up for our first port…Jamaica and ended another day!!

Day four, LAND…Ocho Rios, Jamaica

We were both fresh, bright eyed and ready to go at 7A.M. Had breakfast and waited…we were supposed to dock at 8, the ship wasn't moving at 7:30, and we finally got to leave at 8:20 and joined the herd of passengers.

Forecast was showers and hot, the showers had stopped but the temperature matched the humidity at about 85. Off the ship we found Yardie tours, and told to wait …another wait, in the parking lot with cars and buses coming and going for almost an hour.

Finally, they crammed us into a small bus sized for 8 midgets or models; we were driven up the side of a mountain to a garden where two people were dropped off and we were transferred to a mid-sized sedan with another couple Bob and Betty from Ontario.

We stopped at the side of the road to taste local coconut, mango, nutmeg, and Jamaica apple and visited an elementary school…the kids were GREAT; lots of High fives, and some of the boys intentionally held back…all good fun, fantastic smiles;

We stopped at a coffee farm, were shown how to properly pick the berries, if you don't pick them right the next ones will not grow at that location on the branches. They are red when ripe, I asked how they taste, and he had me pick one and pop it in my mouth. Once past the skin, there is a little gelatinous coating which is pleasantly sweet, then there are two seed, which you don't eat these two are washed and set out to dry, roasted and then mashed in a mortar and pestle, the mix is added to boiling hot water for three minutes, then poured through a cloth bag to drink as Blue Mountain coffee.

Lynn volunteered to mash a handful of coffee beans in a large mortar, she did a great job!

As we drove avoiding the many potholes and bumps, our guide showed us his hair when not braided, it looked like a medium sized bush…he has it done every two weeks; I asked what he does when it is not tourist season and his reply was that he takes care of his grandma…the other seven months. Here, Kentucky Fried Chicken is referred to as K… eep F… rom C… ooking.

We then drove through the countryside pointing out different crop fields and vistas, seems odd they drive on the left side of the road. All major towns have a clock tower. It was almost one in the afternoon when we were asked about seeing the falls, Lynn objected, and so did the other guy, so we passed on them, Lynn still needs a cane and was not happy about climbing on rocks…Stopped in town, tasted rum and rum liquor samples, and picked up those necessary souvenirs! (The other couple did not know another word for marijuana was "ganja"; she also needed assurance that tendering to and from port was not "risky".)

Back in the car, and back at port a little after two in the afternoon; Shared a sandwich for lunch, played a number of trivia's, Beers of the world, Tri-bond trivia, and music lyrics.

Our room was not made up, so we complained the excuse was we had left the light on Do Not Disturb from yesterday…we didn't...the room was cleaned.

Dinner at one of the special restaurants had to wear country club attire including long pants. We met two women there and had a nice meal and conversation. At the theatre a program that did not require a reservation was "Back in the Day" a four piece long haired guy band doing Journey, Styx, Van Halen, and Bon Jovi. The band was loud and very good, a number of the old (er) squints left after the first song, but the theatre was still very full, and the fifty-minute show was full of energy!

P.S. Ocho Rios in Spanish means eight rivers; main attractions are Dunn's river falls, and Fern Gully we have pictures of the gully.

Back to the room, planned out our next day in the Grand Cayman Islands; no tours planned, no swimming or snorkeling either; so we will see what we will see...

Just one small "dark" note, all the elementary schools are fenced with locked gates, parents and guardians must be recognized or show ID to pick up their children...laid back and high, does have costs, I guess...

Day 5, Tuesday, February 11th

Grand Cayman Island. We have been here before, so we will just walk the town, and check out the beach, before returning to the ship, this is a tender port, tenders are running from 7-2 today.

The first tender out was a little after 7; these are the largest tenders we have seen, and they accommodate up to 250 passengers! After breakfast, we used our pass to bypass the "newbies" and jump on a tender (as in everything in life, nothing is equal, since we have sailed with Norwegian several times before we have privileges, this was one of them...on this ship, there is something called the Haven...it has exclusive amenities for the penthouse suites and even more privileged)

The tender was only about 10-15 minutes once loaded to the dock; we took a stroll past the waiting taxis, hawkers for "Hell", Turtle Hatchery, and snorkeling, scuba, and island tours. We have been to "hell" previously, (and we are married) we have also snorkeled here and visited the turtle farm.

We walked the shops, bought a few souvenirs, saw the random street chickens, and a cop with a drug dog watching out for salesmen with long coats, if you know what I mean!

I also found a post office, this was the first of over 30 boats and ships that did not offer stamps; it started heating up both matching temperature and humidity, so we were already tiring, headed back to the dock and jumped on the next tender back.

There were three other cruise ships in the harbor a Royal Caribbean, and two Carnival; ours seemed to be the largest having almost 4000 guests.

Educating Noah...Travelin'

On the way back to the ship we saw a cluster of snorkelers in the water, the water is so beautiful, different shades of blue and blue green and so clear! After lunch I decided to go back to town and mail the two postcards from Jamaica since that was also a British Territory, and Honduras and Mexico are different countries not honoring British or American stamps, put them in the out of country slot, I had just taken my ship pass and no money, so just a bit more of window and people shopping on the way back to the tender.

I joined Lynn for an afternoon of trivia, picto-word challenge, watched another win-lose or draw, and a cruise next trivia with Norwegian ship ports. We opted for a light dinner at the Irish pub, another trivia, and then retired to the room to set up for tomorrow and wait for the Comedy and Magic of Levent Show.

The one-man Levent show was lively, very entertaining, fast paced and everyone enjoyed by the response he got when asked, he engaged several audience members and was very clever in tricks and talk.

Off to play Wheel of Ill Will Game Show; similar to wheel of fortune to fill letters for a phase, but also included a wheel with odd activities or money...some of the activities includes singing answers in opera, rapping to the audience, smelling peoples arm pits or breath, standing like a flamingo till your next turn, etc.

Three contestants; the first game, and I were picked to be a contestant the second, and yes, I won, the phrase was Ice Cream Hot Fudge Sunday!! Lynn was yelling from the back what it was but no one up front heard her, I won an NCL T-shirt!!

We then listened to a rhythm and blues trio, preceding the final show (for us) called The Ultimate Dance Battle. Here six members of the crew, three women and three men were matched up with six members of the audience (Lynn and I are pretty sure two were pre-selected). There was an elimination, and between eliminations the loosing couple were interviewed on camera and shown to the audience, they hammed it up a lot and fun to watch.

The winning couple was determined by the audience, it was a lot of fun, lots of laughs, and the auditorium was full.

That was it for the night, 11:30, but we set our clocks back an hour so woo-hoo.

Noah

Wednesday, February 12th, Roatan, Honduras; We dock at 10, our excursion Garifuna and Mangrove Tunnel starts at 11; we are given instructions on how to find the tour group from either harbor, it will be the Coxen Hole Pier.

Rotan is the largest of the three islands that comprise the Honduras, it is surrounded by reefs, and Half Moon Bay, the best beach, the reef comes as close as 70 feet!

These islands are world class scuba and snorkel sites, the main industry is tourism, followed by fishing. The entire Rotan Island is 37X5 miles with a center spine of mountains and on a map looks like Cuba. The main population arrived in 1797 from Africa, to escape slavery and another tribe that kept winning in wars between them.

We had a leisurely breakfast, played a game of trivia, then got into the line for disembarkation…at 10:00, we finally got off the boat at 10:50, and this waiting in line gets really old!

We walked and walked finally to the exit gate, and found our tour in the mess of taxi's and promoters and quickly moved to a van, it was only us and a tour guide! This is an island that gained independence in the early 1800's we now drive on the right side of the road. Our guide's name is Shorn; current population of the island is 90,000, 20% foreigners.

Coxen Hole was named after the pirate John Coxen who raided the Spanish ships. The hospitals here are both private and government, there are ferries between the islands and there is also a small airport accommodating mainly Italian and American flights.

They have WIFI, eBay and Amazon have a pick-up warehouse on the island. October thru April are the rain months, it is not uncommon to have 45-50 inches of rain during that season. Many still build houses on stilts, since there seems to be always a wind; they string clothes lines between the stilts to dry the clothes.

McCoy is the national food dish; it is a stew of rice, flour, beef chicken, and iguana.

The land here is also taxed, the Islands here were discovered by Columbus in 1502; the schools primary, and elementary are locked here, the same as in Jamaica. Each school has their own color uniforms, this is mandated by the government; Both Spanish and English are mandatory and taught here, however in the small older

African community, the old language is also spoken.

We drove over the center of the island through a number of small towns, lots of corrugated roofs, but a few mansions and very distinctive homes, a small shopping center, even an Ace Hardware store!

We arrive at a small dock with two small rowboats with canopies to take us out to the mangroves. It was us, our driver, and a guide.

There are four types of mangroves, the red being the most popular and used in the past by the pirates to hide before pouncing on their prey. These are all salt water, the passage was just wide enough to let two boats pass either way, is was cool, quiet, and calming, a very nice experience.

They do make a wine out of cashews, which we thought was interesting, and no, we did not have a chance to try that either. Back to the dock, did some shopping and returned to the ship by 2:30 in the afternoon; lunch, Scattergories...we won; find the difference game; got our points and went to the room to type and relax for tonight's activities.

Took Michael Jackson's "Thriller" dance lessons, supper, and finished up the day playing Battle of the Sexes...six men vs. six women,(Lynn was one of them)each person got a number of 1-6, a number was read(12,354) read and they had to put in order, (012354, person holding the zero had to be first).

A paper airplane flying contest , pass the orange neck to neck, form a circle and fill it with as many of that sex as you could get on the floor, and finally sing a song fast...as soon as the microphone was put in front of you and no repeat of anyone else's song...men won three to two YEAH!!!

Tomorrow is Belize, no tours planned, we will just walk around and see what this port has to offer, this is another tender port.

Thursday, Day 7, February 13th, Belize. We arrived at port on schedule at 8, however clearance wasn't till 8:35; these tenders were catamarans, big...250 passengers easily and very smooth.

The transit in was the normal 15-20 minutes, before docking we were warned to keep seated until told to disembark, "You want a vacation, not medication" made everyone relax.

Noah

This is a premier resort, an expansive white sand beach with chairs, cabanas, and even balloon-tired wheelchairs. We walked through a butterfly house, visited cages with toucans and macaws, and an open-air enclosure with "Iggy," the iguana.

Took many flower pictures donated to several souvenir shops, walked the beach, Lynn danced to a native group playing drums; by then we were sweaty, mid 80's including high humidity; back to the return tender, our mission accomplished.

The afternoon was easy, we both got some sun, played some trivia, got a so-so sunset picture, and after dinner watched the "Perfect Couple Game Show" three audience couples, one married 8 days, another 24 years and a final couple 51 years. One contest was rolling a lemon up one leg of his pants and down the other by his wife, a blind folded wife with a long shaft getting directions from her husband to spear the round container between his legs, and finally breaking three balloons, chest to chest, butt to lap, and front to back; the 24 years couple won easily, lots of fun!

Clocks ahead an hour. Tomorrow is Costa Maya, our last port, before heading home.

Day 8, Costa Maya Mexico

We docked at 7. We were actually off the ship by 7:30 and took the trolley to the dock complex.

The complex of jewelry and souvenir shops was extensive, we walked and walked and finally asked people, and they had us go even a bit further to find the proper gate to get into town.

It would be another four or five blocks, Lynn was already tired, so I asked a cabbie the cost for the rest of the way…$8:00 US; I took it, we arrived shortly after and gave our ticket and told to wait. It seems our tour had left without us, about ten minutes prior…Phone calls were made, a van was brought up and driving a bit above the speed limit and slowing down for those speed bumps, we joined the group in another van thirty-five minutes later.

Oh, as the speed bumps increased in the little towns, stalls were set up where the locals sold pineapples (their main crop here), tangerines, jacana, mangoes, peppers, plus honey.

We continued to the Chacchoben Mayan Ruins about 20 minutes

Educating Noah...Travelin'

later.

Please note the directions scale was WAY off in determining the walk through the shopping area. I asked the others, and they told me they left the ship just after seven to arrive at the gathering point at seven forty-five.

We are told the trip to and from the site is a little over an hour, and the tour itself a bit over an hour, at the entrance is another bank of souvenirs, and a bank of toilets we all seemed to need.

It will be a half mile hike into the sites and then a half mile back. Since this is jungle, we were told to wear long pants, long sleeve shirts, and utilize insect repellent. It is now getting very warm, and yes, the humidity is high!

As we walk along the hard earth path to the first ruin, we are told that the pineapples here are sweeter, the core is also soft, and eaten also; the palm trees, there are seven varieties, all here, used for roofs as pointed out, along with various other trees and vegetation.

Peppers are integrated in the local diet, they are "Hotter" here due to the weather, to cut the "heat" salt is used; the cows are skinny here, he states this is due to genetics. The Coke and Pepsi products taste different in Mexico due to the use of cane sugar rather than corn syrup used in the States.

The area where the pyramids are covers almost twenty-seven square miles, and there are 368 pyramids here; most have not been unearthed. It is a National Heritage Site.

The temples are solid; only the top was to interact with God. When a person died, they burned the body along with his/her home. The closer to the pyramid, the better the person was to the community.

All the pyramids were constructed with four corners at the north, southeast, and west; the top was aligned so at each equinox, March 1st and September 22, the sun would be exactly on top.

No business was conducted during the rainy season, and it is normal to have 300 inches of rain at that time! Before the rainy season after harvest, the foliage was slashed and burned to provide continuous rich soil.

The Mayan calendar was the cycle of the planet Venus, 525 days; sacrifices were to keep the earth moving, and it was a privilege to be sacrificed.

The Mayan "zero" was represented as a shell. When it was shown around the world, it became a circle. The math was very similar to the Chinese; their math was based on 20, not 10 like ours, and they counted the toes also!

Solar eclipses were predictable by the Mayans, they were obsessed with astronomy.

According to the Mayans, man started 3114 B.C. Their math was a shell as zero; a dot represented 1-4; a dash=5; the calendar divided into five equal parts, on a tree, female is above ground, male is below, support and strength, the underworld was not necessarily evil.

Fun facts about Costa Maya: The earliest Maya settlements date back to 1800 B.C.; the Mayan's were among the first to use the zero symbol, had a written language, had books, and known for abstract mathematics and astronomy knowledge.

They constructed pyramids and temples rivaling those in Egypt; in fact, the Peak of La Danta is one of the world's largest pyramids. Ancient Maya had their own version of soccer, and there are approximately seven million direct descendants of the Mayan's living in the Americas today!

Back on the ship after 1; we stopped to have a bite to eat and hydrate, both of us exhausted…took naps, we were going to go to a paint class but they wanted $35/person to cover the cost of paint and canvas?? Nope, more trivia, tried to catch the sunset, but the mist rose and started covering the sun before disappearing into the ocean, dinner; watch "this or that game show, and the "Lip sync War Game "show to end the day. Set clocks back an hour tonight.

Day 9 Saturday, February 15th, last day at sea before port tomorrow

I was up at 7, let Lynn sleep in, and lounged around to find out where we exit tomorrow since they canceled our transportation to the airport due to our leaving before 11, the credit for that cancellation, where our passports were, and how /when to get them back, and a comment card to get some of the gripes off my chest.

I hate being negative on these write-ups, but the three-hour wait in line to get on was stupid, the hour waiting in line in a line that went to the back of the ship didn't make sense either, and tables in the lounge was not cleaned for hours, a cabin steward that was MIA, with the cabin not being attended to until afternoon. The smoking lounge on deck 15 was always full. You had to check out a towel on deck, and if not returned, your room was charged $25!

The lounge chairs are only 14 inches off the ground, few higher chairs on the 15th and 16th levels, no "free" water except one place mid-deck on 15 next to a bar.

NCL has gone "corporate." EVERYTHING involves additional charges; even the bartenders add 20% to EACH drink. They do have people at the bar …all the time, half the chairs filled, drinking before 9 A.M.! That's enough, bitchin'!!

Morning is low 70s, cool and breezy, a cloud front east of us, partly sunny, turned to overcast; we walked deck 8 for a short while, actually found a few of the doors locked, played a couple trivia, made origami frogs; a slow morning.

L.M., those with luggage and their own transportation can begin to leave deck 7. We watched an ice sculpture in the making, and we were going to watch the "Best Female Biceps" contest, but looking at the contestants we passed…people got bolder at the end of the cruise. It was one scrawny teenager and four bulky over 50 women…

Checked the drawing for a cruise, nope…cashed in our participation tickets, and ended up with three t-shirts of the five things offered (cozies, Frisbees, cards, t-shirts in lg or xlg, or water bottles), dinner, and one final show "55 To Stay Alive Game Show.

The show asked for volunteers; six were chosen, and each one was given a task; one was to empty a toilet paper roll with one hand in 55 seconds; he did it in 54, racing back and onto the stage and having people hold the end and unwind the roll…his last gasp he left the stage and went all the way to the port side of the ship! Another was to stack empty cups 7 high…she failed; at the end, all the players were called up on stage and had a cracker put on their forehead. The object was to move the cracker to the mouth and eat it without any help except facial muscles, and yes, two did this!

Sunday February 16th, going home. We were told all those with early flights had to take their bags with them and exit after 7. We had planned to eat at one of the early open restaurants, but it was closed…no one was told…we also saw another line forming at 6:30, we went up to the cafeteria which was full, quickly ate, headed back down to the room, and discovered that when we got off the elevator, the line went from the bow elevator bank to the back of the ship and back again to in front of the bow elevator bank…at 7 the line started to move, 25 minutes, just to get off the ship!

It was raining, with some cover, but not a lot, then ramp after ramp to get to the terminal, then once finally in the terminal, we had our passports checked, then three more loooong hallways to the taxis and buses. This is where it started getting better; we got a cab right away, and the driver asked if it was OK to help a woman dragging a large suitcase in the rain to drop her off at a hotel on the way…we quickly agreed, a block later we saw her; stopped the cab, put her suitcase in the back, then drove her 6 blocks to her hotel, she was not asked for fare, but the woman was very appreciative and did slip her (the cab driver) a number of singles!!

The trip to the airport was just another 20 minutes. We checked our bags outside the door, and we went to the desk to get Lynn a wheelchair. Shortly after, we were whisked away through TSA with just a minor search of me, then to the other end of the airport to our gate, 9:15, our flight leaves at 10:28…WOW

The flight home was perfect, the landing text book, our luggage was in the first 15 pieces, we walked from terminal one to the street just after terminal three and saw the bus, it was the Milwaukee coach, we loaded, and the bus left after we boarded, we were back to 13th street an hour and a half later, the car was covered with two inches of snow, both of us very tired, drove home, dragged our stuff upstairs, Lynn crashed, I unpacked most, made a light supper, and both of us in bed by 9.

Tomorrow is President's Day, another federal benefit, and we have only an afternoon furnace inspection to be concerned with to finish unpacking, washing, and starting the week-long recovery. We need, and need more each time!

It took Lynn a full two weeks to recover; a very bad flu, she required extensive nursing, so my time was reserved for her. I went back to driving for the DAV, and I was able to attend my first class as a mentor for Secure Money Futures. It is fun to see the life of these kids and their innocence. I truly missed that from my short teaching days.

I am now also taking Cruz, my grandson, to practice driving. There is so much I now take for granted; it is refreshing to see the learning curve, although after our third run, he is not learning as fast or has the confidence as either of my daughters had, but still very interesting!!

The coronavirus scare is taking over the USA; the president just closed flights from Europe for 30 days, cancellations of sports fans' events, and universities and schools closing. It is March 11th; let's see how long the panic will last!

Noah

On March 17th, all restaurants and bars closed in Wisconsin and across the country; insanity rules!

Educating Noah…Travelin'

Cruise Lines and Where

1.	Caribbean	Royal Caribbean (RC) 1
2.	Alaska	Regency Cruises (1)
3.	South America	Norwegian Cruise Lines NCL (1)
4.	Mediterranean	NCL (2+3)
5.	Quebec to New York	NCL (4)
6.	France Seine (River cruise)	Viking (1)
7.	Brazil -Amazon (River cruise)	Iberia (1)
8.	Atlantic Crossing	Mediterranean Ship Co. (MSC)(1)
9.	Scandinavia	Royal Caribbean (RC) (2)
10.	Caribbean	Holland America (HA) (1)
11.	Caribbean	NCL (5)
12.	Caribbean	Celebrity Cruise Line (1)
13.	New Zealand/ Australia/ Bali	Celebrity (back to back) (2+3)
14.	China/Tibet (River cruise)	Viking (2)
15.	Caribbean	NCL (6)
16.	Greece	Regent (1)
17.	Russia (river cruise)	Viking (3)
18.	Argentina/Falkland/Antarctica	Celebrity (4)
19.	Caribbean/Panama Canal/Central America	Celebrity (5)
20.	Japan/Korea/ S. Vietnam	Celebrity (6)
21.	Carib/Africa/India/Myanmar/	Oceania (1)
22.	Portugal/Spain (River cruise)	Viking (4)
23.	Alaska (second time)	Oceania (2)
24.	Cuba	Azamara (1)
25.	Polynesia (Bora Bora/Tahiti/Easter Island)	Oceania (3)
26.	Holy Land/ Jordan/Suez/Egypt /Oman	Silver Seas (1)
27.	Eastern Europe (Poland/Transylvania) (River cruise)	Vantage (1)
28.	Netherlands to Switzerland (River Cruise)	Amadeus (1)
29.	Columbia River	American Steamboat Co. (1)
30.	Great lakes	Pearl Seas (1)

Countries and States visited:

All the states have been visited: Hawaii, four islands, Oahu, Maui, Hawaii, Kauai, twice, and plus the Highway to Hana, and Alaska twice, including the Yukon territory.

Countries and Islands:

Alsace; Antarctica; Argentina; Australia; Austria; Belize; Brazil; Bulgaria; Canada (All the drivable territories); Chile; China; Costa Rica; Columbia; Croatia; Czech Republic; Denmark; Ecuador; England; Egypt; Finland; France; Germany; Greece; Guatemala; Holland; Hungary; Iceland; India; Indonesia; Ireland; Israel; Italy; Japan; Jordan; Mexico; Monaco; Montenegro; Morocco; Myanmar; Newfoundland; Netherlands, New Zealand; Nicaragua; Namibia; Norway; Nova Scotia; Oman; Panama; Peru; Poland; Portugal; Romania; Russia; Scotland; Serbia; Sicily; Singapore; Slovakia; South Korea; Spain; Sweden; Switzerland; Tanzania; Tibet; Thailand; Tunisia; Turkey; United Arab Emirs; Uruguay; Vatican; Vietnam; Wales , (72)

Islands:

Antigua; Apostle; Aruba; Bahamas; Bali; Barbados; Bonaire: Bora Bora; British Columbia; Canary Islands; Cuba; Curacao; Devil's Island; Easter Island (observed, harbor was closed) Fakarava; Galapagos Islands: (Isla Santa Cruz; Isla Santa Fe; Isla Bartolome; Seymour Norte); Grand Cayman; Falkland Islands; Grand Cayman Islands; Guam; Hawaii: (Maui; Kauai; Oahu; and Hawaii); Honduras; Jamaica; Madeira; Maldives; Papeete (Tahiti); Pitcairn Islands; Philippines; Raiatea; Puerto Rico; Principe; Sao Tome; Seychelles; St. Johns; St. Thomas; St. Martin (43)

Educating Noah…Travelin'

Picture albums of most:
http://theyaregoneagain.shutterfly.com

The Seven Natural Wonders of the World:

1. Grand Canyon — Done
2. Victoria Falls S. Africa — Done
3. Mt. Everest (saw from the plane when we went to Tibet — Done
4. The Great Barrier Reef (snorkeled it in 2014) — Done
5. Harbor of Rio De Jannero (stayed just off the beach) — Done
6. Paricutin Volcano (Mexico) — Done
7. Northern Lights (Ivalo, Finland, glass Igloo 2016) — Done
8. Swiss Alp's experience — Done
9. Amazon river experience — Done

Rivers of the world: Ganga, Amazon, Rio Grande, Rio Negro, Doro, Nile, Yangtze, Yellow, Volga, Thames, Mississippi, Columbia, Rhine, Danube, Seine

Destinations left: Greenland, Bermuda, Western Russia, Madagascar, Shri Lanka, Laos

Noah

FINAL

We are in the midst of social distancing, due to the Corona virus, the total world has been affected, 150 countries now have the virus, as of the 13th of March California has over a million unemployed applications, and the governor is thinking of shutting down the state. Our governor did, only "essential business" open, but I am going to "work", DAV had only 4 patients to bring in and take home, guards at all the entrances, plus a portable police lookout at the south entrance. My follow-up appointment was scheduled as a conference call for my shoulder conference, it lasted one minute nine seconds...good to go!

The stock market went from a high (all time) of 29,551 to 18,231 crude oils to a negative!! ($-37.63/barrel) with oil bouncing back in two weeks to $30.00/barrel; I framed a fill-up at $1.079/gallon! (Never let a crisis go to waste).

It is now the 27th of March, I went in to the DAV; I was the only driver, and acted also, as dispatch, two in, both out by 12:15 and I was told to go home. It is hard if not impossible to find toilet paper, stopped at 7 stores, bought tissue and baby wipes. We are told to stay home; If out, to keep six-foot distance. I had taken in the Subaru for safety checks and they had indicated I needed rear brakes, I called up Mike, my ex-son-in-law, and set a date to replace them.

I picked up the rotors and drums, took over to Mike's and he replaced them for me, nice talking to him again; I found a 4-pack of toilet tissue, also got pork ribs cheap at the Piggly Wiggly, so we will have shredded pork and sour kraut this week! The government passed a bill for over two trillion, our debt now exceeds 25 trillion (that would be $25/second for 32,000 YEARS!) market is starting to recover, the DOW was under 18,000, when it was approaching 30,000 in January!

Staying home is driving a lot of folk's nuts, especially me! President Trump was going to try opening up churches for Easter, but he now is looking to open up closer to the end of April...so hope is in the air! This is election year, the press and democrats hate Trump, since his election, including many republicans.

29 days into this shutdown, last Friday I was the only driver, two guys, and only one entrance open at the VA, no one under 18 allowed or visitors ON THE GROUNDS... we got a deposit from the federal

government on the 13th, dated for the 15th for $1200.00 each…. Woo Hoo!!

I am even getting tired of going to a grocery store, just to get out, we are seeing something this spring never seen before…not snow, not hail, but white flakes too warm to stick, and it is in the thirties…No word as to when things start up again, things are getting stupid, parks closed, drive in church services getting reported, and snitching encouraged, toilet paper coming back, but some meat packing plants closed for two weeks , so price of meat, and limits on amounts now enforced…this is America …I never thought it would ever be like this!!

May 27th, Memorial Day was Monday, no parades, no flag planting. Businesses starting to open…finally! I dropped off some masks, gloves, and sanitizer by Wade, my barber. We are asked to wear masks in many stores, supposed to keep 6-foot distance inside and out, many still wearing masks outside?? Churches are only allowed 10 people in the building…some say masks don't do much good for the health, our two-government heath "experts" Fauci and Burke kept extending isolation time, one, Burke, admitted that she cannot trust the CDC and claiming deaths inflated by 25%; any death counted as death by virus even with co-morbidities, and the most affected are nursing homes. Both VA and Medicare annual appointments cancelled until further notice, our Eastern Europe trip cancelled and moved to next June; there are a total of 328 total patients for this virus in Wisconsin, yet hospitals only taking "must due" items, cancer screenings put off people are afraid to go to the hospitals, some are actually making more on unemployment, if they can get it, some six weeks just to apply!

We took off Sunday and Monday, Door County Sunday, about ½ of the shops open, masks required to enter, and number in building counted.

On Monday we found the 45-degree North-90-degree West geographical marker, took a picture of it utilizing a young girl to give a size reference, and she was a lot cuter than me! There are only four hemispheric points in the world that exist, one in the Pacific Ocean, one in the Indian Ocean, one in the mountains in China and here!

The car was running hot again, I've had the Subaru Forester for four years, and it was time. I called Mike, told him I wanted a 2020

Volkswagen Tiguan, he gave me his contact, I went down and bought a silver one, we will see how this works out! This is my first Volkswagen.

A new crisis took over, a cop killed a black guy by putting his knee on his neck for an extended period of time, and this was captured on camera. It was wrong, he will be put in prison, the other officer and two rookies are also fired and indited. Needless to say, protesting across the country; along with burning buildings, looting, officers and civilians being shot and killed, windows smashed, "social distancing" being ignored, cops at first were being told back off by the "leaders" both mayors and governor's the first couple of nights, now after deaths and extensive looting and vandalism, some laws are being enforced; but the churches and places of worship are under strict distancing and mask rules…every night curfews are set and ignored, it's been almost two weeks, Minneapolis is considering eliminating the police department, other cities defunding police budgets. Hopefully the 'conversations" are held, and something is actually done, as has been promised for decades.

The stock market is coming back fast, already only 2000 points from all-time highs, unemployment down from a record 14.7% to 13.5% for May, last night the mayor of Milwaukee released the restaurants to reopen, without letting them know ahead of time, so many are still closed. (So much for the best and brightest in government).

I upgraded my phone to Verizon, due the continued bad service of Tracfone, although now I am paying $35.00 per month vs $125.00 per year! Amazing how many buys by the month, and have no idea of the real cost.

I also had stencils made for the new car; I have to add or customize to have them "mine"; this is three wild boars running representing the Savanah Express we witnessed in Africa, and they installed, not too subtle, but the car does stand out!

The great lakes cruise was also cancelled, it seems Canada not opening up as fast as the U.S., so that now has also been pushed to next year, seems we will be very busy all summer next year!

Update, June 11th, 2020 a group of Antifa has taken over downtown Seattle, banks and credit unions still only drive up, most stores and restaurants are starting to open, some require masks, and distancing, some not, thousands crowded into the church for the funeral of the black guy that was killed by the cop, but most churches otherwise very restricted…the double standard on how some are treated and others depends on political affiliation….and by the way, over 700 police officers have been injured in the country wide protest/rioting…peaceful??

I put in my notice at the DAV to end January 31, 2021, I have worked there since April of 2014; done…I also turned in my auto signs and quit the Six Cities veteran group; Madison Wisconsin downtown is boarded up, and that project is running out of money, plus I am tired of being only one of two people willing to beg for money.

Met with Art and Pat Kunstler to drive, on one of the motorcycle chapter circle tours, a find and tell outing. It was an old one, took us about six hours, brought back some very good memories, stopped at a cheese store, a great little restaurant, and a good time with good friends.

Went to a Father's Day gathering at my nephews, nice, no woke masks, good food, the kids didn't mention missing Lynn and my birthday dinners, so I e-mailed them that this was the last year of birthday dinners, I guess they are too busy for family get togethers.

I did talk extensively with my nephew Matt about working at home. It is becoming a trend, Chase, the bank he works for, is now encouraging work at home.

I can see eliminating open offices, supervisors, and increases in Uber and share rides, promotion of less interaction, increased isolation, less service, and more profit with much less employee interaction, less interaction with customers, and an increase in deleting entry level jobs…

It is the end of June, a lot of resistance in letting business open up, long lines at the DMV, some people have still not received unemployment checks. I made the mistake of looking for a very part-time job two weeks ago; I have had EIGHT phones' calls from people "on recorded lines" offering jobs; the question is why is unemployment so high? Why are they considering sending out more stimulus checks??

Mid July, sold Lynn's Volvo convertible, the neighbor totaled his car, wanted the Volvo, and I researched, gave Lynn the numbers and let her make a deal. She did great, she was having more and more problems sinking into the Volvo, and when you could put the top down it was either too sunny and humid, or the trip was too short. We contacted Mike our X son-in-law, and went down to visit him with cashier's check in hand.

Lynn now owns a fully decked out Nissan Rouge. It actually is a little larger than "Vicky" (my VW) and she has to get used to it, it is amazing as to what is included in cars now, even this 2017!

The cooped up continues to wear on me, I called my VA doc and she is arranging a mental acuity test for me, after my blood work was great. Lynn also FINALLY agreed to a road trip, so we are visiting some national parks in Utah in August. I went to AAA for trip ticks (they still do this) and now the wait.

Had the mental evaluation, took almost 4 hours, and I am "normal" for my age group...Lynn says; "Maybe for a 5-year-old!!" They did note that the MRI, I had done a few years ago indicated that I had had a few TIA's (Transient ischemic attacks) which makes me a bit more prone for an actual stroke in the future, and may contribute to some memory difficulties

The DNC was supposed to have their convention here in Milwaukee, it was basically cancelled, all of convention was virtual "due to covid" ...so much for business in Milwaukee...

With the continued restrictions, due to the covid pandemic, food delivery is becoming more common, both grocery and restaurant; virtual school is being pushed by one party, actual school attendance by another; EVERYTHING is political now and will be till election.... It is now being leaked that some positive tests for the virus are false, along with the death count....

Check this out

Needed this so bad...Utah State Parks   August 16-21, 2020

Sunday morning, breakfast, put the last stuff in the car, programmed the GPS Des Moines, Iowa, or hopefully Council Bluff, Iowa...figuring 8-9 hours on the road with lunch, 8:00, 2669 miles on the car.

Educating Noah...Travelin'

It was a perfect day, bright and sunny, according to the weatherman, the outlook for the next three or four days in Milwaukee was clear, bright and warm.

Driving through Wisconsin had no road construction until Beloit, a little over an hour out, but we navigated and crossed into Illinois. I had added $20.00 to our I-pass to facilitate drives through the tolls. With the I-pass, the tolls are ½ price, and as noted on other adventures, the I-pass works everywhere but Florida.

The traffic wasn't bad, more than I expected, lots of trucks for a Sunday. And we saw a lot of motorcycles returning from the Sturgis Harley Rally, in South Dakota every first weekend in August, and yes, we took our Honda there years ago!

Traffic moved along at 70-75 mph, most were courteous, not many left lane sitters, only a few construction areas, lots of campers going both ways.

This is flat lands, all planted, all very green, the corn not harvested yet. We pulled off at the Amanda Colonies, but oh, yeah, it is Sunday, the Sabbath, 7 little German settlements, nothing open; However, the Lily Lake was blossoming, waterlily flowers blooming, and the fragrance was worth the stop and look!

Iowa has lots of wind turbines, we saw a couple hundred, about 70% turning, saw a vertical wind blade mounted outside a rest stop, and a couple being transported by semi-tractor bed.

One of the farms had a tractor from a tractor trailer truck mounted on top two silos; saw a few angus beef herds, but that was about all for animals bigger than birds.

Pulled off the road for lunch, had to wait to be seated, our table and chairs disinfected first, then the menus. The place was hoppin'; our meals were more than we could handle, so we tool a box back for supper.

Heavy wind and thunder storms last week damaged quite a bit, we saw quite a few damaged trees, some sway ales of corn blown out, but most if not, all cleared from the roads and highways.

The Quality Inn was in downtown, Counsel Bluff, Iowa, we arrived at 4:55 P.M. Checked in, walked over to a large service station and bought a salad to go with the left-overs from lunch, a couple bananas and donuts for breakfast and cookies for dessert. There was a rain front coming in, the clouds were beautiful, took a picture of those, also took a road picture and one of a bridge we crossed in town lit up in yellow and orange!

Monday, 8/17/2020. All offered at these motels now is juice, yogurt and coffee.... (You know, the covid-19 thing).

Monday morning, we left the motel at 7:30 A.M. It was a rough night, we had a floor level room, close to the highway, a large gas station, and the parking lot. From 10-1, Harley's coming and going, BOOM, Boom, Boom, very loud low frequency of a base from some clown in a lowered car, and a few loud pipes from kids' cars, the air conditioner quit in the middle of the night...yup, she got me up, and I got it running again... I talked to a couple of Harley guys in the lot, yup, they were at Sturgis, had a great time, seems covid didn't affect much as far as The GPS quit working, west of Iowa, so we had to trace our way back the way we came to continue, another 20-minute adventure, but now we are map only....

Iowa, Nebraska, and into Colorado today, easy 75-80 mph, courteous drivers, fields all have walking sprinklers, everything is very green few towns, large farms, more cattle grazing, outside of North Platte I took a picture of the archway Monument over the highway; North Platte turns 1000 rail cars daily! It is the largest rail yard in the U.S.A.

Three hours in we were looking for a place to stretch, an interesting sign and name of town caused us to pull off...turned out to be a marijuana dispensary, looked busy, we passed.

At 12:30 both stomachs growling, both frames stiff, we pulled in to small town, checked and had lunch. Wow...Ole's Big Game Steakhouse and lounge, in Paxton, Nebraska, service food and decor excellent, I believe they had every mountable animal there is except a rhino, they did have a full-size polar bear!

We continued our trip with Denver being much larger than we remembered, and the mountain views fantastic! We wanted to get past Denver and started to see warning signs that the highway to Utah was closed due to wild fires. After weaving up and down through the mountains we found a small town to check how to bypass the next leg, find a place to stay, and get gas. The tourist center was closed...go figure, (on a Monday at 3:15 P.M.) but we found a motel, filled up with gas, and the friendly gas attendant gave us a longer alternate route, but one that goes through. The day was perfect, starting in the mid 60's through the 90's; clear, bright a few clouds in the sky.

Tuesday 08/18/20; we both had a good night's sleep, even though this room had no air conditioning, but a stand-up fan and ceiling fan, the room was very dated, bathroom very small tub at least 50 years old, but the place was comfortable, and we slept well.

We had breakfast at Carl's Jr, after turning in our key, and were on the road by 8:00 our time. (We are in Mountain standard time so from here on and through Utah, they are an hour behind us.)

The detour due to the extensive forest fires was through the mountains, including the Arapahoe National Forest; two lanes up, one down for the slower trucks, many hair-pin turns speeds from 65 to 15, many long climbs, many steep declines including a few run-away truck lanes.

We finally hooked back up with the freeway a little after noon; we found a Mexican restaurant and decided to have lunch, the detour added about 3 ½ hours to the trip, the smell of smoke was heavy in the air.

The entrance door to the restaurant was locked, but people were seated inside and eating. Another customer came in, told us we had to wait till they came, I asked him if he was here before, he said "yes" and he knew the owner. I then said "you get special privileges?" He said "yes" what do you drink? I said anything with tequila, and my mane is Noah and my wife's name is Lynn, He said his name was Sergio, we bumped elbows, and were let into the restaurant.

By now the temperature is in the low 100's, when it gets this hot neither of us can eat much, we ordered an appetizer variety, the waiter brought us a Margareta compliments of Sergio…I looked for him and gave him a thumbs up, and half way through our meal, I ordered a Modelo for him, He indicated he didn't drink but gave the beer to his buddy. We couldn't finish the appetizers so had them wrapped for dinner, and back on the road.

The land is flat and barren, it took an hour to cross into Utah, and another hour to get to a tourist bureau, our GPS quit, only good from Iowa east.

Mapped out the parks we wanted to see with the volunteer, drove down to Moab, found a Comfort Inn and checked in. Then off to Arches National Park to see the arches and rock formations This Park was at least 100 if not 1000 acres, red sandstone formations, a road meanders through most of it with turn-offs and parking areas throughout.

I did hoof it to one arch, in the 105-degree heat, and soft sand I felt both my age and weight, but yup, got the pictures…Lynn, the smart one, stayed in the car!

We only spent an hour and a half in the park, the formations are as varied and spectacular I took a number of photos just as a great reminder!

We stopped at the ranger station on the way out, it as in all the parks start and stop at the ranger station, and clarified where the other parks were, and headed for a fossil store for a friend, picked up a shark's tooth, and iron pyrites (fool's gold) as a memento…Oh, yeah, I did pick up three sample rocks for my rock collectors back home.

Both of us tired and crabby, brought in the stuff from the car, relaxed a bit, showered, bed by 9:30 beeeat!

Wednesday August 19th Left at 8:30 this morning, breakfast offered was a piece of fruit, granola bar, a small muffin and coffee in a bag, the attendant filled the bag… (no, I poured my own coffee, and did NOT put it in the bag!)

Since we did our first State Park yesterday, today we get as many more as possible, the first was Canyon Land State Park; I love this senior park card, saves us the $30.00/park admission!! On our way there are lots of mountains, we looked closely and found a full-sized train 1/3 up, it looked like a toy, everything here is massive!

We stopped at the ranger station after touring the park, most of them are on a loop, you exit where you enter, he confirmed that the red mountains were ferrous sandstone…high school did pay off! He was friendly, knew his stuff, and answered all of our questions immediately, Lynn thought he was very handsome too….

On the way to our third park, (Canyon Land was a 1 ½ hour drive like yesterday's Arches tour); we saw triple trailer semi's, speed limit on highways is 80 mph; in the parks, 35, lots of hairpin turns, few guard rails, but all the roads in excellent condition, there are pull-over spots for major attractions. Third Park Tempe Mountain; great colors, everything just MAGNIFICENT; both in color, and size, most rivers are dry or just trickles, it is very dry, very hot (104F) and driving through the mountains from 6500 feet, then down, then up again, most if not all drivers courteous and friendly.

Time for lunch after finishing the park we found some of the mountains seemed to be carved with figurines, some with columns...Mother Nature at her best, and very creative. Lunch in Hanksville; again, excellent food and great service.

Capital Reef was the next park, here all the rocks are flat (Shale) so I picked up a few for my rock people. The color is getting greener the farther south we are going, what magnificent views, I only hope the camera can convey ½ the beauty!

Our last park for the day was Capital Reef National Park, lots of green now, actually some hieroglyphics on one wall.

It was getting late, both of us tired from driving, the heat was getting to both of us, I did have to hike a bit at several locations to get those "must see" photos, and yep, the camera battery was getting low.

The gas was between ½ and ¼ so we pulled over for gas, Lynn found a basket she liked, then to find a town with a motel to crash and burn. We found one, Cannonville it was 5:20; mileage 1965. This was a "killer" day; both of us exhausted, the room was spacious but on the second floor, no ice machine, went down to the office, "we usually charge for a bag of ice, but we are out" I said, all I need is a handful for our beverages, so he took me back to the ice machine, put in one scoop, asked if I owed him anything, he said no, and that was that. We finished our left-overs from lunch, showered, relaxed, bed by 9:30.

Thursday, we finish the parks and head home today. The office was closed, so no promised breakfast, left the motel at 7:30 our time, and off we go!

First stop was Brice Canyon National Park, our lifetime senior pass saved us $35.00 this time. As we entered the park, three tiny young deer scampered across the road in front of us, this was an omen, we saw at least 10 more alongside the roads as we progressed through the park. The total run through the park was about 36 miles, lots of turn outs for pictures, absolutely no litter, and everyone was courteous. Up and down through the park, elevations to 9115 feet; this is a testament to God's gift to us, paintings, sculptures, the pictures cannot show the depth and magnitude!

Zion, our last park, we entered the east entrance, used the pass, the roads are very narrow, excellent condition, if Lynn put her arm out, she could touch some of the rock sides, we are at the southernmost park, a lot greener, and the river beds have some actual water! We progressed and went through the longest National Park tunnel at 1.1 miles! On the way out we stop at the ranger stations and shops to answer questions, use the bathrooms, here there was absolutely no parking, on a Thursday at noon! Can you imagine the weekends?? I dropped off Lynn, tried two more passes, then found a 15-minute parking spot, ran in used the facilities, found Lynn and back on the road.

We looked but could not find a restaurant, so we stopped at a grocery/hardware/liquor store bought a lunch, ate and started our trek home.

At 6:30 we pulled of the road, Coalville, Utah; just a few miles from the Wyoming border; yup, both tired, the traffic around Provo and Salt Lake City was six crammed lanes each side…

Friday; 08/21/2020; The breakfast was a donut, toast, yogurt, and coffee and almond milk…not bad. We left late, slept in, so 8:30 was out the parking lot time.

This is going to be a travel day as the balance of time, I was shooting for Saturday, but it is looking more like Sunday return.

The trip has a lot of scenery, very few towns, some cattle, some horses, and we saw two antelope along the road. The speed limit is 75 or 80, and most pull over to the right, lots of trucks, both pick-ups, and semis, and campers. A little after 11, we passed the continental divide, every few miles we see small oil wells.

For lunch we stopped at a roadside tavern, had a good time talking to locals, our order was wrong, so drinks were on the house…we were OK with that, and the company was very good, spent the good part of an hour there for lunch!

Running close to a quarter tank, (averaging a bit more than 30 mpg) pulled off the highway, we are close to the South Dakota border, the end of Wyoming, so we decided to call it a day. Filled up with gas, and checked into the Best Western next door. Total mileage 3004

Educating Noah...Travelin'

Saturday, it will be very late today or mid-day Sunday when we return home. Breakfast was offered in the restaurant only, no free breakfast, so we had a very nice breakfast, the waitress was very nice, and since everyone else is on Rocky Mountain Time at 7:00 our time 6:00 theirs, we were among three tables.

Off at 7:35! As we are heading east, everything is getting greener, we are now seeing sunflower and corn fields, along with beef cattle. I planned to go to Sturgis, to see what it looks like after the annual run every year for motorcycles. The town looked empty compared to the 10-12 years ago we drove here on our Honda! Please note, the town was immaculate, no littler, no indication that there were thousands of bikers here just 1-2 weeks ago! We stopped in at a biker shop, and scarfed up a couple deals and left.

Next stop was Wall Drug. We were here also when we went to Sturgis, spent an hour and a half in town, scarfing up a few more "must haves", plus lunch. I found it hard seeing how far in between these towns were, plus how much we did cover on that bike in such a short time...I was much younger then...

It was getting later, we pulled into a small town, Lynn tried to use her Choice Hotels rewards for a room, only to be told now, that she needed to be signed up first, even though she had called a few days earlier during lunch to confirm that we qualified, so she said "find me a Super 8." One half hour later, we found one, we are now in Minnesota, had put on enough miles, and she and I were getting' "bitchy", so we got a room, found a restaurant open inside eating (covid you know); we ate at a Perkins Restaurant. We both wanted the chicken pot pie with salad, but of course they were out. The waitress said they run out every day. Don't you think someone would let management know they have too few? We would have let them know they needed 10-12 more made each day!! Done for the day, tomorrow we will be home!

Sunday, the final stretch; about 450 miles to go, left the motel at 7:05; after a muffin, yogurt and coffee. The morning has a morning mist, the sun rays piercing through the clouds, touching the ground, a really nice picture to drive into. Once into the mist, it was only 10-15 minutes before the sky was clear, and the sun shing bright!

We passed many wind farms, many of the turbines were sleeping, no movement, not much wind today. Our favorite cheese store in the

Wisconsin Dells area appeared, so we had to stop, made a good donation, and received a good supply of cheese in return; we also tried a lemon meringue soda…. yeah, it was very good!

Home at 2:00 in the afternoon, another great road trip!

Total miles: 4012

Average mpg: 30

Motels: $624

Food: $319

Had to have stuff: $270

Gas: $292

It has been two weeks since returning, met with the Medicare doctor; I am officially now only 10 pounds from all-time high, and eating half what I used to, need to count calories, exercise more. Met with a friend and had her arrange a time at a shooting range, to show her how to handle a hand gun.

The gun lesson was cancelled, she was uncomfortable going to a range without a mask on.

Cruz turned 16, I gave him driving lessons, had cones to navigate

Educating Noah...Travelin'

in a parking lot, practiced backing, parking, parallel parking and driving. We then drove when he had confidence on three major trips of 3-4 hours, the first was to Beloit and Fort Atkinson, the second was through the north side of Milwaukee and all the way to Plymouth Wisconsin, and the last to Madison Wisconsin; southwest, north, and west. Yup he is ready. The problem is grades, his mom won't let him get his license till they improve; the problem is school is in class, then virtual due to covid...difficult for him!

It is now the end of November 2020; the election is finally over, still being contested and the democrats are gloating. I and one other driver drive every Friday for the DVA; we held disinfect the vans and cars, and we only have 3-5 people between the two of us to transport.

We have been under a mask order since August 1st, the covid cases are peaking here in Wisconsin, no information on how many is A-symptomatic, saying some hospitals are close to full, a few more die every day, I guess there is no seasonal flu this year, and all other deaths are down...very suspicious...We had notices that three vaccinations will soon be available, waiting for FDA approval. The governor is asking everyone not to have Thanksgiving with extended family to keep to a total of 6-8 people. In Oregon, their governor is asking neighbors to report any gatherings they see of more than 6-8 people, California is closing down restaurants and putting on curfews; this is all after a summer of rioting and looting where nothing was said.

I got a call from Basil regarding the final demise of Six Cities Veterans Group, his wife died 2 weeks ago, out of the last $700.00 spent on mailings for support, he had 30-40 answers and they were usually moving notices; his liver has cancer also, he will be getting chemo early next year.

I entered into a business with Tiffany's new boy-friend in May; Hopefully it will be over very soon. I have lost complete trust in him, he fits a "flim-flam man" pattern to a T. Doesn't answer and screens his phone calls and takes a week to answer e-mail. Since she has known him, he has had back problems, leg problems, and recently a stroke, his BMW is always needing work, he works for a while, then off...

I will be ringing a bell for the Salvation Army for 9-days to finish up the year, signed up with another volunteer program to keep busy

Noah

next year, plus since all out scheduled travels that were cancelled from March on, it should be a busy 2021; and both Lynn and I will be very happy so see this year end.

Educating Noah…Travelin'

2021

It is New Year's Day, spent New Year's Eve with Lynn's brother Perry and Janelle his wife; we went out to eat, then played games at their house; had a good time we got loud and drunk….

Everyone is still confused as to this covid epidemic, we have two vaccines now, the roll out is slow due to slow State planning; care givers are first, some states want criminals next?? Some want the old folks since they are the ones the virus is so deadly with; but who knows. Many of the deaths classified as covid are being "as" rather than "with" it seems when politics gets involved nothing is trusted, people all wearing masks, trying to keep distances, each State has different rules, there is still a big push to defund the police, crime and deaths due to crime at least doubling. There now is a renewed effort to legalize marijuana "to increase State revenue" ignoring petty crime increases and health warnings about it. This will be my last month with the DAV, it has been 6-7 years, I am now driving for EROS two to three times a week taking seniors to appointments, we will see how that works out.

We got our new dates for the cruise we had cancelled due to Covid; it will be February of 2022. No news of the other cruises this year besides the eastern Europe one being moved 3 weeks later. Everything world-wide is in limbo, hopefully by spring there will be a lot more positivity.

I gave notice three months ago about leaving the DAV. Today I pulled the plug. They had a meal for everyone, and gave me a gift card. I started 08/24/14 and have consistently worked 1-2 days a week since. This end date is 01/29/21. (You can do the math if you want.)

Yesterday I received my second covid shot, little if any information given as to how this affects the mask mandate; there are rumors that covid tests are required three days before and three days prior to leaving overseas on travel. When politics gets involved, everything is confused, no one knows, our new president in the first week has issued a record number of executive orders; new policies are being implemented, confusion reigns, hopefully by May this will be straightened out.

I am driving for EROS helping seniors with transportation, plus I renewed my nursing license to help out the Franklin Health department for 4 weeks on Tuesday afternoon for 4 hours. I also signed up Lynn for a number of hours, mainly for her to get her shot early also. The VA is now giving shots to older vets, Wisconsin is one of the slowest to give out the vaccinations in the mid-west, the governor is blaming the Feds, even though he has only used 1/3 of what he got in December of last year. There are still some cases in Wisconsin where the unemployment from March and April haven't been paid; what a shame.

First "It was time" in 2021

After the horrible year of covid last year, the government shut downs, the moving of goal posts, an election year riots in the streets, hate for small business, police, and differential enforcement of laws to some and not others, every other commercial on TV is either insurance companies or lawyers, we needed a break, and a get-away.

Lynn suggested a road trip, one to Laurel Mississippi, the place where the ben and Erin Napier "Hometown" home renovation TV show is produced. I contacted AAA for trip tics, and after two weeks finally met and obtained the maps and information. This will be the last year paper will be used, like maps, trip ticks are old school, phones and internet from now on after stock is depleted.

Our plan was to leave after Lynn's dental appointment Thursday February 18th. Previously that week a cold front went through the south, ice storms and snow, 6-12 inches of snow throughout the south, massive power outages in Texas, and plenty of road accidents. Not ideal for travel, PLUS, the covid restrictions nationwide.... BUT we "gotta go!"

While Lynn was at the dentist, I packed the car, fueled it up, and set up the GPS. Ten thirty we were on the road. I had Lynn plan the trip, and asked her how far down in Illinois we could get for the first day. I had forgotten that I originally set up the trip so that it would take longer to get there than back, so after we passed Chicago, we were actually doing the trip in reverse of what planned.... arghhhhhhh

The day was clear, upper 20's F, and traffic, given it being Thursday, was light. We passed Chicago midday, no traffic back-ups, and continued south. As always, I tend to push it a bit, and really wanted to get past Illinois, Lynn relented, and our first night was spent in Havik, Missouri.

Educating Noah...Travelin'

Friday morning, no promised "free" breakfast from the motel, but got a bite at Arby's after filling up... (same place we had dinner, not too much indoor eating yet!). The roads became worse, many snow and ice patches, at times the entire left lane was ice and snow packed, we joined single lane truck convoys a number of times, traveling from 35-60 miles per hour.

We pulled off the road in Memphis, wanting to tour the Rock and Soul Museum, but the visitor center was open but the walkway to the doors were not shoveled (not even a narrow path) and the 4-6 inches of snow was slick and irregular, so we pushed on. I had an idea to look around downtown, found the address and NOPE, everything closed, it is around noon, no one on the streets, barricades closing off main streets, few if any open signs, so back to the freeway and head to Laurel!

We arrived just after 3, and toured around the city. This was much larger than we thought, went up and down a number of streets looking for the remodeled homes they had refurbished, and found some very nice homes. The second time looking, I stopped and asked a very friendly guy with his dog and daughter. He pointed out the shop points of interest, and pointed out a red Chevrolet Chevelle SS 396 that went by with Ben Napier behind the wheel...excited Lynn a bit!

We took pictures and found a restaurant for a supper of fried green tomatoes and duck won tons.

Saturday morning off to Nashville. It is in the mid 30's the roads are clear, and the temperature is climbing! We had contacted my niece to see if we could detour on the way home to visit with her and her family, we asked how far from Nashville and she said two hours. Lynn referred to our guide book and booked a motel room for tonight in Crossville, east of Nashville.

As we drove north, the temperature was in the upper 40's now, highways were dry. Midday we arrived in Nashville, toured the town, here it was open, but a lot of barricades, no real parking, lots of people on the streets in and out of bars, blaring music, everyone in masks, but nope on the social distancing...

We drove the streets, but really not in the mood to bar hop, so off we went to Crossville. Toured the town, again much larger than we had imagined, found our motel, then went looking for a "rib Joint". Found signs leading to Lefties Bar B Que" and enjoyed a perfect meal!

Noah

Sunday morning, we drove over to Cindy's place, met Paul and his son Malachi; her two daughters Gabriel and Serenity (they grew quite a bit since we last saw them) when they came up to visit ma before she passed. We had a good conversation, the girls and Malachi usually with noses in their phones, and the (4) dogs caged, one of the two cats came out occasionally. Devin had to work so he couldn't meet up with us, reservations at an open restaurant Cindy arranged, pictures and food. Nice conversations, all day, everyone at ease, warm family, nice!

After the restaurant we took off for home taking the less traveled highways toward Indianapolis and drove until "it was time", just south of the city. We did take a few pictures, beautiful country, even snow covered, we both noticed how much land there really is! We checked out, we were going to stop at a restaurant just before the Wisconsin line, the signs said it was open, but the door locked, we left, Lynn called, they answered, and said the door in the back was open…. DUH…she let them know a bit about signs! Treated ourselves to Cracker Barrel, always good, very nice people and staff, home by 3 PM Monday, 2050 total miles.

It is now May 4th, 2021, our Bermuda and transatlantic are a "go" FINALLY! All other cruises have been moved to next year. We are told we do not have to wear masks outside if vaccinated, but we still have been wearing in restaurants before sitting down. There is definitely a mood to "get out" and we are seeing more and more of the restaurants filling up (within GOVT. guidelines); those that still exist… Many vacant commercial buildings, malls dying faster than we thought; crime increasing geometrically and our southern border is basically open, with little or no concern by the government or the press. In several conversations, the investing in silver was brought up, so I did look into, what I found was a shortage of 100 oz bars; actually, not available, and at $27.00 per ounce you cannot find a buy for less than $5.00 over per oz. I will be watching. The government now says if we are vaccinated, we don't have to wear a mask inside or outside. However, on buses and trains still required.

The housing market is insane, new listings have offers within 24 hours, all above asking price, and cash buyers offering way over assessed values, a lower condo here selling for 210-215k just sold for cash $250K!

Educating Noah…Travelin'

Happy Times 3 Day Amish Country Tour May 17-19th 2021

The actual tour was called "Garden's and Gifts in Indiana's Amish Country, and when we returned, we had a new chair plus three bags fully of goodies, gifts and food…. So here we go!

Monday morning the bus pulled up to the park and ride on college to pick up us and another couple. We were the last stop, a total of 19 people including the driver and tour guide. Since Covid restrictions still enforced, many seats were blocked off and masks were advised, when not eating, since breakfast (boxed) was provided on the bus. A box breakfast was provided, then a Bingo session on the trip down.

We did stop at an oasis for a comfort break, then our first attraction of the tour, Wellfield Botanical Gardens, thirty-six acres, eighteen of those acres water. The gardens include fountains, metal origami nesting geese, we even found a rather large ground hog! We spent an hour and a half, guide provided, along with two golf carts for those unable to walk distances. weather was perfect, those that wanted to go off on their own was tolerated, and yes, I took pictures of various plants and sculptures.

Back on the bus and off for a short drive to our next attraction, the Fruit Hills Winery. They had a covered patio set up, tables "socially distanced" and a variety of high medium and low chairs for us. We were presented with a history of the family, started out as an apple orchard farm which gradually became a winery, multigenerational and now primarily wine based. We were offered snacks of sausage, cheese, crackers and bread to clear our pallets as we tasted a total of EIGHTEEN wines, from dry to sweet! Nice selection, yes, I tried them all! Lynn tried a few, she liked two, I did buy a bottle….

We loaded up and checked into the Essenhause Inn and Conference Center; dropped off our bags and oriented as to where our rooms were, bathrooms, and breakfast areas. Then off to the last stop of the day, an Amish Neighbor's party!

The farm had a separate building for this, and I suspect this was to give the "English" an insight to Amish life. The family consisted of husband, wife, grandma, and two children, boy 6 and little girl of 4. The food was served family style, freshly baked bread, home-made apple butter, fresh salads with grandma's special dressing, roast beef, gravy, mashed potatoes, fresh beans, coffee, a special spiced ice tea, with apple crisp and rhubarb cake including a caramel sauce…seconds offered on EVERYTHING…wow!

After diner a Bingo game modified to be JONES game with the kids pulling the numbers, prizes consisted of local and homemade stuff, Lynn won a family recipe book, and I won a bottle of champaign vinegar! We were given a half hour to walk the farm yard, up close encounters with mares and colts, everything was relaxed and friendly!

A short ride back to the Inn, showers and bed…What a great first day!!

DAY 2

We thought Monday was busy.... HA!

Breakfast at the inn, bus loaded and ready to roll 8:15 A.M., and off to our first stop, an Amish, Red Roof Bakery. As we entered, we received coffee, bread, and a donut! We surveyed the various baked goods, a great variety, everything fresh, yum!

Back on the bus, toured the back roads all the time being filled in to the Amish culture and practices by a local guide. Next stop was another Amish shop, as we entered the parking lot, we saw a flower quilt on the side, this is a garden area, about the size of a bus length square, made to look like a quilt made out of different flowers! Inside, we could watch noodles being made in a commercial setting, fresh jams and jellies, and candies, caramel barks with nuts.... uh.... yum!

Load up for more touring to our next stop, an Amish wind-chime company! We were met by the owner, given a tour of the company with the history, we were instructed as to how and why different parts are installed, the different tones produced, and materials used. Of course, there was a gift shop, many unique chimes, and the staff were friendly and helpful.

A woodworking company was next on the stops, specializing in wood baskets, including a cutting demonstration, and showing how the products were assembled. This like the previous companies, was Amish run, and had only 3-5 employees outside the family members. All these tours had something to teach, and entertained question and answer periods, all positive and smiling!

It was noon, so we had to eat, this was a stop at the Kinder "World's Fair" Garden. Another boxed lunch...too much food...but delicious! After eating outside at a covered picnic benched area, we were given a walking tour of the garden, two separate groups, we were lucky enough to have the grandson of the garden creator. Like the other tour yesterday, the guide was well versed, knew all the plants, and filled us in on the development of the gardens over the years. This nursery was designated winner of the 1933-34 Chicago's world fair garden competition.

We now had our fill of food and a bit of walking around, so we now toured more of the country side and found yet another store, this was a feed and seed store. Here we learned about Bee keeping, different birds and what they eat. Lynn found a collapsible rocker she just had to have, and the bus driver said there was plenty of room under the bus, so the owner provided us a boxed one and put it in the bus for us. (The reason why no mustache on Amish men is that Hitler wore one...)

This was the last bus stop for the day, back to the Inn, some time to freshen up, then a short walk, about two blocks (I actually heard some groans as to the distance) to a buffet dinner, then a shot three block bus drive to a theatre where we watched "A Red Plaid Shirt" a play about two retired husbands coping with retirement. The play lasted almost 2 ½ hours; bussed after the 3 blocks to our Inn.

Before they let us off the bus, they announced that the remainder of the cheese and sausage and a bottle of wine was available on the patio, hosted by the guide and bus driver. A group of 6-7 were interested, we went back to our room. Our neighboring room did attend, it lasted over an hour...the one bottle seemed to be plenty? And the cheese and sausage disappeared... (There was a total of 4 men on this tour including the driver, this is why I suspect one bottle of wine was enough!!)

Day 3

Wednesday morning, luggage out, breakfast, all meeting and in the bus at 8:45. Luggage was checked and loaded, a half hour trip to Shipshewana Flea Market and Auction. This is 40 acres of auction barn and almost 700 flea market vendor spaces. The auction was happening as we arrived, so the flea market area was much less crowded. We had about three hours to explore. Some opted for a scoter rental of $10 per hour which according to many was quite cheap...Lynn lasted about two aisles then headed for the covered benched rest area, I did trek the entire fair, and yes bought a few items that we "just had to have".

We were told to be at the bus by 11:30 all were on the bus at this time, I know it was a small group, but at every stop during this tour, everyone was on time, no laggards!

Lunch time; Ben's Pretzel's was where we were all given a talk on the history of the company, history of the pretzel...Were made by monks, arms crossed to represent God's love, and were given to children as a reward, and they were soft. Hard pretzels were made by one guy who fell asleep and burned a batch, he gave them away, then

Educating Noah…Travelin'

found that many actually liked small hard pretzels!

We all sat at sanitized tables given a small rope of dough, then instructed as how to roll and form our own pretzels; we made each creation, they collected them and put them in the ovens to bake and salt, as we waited, we then were served pretzel pocket sandwiches and choice of beverages. Most of us were stuffed so they provided us bags to keep our pretzels for a snack later. (I claimed mine was the best formed…but I was booed!)

Across the street was a large Amish Bulk food market, and gave us a chance to mingle, Amish and English. There was a good mix, everyone was courteous, a lot of smiles, even the cahiers, so nice and laid back!

We met only two back-ups on the toll roads, a relief stop mid Illinois, and we were back at the park and ride on college by 5:30 P.M. One suitcase, one box of a chair and three grocery bags full of goodies and prizes; for supper we shared my pretzel and half each of a cookie. Tired, and into bed early!

Total with the driver of 19 people, the tour was well planned, carried out flawlessly, the additional tour guide on Tuesday was well informed, friendly, and structured a very busy day flawlessly, and seamless! We both endorse and recommend Happy Times Tours, this was our second tour with them, and look forward to future travels with them.

When I opened the carton, I found two chairs…I called the store, he told me he was confused and said to send back or send him a check for $50.00; I told him a check was on its way…he was not surprised I called, being honest is expected…. NICE!!

Another week before our Southwest trek, Lynn tried calling cousin Fred, but his wife has been sick, now that Lynn has had a taste of getting' out, she was a bit antsy today!

Road Trip Southwest USA June2021

The day after Memorial Day was to be the start. Everything is slowly opening up after the covid shutdown, and we are antsy, had that earlier trip to Laurel Mississippi, our Bermuda and transatlantic back-to-back cruise was cancelled just last week due to New Jersey and Europe opening up slower than everywhere else, AND about ½ the people wearing masks outside and inside……. Including their own cars...ALONE.

Gas prices didn't jump up for the holiday weekend, right now about $2.89/gallon; I had the oil changed since the second one was included with the car purchase, and I wanted everything set for the trip. They are now recommending change every 10,000 miles, the computer keeps track of when to change, and even with the 4cylinder engine the VW Tiguan takes 6 quarts. I had the first change at 8,000 miles and now again at 16,200...yeah, I'm anal!

We left the house at 8:20 a.m., and we are so into this! Lynn did most of the planning, so let's see how it goes... Turns out we need to stop every 2 hours or so due to bladder age (both of us) .... the trip through Wisconsin went well, medium traffic, a bit confusing due to road construction going south into Illinois, but we did it, as we progressed through Illinois, we saw quite a few wind farms, seems if you pay 1-2 million for each with a life span of 15-20 years you would see them working...naw...not one was turning. The price of gas in Illinois ran consistently around $3.25 per gallon, in Wisconsin it was about $2.89, and in Iowa; yeah, I filled it back up before leaving Iowa at $2.66/gal. As in mid Wisconsin, Illinois, and crossing Iowa, flat land, nice a green farm fields 70-75 degrees f, and we did have one short spurt of rain, lots of trucks, mostly semi's, we did see a number of wind mill blades and one tower being taken east, on trucks.

By the way; When we entered Iowa, we passed the World's Largest Truck Stop in Walcott, Iowa, just after crossing the border a few minutes after noon. We saw more wind farms, here the blades were turning ...slowly....

After 5 P.m. Lynn had had enough, so we checked into a Best Western at 5:30, in Lincoln Nebraska. The desk clerk recommended a restaurant only a block away, we hoofed it over, had a small meal, came back, set up the GPS and retired to the room. Total mileage 553.

Day 2 Wednesday June 2nd. Up early, brought up breakfast for Lynn, apple juice and a banana muffin, I splurged on a Jimmy Dean breakfast on a stick, and orange juice; closest thing to hot...no waffles, eggs, sausage offered due to not quickly returning from covid restrictions.

On the road by 7:30, lots of trucks, semis and traffic, speed limit now 75, most cruising at 78-83. Yesterday and today, we still see Trump election signs, even one to remove Pelosi the speaker of the

Educating Noah...Travelin'

house, no Biden signs, much like before the election.

We passed the Arch over the freeway as we entered Nebraska, we took pictures previous trips, drove past North Platte, the largest railroad junction in America seeing over 10,000 rail cars a day! We toured this before, so kept on going to stop for lunch in Paxton, at Ole's Big Game Steak House. It was weird, we had stopped at this very small town before and ate here and here we were again! It was busy, we were seated at a table and the waitress was very nice. We ordered our meals, and she put in our order, as we waited, we watched the crowd, the kids taking pictures of themselves with various mounted heads of game, over 50! I saw our waitress bussing the tables also, called her over and asked why, she stated that the last time the bus people cleaned they lost two order slips! (No order slip, no way to tell tip!)

Our meals were perfect, pulled pork for me, crispy chicken for Lynn; the total bill was only $27.50; I left a $30.00 tip to cover our meals and help her out on lost revenue.

Down the road we stopped for gas, clean the windshield, and visited a curio shop...needed to walk and stretch!! The shop had everything! Talked to the owner and daughter-in-law, an elementary teacher, who works there in summer when school is out. They had classes, in person, since September of last year! Lucky Nebraska kids!!

One more stop, yup, both our backs were killn' us; so, we pulled into Fort Morgan. Last time we pulled over at the same place and went north to find some attraction that was not there... this time we went south, into town, and toured the library and museum. We talked to the librarian/ museum person and asked where the Indians got the beads seen as decoration. Seems we were both right, I said bones, Lynn said they traded for them....

We did tour the town, took pictures of a sculpture, and old train engine, and a beautiful park that had a lagoon, wild ducks and geese, a very large pool, a large playground, all manicured and yes, the pool was full of adults and kids!

Finally pulled off just after Denver; 5:30; we are wearing on each other's nerves, pulled into a Comfort inn Suites, at this point we really didn't care about the rates (which is really rare!!) Moved in, left over Lynn's chicken and energy bars was plenty for supper...both of us crabby... Lynn went down to the hot Tub (It was actually open!!) My suit was in the car, buried in my suitcase so I opted just to relax in the room, oh, I did take a picture of the mountains out of our window...MAGNIFICENT. Total milage 1102

Day 3 Thursday June 3. These bodies will not take another road trip like this...we both agreed! Lynn's 15 minutes in the hot tub worked very well she came back smiling!!

We were on the road at 8:30 our time their time 7:30, breakfast again very abbreviated, coffee juice, milk, cereal, and a breakfast sandwich we both opted for. Getting back to the highway turned out easier than we anticipated, and now that we were past Denver, much less congested. The ski towns all advertised high end brands, and gas was in the low $3.00 range. Speed limit varied between 65 and 80 depending on the grade, two or one lane, and yes, some road construction. The rest of Colorado was mountain roads, most the drivers working with the truckers to keep everything moving. I did fuel up before leaving the mountains, the warning light was on, I tried to fill up at the pump, but the pump would not take my charge card without a 4-digit code. I told the attendant that I did not have one and that no other place required one. She told me the State of Colorado was requiring it from all gas purchases at the pump by the end of the year. I told her to charge me $40, and I would stop the pump there. She did, I did, at those prices, no problem...note to self, get code from Bank!

Utah is barren and beautiful, took more pictures, pulled off the road now for pictures, leg stretches, and souvenirs, and gas of course (no code needed in Utah). After 8 hours or so and I liked the name, we pulled in to a Comfort Inn in the town of Beaver...yup, spent the night in Beaver!

We registered in, checked out a place called the Creamery, had dinner, shared ice cream, came back, filled the car, used their computer for directions to addresses of the folks we are to visit, hit the whirlpool, swam a few laps (yeah, people still scared, so we had the whole pool area to ourselves!)

Typed notes made the calls for tomorrow and called it a night. Also had to charge the camera, lots of great landscapes! Milage 1644

Day 4 Friday; the visitation starts!

Educating Noah...Travelin'

We started off at 8:40 their time, we finished up Utah, crossed into Arizona for a short while and then Nevada. Yesterday and today seeing cattle stock yards, some large solar farms, no turbines. The southwest is experiencing a draught...blaming on Global warming, even though this happens every few years, but it is really political now so....

Gas prices mid $3.50s range, regular gas higher than diesel! I have never seen this before. We were going to stop at the St. George dinosaur museum, but it was closed; the bridges over the highway were beautiful, Las Vega gas up at $3.73/gal.

We checked out our friends address and tried to call, phone disconnected, went to the community information, our phone number was correct, but that is all they could provide.... another connection/friends gone!

Met with our niece Sarah and her son, Michael, enjoyed our conversation, they have a very nice mid-sized dog, and a desert tortoise they got from my brother's property. The tortoise prefers the back yard and when in the house has a special place! She has a shell a good 24-30 inches. P.S. The turtle has to be registered with the State. We went for supper. We tried to get a motel room close, all rooms taken! We tried many, found a strip room available but $230 plus, didn't make sense, asked Sarah for help, she found a room in Pahrump for two nights so at least we didn't have to sleep in the car! Vegas is a big weekend destination! Traffic horrible, tailgating encouraged otherwise you will be cut off even at higher speeds, and yup, almost hit a guy!

After dinner, thanked Sarah and her son, and headed out to Pahrump. The on ramp to the freeway stopped dead, after 25 minutes waiting on the ramp, I turned on to the graveled approach and drove to an off ramp that was moving, and someone actually let us back on the road, then through Vega, bumper to bumper for another 45 minutes, low on gas, and needing a bathroom break found a gas station, filled up next to a sheriff and asked him directions to Pahrump besides the plugged freeway. He told me the old Blue Diamond Highway would take us right in, and was only a couple miles down the road! Thanked him, picked up Lynn at the restaurant next door (the one bathroom at the gas station was closed and locked) and off we went! We found the motel, found where to check in, a notice at the desk stated "You can keep your gun in the room but it must be empty) and ended the day in room 10:30 their time. Both of us exhausted mostly due to the HORRIBLE TRAFFIC, including obnoxious drivers and nose to back SLOW traffic. Mileage 2014

Day 5 Saturday June 5th; 2021. We had called my brother Ted and asked when to see them yesterday. He said, "No earlier than 10:30, so we planned to be there at or a little after. This motel had no included breakfast so we had energy bars and water, coffee for me from the room. We first went to Walmart, yup, found one when we were looking for one, bought two doughnuts and a bottle of Gatorade for Sunday morning, and windshield wash for the car, we used the self-checkout since only two other registered open with lines, we were also told that we could use only credit or debit cards, no cash to check out….

Filled up the windshield washer, it stated it was only good above 32 degrees, so I only put in ½ gallon, and donated the rest to Ted. One guy did approach me and asked if I needed help, ("need some help bro") I told him "No, but that I appreciate him askin'"; nice way to start the day. We then checked out the lot I had bought as an investment or possible move, and to our surprise, it was still vacant, actually the whole area was the same as when we bought (great investment, finally sold it a few years ago for a $42,000 loss, not including the $400-$500 annual taxes!) I picked up a rock to keep and remember, then off to Ted and Carol's house.

OOPs, Pahrump is Pacific time, what we thought was 10:40 was here, 9:40…yes, we were reminded of this by Ted. We sat at the table, Carol joined us within a half hour and we discussed kids, ailments, deaths, and even politics. At 11:30 THEIR time, we went to a Chinese place called China Wok; the food was excellent, plenty to choose from and served buffet style…everything including Sushi was perfectly presented and great. Ted insisted on treating, we returned to their house, Ted's sight is faltering so we took my car. We continued family discussions, then called it quits. Back to the motel, called the last two families as to when we may show up and back to the motel.

Neither room card worked to get us in, so I had to get both recoded, FYI, do not place coded room keys next to credit cards or a phone! The heat outside is over 100 degrees, I have no idea how people can wear a mask here outside, yet we still found quite a few! The heat tired us, we refreshed in the room, went out to Taco Bell for a dinner snack, back to the room, checked on any return phone calls, showered and relaxed, went to bed early for an early start. I am also warned by my brother that the speed laws are strictly enforced. Another note, except for a few more casinos, nothing has changed in the ten plus years we were last here, we even drove past the Chicken Ranch and yes, they are still in business! (This is the oldest brothel in Nevada, and no, I did not check out things...) Mileage: 2064

Sunday, June 6th, re-visit Hoover Dam and visited my cousin John and his wife Lisa. Left the motel at 8:20; Sunday morning traveling is great, much less traffic, getting through/past Las Vegas was no problem at all. Traffic good, as we turned south noted the lack of tractor trailers. The roads around Boulder and the dam seemed all new, we shopped the town, took a drive around the dam, security stopped all cars at the dam, this seemed new, this didn't happen last time we were here! The largest flag that we came to see is only flown Memorial Day weekend, the school is out as to being flown again on the 4th of July.

Got some great pictures, road, and country. At every look-out point some local Indians were selling trinkets, and yes Lynn looked at all, and even donated to her collection. We stopped a few more places including a jerky shop, for me and Cruz.

Lisa wasn't due home till 2 P.M., we arrived in Kingsman at 2 OUR TIME; so actually 12 their time, so we found their home, checked out the fuel prices while finding our motel for the night, checked in, and relaxed, figured out the rest and night stops for home after our second cousin visit, organized the car and waited.

After checking in, setting up the room, dairying the trip and re-organizing the souvenirs and car we dropped in at the Zimmerman's actually on the way over found gas for only $3.18 /gallon!

Spent an hour of so chewing the fat, took them out for a dinner of their choice, then back to their house, splitting up Lynn with Lisa, me with John. They talked about gardening and flowers, we talked about old cars, he is currently working on a Hudson, a Crosley, an old fire truck, a 56 ford, and a 57 chevy. He was in the Air Force for 4 years, then his buddy told him to go into the Reserve, where he worked for another 17 years and with extra duties, got full retirement!

We had plenty to talk about, old times, the service, and cars...what else is there, women are just thoughts now!! It was after 10 our time, Lynn giving me "the look" so we said our good byes, and headed back to the motel, Lynn needs to send recipes, I need to send a jar of herring. Both of us had a great time!

Milage 2248

Monday June 7th, last visit to those "must see" folks for early afternoon and lunch. This Best Western had a served breakfast, cheesy potatoes, scrambled eggs sausages, corn bread, and a variety of breads, cereals, juices, milk and coffee, best one yet!

On the road at 7:30 their time, passed gas stations on the road selling regular gas for $3.99/gallon, the diesel fuel twenty cents less…the Saguaro cactus are blooming now, this was the first time we have seen this, saw two dust devils, and the temperature was in the upper 90's.

We arrived at Mary and Franco's place a bit after 10:30 A.M. We were welcomed in, sat down at the kitchen table for an hour or so, then we all ate lunch, which included a Caesar salad, pasta w/Ragu, garlic rolls, a fruit torte, and ending in cappuccino, WOW…great food, great company, and non-stop conversation. They are doing fine, Franco keeping busy volunteering, Mary also, they are concerned about lake mead being only at half level and the current draught conditions in Phoenix and Scottsdale. Mary was very proud of only being 69 and everyone else "old"; we had to leave after 3 1/24 hours to drive to Flagstaff, our jump off for our return home. Both of us are tired of traveling, our arthritis is winning, so yes, indeed, this will be the last of road trips more that 1-3 days.   Milage 2635

Tuesday June 8th eight days of travel and really showing! Breakfast at 6:30, on the road by 9 (our time) 7 Phoenix…After leaving Arizona, the gas priced for regular was under $3/gal; and diesel was 30-40 cents higher. Lots of Navaho reservation, still seeing some Trump signs, depending on elevation, the temperature is 95 to 100 degrees f. stopped just after New Mexico for potty break and fill-up, found the New Mexico still strictly enforcing mask mandates, no mask, no entry! The station had no water also, so no cleaning windows, and Lynn actually walked past the attendant saying she could not use any toilets…She said she would use if the toilet flushed or not! (It did).

We had gone through Santa Fe, New Mexico when we did Route 66 years ago, and we found Cowgirl BBQ for lunch…Yummy! Excellent food and service, we had guacamole and sliders, we actually

Educating Noah...Travelin'

took two sliders home to eat for dinner, much larger than we thought. Lynn also got a Cowgirl shirt to wear. The homes in Santa Fe were mostly adobe, and flat roofed, took several streets to look the now, much larger town, then off, we were running late and this may be our longest leg on the return trip. Crossing into Texas we saw acres, 100's of acres of wind farms, both sides of the highway from the border to 1/3 of the way to Amarillo, even saw a stack of damaged blades by the highway, waiting to be disposed of, from the last hurricane.

Farms followed, then cows in the fields, even a huge stock yard... Everything is big in Texas! We checked in at 7:20 P.M. Our time and their time are now the same, we are tired, we now have to stop every 2 hours for potty beaks and stretching, and both need at least a ½ hour "alone time" to decompress.   Mileage   3304

Wednesday, getting closer to home, and we are anxious!

We saw a lot more windmills in Texas, as we drove, we first encountered cloud cover, then lower and lower clouds, you could see the bases of the turbines, but the blades hidden by the clouds. On the side of the road was a sign "Hitch-hikers may be escaped Inmates", no we did not stop for any, and there actually no one hitching this whole trip.

Oklahoma was windy-er, in the 70's and humid but felt much better. Lots of green, trees shrubs, and red earth. We stopped at The Cherokee Trading Post. Shopped, took pictures, there were more sheriffs on the highway, the bridges are fairly new and are nicely decorated to blend into the landscape and offer some art.

Lunch time, pulled off to Chandler, at the Boomerang Diner. We missed this on our Route 66; it was decorated in 50's and 60's paraphernalia. We had a grilled cheese sandwich, Frito pie, fried okra, and fried pickles. Great lunch, nice staff! Lynn also shopped a local store and snagged a dress also.

We reached our destination of Springfield Missouri, at 5:15; this will be a Baymont Inn, we had enough points to get a free night 😊 Enough for that, swapped GPS for fastest route home, should be about 8 hours!   Milage 3924

Thursday 6/10/21 Last leg, make it or break it! Breakfast at 6, on the road by 6:30...yes, we are both anxious. As we head northeast, the land is getting greener, more trees and shrubs, and river beds with water! Some scattered windmills, some turning, some not, small groups of them nothing like Texas. We made Bloomington Illinois a bit before noon had lunch at a place called Woody's. Like every other restaurant a help wanted sign in the window, our waitress seemed pretty tired, but she was efficient. Crossed the Wisconsin border around 3 P.M. filled up with gas, stopped by the post office to pick-up and restart mail, and home by 4:30…DONE…Total mileage 4448!

Educating Noah...Travelin'

Columbia River Escape
08/08/21-08/16/21

Our Bermuda/Greenland back-to-back cruise was cancelled due to Covid; I worked with Mike at On Line Vacations to find us a cruise that would not be cancelled.

Everything is now politicalized, especially this covid, masks on, masks off, the government pushing everyone to get vaccinations whether you have had the virus or not, I had our vaccinations cards duplicated and put in plastic for further use, and hopefully no more cancellations!

I was notified on the Tuesday before leaving that we will be tested for covid at the hotel we are staying at the night before we are transported to the ship. So yes, I made the appointment for late in the afternoon...so if we fail then what???

On the day before, I checked into the flight with American Airlines, and printed the tickets, no Trusted Traveler was noted, so I tried to call...oops, bankers' hours, only 9-5 Monday through Friday...so I guess I will have to approach the desk when we check our luggage. Yup, customer service no longer matters...

Then I wanted to check the bus schedule to O'Hare from Milwaukee and see how I would get a parking pass, since we would be gone less than two weeks. Again, no information on the web site, but I was able to confirm the abbreviated schedule and made the phone call, AGAIN; wading through the auto responses, for minutes, I finally got through, the contact assured me that I could just leave the car, no ticket was needed. To make sure I did e-mail Coach USA let them know I was given permission and identifying my car, plus passed on how "happy" I was with their poor customer service.

We have checked and double checked everything; we are good to go; I will continue on the journey.... wish us luck!

Sunday, here we go! Both of us up before the alarm set at 5:50; breakfast down, clean-up and out the door at 6:30. Arrived at bus station at 6:50, bus showed up at 7:10 on schedule, confirmed parking without permit, and joked with the driver. We were off! Driver friendly and efficient, instructions clear every stop, and even put the luggage above the curb, his name, Kevin, and yes, I will comment to the company when/if they answer my e-mail.

We checked in outside the terminal, and got a slip for wheelchair transport for Lynn. We went to the indicated area to wait, after a half hour we asked again, and after the other people were taken, we got someone.... The ticket did not indicate trusted Travelers but we went any way, yup shoes off and computer out, both of us patted down, but we passed and off to the gate. We tipped the wheelchair guy, and I asked about the ticket not indicating trusted Traveler and was told it is inconsistent, some stamped some not with a shrug and "sorry".

We ate our power bars and I went off to walk as I always do to kill the 1 1/2 hours till takeoff. I did notice that CNN was no longer on the TV's, seems the airports went the way of the VA and showing only airport or nature stuff, everything is way too political!!

I exchanged my masks, till I found one that did not bother my ears, the airport was packed even for an early Sunday morning, all kinds of masks and people!

We took off on time, a three-hour flight, actually arrive 10 minutes early, but then had to wait on the tarmac 40 minutes for our docking station...seems corporate getting more like government every day.

Luggage was one of the last on the belt, grabbed a cab and off we went. The driver was from Bagdad, Iraq; worked with our military as an interpreter, and was brought back to the USA, he is also now a proud citizen! Very nice, very accommodating and delivered us to the front door...yup, I over tipped him, he deserved it!

We checked into the hotel; seems this is the spring-off place for the steam ship. Dropped off our luggage rested a few minutes then got in line on the second floor to check in, and get our covid check. Loong line and slow, but we met a number of couples to couple -up with on the cruise, one woman was a typical east coast loud, authoritative woman (reminded me of our last president) that stated we must be from the Midwest being so nice and polite...I believe too many in America didn't realize this style...she was nice, we talked and exchanged ideas. One hour ten minutes to check in, then another ½ hour for the covid swabbing...It seems they only had two people checking in everyone, two people selling excursions, and 6 people doing the covid tests...priorities???? Oh, I also found out in talking to others, that the assigned appointments were kind of ignored, and actually on a first come first served basis, two other couples had appointments 1 hour and two-hour s later....

Asked about local places to eat, found a local pub, service slow, short on help, but the food was excellent, walked back to the hotel, both of us tired of waiting in lines, flying, and yeah, we are getting older...

Monday morning, an early start of the day, the room was very "ritzy" big king bed with high Davenport mattress marble bath with a walk-in shower; we were on the 8th floor, but still a lot of traffic and yup, a train came through eight times reminded us of Mexico City where traffic never stops!

Breakfast was a simple serve yourself buffet in the hotel (included) we packed our bags, left the suitcase inside the door for a 6-8:30 pick-up, and down to the desk to have our carry-ons secured due to the bus leaving at 2:45 and check-out at 11.

The river front was only a couple blocks away so off we went, temperature in the upper seventies and sunny!

We found the park, walked and observed, pictures of the park and river, then back to the hotel...Lynn was tired, had her book, I was too antsy, so we agreed I would return around lunch to check out a little coffee shop.

Back to the river for me, I wanted to see the Spokane falls, and the garbage goat, and yep, found them plus an operating carousel, and a yelling homeless person.

I also explored the transit station, they wanted everyone to double mask! Most shops opening a 11, a number of vacant storefronts, and a small smoke shop that was filthy and crowded with merchandise next to the bus terminal.

I picked up Lynn, we walked to the Brews Brothers, shared a drink, avocado toast and a bagel. Back to the hotel, and waited for the bus.

The bus ride was a little over two hours, lentil, wheat fields few houses and barns.

Boarding was a breeze since we had our passes and all the dissemination taken care of at the hotel. We are on the second deck forward, everyone has a balcony, it is a small ship even though it is the largest stern wheeler west of the Mississippi. Within a half hour, we had to muster for the mandatory life vest drill, met our neighbors and in ten minutes it was over.

We checked in at dinning and found we were assigned 7:30 dining, which we proceeded to change. This being the first night, everyone went to the bar for drinks, and everyone with our exception dinned in the dining room. Lynn was not going to wait, so off to the grill, we were of the few there, we ate, back to the room to unpack, then to the orientation. I left ½ way through, I was tired, all the walking I did before the bus trip paid heavily by my ankles and hip, my key refused to work, and the safe didn't work. Finally, after 4 people tried to fix the safe, it was, and the key card worked, early rise, the Hells Canyon jet boat ride leaves the dock at 7:30 A.M.

Tuesday august 10th; both of us at 5:45, dressed, found camera, Lynn's phone, tickets, and off to the grill for breakfast. It seems a lot of people had the same idea, it was very crowded, had to sit at the bar, and yes had to be ladled out by staff. My plan was to get on the bus first or among the first to get a side seat on the boat…It worked, but what I didn't know was that there were three boats…half the ship signed up for this excursion!

A ten-minute bus ride to jet boat dock, loading went quick, and we were on the first jet boat out. Hells Canyon is the deepest gorge in north America, many rapids, crossed three states, Idaho, Washington, and Oregon. The jet boat seated a good 30 people with a guide/driver and helper. The boat has a draft of only 18 inches, some of the rapids are only 24 inches deep!

We saw deer, mule deer, osprey, eagles, wild turkeys, goats, ducks, geese, and pelicans for wildlife, the Snake River has a wide variety of fish, from sturgeons to pan fish with bass and others between. We also stopped to view petroglyphs which were found when some high schoolers were spray painting graffiti on a rock protuberance. The five-hour excursion was beautiful, well narrated and the crew member even jumped off a cliff for us, (into the water below, and yes, he got back on the boat). The more we travel the more we love this country, it is so expansive and beautiful with outstanding variety.

We were returned to the ship, had a lunch then a native American presentation from the Nez Perce tribe. The presentation was enlightening and very entertaining. He explained that much of the knowledge was conveyed through stories, why animals and plants were shaped the way they were, how landmarks were used to guide. Geologists and other "experts" have studied these stories and are finding out that the accuracy was surprising. The presentation was clever, varied, and informative, the ship was casting off, so there was no time for questions and answers, but if this is an indication of caliber of entertainment, we are IN! two last things, this tribe was known for their breeding and keeping of horses, the Appaloosa breed, treasured around the world, and this tribe negotiated treaties where they were allowed to hunt and fish off the reservations.

Dinner at the dining room with our converted reservation, showing up at 5:30 made us one of the last to be seated. We were joined by a 100-year-old vet and his daughter, pleasant conversation, went to the lounge afterword for a piano show, checked into the purser's office to make sure accommodations for the vet's 101 birthday Thursday, got our tickets for the hop-on-hop-hop off bus and retired for the evening.

Wednesday, August 11, 2021; last night we went to bed early again! (Early is before 10); so now we are the folks we complained about on our other adventures…karma??

Breakfast 7;30 ish, we ate at the formal dining room because Lynn's eggs were cold yesterday, and yup again her eggs were cold, no waffles offered either place. Our bus tickets for hop on hop off were for 9 AM so we got down to the loading area twenty minutes early. Others joined us, jockeyed around us, clogged up the hall and entrance to the restaurant, finally off the ship at 9;10.

We again had to wear the stupid, stinking masks for the bus rides, in reviewing the three stops, I thought it would be best for us to take the second stop first since it was a park and mostly outside and the first one second since that was inside, and the forecast was for low 100's.

On the way, we had a guide that filled us in on the towns, let us know that Bill Gates of Microsoft owned most of the land where all the potatoes were grown, the wheat harvest was so good that the wheat was coned in piles outside the full silos, (I have picture) The Lewis and Clark expedition was charged in finding the easiest path for commerce from the pacific to the Midwest, in 1805.

The first stop for us was Sacajawea State Park. It is at the

Noah

confluence of the snake and Columbian Rivers, outside were canoes used made out of solid logs with the inside carved out, a 1940 restroom (it has been updated, I checked when used) inside the small museum was the Lewis and Clark story, seems Sacajawea, the native American was 16, married to a fur trader that also joined the party. The Indian tribes the expedition met were mostly friendly and helpful, they were surprised to see the one black slave brought along by Clark. During the over two years of the expedition, Sacajawea gave birth and carried the child through the entire ordeal including low provisions, hostile weather and a confrontation with one tribe…talk about tough!!

We spent about 30 minutes at the park, inside and outside, and just missed the next bus, I waved but it seems the driver did not see us…

After waiting almost 45 minutes the next bus came and picked us up to take us back to the ship since we skipped the last Franklin County Museum, as we drove through town, we were shown a catholic hospital that was three stories high…the operation rooms were on the 3rd floor. The nuns had to carry the patients up to the third floor for procedures…why? NO ELEVATOR…AGAIN THE TERM "EXPERTS" COMES TO MIND!!!

We arrive back at the dock, let them know we wanted to go to the actual first stop on the loop, and were told that now there would be 45 minutes between stops and pick-ups, and after a short while we were off again to the Reach Museum; (The Hanford Reach Interpretive Center) this was the top-secret area where 2/3rds of out plutonium were enriched for the Manhattan Project. (1942-1947)

There was a lake that covered $1/3^{rd}$ of the state, now just a couple rivers! The rocks I pick up for those asking may date back to the basalt lava Flows, 16.5-5.5 million years ago, and sure look like lava to me!

The must see short 15-minute movie about the Manhattan project, was another secret, there were government spies in with the workers, all mail was funneled through one post office, and everyone was forbidden to talk about their job or what they did, and within completion of the project three weeks, the bomb was dropped on Hiroshima.

During the cold war, nine nuclear reactors were supplied from here. The workers lived in trailers, a 170 sq. ft. trailer had an average of 2.7 people in it, there was also ABC houses for the management and box houses for the executives. No one could come to the facility with their own vehicles, everyone was bussed on to the sites and bussed home, the bus fleet was larger than many major cities in the U.S.

We finished the museum in about 45 minutes, and waited again for the hop-on bus. In total, we spent less than an hour and a half at the two sites, m the rest of the 5 hours on shore was waiting for the buses and bus ride, we were not too happy.

Back on the ship, went hunting for food and drink, after waiting in the Grill, the four people actually looked up and one told me she couldn't help, they were no longer serving beverages until later…I went down to the lounge, got some popcorn and a beer, returned to the room joined Lynn on the veranda who had two Sundays, and watched the river go by.

They had an event honoring veteran before supper (or actually the first seating), there were 80 vets and family of the 188 passengers on board. Nice presentation, the mike was passed around for which war, which service and when…there were two WWII vets.

Dinner with two other couples; then attended dismemberment talk…I found that rather odd, you had to make one of 6 choices, and this was the second day, we boarded late in the afternoon Monday!! Trying to get rid of us already??

The presentation was followed by a four-piece band doing various country western songs from the 60's and 70's, enjoyed by all.

Hey we lasted past 9:30! Oh, and there is no casino on board, so no people sitting in front of slot machines all day and night!

Thursday, August 12, 2021. Temperature forecast 109/72 mostly sunny; we will be less than 2 hours east of Portland, the native population used this area now known as the Dalles, Oregon as a major trading center for at least 10,000 years.

This is the end of the wagon road of the Oregon trail, from here if desired, you had to proceed west via raft, and there were many rapids!

This was finally solved with the construction of the Barlow Road in 1846. This area was also meant to house the U.S. Mint for the processing of gold from the Canyon City into coin, but do to cost overages, flooding, the creation of the central Pacific railroad, and the tapering of gold discoveries, the project was abandoned.

Noah

We had selected two destinations on the hop-on-hop off bus provided by the cruise line. A narrator is provided during the trips to fill everyone in. What we were told on the way to our first destination The Columbia Gorge Discovery center and Museum was, that the soft white wheat grown here is manly for export to Japan and Korea for noodles; Dalles is a French name, from the fur traders meaning the rapids in the river. The river here has 44 species of fish, 200 species of birds is the center of Google headquarters mainly due to the cheap and available hydroelectric power. Usual rainfall is only thirteen inches per year, the air is dry. Eighty percent of the cherries used in Ben and Jerry's cherry ice cream comes from here, another major crop of this region is cherries.

We are actually at sea level, surrounded by bluffs, regular gas sells for $3.61/gal. where it sells for 2.95 /gal at home at this time, but this is common on the west coast including Oregon, Washington, and of course California. A comment was made about all the blooming rose bushes, and we are told that Portland is known as the "city of Roses". The ponderosa Pines have been disappearing, due to a bug, (western pine Beetle) however, it is a tree that does not like other ponderosas nearby.

The Discovery center was very interesting. When we entered, we were told to follow the river, which was colored in the marble flooring and "flowed" to the various exhibits, multimedia and interactive displays of cultural histories, development of the eco systems.

Today our timing was perfect, as we exited the museum we saw the bus, and proceeded to the other stop, The National Neon Sign Museum. We were treated to a film that showed how neon signs are made, provided a guide, the owner explaining the progression of bulb and neon signs from 1880-1920s and further…the neon sign was introduced in the USA in 1923. All of the early bulbed and neon signs were one word…why? Because of the immigration and limited knowledge of reading and writing English. Neon has always been expensive as well as the early light bulbs, an early sign advertised a 32 light socket sign for $157.00!

Th gas is either neon or argon. Neon red, argon is blue, other colors were developed by tinting the glass or adding chemicals. White phosphorous added to get the white. Neon usually lasts at least 20 years. The depression was the hay day for neon, those that had goods to sell needed to advertise and attract what little money that was out there!

Last note on the way back to the ship, Oregon has been voting by mail since 1988, you cannot pump your own gas in Oregon, there was a major scandal here where Bio-terrorism was used in an election, and in 1905 the last public hanging in the USA was conducted here, he was convicted of killing his seventh wife

Back on the ship, lunch, Lynn needed cough drops so I hoofed it back into town, took a number pictures of the wall dog murals, found her drops, and noted many of the downtown storefronts shuttered and vacant.

An easy afternoon, the presentation this afternoon on the Oregon trail. It was partially due to the 1837 depression ,800 to 1200 made the trip a year, most of the trail was by water, along rivers with connections to fur traders. The British traders were instructed by England to kill all the beavers found to eliminate them in America.

Fort Austria was the first trading post on the Pacific the main commodity on the trail was water and grass. Besides the meat, buffalos provided chips for cooking, so yes, there was a special place in the wagons to dry the "cow pies" …

The start of the trail, in the Midwest, St. Louis and Iowa, fort Laramie was a supply point, Portland, Oregon was the final destination. 300-400, an entire year, mostly wagon trains, the wagons called Prairie Schooners; team of 8 oxen was $200; 6 mules $600.

Four to six percent died, safe drinking water at a premium, cholera, dysentery common, kids' diphtheria. Most Indians were friendly and traded for supplies and food. But, as time went on, the relations became more stranded, 1850's showed increased negative encounters.

The Mormons took a path south in Idaho with Narcissa and Marcus Whitman establishing a Mission. The Mormons utilized hand carts.

The beginning of the end was the Transcontinental Railroad 1843-1857.

Dinner with our now assigned table with two other couples, then a brief orientation on the next day's activities, checked out the printing computer on deck 2 for printing return aircraft tickets, and enjoyed a

Noah

very good one singer backed up by the ship's quartet.

Friday 08/13/21. We will be docking around noon today, in Stevenson, Washington, so we attended a lecture on salmon and fish of the Columbia.

Salmon migrates to the ocean as soon as they are able, and stay there for one to four years before returning to their place of birth to either lay or fertilize their eggs and then die.

The females lay around 4000 eggs, then a male foam the eggs to fertilize them, then the female returns to cover and hide the eggs, then both go off to die. The survival rate of the eggs is only 20%.

Both male and female turn color when coming back to lay eggs, the males have a hook nose, they turn from silver to shades of red. Three major salmon are the Sockeye, Coho, and King; how they return to the place they are born is a combination of magnetic pull from the earth, and the salinity of the water.

10% of the salmon lose their life to the dams, predators include sea lions, cascade terns, herons, crested Comorans.

Record salmon caught 97#s; most mature salmon run 30-403s.

Craft corner making cards (Riverboat Greeting cards) at ten.

The hop-on hop off took us to two locations, The Columbian gorge Interpretive center and the Bonneville dam. It is hot and sticky again today, low 100's, it is hazy outside due to the fires, and so much of the scenery is behind smoke clouds. This is the first time the last ten years smoke from the south, there was a major fire here caused by a couple of kids with fireworks, that caused 10's of thousands in damages.

Stevenson is the gateway to Mount St. Helen; when it erupted may 18, 1980, the complete top blew off, the elevation changed from 10,000 feet to 8,600 ft.! According to "experts" the next local mountain to erupt is Mount Rannier...

The center was a small museum, some very interesting artifacts including sculpted poles, old farm equipment, a pill box by the river, fish wheel, biplane, early flat- bed truck, moccasins/boot made reeds with a reed carrying sack, not to mention a display of just under 4000 rosaries!

It was a good day, finished the museum walked out and five

Educating Noah...Travelin'

minutes later, the bus arrived. Off to the dam, we went to see the fish ladder, it was similar to the one we saw in Scotland, but there were far more fish and lampreys in this one.

This dam was another one of Roosevelt's new deals, built in 1930

In 1813 there was a western trail from Portland to St. Lewis, however it did not get the press of the government sponsored Lewis and Clark starting from the Midwest to the pacific.

Way back when, millions of years ago, sheets of earth shifted from Washington to Oregon, Washington got earth shifts, Oregon got waterfalls, liquid lava flowed from western Idaho to both Washington and Oregon...I'm guessing continental plate shifts...

Salmon run three times a year, we passed the bridge of the Gods that for many centuries was a natural bridge over the Columbia, now a toll bridge. The guide did show me a picture of the natural bridge and I would agree with the Indians, it was a bridge created by God!

Back on the ship, blackjack tournament at 4:30, as of 2 P.M. only 7 people signed up including Lynn and myself...

Blackjack 14 people, delayed a bit for the last excursion return, $10.00 buy in, at end of session, last player with most chips wins all the money. Lynn lasted longer than I did, the guy on the end won the $60.

Dinner and company were very nice, walked the deck, watched the sun set, and the entertainer was excellent, another day gone.

One more thing, talking to the Double Bass fiddle player in the lounge, when he flies with his instrument, he is charged $375.00 for transport it. We also learned that the kitchen and serving staff was 15 people short for this cruise...I did the math, the company could have easily covered the required tip per person with a bonus for those that had to work harder and make up for the cold eggs and slow service, but then reality hit me...never mind!

Saturday, August 14th; no stops today, we will be cruising the river. The shore line is much greener now, refreshing and feels cooler, forecast 96/67, mostly sunny. Today we are in the Columbia River Gorge, up to 4000 feet deep and over 80 miles in length. In the west there can be 100 inches of rain per year, here in the eastern part, only 80 miles, annual rainfall only 10-15 inches, this year so far is very dry

Noah

and under 6, in mid -August!

Two further lectures a little over two hours combined, here are the items I found that were interesting, besides prior notes.

In 1802 there were only 16 states, the world -wide fur trade valued fur, which you could purchase from the natives for 1$ and actually sell to the Japanese for $100.00! The Columbia River was actually named after an early explorer, Robert grey's ship, the Columbia Riviana.

This was the Louisiana purchase, President Jefferson picked Clark because he was the exact opposite of Lewis, who was an introvert.

One of the must haves for the trip was "Dr. Rushes' Thunder Clapper Pills", a period cure all, a thousand pills were taken!

They took keel boats and perogies assuming the trip would all be on waterways. To trade they brought Indian Peace medals, fish hooks, beads (the blue beads being the most valued by the Indians.)

Weaponry included pistols, 20 round repeating air rifles and a swivel canon. It took 20 pumps to fire one round...

The first two months they were still in Missouri, three months to get to St. Louis!

The Great Plains fascinated the whole party, prairies stretched out forever with not one tree in site, never seen coyotes, antelopes, jack rabbits, prairie dogs or buffalo.

First Indian tribe encountered was the Otoe and Little Thief the chief, the greeting was peaceful, and he was presented gun powder and whiskey.

The tribes allowed more than one woman as long as you could care for them, they were also traded like a commodity.... Except for the Shoshone tribe, where women were treated more equally.

The Sioux were hostile, powerful and fierce, they charged tolls to the expedition as they did other tribes, they accepted mostly tobacco.

Clark's slave that accompanied the expedition fascinated the various tribes in that they had never seen a black man before, he let them examine him closely and played with the children.

When they came upon Sacagawea (means Bird Woman) she was actually 15 and 6 months pregnant, married to a French fur trader and she wanted to be re-united with her tribe, where she had been taken

Educating Noah...Travelin'

by another tribe, and then bargained for by her husband.

It was rigorous, some of the expedition men were known to eat up to nine pounds of meat a day!

She and other tribes told to look for great water falls (5) and shown from the white cliffs looking toward the Rocky Mountains. The continental divide is just east of the Rocky Mountain range.

When the met with the Shoshone Tribe they were in for a big surprise, seems the chief was actually the brother of Sacagawea, made trade much easier, bought 29 horses from the tribe.

They also encountered the Salish Indians who they called "flat heads" the babies were put under a board that would actually flatten the forehead of each child! We saw an example of what they looked like and the device used...

They were starving, the Nez Perce fed them, and in exchange, took all of their weapons. There was actually a plot to kill all of them but Watkuest, an honored elder woman who had been previously captured, enslaved by both the Creed and Chippewa, escaped and returned convinced the tribe to let them live! (Never heard about her did you!!)

Salmon was available but many of the party actually resorted to eating wild dogs for the meat. Rapids after rapids, five fish hooks for 2 beaver skins the entire trip, 4,162 miles, 19 months. President Jefferson wanted an all-water route, didn't work out! On the return trip, the natives kept stealing, even the pet dog, so when the horses were bought again, the expedition burned the canoes rather than leave for the tribes. The two leaders split routes for a while hopefully to shorten the time back Lewis by water, Clark by land; They rejoined with no great savings of time either route.

During the entire expedition the only real fight was with the Blackfoot tribe, but it was settled with minimum blood-shed.

Those that completed the ordeal were rewarded with double salaries, and considerable acreage in the new land, Sacagawea had a second child, moved to St. Louis and died at 25, her children were taken into custody by the Clark family, the second child died at the age of two. Yea, no compensation for either woman who actually made this adventure a success!

Noah

Remember York, the slave? He asked Clark to free him, Clark refused but five years later actually did free him.

The average life span in the early 1800's was 50 years old, Clark lived to his 50's, Lewis suffered from various ailments, became addicted to opium and morphine and actually killed himself at 35.

Played the Match Game with the band, there were 12 teams, nope, we did not win, not even close, but it was fun!

Bingo! We played two cards each, Lynn won the first Bingo, (along with two other players) gave me $10 for her cards and pocketed the left over $5. It was fun, everything collected was given back, 5 total games, the last prize was $160.00!

Dinner with our group of three couples, from appetizer to soup took 45 minutes, I heard others complain about the slow delivery also in the main dining room, the singing! In the grill cafe, you have to stand in line to be served due to that stupid covid crap, and if lucky the food in Luke warm... however, the food is very tasteful both places, and a good selection of excellent choices.

At dinner, they brought in a cake for the WWII vet, Walter who turned 101, Lynn even made him a card from the craft session that morning, everyone got up, and wished him a happy birthday, balloons and hats, all singing! he was very appreciative.

Showtime tonight was "I'm A Believer" 60's music, we even danced! Great time!

Astoria, Oregon; named after John Jacob Astor whose American Fur Company founded Fort Astoria 1811. This is a deep-water port at the mouth of the Columbia River and the Pacific Ocean.

We took the hop-on, hop off bus and our first stop was The Flavell House, built in 1885 for Captain George Flavell. Several of the trees on the lot are original, two main floors with a four-story cupula. Interesting building with furnishings from that time, I took pictures of the kitchen and bathroom, also noted that he had his own bedroom. There was a play room, music room and dining room with an extension, windowed overlooking the rear yard. I was also able to take pictures of some newer flowers I haven't seen.

Next stop was the Astoria Column, sitting 600 feet above sea level, providing great views of the river and bay. We were given small wood aircraft to shoot off the top rails, but my knees and Lynn's back barked too long and loud so we kept the planes and just walked around.

The last stop was downtown and we walked an extensive open-air market for local produce and artistic goods (about three blocks).

Here is some of the information gleaned from the narrations on the busses. The fish and fishing here are plentiful; through Astoria's history, there has been thirty canneries, before that, fifty taverns, and fifty brothels, if you were penniless, the brothels had a fish box outside and fish were accepted as pay! In that there was a large bear population, side arms were common, especially if you transported your catch a distance on land. As far as the taverns, this was also a place where men were shanghaied as crew on ships. If you were drugged and taken to a ship, you could expect captivity to last TWO YEARS!

The Chinese were here trading with the natives many years before the Europeans, usual rainfall is 55-75"/year; this is the oldest city in the USA west of the Rockies, and as mentioned the shanghaiing capitol of the west coast.

I also took a picture of the jail house the movie Goonies was started in the opening scene.

Lazy afternoon, printed airline tickets, set up cab, finished notes, winding down of the cruise, started packing etc. Dinner and a 70's show tonight.

Sunday, August 15, 2021 73/50 partly cloudy; last day arrive before dawn, all day docked All onboard 4:30; Monday we are to be out of our room by 8:00; we have a cab waiting at 8:00 at the port.

Monday, the restaurants were open at 6, everyone was to be off the ship by 8 A.M. SOOO the two elevators were always full, we had our luggage so we had no option…they let us cram in for the one floor up exit. Three buses pulled in and out, our cab arrived promptly at 8, one couple wanted to share (he basically claimed it was him, it was a compact cube, not much space or luggage area so we said "sorry".

Twenty minutes to the airport, talking to the cabbie all the way. He stated that the last three years has shown a tripling of the homeless, and they are getting aggressive, camping everywhere, leaving needles and trash everywhere.

Noah

We checked into the airline, found Lynn a wheel chair and headed for TSA. We have the Global Entry renewed last year and assumed the airlines would also update. We got to the check-in and the officer said no, the ticket did not show TSA express, I told him the Global entry IDs were on the back of the passport, but he didn't care, and we were directed to the regular backed up line. A very nice couple of folks let us in, we went through, and at the gate a little after 9:30.

Our flight was due to take off at 12:15; up until 12, we were told that the plane had finally docked and the boarding time changed to 1:15... We loaded at 1:15 and landed four hours later only to taxi for a half hour, then finally parking at the terminal. Luggage I/2 hour later, then over to the bus station, and yes, the new covid schedule we had another 1 ¾ hours to wait. O'Hare was a bit jammed up, but off we went, just after the state line the freeway went down to one lane from 4, slow and a lot of jockeying. finally, we got to the station where the car was parked, we finally got home 11:00 P.M. Too long, crabby and showers!

We have been busy since returning, Lynn arranged two different weekend events for the motorcycle club, no bikes, only three couples including us, but it is good to get out with friends! One was Pizza on the farm, in Athens Wisconsin, a four-hour drive, including lunch at a small polish diner, the pizza is made in outdoor ovens; we got there a bit after 5, the pizza was excellent, two pizzas for 6 people, and yes, we did contribute a couple slices to the pigs…we can't eat anything as much as we used to, when we left, the parking area was completely full! Back to the motel, then walked across the street for a dessert ice cream. The next day, visited a Jurassic sculptor garden, we stopped in at a picnic put on by another chapter to say "hi" and then home early in the afternoon. We did have the opportunity to talk with the owner of the motel, this Covid devastated him, especially being in a small town, he had to take out a $100,000 loan just to keep the doors open, and yes, only coffee and juice with prepackaged donuts for breakfast, even though pictures of "full breakfast offered" I guess breakfast is now also re-defined!

The next week, the "group" went to La Crosse for a lunch at Rudy's Drive in, old fashion tray on window, roller skating waitresses, great menu, excellent service, then a walk through an international garden, a visit to a Lady of Guadalupe, shrine, a visit to an indoor auto classic museum, and an excellent dinner at a local restaurant. Here the motel in poor condition, dirty vents, the restaurant closed, the banquet area abandoned, all outside door locks taped open. We asked the desk for an additional bath towel, and were basically ignored and yes, we were very careful in checking for bed bugs! On the way back the next day, breakfast again was offered but not really delivered, we stopped Country Barrel; always a good choice, sopped at a cheese outlet, and an outlet mall…spending time with good friends is way under-valued!

Noah

McGivern Rhine Adventure 10/06-16 2021

AFTER A LITTLE MORE OF A YEAR AND A HALF OF COVID, COVID, COVID: we were finally able to leave the States and to say it was easy or un-stressful would be a fairy tale!

John McGivern is a local comedian and also hosts a TV series exploring different towns and cities in Wisconsin. We saw three of his staged shows, that were very good, and his TV series has a very "homey" familiar flare, relaxed and enjoyable along with being informative. We have done other adventures with radio personalities, but not TV hosts so of course it was worth a try… (we are not getting any younger).

Three weeks before we were to leave there was a general meet and greet meeting of all the people going in the group. We also received a list of all the names. Where we were to be picked up by the bus on the trip to O'Hare in Chicago, a meet and greet with John and his partner, and a distribution of insulated vests for all provided by the tour company.

10 days before leaving, we were told we needed to fill out a form and provide copies of our passports, vaccination cards and return flight information in order to get permission from the French to visit France. Glitch after glitch, I called our tour guide, I forwarded the info and copies to her, and she took care of that.

We were all required to be vaccinated for covid, I learned that the third vaccination was available through the VA and also got that, but Lynn called Franklin Health department for hers and nope, not available….

Five days before leaving, we were given a few locations that provide immediate covid testing for the flight, of course since our flight leaves on a Wednesday at 6:30 P.M. we needed to schedule a test on Tuesday that provided same day provable results. (48 hours test results required to fly) I walked over to the testing site on Rawson, and asked, I was directed to a web site to sign up and told if I wanted same day printed results, it would cost an additional $100/person. So back to the computer, it was the Friday before leaving, after not being able to get a Tuesday appointment, I called, I was told they only schedule the day before and I had to do it by computer.... the stress started to build.

After a toss and turn night, I would not be defeated, after fighting Google for the proper site recommended, and then fighting my way to Wisconsin sites, not Chicago sites, I again tried to schedule an appointment, and again was not able to get to Tuesday, much less Monday or Sunday because the location was closed for the day??

Finally, after three attempts through different avenues, I went on a chat line, and after explaining everything twice, got appointments for Lynn and myself 8:10 and 8:20 Tuesday morning in South Milwaukee. They sent a pre-registration inquiry via phone, which asked to forward pictures of driver's license and vaccination cards, which neither of us knew what to do on the phone, so we waited till Tuesday with cards in hand.

Tuesday morning, the day we were to leave we had appointments to be covid tested, there was another couple from the group there also, they recognized the car. (With the pigs on the side). The site finally took us in at 8:30, we had to wait in the car and fill out paperwork for a while, then everything was done in 20 minutes! On the way home we were second guessing on the names and picked up our passports and yep, they had the full middle names in them, so back to South Milwaukee to have the names exactly match the test and the passports...We don't need ANY more stress!

One more day of fretting, one last concern as to being picked up on time to meet the bus....

Taffy called and said she would be a half hour early for pick-up, she was, the car was loaded, and we arrived at the designated park and ride an hour early. The leader of the group was already there, and John McGivern and his partner, Steve showed up soon after us, so there was plenty of conversation, and the weather was upper 60's and sunny, perfect!

Uneventful trip down to O'Hare, we had 40 people signed up, ended with 22 total; as we checked in for our flight, we were asked for a Netherlands Declaration of Health, so we had to call in help, he promptly provided the form, we filled out one each, he had to sign-off and verify the forms, then we had to re- enter everything to get our tickets. The attendant told us that we were lucky to be there early in the afternoon, the crowd was small, especially with all the additional paperwork, the lines grow fast! This time the tickets were issued with the TSA-Pre-check approval, and since we had wheel chair assist, we breezed through the TSA even kept our shoes on!

The trek to the gate was, at least seemed to be the entire length of the airport,

We got to the gate 2 ½ hours early, but passed the time talking to other people in the group. The flight to Amsterdam was 8 1/2 hours, and there is a 6-hour time change, most of us did not sleep well on the plane, disembarkation went well, and the group formed and out to the bus with little trouble or problems, Amsterdam and the Netherlands no longer had the mask mandate as of two weeks ago, inside or outside, everyone was glad to take off the masks as we left the airport, wearing them over 12 plus hours was not enjoyable! We did have some others that thought we were a local bus and tried to get their luggage on, but the problem was quickly solved.

On the bus a little after 10:30 Friday their time for a tour of the city and some information, so here goes as far as I remember…

Most of Amsterdam is actually below sea level, (Netherlands literally means low lands) the winters are in the low 20's F, summers in the mid 70's F, Amsterdam is the most populous city in the Netherlands, only 50% of the adults are married, the gay and lesbian population is about 15%, this country was the first to legalize gay marriage in the world in the early 2000's. The apartments are very small, actually only large enough to accommodate one person. During the cruise I talked with the desk girl and asked about her apartment, she told me she was single and had upgraded to a larger apartment after getting this job, I asked how large was the new one, she proudly told me it was 15 square meters…I did look this up, converted to feet it was 150 square feet!) We were told by our guide that there are more bicycles than people, most residents use two bicycle locks to secure their bikes, and the locks sometimes exceed the cost of the bike. theft is high, under $1000 is not pursued by the police, parking is at a premium, it is not uncommon for someone that parks on the street to spend 20-30 minutes in the evening to find a parking spot for their car. The Dutch are very frugal and orderly. This was a problem at the start of the second world war, when the Nazi's invaded, of the 70,000 recorded Jews that had emigrated here, 60,000 were put to death!

Amsterdam has more canals than Venice, so actually Venice

Educating Noah...Travelin'

should be the southern Amsterdam!

Our first stop was a vintage wind mill, we got 20 minutes to stretch our legs and take pictures. We then were taken to an included restaurant for lunch. Most of us thought the first servings was the only one, but no, it was a split pea and potato soup, (full size bowl) then followed by a platter of mashed potatoes covered by veal in gravy, followed by a large bowl of whipped cream yogurt, and fresh fruit... We all waddled out of the restaurant, since bikes do have the right of way some are rather obnoxious about it, not only to pedestrians but also to cars, trucks and buses one of the women in our group was brushed by a speeding bicycle (they have the right of way!) on the way back to the bus.

One last stop before the ship, was the flower market, we had about an hour to explore the two blocks of flowers, bulbs, and souvenirs along one of the canals, so we were able to buy bulbs, thimbles, postcards, collect stones and pens for the people back home and make it back to the bus on time. One last thing was pointed out to us, was that some of the older building actually slanted forward, this was due to people on the upper floors having to hoist their furniture through the windows when moving in due to the staircases being so narrow and steep, and yes, I got a picture of one!

We boarded the ship after 4 P.M., the safety briefing was in the lounge, a full dinner was at 7 P.M., and most of the group headed for the cabins after, to catch up on sleep, we were in bed after a welcome shower by 9 P.M...a need but rough night due to time change extended flight, and too much food! However, we were informed that masks were required on ship in the hallways☹....

Friday! We both woke at 2 A.M., I logged, Lynn read for an hour, then back to sleep till 8:30 where we woke to a foggy day next to a pier, refreshed and feeling much better. There was an optional tour available from the ship, but it was basically the same as the included tour from the agency yesterday, so today is just walk around and stabilize. We had a lite breakfast and lunch, the fog lifted just before noon, and we docked in Hoorn to pick up the folks that had taken the optional tour, then back out on the river. This was a "laid back" day, not much to do but watch the shore go by, at least it was sunny, the temperature was in the mid 60's.

We had an on ship "meet and greet" with John McGivern and the rest of the tour group which included drinks, got some background on him and he pointed us out as the most traveled couple. After that, was the captains "meet and greet", supper had the best appetizer I have ever had, and then bed again for us…we are old now…early to bed and late to rise!

Saturday, October 9, 2021 We had another almost full day of ship, light breakfast and lunch, it is sunny and cool, low 60's, so we did walk the deck, watched some play shuttle board, and an apple strudel making culinary demo before disembarking in Cologne for a three-hour walking tour of the city.

Well, that didn't work, three ramps 108 steps just to get to the other side of the bridge, plus a half hour walk, so gauging by the map we would have had another 45 minutes to an hour just to our first destination, the chocolate factory. After we rested Lynn decided it was way too far so back, we went, it was now in the 70's and we arrived on ship an hour and five minutes since we left, 216 steps of dragging the walker, both of us sweating, Lynn asked the captain about the other ports, and he told her this one had the most steps! I did get a couple pictures of the locks on the bridge, two Corman's, and the church which was the highlight of the tour besides the chocolate factory.

All aboard was 7 O'clock so we probably would not have made it w/o a cab partially since we actually only had originally two hours and 45 minutes ashore. (We docked fifteen minutes late!)

Dinner was at seven thirty due to the excursion. Way too big of servings, but yes, the food was excellent. It looked like some of the group skipped dinner, or had a snack for supper. After we went up to the lounge to play a game where you named the country the song came from, and you got extra points if you danced to the songs. Yes, we were over the jet lag, we did get all the dance credits, we danced to all the songs with most of the folks there, but we missed two countries, we guessed Norway instead of Sweden, on one song, and Mexico instead of Cuba on another…the dance floor was full, most everyone "got in the mood" and we voted one Spanish woman, Petra, as the winner, she was the craziest!

11:45 back to cabin to shower and sleep, another day done.

Sunday, October 10, 2021, up late at 8, breakfast, again too much, then we entered the lottery, 5 tickets for 10 Eu and I got to break down a 50, 11 o'clock, they had a German snack. Sausages, kraut, potato salad, coleslaw, with ½ pretzel, yes, again lots of food.

To the upper deck, we are going down the Moselle River, the largest tributary of the Rhine to the old town of Cochem and half way we reversed at a wide spot so that we could return bow first. The fog, like yesterday, finally lifted, the temperature climbed again to the mid-sixties from the mid 40's F. the sun shining. We decided to skip lunch at 1, how much can you eat??

We anchored in Cochem, it was a walking tour, so Lynn decided to stay on board, I joined a group. The walkie-talkies have large ear pieces and do not work well with my ears, they don't stay in the ear, so most of the talk was not heard. The walking was extensive, steep hills, cobblestone, and NOTHING is close by, we did get a bus ride to the castle, and the tour inside was beautiful. The vistas from the castle were beautiful, and like the previous day, the fog line had lifted and the sun was out. Storks are protected here and people feed and attract them to nest for good luck. Following the 2 ½ hour walking tour, we had a wine tasting at a winery, we tasted three different choices of wine, but our hostess was the only one giving the tastings and she had two groups, so it was a good 15 minutes between tastes. Back on the ship, the dinners are all at least 5 courses, and the portions are generous to say the least. (Did I mention, the portions were quite large?)

After dinner we participated in a riddle game, our team got 8/10, the only other team to beat us had 9/10, music and dancing followed.

Monday, October 11, 2021 early (7:30) rise for a walking tour of the city of Koblenz, this is the last tour on the Moselle, and the town is on the confluence of the two rivers. Most of the walking tour was on flat cobblestones, we learned the influence of the Romans, the Franks, the Holy Roman Empire, the French and the Germans who all built this city's 2000-year history. The massive statue is of the German Emperor Kaiser Wilhelm, we also visited several churches including St. Castor Basilica, the church of our Beloved Lady, a fountain with a little boy spitting out the fountain water at different intervals and a building with a face that had eyes that moved and an occasional mouth movement. The tour did last the full two hours, Lynn was able to tour with a smaller group and so she too enjoyed the sites of the town.

We cast off at 10:45 to join the Rhine for the rest of our boat trip.

Noah

As we traveled the river, we were given a map of all the castles we were to encounter with kilometer markers, and which side of the ship to expect to see them, and century they were from, from the 10th to the 14th century, 23 in total, names and towns.

At 4:30 we arrived at our second destination, Rudesheim, a quaint little town, the walking tour offered a small toy train to take everyone to the museum at the other end of town, we opted to explore the area ourselves, gift shops and restaurants lined the area just up the river's edge. We found what we "needed". Headed back to the ship, met and talked with another couple on the ship, not part of our group, who had done the same, back on board, many had opted to eat in town, we enjoyed dinner with John McGivern and his partner Steve.

After dinner we joined everyone for the raffle, we were surprised on only half on board actually bought the raffles tickets, and actually only a few people won the prizes, none from our group, and no we did not... Bed by 10, we were both aching from the day's activities.

Lynn was up half the night with bowel difficulties so neither of us had much sleep.

Tuesday, October 12, 2021 We straggled out of bed and had breakfast at 8:30. Due to the night before I decided not to take the tour and stay on board with Lynn for the morning. That didn't last long, had breakfast with two other couples, we are all eating much lighter on many meals. Since Lynn was feeling better, off I went to explore the bustling metropolis of Mannheim. This is a university town, I walked 10-12 blocks, sidewalks are all brick, narrow streets, no or little parking spaces, and half the car parked on the street, half on the sidewalk. I took a picture of one of the cigarette machines hanging on a wall, explored and Aldi and other discount food store, and headed back, only half the stores were open, and not that many people on the streets... met up with Lynn, documented and talked to staff. She told me rent is about 80% of what one makes, her apartment was about 15 square meters, (150 sq. ft.) bedroom, bathroom, kitchen, living room and porch. A parking spot is included, three months deposit required for apartments in larger complexes.

It was drizzling most the morning but the temperature was in the 60's, tolerable, especially for October!

Lunch was way too much as always, salad, or soup, dessert, and a full rack of ribs each, I asked, and yes, we could all ask for ½ portions from now on...I will make a point to note this in the comments because everyone in the group commented on how good the food was, but most of us ate ½ or less and we really felt bad about the amount thrown out.

Briefing midafternoon on tomorrow's activity in the morning, the afternoon will be cruising through a series of very busy locks, and then Thursday morning we debark for the two nights stay in Switzerland, touring through the east of France.

I asked, and we will be covid tested at 3:30 Thursday, required by the airline before boarding on our flight home Saturday morning. After 4 P.M. we docked in Speyer, (the auto correct does not agree with the German spelling of these ports!) another walking tour.

Turns out we docked the furthest away, of the four river ships, after 20 minutes of walking we were lagging behind the group quite a bit and the guide stopped to point out the steeple of the church which was to be the start of our tour, about 3-4 blocks away. Lynn had enough, I excused us from the group and we went back to the ship, it was still in the lower 60's and off and on light rain, with any luck the excursion on Wednesday will be less rigorous; please note when in Europe a ten-minute walk is brisk and usually at least 15-20 minutes!

Dinner, I asked for half portions both on just an appetizer and main course, they complied and it turned out perfect...everyone at the table will be asking for half portions at our table, even one other guy!

The lounge game of Majority Rules was delayed due to many eating late, so the host went down to the dining room and reminded them, but after one half hour we started... all participation games are presented in English, Spanish, and German, along with everything on the presentation screen. Our team won with 8/10 answers, tied with another team, we then had a dance off with an orange between our foreheads, we lost that, but both our team and the winners were presented with bottles of Champaign, we opened both and poured for everyone to enjoy, and left to end the night.

Wednesday, October 13, 2021; last fully day on ship. Our excursion to Strasbourg required additional paperwork, is rated only two dots as far as difficulty (out of four), so hopefully Lynn was be able to complete.

Strasbourg is the capitol city of Alsace, this was part of the Roman

Noah

Empire, then French, then German, then French, then German and now kinda' French, Alsace. Canals intertwine this city, the largest one we have been in since Amsterdam, with 22 bridges crossing the network of canals. By the way, the canals were actually the sewers of the town.

We took a tour bus to the middle of the city where we disembarked and started walking through the narrow streets, with buildings from the 15th century on up. Our first stop was the cathedral Strasbourg Munster, we had to wear masks inside, also show vaccination cards to enter. It was a huge church, first catholic, then protestant, then back to catholic, then both and now it is just Christian, just kind of followed the occupation of the town. We then walked down to a canal where we had a tour of several canals on a canal boat, again different centuries of architecture with even a lock to meet a 1.8-liter difference in water heights. The boat tour was almost a comfortable hour, with the last portion showing the newest, most modern complex of the European Union, Parliament.

After the canal cruise, we walked the Petite France quarter, the former mill and tannery district that still had the medieval charm, however watch out for those bikes that have the right away, and some crowds of people who do not move when you are trying to get past, or cross a street! Here also, the street signs are in both French and Dutch.

We got to the bus, loaded up, and the rear door would not close completely, after a number of attempts, the bus driver behind tried to fix, to no avail, The country does not allow buses to transport people with a defective door, so we were all transferred to another bus, taken to the ship, and were just in time for lunch.

The afternoon is just cruising, 6 locks, and on our way to the last destination on the ship of Lucerne, Switzerland. This being the final night, all tabs to be paid, and a captain's reception followed by a final Captain's dinner.

All the food on this cruise was excellent, and the ½ portions was perfect! The captain's reception included Mimosa's and appetizers, the dinners, Lynn's steak was perfectly cooked and moist, my salmon was the best salmon I have EVER had, we shared a baked Alaska for dessert, packed up our stuff and ended another great day by 10!

Thursday, October 14, 2021

Educating Noah...Travelin'

We bid farewell to the cruise portion, docked next to a ship on the pier, had to go up to the top deck, across theirs, and then down to the pier, and then up to the top of the river bank, not the easiest with the roller and two carry-ons. We found our bus and were checking our luggage, Lynn's couldn't be found, checked everywhere, then discovered that her's had been put on the bus before we got there???? So much for security!

We then had difficulty getting the bus out of the cull de sac, due to other vans and dumpsters in the way, but we managed, no big rush by those outside to help guide...seems the more you are in Europe, the more "me" people than in the States!

To finish Basel, we walked the town for a good 1 1/2 hours, then we had free time to find something to eat and explore the sites. I did find a post office, found someone to translate, and was told where to put the postcards to be sent to the States plus purchase 3 stamps for 2 EU each (about $2 US). I also found Lynn a flat- bed folded pizza sandwich, took pictures of the waste bins and the public toilets, inside and out. McDonalds had no restroom for the public, Swiss do not eat ice cream in the winter

The bus trip to Lucerne was un-eventful, lots of tunnels, some farms some with cows, chickens, and fields of corn, we are told all are "organic".

In Lucerne we visited the rock relief of the Lion monument, hand hewn in a cliff 1820-1821 by Lukas Ahorn. We were then driven to the hotel, dropped off our luggage, locked up our carry-ons, and proceeded on a walking tour in downtown. We walked a few blocks to the river's edge, walked across an ancient wooden bridge and through other parts of town until arriving at our designated covid testing site for out flight home. Forty minutes later and $37.00 ea. we proceeded to struggle back to the hotel. They promised to get the results to our group that evening.

We took our carry-ons to the room, opened the windows (no A/C) and we rested awhile. I still needed to find a chocolate place, some stones, and a refrigerator magnet, so I set us to finish the "Necessary "shopping. Bikes here too have the right of way, and being brushed by pedestrians is not uncommon. I found a "Chocolatier" and a souvenir shop for the magnet and chocolates, and also a rock pile to complete my tasks. The Swiss bills start at $10 (Swiss Francs) below are coins, $5, $1, 25 cents, dime, nickel, no/few pennies. Dinner was served by the hotel, everyone got soup, beef stroganoff with spätzle and veggies, followed by a caramel flan.

Tired and need to un-pack for two days, our tests came back negative…YAA, the group has been pretty cohesive, everyone followed instructions and were always on time, we called it a night. After figuring out how to use the internet, safe, and lock the door…

Friday, October 15, 2021 before bed, we figured out the safe, the internet had over 100 e-mails to delete, we do not do any banking outside our own network or over-seas, and I am using my credit card a little just to see how it works out, with exchange rate and such.

Buffet breakfast, first we have seen since covid, however scrambled eggs almost gone, along with the bacon; typical European service, slow, and you have to ask. After breakfast we strolled the town looking for a place to have dinner on our own, once we found one place, we found several others.

At 10 A.M. we all walked about four blocks to Lake Lucerne, I am still amazed how clear this water was, every stop you could see the bottom, crystal clear at 3-4 meters! We boarded a passenger ferry to cruise the largest lake in the country, after an hour and half of visiting small communities to drop off and pick up a few people, we landed at Alpnachstad, to take the world steepest cog railway in the world to Pilantus Kulm, at 7000 ft above sea level, in a ½ hour climb, welcome to the top of the Alps!

We were treated to lunch, consisting of pumpkin soup, a puff pastry with veal stroganoff veggies and rice finished off with a caramel pudding tart…WOW! Included was a local beer or wine.

We had time to walk around, take in the fantastic views from all vantages, then proceeded down in two cable cars the first 15 minutes, holding about 30 people, the second thirty minutes, holding four people each. We actually had the tour guide on the second car, and we got some personal in sites on history and Euro-politics, where she noted the decreasing respect for others and "Me" people, especially with increasing boldness of those on bicycles.

The price of gas here about 1.81 EU/liter. I didn't want to say anything but a number of others commented on how expensive even the small stuff was, and the number of people still smoking.

It was a short drive back to our hotel in Lucerne, we had a small reception to discuss tomorrows check out, travel to the airport and flight home. We have to leave the hotel and be on the bus by 6:30 A.M., luggage out of room by 6:15…we plan to get up at 5:45, breakfast at 6…that's the plan…

We decided that both of us were still full from lunch, we had to call the desk, the maid had turned off the power in the room, with power back on, we packed, showered and hit the hay early…tomorrow will be a Loong day!

Saturday, October 17, 2021; goin' home. Up at 5:15, luggage out at 5:35, everything checked and rechecked, joined everyone for breakfast, baggage checked and on the bus by 6:30, everyone was prompt and on time. The hour plus drive to Zurich was easy being so early, lots of tunnels.

The airport was pretty empty, the person we checked in with was quite slow, by the time we were finally done, everyone else was on the move to the gate. We went over to the wheelchair transport, fought back and forth with "gate check" for Lynn's roller, then had to wait again for transport. Transport arrived with a golf cart, we loaded on, then he drove 40 feet and picked up two more folks and their gear, (he neglected to tell us of more people, so both of us had to move and re-arrange. Both TSA and Customs went well, and from the ticket, through TSA, through customs, to the gate took a good 45 minutes, made it to the gate with 20 minutes to spare, and explained gate check for the walker again, it finally worked.

We got settled in for the 9-hour first leg, two meals, beer and wine only with meals, I watched 3 movies, and 5 sit-coms till landing. On time, in New Jersey.

We exited the aircraft and waited for the walker, finally got a gate attendant to follow-up, and finally after everyone including the crew had exited the plane, the walker was delivered. Then through customs, had to transfer the luggage from one area to another, the through customs again, then the wheel chair guy put us in the regular TSA extended lines, and then through a number of elevators, taken outside by wheel chair once, then back in to pick up a monorail, more elevators, finally to our gate with 20 minutes to spare…We had a lay-over/transfer of about 2 ¾ hours and used all but 20 minutes! Last flight left late, but arrived in Chicago on time. The roller showed up just before the crew left the aircraft, and the 25- minute walk including a toilet stop, got us to the baggage area where we bid the last transporter, "A-Do". Gathered our luggage, out to the bus terminal, back at the College exit by 6:30, Mike our grandson's dad picked us up, and we were in the house 7 P.M. Another adventure done, another goal, top of Alps accomplished!

Back home now everyone should get covid third shot, now giving to kids 5-11; many states requiring public employees who were heroes before now fired for not taking shot even though they have antibodies, may be pregnant, or have religious objections, things are just getting stupid, everyplace looking for workers, unemployment keeps getting extended.

November, Lynn had some minor foot surgery, in a boot for 2 ½ weeks, transporting for ERS twice a week.

December, Christmas, more government scares, airlines cancelling flights due to no manpower, people sitting at home collecting unemployment, job openings everywhere, just people don't want to work, even with wages up, and $2000 on up bonuses. I am hoping things will calm down in 2022, we have a cruise in February, March, June, and August; tried to get an upgrade on flight with Cruise and Tour for our march cruise, but they are having problems booking a flight also, and it's not the same company, they were upset that I was persistent on requests after the third inquiry. They are now talking a second booster shot, that would be four al together, we had the original, then delta, now omicron variation, which is far more contagious, but far less lethal, many still wearing masks in stores, cars, required on buses and aircraft and airports.

Christmas was three hours at the Pegoraro's; New Year's home....

Noah

2022

It's the end of January; the re-scheduled cruise with Royal Caribbean has been cancelled again; I have received most of the money back, and trying to reschedule the Bermuda, and Greenland back-to-back in 2023. The Mark Belling cruise is still on, my e-mails to Cruise and Tour not being responded to yet, the covid mess still being pushed, and now build-up of soviet forces next to Ukraine; offers more challenges. We started visiting cousins again, visited Lois and Glen, (The Polly family) had a good conversation and checked them off the list.

America is highly politically divided, racism being touted; most TV commercials now have to have mixed marriages or gay representation, and all groups must have at least two if not three races represented.

We leave for the Belling cruise the end of this week, visited Mike and Charlene of the Polly clan, our monthly dinner out with Lynn's brother and his wife Janelle, plus the domino's group. Had a presentation scheduled for Money Sense but the last week it was cancelled and rescheduled; typical Milwaukee Public School system, so I rescheduled for late March. Neither daughter could help in creating the presentation, even the volunteer "expert" said it was years, and he wasn't current enough to create a presentation. I did go through Money Sense and forwarded the word documents for the presentation and even said they would give me 40 minutes! Oh, and yes, I got the Bermuda, Greenland and West Russia cruises planned, plus a road trip, The Great River Road (Mississippi) is in the planning stage.

Mark Belling Caribbean Cruise, March 2022

Finally, After Royal Caribbean cancellation, and now the Ukraine invasion by Putin jeopardizing our June River cruise the stress is showing in both of us.

A week before, our suitcases are packed, everything checked

Educating Noah...Travelin'

twice, confirmed our covid test time, our friends Pat and Art are willing to take us to and pick us from the airport; I am actually going to trust the results forwarded to our phones, cost of the test $70 each, not sure if we have to test again on return!

This is our first chartered flight, so this should be interesting, I upset the Cruise and Tour coordinator, Charlie for asking about accommodations and upgrades, personally found that rather unprofessional especially since we have traveled with this company at least three if not four times before, so I just call now if absolutely necessary with a yes or no question.... seems customer service is dead here too!

Mask mandated are lifting, hoping for aircraft mask lift is soon, the ship announced relaxed mandates with only a few exceptions. We have had a mild winter, the week before our flight was to be clear and in the 30's and 40's F.

Friday March 4, 2021; As usual, my internal alarm went off at 0500 (A.M.); and checking on Lynn before the 5:15 alarm, I turned that off while she was in the bathroom. Accomplished everything on my check list, made smoothies for breakfast, and we were off for our covid test at 5:50! We were third in line, took a full ten minutes and we were off! Returned home, put out the luggage for our 7:45 pick-up and they were a bit earlier, and we arrived a bit after 8, to join the line of all the others. Since this was a private lease, we had to go through a full TSA check, it went smoother, and off to the gate.

They loaded the physically challenged first, we had seats in the 33rd row and squeezed ourselves in, it was tight, not very comfortable and the whole plane was ours, 160 people. The travel company did buy a round of drinks, and provided a snack on the 2 ½ hour flight. We landed to a windy 79 F degree sunny day in Miami, loaded on two buses and headed for Fort Lauderdale...during rush hour, 1 ½ hour later we arrive at the beach front hotel where we are to spend two nights, nothing planned for Saturday...we are on our own. We met some friends from the vagabond club and walked out to a Mexican restaurant for dinner and talk.

Back to the room and early to bed, we were supposed to get results for the test, but nope, hope we can get a copy from the group leader who did receive results!

Saturday, March 5th; a buffet breakfast included, actually with a group this size we had our own area on the penthouse floor, the view of the ocean is spectacular, however, being so windy not many on the beach. Since the covid test place was not consistent with providing results to everyone, besides the group leader, the results were printed out for anyone who wanted them, ours did come via e-mail from him, our group leader last night, so we are set for tomorrow, when we board.

Nothing planned by the tour group today, it was 75 degrees and clear, but the winds from the east are at 20-30 mph! After breakfast we picked up some brochures from the desk, and seemed everything was NOT in walking distance except for the beach, 30 miles of sand! Wow; and a park just a block away. I talked to the security guy in the lobby, and asked, he told me there was a golf cart escort available so off we went.

It was only 2 blocks to the entrance, and for $4.00 each, we got an escort driven golf cart with a ramp to load "Rolle". (Lynn's walker) We were given a history of the place where the tortoise holes were, the inlet where the channel to the luxury homes were, lagoons for those that wanted to kayak or canoe, and the untouched swamps, foliage, and banyan trees. The tour was well worth the money, gave the guide a nice tip and headed back to the hotel. I know in real estate and business it is location, location, location, BUT we were at a junction of two major roads, and even on the third floor, you could hear a lot of cars revving and loud music.

We rested for a bit, then went out for an ice cream and checked out the neighborhood. Checked out a couple souvenir shops, narrow aisles, lots of stuff and too crowded especially with the walker! The ice cream was great but the $15.00 for two single scoop cones seemed a bit much! We walked a bit more, too windy, and back to our room. I tried to use the phone application but it got too complicated with scan this, take my picture, answer this, present this; Answered the health questions and frustrated ended it!!!

Sunday March 7, 2022; still windy, clear skies, 78 degrees f. Buffet breakfast, luggage out at 8. We had a presentation by Mark Belling, made some new friends, and we were told there are 260 in the group, NONE had tested positive and denied, the meeting/dining room crowded, the presentation brief, and then the challenge to go back to our, rooms, get our carry-ons and line up for the 6 buses to take us to the port. As with the plane, no accommodations for people

Educating Noah…Travelin'

with handicaps or disabilities first come, first serve. The ride to the port was longer than anticipated almost 45 minutes, but going through reception to the ship went very smooth.

This is the newest Celebrity ship, no maps provided by the elevators, many venues are 5 steps up or down, not stroller friendly, so we left Rollie in the room and used Noah and the cane I brought.

Since luggage takes a while, we found a hamburger place, toured the ship a bit, and tried to familiarize ourselves to elevator locations, food, bar, Théâtre, and various decks.

Dinner was at one of the restaurants, first day, only tables for two, so we both had escargot and I had Ceviche she had lamb, all was prepared perfect and excellent service.

We roamed to an outside deck for the sail-off, drinks and talk to various people, had the badly needed drinks, then down to the martini bar for the music, after that went to The Club and played Yes Or NO, and Trivia; we were not winners!

Back to the room, unpacked and met our Steward, figured out how the TV worked, the window and shades; that was the first day on ship.

Monday, March 7, 2022 Set our watches ahead one hour, up at 8; had some swaying last night, being on the 7th deck enhanced the sway!

15 ft/3 meter waves, makes walking around a bit more challenging…we found the buffet Ocean View Café on deck 14 aft; four aisles, most any pastry, breads, eggs, waffles, fruit, plentiful and generous; walked around a bit more, found that 4th and 5th deck connect bow to front without steps, played S.A.F.E. Archery, we were the only team that didn't hit one of the targets in the one minute time allowance; ALL the other teams (of 2) scored at least one; the winners scored three hits in the minute allowed….oh, well…swallow the pride…

Lunch, this was an assortment of fruits, breads, Mediterranean dishes, pastas, and Greek, what a great selection, and even with both of us taking ½ plates of goodies, we again seemed to over eat! Afternoon activities included name that Tune; game show "Deal or No Deal"; Music quiz; and a tour group cocktail hour with meet and greet the tour hosts and Mark Belling, the WISN talk show celebrity. Dinner again at the Cyprus restaurant, table for two, both of us stuffed with each of us only ordering two appetizers each…all four excellent!

Noah

We made it to the dinner show "Kaleidoscope", dancing acrobatics, and singing. An excellent show, amazing how some can bend so much!

Last item was a game show of Friendly Feud. We were not picked to be on a team, but it was fun to watch, I had won some points in the deal or no deal cards I bought, 3 for $45.00, so we went over to the casino to cash them in…$25.00 credit! Yup, took it to the slots, cashed out for $2.67 only 7 minutes later…ON A PENNY MACHINE!!

We went to the room, tired, we have become those "old fogies" we complained about just a few years ago!! Showered and off to bed by 10;30…. groan!

Tuesday March 9, 2022, up without an alarm at 7:30; the waves persist, so walking a little challenge.

We will be out at sea most of the day, since we left the port two hours late due to a medical emergency, the captain has been trying to make up the time, but we will still be getting into port late in the afternoon, projected at 5 P.m. rather than the originally scheduled 4 P.M.; it gets dark around 7-7:30 and since it is so late many do not want to explore deep into the island since the boat waits only for shore excursions booked through the cruise line.

Informal breakfast, tons to choose from, then off to the activities! Deal or no deal again, Music trivia, Theme "woman's day" trivia.

I left the ship to plant my feet on the island, we have been here at least twice before, and I knew the walking would be hard on Lynn and the ships excursions were not exciting or passive enough for us. Covid screwed this up, streets were not crowded, the vendors mostly selling the same things, I found the rocks for the rock hounds, the pens at a Walgreens, (local souvenirs like pens and postcards now very hard to find! I finally found a souvenir shop back at the terminal, got the other pen, coffee, and post cards. I probably walked a bit more than a mile, we had dinner at the café, played another game show 'level Up", joined friends for a tribute to Aretha Franklin, and called it a night. (We had planned to join others for the Electro swing party but both of us pooped out), yeah, it was after 10:30… ☹

Wednesday March 9, 2022 breakfasts at the café, by 8 A.M. we are docked in Tortola, BVI; This is the 4-hour beach Bar-B-Q starting at 10:15. All of us crowded into various open and closed vans, and up and over the mountain to the beach at Myatt's on Cane Garden Bay for a day at the beach! The barbeque and drinks were included, the sand was warm along with the water. Temperature 78-80 degrees F, sunny warm, covered area with tables for some, beach chairs for others and two bars set up. Food included but not limited, salad, rice, BBQ chicken, ribs, and Ahi Tuna, vegies, followed by a chocolate or lemon cake. As with everything now, there were a few glitches in serving the food, notifying when it was ready, along was to when and where to leave to go back to the ship.

We were entrained by a very good Caribbean band, and 20-30 pelicans and other birds diving for food. We caught a van on the way back, most of the cars have steering on the left, but the roads are English, so they drive on the left too…. The drive to and from the beach was on a narrow two-lane paved road, no shoulders, and no center line, few guard rails. The drivers to and from very friendly and liked to talk about their homes…here land is valued the most, most build larger houses to live on the top floor and rent out rooms below.

The ship confiscated the two rocks I had in the carry-on bag, but let me in with 4 in my pocket?? They didn't confiscate the sand on my legs either??

Rested for a while, went down and played visual Trivia, followed by a general knowledge trivia, we got Bronze or less…duhhh

The show was four singers, they won England's Got Talent, "classically trained, and sang songs blended between classical and Blues, very nice and entertaining.

This night also we stayed up for the liars Club, adult version. Four words where the three players make up stories to sell what their definition of the word was. The participants were the captain, cruise director, and an officer. Their stories were complicated, very well presented, and quite convincing, until the last one where they were just having fun digging at each other's stories. One of the best 1 1/2-hours of the cruise!

Thursday March 10, 2022 Up early (relatively) to be fed and out on the pier for our only prepaid excursion, the trolley train, a two-hour tour with stops at a Dutch cheese and liquor store, then to the middle of town for an hour to explore the shops. We were out on the pier at 8:05, ten minutes early to be joined by the rest, and finally walked the 3-4 blocks to the train in the port. We were lucky to take Rollie along, and we got a rear seat alone with Rollie!

The first stop was cheese and alcohol, we got some of the souvenirs, a green cheese and a limoncello cheese. After 20 minutes at the store, practically everyone bought something, we toured the city, not the best of neighborhoods, some crumbling houses and buildings and many boarded up storefronts, due to prior hurricanes and covid. Like the last island, land is extremely expensive since most has been handed down, most building materials are shipped in, and the kids and grandkids, and great grandkids don't sell, rent, and if the building falls apart, they are not there to fix or repair since the value goes up yearly…per our guide a small house sells for $500,000! As in the other islands also not mansions are rented out below the top floor by the room.

During the hour in town, Lynn spent most of it sitting in the square talking to the guide and getting information on the island, I was in search for postcards and even more scarce, stamps! The guide was fairly new, she only guided for 3 months, she was a cook but she developed trouble with heat and cold on her hands. Born in Antigua, moved here, with family, expensive to live on all the Caribbean Islands, and share her breakfast with Lynn. All the while I was trying to find the stamps! Since the internet, kids don't use mail, REAL MAIL, except for buying merchandise…so long Hallmark!!

I was sent 3 blocks this way, 4 blocks that way, "just behind" turned out to be 3-4 blocks, and when I finally got a cop, the post office was another 3 blocks away, and I needed to get back to the group for loading and back to the pier.

At the pier and after four different shops, I found both cards and stamps, and a mail box, so I finished all the post cards, stamped them and in the mail box hopefully to beat us home!

I was stopped again at the gate asked about the stones in my pocket, but I gave this guy the look and he let me go with the stones! I wonder if the same rule applies to local hand crafted painted, and made to sell to tourists…. duhhh!

Complained again about the confiscated stones, got two pens for the pen collectors, and they told me that without a ticket the stones were gone…they were nice enough to check again. They left a message on the phone…nope, so sorry!

Educating Noah...Travelin'

Ran to get to the next trivia which was a difficult visual trivia, people and landmarks, then another general knowledge trivia, dressed and dinner in the café, took in a magic show in the theatre, he was good, but a bit cocky. From 9-11 was another group get together, with a live band, and drinks...I left early with two fingers giving me "freeze" problems, Lynn joined me in the room a bit after ten to finish the night.

Friday March 11th, 2019; First of two days at sea to return to Ft. Lauderdale, the ocean here is 1500 meters deep, the temperature in in the upper 70's, sunny, 70's humidity and light winds, a perfect day!

We are waking up and up and out regularly at just after 7:30 A.M.; café for breakfast, walk around and soak up some of the sun before our first trivia with our now consistent group of 7.

After losing again, we actually just sat in the sun, watching the waves until, yup, I GOT ANSEY, so we went back to the pool area to play free Bingo, followed by a ring toss competition, yup lost to the young folks, a lunch, then to join another game of Deal, No Deal... I didn't buy any cards, so we just watched. One of our Trivia groups got picked, and actually won $. 01.. yup, the lowest amount!

Two trivia followed, ...what a bunch of losers! Prep for dinner, this was a specialty dinner at the Eden restaurant. We usually don't care to go to the exclusive restaurants where you actually have to pay for food and drinks, but what to heck...We were treated like somebodies! Given a choice where to sit, complimentary drink, and a two-column menu...the left side was the high priced and high-end drinks!

Five courses two appetizers and midmeal, and an entree, and desserts; My selections included the Descending Frost which was oyster, sea urchin, three items with Chervil, wasabi, and tomato compliments served in 1\2 shells; Lynn's Raindrops comprised of lobster, gribiche tarragon and orange. These are relatively petite portions, with a perfect display, feast with your eyes! Main course Lynn, life after death, Tenderloin, fondant potatoes, Café' de Paris, Beurre, Asparagus, and watercress; Mine was the Mangalitsa, which included braised pork cheek, polenta, seasonal mushrooms, snap peas, and bonito flakes. Yup, perfectly displayed!

THE OTHER ITEMS WERE: SOLEIL: tomato tartar, capers, fingerling potatoes, and tomato water. NAMASTE: Shrimp

Noah

cauliflower, garam marsala, cashew nuts and cilantro; TIDAL POOL; catch of the day, marcona almond, green apple, grapes, crystalized fennel, yuzu beurre blanc; COVE: scallop, egg yolk, celery root, brown chicken jus, caviar, chicken skin;

Desserts: Lynn had the LOOKING GLASS, which was pistachio cake, chocolate, Raspberry and lemon, I had the FORBIDDEN FRUIT, which was apple almond and caramel. They also presented us with another specialty dessert which was a round white ball a bit larger than a soft baseball, and when the hot chocolate was poured over, it opened like a flower to expose a small cake, cream, and foam…WOW!

The cost? With tip a bit over $100.00; but neither of us have any regrets, the most unique food experience we have ever had!

The game show "majority Rules" …we won!! Later a pub quiz and that was it for us, typical 10:00-10:30 old foggy go to bed time!

Saturday March 12, 2022; our last day at sea, finish up loose ends, eat what we can and hand out the extra tips, to the bartender, waitress and room attendant that were so special to us during the week on board. After breakfast Lynn joined the fun and fit class by the activity manager; sat poolside, then in the solarium, a special show by mark Belling the host of the cruise, lunch, start packing, luggage out by 10 P.M. tonight.

Baseball signing event by Belling, three in a row trivia with our group of friends, dinner with another group at 6.

We had a nice dinner 6 others 4 from the Vagabond club we used to belong to! Great conversation, after two hours we had to leave for another event, where Lynn and I participated and yes, we lost again!! After words we went to one of the best production shows, with colors, acrobatics, singing and dancing! Back to the cabin, luggage out before 10; we were two decks above the Club…the drum pounding stopped around 1 A.M.…

Sunday, March 14, 2022 up early, we were to be at the gathering site outside one of the restaurants by 7:45. OOPs; another cruise ship was late, so they shifted us to another pier…our group finally allowed to disembark in a little before 9. Found our luggage, most cheat in getting off, so ours were really easy to see since everyone else proceeded us, our group had four buses, that went well, the bus ride

Educating Noah…Travelin'

was a lot quicker since it was Sunday and not rush hour!

Miami airport has always been poorly run, the line for TSA was 45 minutes, we were lucky it was a charter, instead of leaving at 11, we lifter off a little after 1. The luggage pickup was crowded, all the handles were running at the bottom and hard to get at, plus since all had the tour locking belt, hard to distinguish the large number of black suitcases, plus the aggressive ones that just had to have their luggage first and did not care for others when they pulled the wrong black case. Our friends showed up quickly, offered to go out to supper, but we had other family issues to address too they dropped us off, and art even helped take the luggage us. THANKS ART!! We owe them a dinner!

This was quite a different get-away, than in the past, we were with each other far more than others, there were less activities offered (other than trivia), the largest group we traveled in, but the Canadian couple, Melisa and Dave, we worked with as a trivia team were the friendliest!

Our limitations are showing, Lynn wants the walker most of the time, and I am starting to understand how others care so little for those with limitations! My knees and back barked a lot, we pooped out about the same time at night, most of the chairs are low, without handles to help get up, and many places are not easily accessible with any aids or impairments.

It was a short cruise, one of our shortest! Met some new people, and old friends. It only took 2-3 days to recover, which is a good thing since I had a presentation on money for Money Sense; an organization that educates Milwaukee Public School kids on how to handle money and basic money skills.

I had four documents to be projected on a screen to facilitate the talk forwarded and the teacher assigned ran the computer. The talk actually was closely timed, I only had 2-3 minutes of the 45 minutes for discussion, however, there were no questions, not even one!

When I gave away two bogus Billion Dollar bills, only 3-4 kids of the 20 participated, and only 3-4 kids actually followed along, at least ½ of them slept through the presentation. So much for interest…Plus they actually asked for the discussion!

The postcards sent on the 10th March, arrived in Milwaukee the 5th

Noah

of April…extension of "Island time?"

I received a call from Stars and Stripes Honor Flight that I have a seat May 21st 2022. Camille and Kelly were over for Easter, I told them and asked if she wanted to be my "guardian". That night she called back and said yes! I called Stars and Stripes to get the info as to where she gets and submits application, forwarded it to her, and let her know how much I appreciated, plus any expense I would cover…WOW!

It's the end of April, 2022; I paid for my daughters' participation in the Stars and Stripes flight, she has to attend a seminar the Saturday before as a requirement also, and she has agreed.

Russia still at war with the Ukraine, putting a lot of stress on that eastern Europe cruise coming up in June: To say I hate this wait and see crap would be grossly understated! But it is still on; I am doing repeat transportations with some of the ERS clients; they now know the car and me.

Stock market way down at its high it was at 3500, now down to 3000; first negative quarter, one more and we will be officially in a recession; our southern border is basically open, 2-3,000 coming over every day that are accounted for, gas prices now hoover around $4/gallon, I hate to think what it is in Europe!

Enough of a brief update, next will be the results of the Stars and Stripes flight!!

Educating Noah…Travelin'

Stars and Stripes Honor Flight 05/21/2022

A number of years ago, Lynn, encouraged me to sign up for this honor flight with a good friend and fellow vet friend of ours, Arthur Kunstler.

Two months ago, we found that Art was invited to go in April, just after his flight I received a request for the flight in May. All of us invited are asked to have an escort to travel with us, not our wives, older than 21, and younger than 60, due to our advanced ages and infirmities. Of the 77 vets on the first of two flights today, 40 required wheel chairs, 4 medical doctors were on board, 4 med techs, and four support people, all branches were represented, average age of our group was 75, all but three were Vietnam vets the other three Korean war vets.

My grandson wasn't old enough, but my youngest daughter said she would like to do it! They require the escort to pay their way, which I gladly offered and did cover, and we were set!

The required paperwork was done by both of us, vaccinations proved, and forms signed; Camille had to also attend a class for escorts the week before.

The day of the event, we picked up Camille at 4:30 A.M. arrived at the airport a bit before 5; greeted outside and directed to the gate. Both Camille and I were impressed by the cheerfulness of the people providing direction, the TSA was abbreviated to basically ID; and then receiving our seat assignment, with escort sitting behind the veteran, and middle seats in most cases left empty for comfort!

While waiting for the aircraft to take off, we were served a bag lunch at the gate. During the 1 ½ hour flight we were offered water, juice, or soda. On the tarmac the fire department doused us with a water cannon as we passed in respect for us, and we were accompanied by two small airplanes to see us off!

We landed in Baltimore, having seen the beautiful Chesapeake Bay and over the Pimlico Race Couse where the Preakness Horse Race was also today!

Noah

The weather is clear, dry and a bit hot at 95 degrees F. The Disembark from the plane and will be from the busses along with embarkations due to the number of wheel chair requirement is a bit slow30-45 minutes on and off plane, 20 minutes on and off the buses, but both Camille and I noticed no push and shove, and patience by all participants, and guides.

We arrived at 9:40 A.M. Eastern time, we waited for the second flight when we were escorted to the waiting buses; with other states also having flights for vets in, we are told that there will be a total of 584 vets touring today!

Once all abord the buses, we are issued bag lunches, beef or turkey for choice including a sandwich, chips, and a cookie, we are always asked about taking water bottles and this will be though out the day, and reminded before exiting and entering the buses at the various stops, and encouraged.

On the bus trip to our first stop in D.C., the escorts were encouraged to provide a brief Bio on the vet they are accompanying. Like others I gave Camille a few notes to use.... Air Force, 1968-1972, Vietnam, Guam, Philippine Islands, and then K.I. Sawyer in Upper Michigan.

As we approached Arlington cemetery, we slowly drove around the statue of the raising of the flag on Iwo Jima, and were told to watch as we went past. There is an illusion of the flag actually being straightened by the statues as you pass the monument! And, yes it did look like that!

The size of Arlington Cemetery is immense! We traveled to the tomb of the unknown soldier to watch the changing of the guard at 1 P.M.

The precision, the inspection, and the change of one guard to another was a great show! We also explored the tomb area, walked the actual marble colosseum style theatre behind the tomb with seating for at least 300!

Rejoined the group, loaded up the bus and moved on the Marine, monument, tour, pictures, back on bus, Air Force monument, tour pictures, back on the bus, then to the Lincoln Memorial and the Washington Monument. Here we had an hour to tour. After looking at the Lincoln memorial up close we walked the reflecting pool, about

7/8s the way I needed to rest, we sat next to a nice lady who invited us to sit and asked about the name tags and all those dressed in blue and red shirts, we explained that the blue shirts were vets and the red shirts were the escorts, all in our group from Milwaukee for the day. We asked her, and she told us that she was here for three years and is hoping to finally have her kids and husband join her from her home in Africa. She was very nice, we answered all the questions she had, and we wished her well in seeing her family soon, now that the covid restrictions are being lifted. We continued our walk to and around the World War II Memorial to meet up again with the group and the bus.

One last stop before the return home was the Navy Museum and exhibit, which was opened late for our group to take pictures, explore and enjoy.

It was now evening rush hour, half way back to the airport we picked up a police escort and also served a bag supper, this was a Chic-filet sandwich, chips, and cookie, always with water available delivered to your seat!

Back at the Baltimore airport, special TSA aisle, gathered at gate for departure, our seats were printed on our name tags (same assignment as the flight in); we were delayed a bit due to the 40 wheelchairs that had to be loaded, then off we went, again the fire department hosed us down with a water cannon as we passed as a sign of respect, and the flight home. There was a delay after we approached the gate, waiting for the wheelchairs, then slowly released to see hundreds of people greeting us shaking our hands, waving smiling, a Scottish band, flags waving, WOW!!

Met up with Kelly, Cami's hubby, Melissa a great cousin, and Lynn. WOW great, home at 10:30 long day, but unforgettable! AND Thanks again Camille!!

Eastern Europe Adventure June 2022

We made our first deposit on this finishing Europe in 2019. It was moved twice, with the pandemic and so even though Lynn and I have been on both the John McGivern Cruise and the Mark Belling cruise we still sweat the mandatory Covid negative tests required.

In the last three weeks leading up to us finally leaving, I volunteered for a Franklin Run, working with registration, replaced my main computer in that it was advised to replace them every 3-5

Noah

years, mine was 7 years old. I went to Best Buy, found a good cheap one and paid the extra $200 for data transfer and one year GEEK coverage.

After having to return three times to get the computer working properly and having to buy a new WORD program for $150 and a disc converter for $30…the new computers don't have disc drives any longer; no, I wasn't told……

Then my phone was updated by Samsung…all calls did not ring just went to voice mail, and my hearing aids were no longer synced; Visiting Verizon twice, chatting with Samsung, and reading and connecting to the hearing aid people I got that all taken care of in two days!

All the while, I was also chatting with Swiss airlines and Vantage regarding having only an hour between flights from Switzerland to Poland; I was really concerned given this happened before with our cruise to Greece! A week worth of chats got us a wheel chair for Lynn in Switzerland airport, along with the ones in Poland and Chicago, and Rollie, her walker is to be checked with the luggage.

I charged the four batteries for our cameras, and this lap top; our two covid tests were arranged the day before takeoff, and only the ride to the bus terminal on Wednesday needed to be arranged, our friends, the Kunstler's will be picking us up on the 28th after 10 P.M.

I was also in contact with Vantage with both post and pre-excursions in regards to the walker…everything is slow, and everything has to be explained carefully!

I ordered copies of pictures from the photographer on the Stars and Stripes trip, then went back and forth with them to send the pictures after the 28th of this month, Camille came through with a couple pictures to finish up the Shutterfly album order, it was another couple hours challenge to download those pictures from my computer files, but after several attempts I got it! Tried going back and forth with chat, then after frustration, got an actual human on chat then took too long to answer and was cut off…so I will just let that photo album sit until we return. I am starting to feel like a grumpy old man, but service is not as good as it used to be.

Called one cab company to see what kind of lead time, had to leave a message?? At noon?? After an hour I called another cab company,

Educating Noah…Travelin'

he told me at least an hour before, I asked about his competition, he told me that that was common in that they want the medical transports that pay better. By the way, still not able to call an Uber since I tried working for them years ago…no local numbers to correct, never responded to my e-mail years ago in California…is it really me??

I confirmed our flights, it is now 23 hours before flight at the airlines, instead of 24, had problems printing luggage tags, and boarding passes were on two pages…. Lynn talked to our neighbor Jim about being our taxi and he readily agreed!

Wednesday June 8th; day 1; checked and rechecked everything, the allowance in Europe for checked bags is 20 Kilograms (44lbs) vs our 50 lb. limit, both of ours came in about 37 pounds…Rain on and off all day, Jim picked us up promptly at 2:30 We arrived at the bus station at 3:50for the bus scheduled for a 3:10 pickup. He agreed to stay with us and shelter us in the car do the on and of rain shows and since Covid, the terminal was closed so everyone has to wait outside…The bus was 15 minutes late which put us even closer to rush hour in Illinois, but actually it was smooth sailing all the way to the airport!!

The luggage check promised for Swiss Air did not exist, so we joined the lines to check-in. Since we now fly business class, so the line was significantly shorter, they issued luggage tags and also a special one for the walker, and the walker we had to take to the other end of the terminal in the "oversized luggage" there was no extra charge…

TSA went well, our gate was a pretty good hike from TSA, but with the wheel chair assist, Lynn wasn't hindered, and the attendant was very nice!

We were scheduled to leave at 7:10, actually taxied from the gate and out in que at 7:40 and off the ground just before 8…yup, more anxiety about the short one-hour transfer time in Switzerland!

Flight went smoothly, food was good, and the Swiss beer very good with the meals. An hour before landing the lights came back up in the cabin, our watches were adjusted to local time (about 8 hours ahead, we flew east, will get them back on our return flights!)

We landed and at the dock at the time projected…the pilots made up the lost time, and we found the wheel chair assist soon after leaving

Noah

the aircraft. We actually landed and docked at D gates, our connection flight...Zurich to Warsaw...you guessed it, was at the A docks and on the tarmac!

We actually were golf carted to the A section, then given the option of elevated plane entry, so we took that, this was a new experience, the vehicle was the size of a small school bus, we got in, took our seats, and were driven out to the aircraft where the whole compartment was lifted to the rear door where we walked right into the aircraft...wow. The rest of the passengers were brought out in three buses and walked up the steps to the aircraft, the weather? Sunny and warm.

We left a bit late from there also, the food again was very good, landed in Warsaw about 15 minutes later than projected, went to pick up our luggage and found we had to go to another area to pick up the walker... (the oversize area) which we did.

Processed out, where we were to meet the hotel pick-up...no pick-up person, so we went toward the exits, hoping to find ... (asked the wheel chair guy to call the hotel number and try to coordinate, after the second call they agreed to send someone, I gave the attendant an extra tip for using his phone and sent him off.) I left Lynn and went back to the first luggage exit and asked the few persons left with clip boards if they were from the hotel, on returning, Lynn was standing with a guy from the hotel.

This was all within 10-15 minutes, the driver was not talkative somewhat short in speech, and the car was parked in the garage...it took a good 30 minutes to get to the hotel, the drivers here are as aggressive as in the U.S. now, he called ahead for a doorman, and then told me to sign a slip for the charge of picking us up.

We went inside, found the Vantage representative, gave her the bill which she promised to take care of and received our keys to our room, and told to meet in the restaurant to get a brief orientation, and included dinner. It looks like about 30 people signed up for the pre-trip, we are given our listening devices, told that if we lose them, it's $100; and that her time is the time, most toilets require money to use, so we are told to carry small local money, if we do not show up on time, it is taken we are opting out of the excursion!

The meal was very good, met some of the folks, found some had arrived on Monday, and some actually joined us after 8 PM coming in later and had to still wait for some luggage.

Well, after dinner we headed up to the room, long tiring trip, in bed by 9:15, the weather in Poland now…summer 75-80 degrees F, light clouds.

Friday, 10, June, day 3; First adjust night, our bodies not caught up to the change in times, so around 2 AM we were both awake, got up, read for a while, back to bed and slept till 6:45.

Breakfast at the hotel was abundant, rivaled a cruise ship, tables with various breads, rolls and croissants, fruit table, cheese table, hot buffet line with potatoes, beans, eggs sausage, bacon, pancakes and waffles, also fresh salmon and herring, a variety of juices and of course a couple coffee machines.

I asked at the desk about a white page and got a stare back…from all of them, also asked where on the supplied map was the hotel, the woman took the map and found it while three guys watched…young people…. ugh!!

A bit before nine o'clock the bus came for our morning tour, we were all on the bus at nine as requested and off for the city tour.

80 percent of this city was leveled and completely destroyed by the retreating German troops. Warsaw is the largest city in Poland, the population at or above two million, the second city we will be visiting tomorrow is Krakow and that is about the same as Milwaukee sitting at 800,000. The total population of Poland is eight million.

Poland lost its independence in 1795, and finally won it back in the late 1800's, then again in 1984. A very rocky relationship with Russia, and before the second world war had the highest population of Jews, in Europe, and second only to the Jewish population in New York City, USA.

Presently, in Poland, you are first polish, and then Catholic. The concentration and killing camps are basically all gone disassembled by the Germans in retreat, 1,000s of Jews were killed as soon as they arrived at these places.

The English language is now compulsory in all he schools here so all the young are bilingual. We had three stops, the first was at a park with a statue dedicated to Chopin, the second was a stop for rest rooms and the Jewish Museum and monument, and the third after the city tour was Old Town, where after an extensive walking tour, we were given 2 hours to explore, eat, and get those souvenirs we just had to have!

Architecture in this city is quite varied, a lot of Russian socialist plain "functional" buildings for the 'working class" which were small cramped apartments in very plain large box buildings, a lot of statues, and a couple of fancy government buildings. The city symbol is that of a mermaid, Poland's symbol is the eagle.

Met up with the group, back to the bus, we were in the minority, it seemed that 2/3 of the group decided to hoof it back to the hotel rather than ride…Lynn and I had agreed to take the bus her with Rollie and me with a painful back…I guess we are getting' too old for this stuff!!

Afternoon nap… (talk about getting' old,) then off to find someplace local for a light supper. About two blocks from the hotel, we found a local eatery, Lynn had turkey veggie wraps, with a 7up; I had a sour soup that also had sausage and egg in it and as a bonus, it was two for one on the drinks, So I ordered a sour beer which was really good; in fact, both of us enjoyed the meals, and watching people.

We took the long route back to the hotel, luggage out at 8:30 tomorrow A.M. We like to watch the international news, nice to see "the other side" and it seems no one is happy with their governments, as we passed the polish parliament, the guide indicated it was the "circus district" and the clowns that occupied it…

everyone on the bus seemed to agree…reinforcing the Viking cruise line saying that on home visited, discuss past occupations, and background because their governments are as bad as ours….

One last thing, on the war in Ukraine, I asked how far to the Ukraine border, and the guide stated "about 5-hour drive" …. given 100-120 K/M (about 60-70 mph) would put the border 600-700 km away …about 500-600 miles; no evidence of a war here, at all!

Saturday, June 11th, 2022; Day 4; Another great breakfast, just on Saturdays, the hotel restaurant doesn't open till 7 AM so we had to wait a half hour.

Suitcases out by 8:30, ours out at 8:10 went down at 8:45, suitcases still there …oops meet time 10! Talked to other early birds watched our luggage loaded and everyone on the bus at 9:55, impressing our guide!

The bus trip with two "rest" breaks took 5 hours to our next Polish stop in Krakow; on the way we learned that the Polish language is the second hardest to learn in the world next to Chinese, we were given a Polish language lesson on the bus along with watching a movie called the Zoo Keeper's Wife, about a family that helped Jews escape the Nazi's and Soviets during WWII…. a very good movie!

Gas at home is about $5.00 per gallon, here, $7.79 K/liter…comes to about $8.00/gallon!! WOW!!

After checking into our room, Lynn played nurse, my back was killing me, and about an hour our, a roundabout turn brought another passenger's carry-on off the top rack and bouncing off my left arm...ouch!!

Dinner was on our own, so on the way to a recommended restaurant, we stopped at another souvenir shop to get the rest of Polish souvenirs for friends!

What a great stop! The owner took a liking to us, I bought some additional shot glasses along with Oher trinkets, and by the time we left the shop, I had three shots of Polish vodka, Lynn was kissed and hugged, and he threw in a shot glass and thimble for free!! WOW! I also had shown him the list of polish names, and he confirmed ALL of them were very common, including the two spellings of Scherlowski, and Scherlovski; Krzyzanowski, Przyzanowski, and Yaroszewski…

The restaurant recommended was closed for the day, we decided to return to the hotel, got an additional pen (yeah, just another souvenir we needed to collect) and had dinner; I had fried sea food, including calamari, octopus, and shrimp, and zucchini, Lynn had a margarita pizza; both excellent! To the room, long tiring day!

I had planned to take the salt mine tour, but due to my continuing back aches, and my hip acting up, the 800 stairs and initial 320 steps to explore, I whimped out. It would have been interesting though, the mine was opened in the 13th century, one of the world's oldest salt mines, 1073 feet below the surface, and encompasses 178 miles of tunnels. You can only explore this with a guide and the tour lasts a bit over two hours. There was supposed to be a provision for those unable to navigate that many steps, but trying to use Google, for my mail or information, the security required a phone number to verify, and no, I didn't get the European chip for our phones...

Sunday Day 5; June 12th. we are to meet for a bus and walking tour of the town, meeting in the lobby at 8:30; I don't know what happened to the city pub crawl that was supposed to happen last night with our city host....

The tour was of all the old town where the Jews lived, some of the buildings still standing, symbols of the community including a Minora and a Chanukah candle holder (one has two less candles...see the pictures)! I took a picture of a stone commemorating the 1,000's of Jews burned to death, symbolizing the stone lasts much longer than candles.

Most of the Jewish section was free of graffiti that seems to be everywhere in this city, and we are told that the synagogues and Churches were put high in the air, including steeples so that locals got their bearings in that there were no maps, and few compasses, so this oriented the community.

When the Jews were rounded up, they were restricted to a maximum of 40Kg. of luggage; when they arrived at the trains, the baggage was taken away, and every man, woman, and child herded into box cars. The luggage was emptied and all the valuables found taken to Germany, all bags were roughly searched and examined for hidden treasures.

The river was the dividing line between the residential areas and the factories, the Jewish were the builders of commerce, BY THE 17th century and beyond so there was quite a complex of factories. We stopped to observe straight back chairs in an open area, placed there to represent those that lost their possessions and lives to the Germans and Russians.

When the factories were closed, all were required to report at 6 A.M. and marched to the railway, anyone non-compiling was shot dead on the spot.

At the railway station, the crowd was sorted, those that had specific jobs were sent back to work in the factories now,' 'owned" by the Germans, and used as slave labor, unskilled were placed on the train for extermination.

Educating Noah...Travelin'

Off to the Wawel Castle complex, which was the coronation and burial site of Polish kings. We walked through a park, and shown a rather long incline to reach the gates of the complex. Lynn and six others stayed below as the rest of us followed our guide through the complex. Pictures accompany this UNESCO site the complex consists of a series of buildings and a church, cobblestone drives, and beautiful architecture. Once in the complex we explored the outside of all the buildings even had a short potty break where the cost to use the toilets was Zoles's (about 50 cents,) change was not provided, and if the two single coins were not available a credit card was needed...image how many 50 cent charges!!

We descended down after almost an hour and a half to the main streets below, picked up Lynn and the rest of the group, to walk past other churches, store fronts and restaurants to the huge medieval square, having another church, tents of venders, store fronts and rental carriages, after orientation as to where the better restaurants where we were left to ourselves to find and enjoy lunch on our own. Lynn and I found a recommended restaurant, I had beet root soup and Lynn had an almond tort, we shared her soda, and both were excellent!

At 1 o'clock we joined the group to walk to the park, where we picked up the bus to make the somber visit to the Nazi concentration camp, Auschwitz, to be followed by the "death camp", Birkenau.

The camp is about an hour and a half drive which gave us a bit of a break from almost continually walking for 2 plus hours, yeah, we're getting' older fast!

At the camp you must present a photo ID along with the pre-purchased tickets. The guides, we are told must go through a rigorous training period for three months, then pass a thirty-question test with no more than 2 questions wrong, and then an oral exam by a panel of 6 to be approved as a guide!

Our group was split up to 16 in each group, and atter going through screening similar to TSA at the airport, we were off!

The Germans picked this place because there were a number of barracks from it being a Polish military training camp, with security fences, and extensive buildings, including a rail station and tracks.

We toured several buildings, those that could, or were able to work, were sorted again, the others, told to strip down for showers and after entering the buildings poisoned, women, and children. In some cases, this was within 3 hours of arriving at the camp.

In the beginning of the camp, it was just for political and captured soldiers in the Polish government, but then from 1942 on it was a death camp. On average since the seasons ranged from high 80's and 90's F to below zero in the winter, and the only clothes were on their backs, women lasted about three months, the men 8 months, of those chosen to work.

In the first year or so the prisoners, then executed, included those prisoners of war, the political opposition, church priests, and Polish resistance, from there came the Jews, so there were not only Jews exterminated, on a scale of tens of thousands some days in excess of 10,000 were exterminated, bodies cremated.

We were shown rooms, 20'X 50-60' half filled with shoes, men's women's, children's, fancy work, and casual, another room with the destructed luggage and bags searched for valuables, and one other, the same size 1/3 full of human hair, shaved off the corpses before disposal to be made into material....

A few did escape, however, if caught you were executed and a number of others were also to set an example, and of course the execution was in a public forum by various means, hanging and left for days was only one example.

We asked where and who supplied the Nazis with materials, and were told many corporations supplied, including American corporations, one he mentioned was Coca cola, sounds like the same now with the companies dealing with China, like Nike, Apple, NBA and others. The tour was extensive, we even toured a gas and cremation structure to finish the two-hour tour; on the bus to Birkenau; Lynn and I had seen similar, so we stayed out in a small café to skip that 45-minute mile walking tour.

The rest room here demanded two zoles exactly, again no change for a five zole coin (~$1.25) and we had to use my credit card...well it worked the first time, then we were having difficulty having it read, two bus drivers used their passes tried to help Lynn with the card, finally I came out and figured it out...I thought it was interesting that neither driver just used their pass for her....

We returned to the hotel, after the 1 ½ hour drive at 7:30, given

Educating Noah...Travelin'

our time for covid tests required for the cruise ship, ours was 8:40 A.M.; a long walking day, turned in our listening devices, had a light supper and called it a day!

Monday June 13th, day 6; breakfast, finish up the documentation, and covid testing. Good news, everyone passed...just like the other recent cruises, we found that quite interesting considering the "news", and panics....

The rest of the day was on our own, so off we went back to the shopping area where Lynn wanted to explore more shops. I was able to take a few more pictures of the castle complex, we did notice a lot of groups of kids both going up to explore the river's edge, the castle complex, and the square. We have noticed that other countries seem to get the kids out more than in the states.

Most of the stores open around 10 A.M., most did not have posted hours and some didn't open until just before 11. We were both reminded that personal space is much closer in Europe, including light brushes, and a lot more aggressive bicyclist!

We found some additional must have souvenirs, collected the rocks for folks and postcards, went back to the souvenir shop to get the name of that polish "Wodka"; and I gave him some toilet paper $100 USA bills.

We were going to take a small river boat cruise, but walked the wrong way on the path, and it was very difficult to get down to the water's edge due to too many steps without hand rails, and only one or two very steep dirt gravel paths...we did it, walked the path along the river, brushed twice by bikers, and close encounters with groups of middle and high school kids.

We realized we had gone too far in the wrong direction and it was already past lunch, so we explored a grocery store (I like to check prices and selection), found a Pepsi with Mango, a juice drink with pomegranate flavor, a donut with cheese, one with raspberry, two cookies and I was able to add a bottle of the vodka ...ZUBROIVKA...No bag was provided, everything was just pushed into a bin just beyond the credit card device, and the cashier had an attitude, he was there just to get paid I guess....

We took our lunch home, there were a few parks or green islands but only one park bench and that one was occupied. We did notice

UBER and BOLT cars, food delivery people on bikes...and a McDonalds.

Back at the room, we rested and ate our lunch. The news is basically the same, here, (no Fox network) food supply shortages due to the war between Russia and the Ukraine, England expelling illegals but not having enough workers for food harvest, and yes, the Climate crisis.

I asked how far was Warsaw from Chernobyl, and it was only 780 kilometers; both cities seemed "business as usual" except for a small report on the war occurring just a few 100 miles away....

Enough sitting in the room, the forecast was for rain but it hadn't started yet, we asked Marta our guide what else was within walking range, and she suggested visiting the dragon...so she gave us directions and off we went. The dragon is metal, about 12-15 feet tall, and yes, we asked, its breaths a puff of fire on the half hour...yes, we stayed for it!

Lynn had wanted the river boat ride, we saw a girl with an advertisement, and she took us to the river boat. It was an hour tour up and down the river guided in polish and English. Halfway through it started to rain, we got under cover, and finished the cruise in a lighter rain. It didn't look like it would get any lighter, and we didn't really want to chance heavier rain, so we hoofed it back to the hotel. Both of us a bit wet and cold but not everything can be perfect!

We changed clothes, had a light supper at the hotel, finished up the notes, packed up our suitcases for the 6:30 luggage out request and settled in for our final night in Krakow!

June 14th Day 8; Wednesday; This is an extensive travel day, breakfast, then on the bus, all aboard at 8 and off we went. There was a toilet break every 1 ½ hours of travel, we were stopped for papers as we crossed the Slovakia border, (improper papers cost about $1600 US which the bus driver would be responsible for) and at noon we had lunch at a unique restaurant, part of a ski resort, that had a 5-page selection of food!

Lynn had chicken with cream sauce and vegetables, I had the garlic soup with a local beer, that too was excellent. There a number of groups of kids in and out of the complex, and it seemed they were all going nuts over hats with ears, so we got them for the Bopp's,

Educating Noah...Travelin'

Oliver got a bear one, Elenore a unicorn, Benny a rabbit...they all have extensions that when squeezed the ears straighten up.

We observed jerk drivers, as in the USA, went through a number of speed traps (video cameras) As in other European countries, mostly video highway patrol, and the local police take care of violators in their jurisdiction. All three countries we were in do not to be called Eastern European, they prefer and insist on being central European, Eastern European suggests communist/ socialist which they resent.

At 5:30 we finally stopped at the dock, greeted by the captain and crew, turned in our passports, room keys, found our room, everything in, a welcome by the captain, dinner, and finally unpack for the night.

June 15th, buffet breakfast, yes, extensive, in the time we were gone, our room was made up, exchanged some US dollars for Euros, and signed us up for the slow Pest side of Budapest morning tour.

The slow walk tour here would be a regular tour, these Europeans all tend to walk fast! Must watch out for bicycles, the tour was ½ by bus and half walking.

Budapest is the largest city in Hungary, two million people, in a country of eight million, it is the combination of two cities on the river's edge, Buda, (means hill) east side of the river, and Pest, (flat) the west side of the Danube River.

Three semi-circle main boulevards, representing where to old city walls were, all have trollies, cabs buses, and an underground subway, and any possible parking spot taken by cars!

Mostly catholic, some protestant, and some Jewish, we drove past the second largest synagogue in the world, the largest being in New York city! This was turned into a Jewish ghetto; all of the Jewish possessions were confiscated, and thousands of Jews were killed here; During the holocaust over 600,000 Hungarians were killed or sent to death camps.

We also visited the tomb of the unknown soldier; located at the end of a major boulevard, I took a number of pictures to show how grand it was, and even one close-up of a mounted soldier with a horse having antlers incorporated in the reigns, the inscription "Huba".

In 1999 Hungary was officially an independent democracy, in 2004 Hungary became a member of NATO, HOPEFULLY, never

Noah

again be threatened by communists...

Back on the ship, we had a great lunch, found out that the ship will stamp and send out postcards, so back to the room, filled them out and took them back to the front desk, after a nap...we are getting old!!

We had another orientation as to our program tomorrow, dinner, a folk-dance show with a very talented quartet of string instruments, and it looked like the guy did all the hard jumping and boot slapping, she just mainly followed along and yelped a couple times. I thought it was similar to Irish foot dancing, just a bit more leg and boot slapping.

Went up to the top deck to take pictures of the Budapest at night, and we called it another day!

Thursday June 16th; day 9; this is the exploration of the Buda side of the river. We were signed up for one of the later tours since we had some of the assistive folk; Lynn decided not to go after talking to a few people, and lucky for her she stayed back! many multiple staircases, inclines and extensive walking, even in our group, the pace was European, at times I was almost a block behind the leader who rarely waited for the group to reform.

Our first stop was the Parliament building, outside was a sculpture of a lion and a serpent, asked, and found the lion was the leadership, and the serpent wrapped around was evil or the devil. The guide repeated quite a few times that the Hungarians are proud to finally be a democracy, they are basically agrarian, and their spice is paprika! Since the Ottoman Empire conquered them from 1526-1666; then the Turks took over!

An idea of how many times the Hungarians have been subjected and lost to wars, the castle has been seized 33 times!! In fact, their national anthem mentions all the different rulers!

The government buildings are in yellow and gold bricks, the parliamentary building took 17 years to complete has over 40 kilograms of gold, and used an average of 1000 people to complete the construction, and has 365 spires, one for every day in the year.

The center of the complex is a large inside domed room, with an exterior dome over it, at the center is the Hungarian crown and scepter, guarded by two soldiers standing at attention. The changing of the guard is hourly, we were there to witness if. They guard from 5 AM to 6 PM when the building is open, no photos allowed in this room, the crown weighs 2 kilograms!

We toured various other hallways and legislative rooms, on the outside of one of the major meeting rooms were a number of gold-plated rectangular ashtrays, each capable of holding 8-10 large significant cigars…it was the fashion then, large in both diameter and length, was "impressive".

Back on the bus, we finally crossed the river where it was pointed out the cliff top where the first bishop pushed too hard in converting the" heathens" and was placed in a barrel full of nails and sent rolling down the steep hillside.

Hungary is known for weaving and flower decorations, pyro-granite pottery, water polo, and water sports, and actually a leader in water purification.

There was not enough clearance for the bus, so we all used the cog tram to get up to the castle grounds which are extensive. Castle hill includes shops, gardens, the main castle, plus of course a number of statues, a good 1-1 1/2 miles of walking there and back, look out over the river from Fisherman's Bastion.

Back to ship, All on Board is 1:45; set sail for Kalocsa. After lunch we had a bit of free time before our cooking class in the captain's Lounge. We were treated to making Lagos, which is very popular and was a peasant's food, simple flour, salt yeast, and water, deep fried in sunflower oil, and garnished with sour cream, and feta cheese. IT WAS DELICIOUS…everyone cleaned their plates.

Just a note, Hungarians want to use only products made in Hungary…sound familiar? Also, on a TV documentary it was shown in England, stations are being set up to replace car batteries for electric cars where you park in front, the car parks itself in the station, and the spent battery is replaced with a fully charged one in less than 15 minutes, start to finish…They bragged that it took less time than fill up with petrol…but left out the price…

Supper, we now have the same regulars at the table, dinner excellent, I city tour was after 8, so back to the room…crash and burn.

Friday June 17th; Day 10; Early start, we left on bus to Kalocsa, Hungary; as we entered the town, a stork's nest was pointed out, and it was pointed out that the stork's mate for life, are migratory, fly as far south as southern Africa, the male proceeds the female, and prepares/repairs the nests; same location both north and south. They leave late September-mid October, and return Late April early May to the same place.

Our first stop was a church, this is the fourth church on the same location for 1000 years ago, it is baroque style, the outside very plain, but the inside was outstanding in white marble and gold plate, one of the most stunning we have seen, and we have seen a lot of churches! The other churches destroyed by the various invading armies; this one erected 1734-35.

As in most if not all Christian churches the alter faces the east, where the sun rises; we were treated to six songs on the pipe organ with a surprise of the Star-Spangled Banner!

Next a bus ride to Kalocsa to engage in folk art workshops! I made paprika bread, Lynn embroidered, I sample Silva Palinkas a plum brandy, quite good, and counting the number of ½ shots I was feeling' no pain!

I made my loaf and will make one at home, we were not there long enough to bake them but we were provided with wine, onion, peppers, cheese, sausage, and previously prepared loaves, and yes, well worth the effort and delicious! There was also painting of egg shells, but we doubted if they would make it home!

Back on the bus for our trip to Pecs for lunch at a local restaurant, which included wine, beer, a balsamic salad, and rust bread with butter, and the main course of chicken paprikash on spätzle.

We had an hour to tour the town on our own, we did some people watching in the square, found a number of food delivery bicycles darting, Panda Box and Wolt whizzing by; then we boarded a miniature train for a ride seeing the highlights of the town. Finished up by the buses, met our ship, and down the river we went. As we crossed the Croatian border, we had a face to face with the border patrol, late, 9-10 PM to continue our journey.

Miscellaneous information while on the buses: 58% Hungarians are Roman Catholics, the area we were in is considered the great plains of Hungary, adult storks have orange or reddish beaks, the kids have white or grey beaks, main crops paprika, feed corn, wheat, sunflowers, beef pork and chickens. When the communists took over, everything was confiscated, property, land, and animals; when they were finally defeated land was sold by the government in shares. Capitalism finally in 2004; in the many wars, by different armies, it was not uncommon to have 1 in 3, or 1 in 5 killed; man, woman and child. When the ottoman empire conquered, all churches were converted to mosques, or destroyed, later when defeated most mosques changed back to catholic churches. Houdini was a Hungarian Jew who emigrated, and most of Hollywood were Hungarian Jews.

The price of gas right now, 490 HVF/liter; the price is government controlled, if you want to pay this amount you must have a Hungarian registration or license plate and show you are Hungarian, the guide said he had friends visit from Germany and it cost them twice the rate...P.S. $1 US =381 HVF, 4.5 liters per gallon.

Since we have been on the river, we are always banked at least on the river side, by another boat, open the curtains and you are looking into another room or another set of curtains...disappointing! I am also noticing that when walking in a group, many disregard the bike path markings; bike path as wide as pedestrian, and then complain when they are brushed by those obnoxious riders! It is interesting that any available parking spot on street or over the curb is still taken, and although a larger number of bikes in Europe, it only seems about double we see in the cities...

Saturday, June 18th; day 11; Volkova, Croatia; meeting time on the dock was 9:00 but we were anchored two ships out; take the elevator up to deck three, stairs up to top deck, across other ship, down staircase, up another stair case, down again, then the 50-foot ramp to another 6-step staircase...not so fun with the stroller!

This city was 90% destroyed in the 90's, buy the Russians, the war lasted three years, the settlements took another 4 years, the country is now a democracy and in the 2000's, a member of NATO. The hospital here was evacuated by the Russians to a "safe place" which just meant all were exterminated. The language here is a mixture of several languages, but most also know enough English to work with tourists. Most the industry was also destroyed but the country is making a slow comeback with tourism, farming, and hopefully more industry.

Our first stop was a Monastery that has been rebuilt to about 90%; we were given a history, and then treated to a flute and guitar musical. On the bus trip to and from the monetary we noticed no graffiti, and no bike lanes, extremely clean, all streets and yards, all restorations

Noah

must be approved by a government panel of experts...

On the ride to a culturally exchanged local family lunch, we are told a few more items about Croatian life, we are told not to bring up politics, the war was not that far back! Everyone has employer paid basic health insurance and most pay an additional supplemental policy, the crime rate is very low, farms are individually owned except for the large farms owned by corporations. Sunflowers, sugar beets, wheat, barley, feed corn; pork is the main meat, dairy cows for milk. Minimum wage was 450 EU/month, and has been increased to 600EU; eight grades then 3or 4 years of high school three, for trade prep, four for college prep. An exam at the end puts you in college with a major or tech school trade. s

The lunch with a family was outstanding! There were 11 people in our group, we were greeted with cherry flavored brandy, (Latia; a shot a day keeps the doctor away) and given a short tour of the house. It is their summer house, and they do rent out when people are interested,

We were served with a vegetable soup, choice of wine with dinner, a stuffed yellow pepper in gravy, coleslaw, and creamy mashed potatoes, ALL EXELLENT!

This of four hosts for our bus was a husband, wife and 10-year-old daughter. They own a small winery, were very pleasant and we exchanged a nice conversation. We were picked up after finishing and taken back to the dock, later we were treated to a local string band for entertainment during cocktails, and that evening, wine matched with each serving. Lynn stayed for the "no jazz band" to get those dance steps in, and joined me later to finish out the day.

Another outstanding day, exploring different cultures and realizing how similar we all are in goals and wants!

Sunday, June 19th, day 12 Belgrade Serbia. Forecast was 88 degrees F!

Our first activity after breakfast is a lecture on Serbia, 8 countries now, the Balkans on the east and west resulting from the Ottomans vs the Christian empire, the Serb's being the defenders of the Austria, and people here are defined by ethnicity, not country. After the first world war Yugoslavia was recognized by the USA, then dissolved into 8 individual countries after 1991-1999.

Educating Noah...Travelin'

The city tour began at 9:45; the city of Belgrade is located on the edge of the Carpathian Basin, at the confluence of the rivers Sava and Danube. The first settlement was founded in the 3rd century B.C. by the Celtic. In 1842 the city of Belgrave became the Serbian capital and in 1918, the capitol of the kingdom of Serbs, Croats, and Slovenes.

Our first stop was a park next to the Kalamunda Fortress, there was also a dog festival in the park, all the dogs were very well behaved including those all visiting! The second was the Church of Saint Sava, which is one of the largest buildings in Christianity; white marble imported from Greece, it can hold up to 10,000 people, no musical instruments, only choirs.

The average wage here is about the equivalent of 500 EU/month.... retirement is 250 EU per month...with the cost of living most are barely making it on one job alone.

Back to the port, lunch, the next activities, Noah a Pub crawl with a group led by the cruise director, Lynn an interactive cooking lesson: Serbian White Bean Soup.

The pub crawl turned out to be two pubs on dock, there was 18-20 of us, they sat us down, took orders then followed up with the beer they were pushing and one of two different shots of flavored brandy, one apricot and the other cherry; then asked anyone if they wanted to try the other, most did, they also served small buns, cheese, salami, jam, relish peppers and toasted pork belly.

Then we waited, finally the bill came and the waiter presented a bill for the table, in Serb money.... we agreed that two people pay with their credit cards and everyone else threw in $20 each, the other table paid each one by credit card, the second pub, our guide wrangled with the manger to let us eat inside, then we were each served a Serb beer, from the tap...our guide said she had to go...finally I signaled one of the five waiters at the bar to come and present bills. AGAIN, we were told what the bill was in Serb, when asked, the waiter said $2.50 in EU, but no change accepted, just paper money...the guy next to me this time said he would pick up my 42.50 tab, but I owed him! (I did get the waitress to deliver two beers to him during supper!)

Back to the ship for dinner, Lynn said the cooking demonstration was very good and entertaining, and included the recipe.

After supper a folk-dance troop was there for a forty-minute presentation in instruments and dance, it was outstanding, both in music and performances.

Back to the room, another day gone.

Monday June 20th, day 13; Donji Milanovac, Serbia, forecast sunny 87 degrees F. a bright and sunny day, left the ship at 8;45 for a 1 1/2-hour walking tour of a very small 7000 people 17th century town, rebuilt in 1840, and then again in the 1880's. At the beginning there was a small local market set up with linens, blouses, and a few other things, Lynn got a hat and a blouse. Off on the tour, we visited a school where the Serbian alphabet was explained compared to ours. Then on to the Church of St. Nicholas, where we were briefly welcomed by the priest, given a short history and then asked for a donation…. A three to four block walk back to the ship. As with most European towns this was not handicap friendly, the information at the school was basically a group leader talking, we expected some kid participation, but it seems these are the last days of school, and many kids were just roaming around. Lynn could not go up the two flights of steps to the classroom our group was meeting so we joined another group on the first floor, again at the church, eight stairs up to the grounds without hand rails left her at the entrance for a while.

Back on the ship, nothing really left to look at, all on board 1:45; there are two ships next to us, they pulled out and forward, we backed up and back on the river!

86 miles to the locks, snapped some pictures of a rather pristine shoreline, both sides, gorges, the face of Decebalas, a Dacian ruler and a Romanian national hero who fought the Romans, carved into a mountain side. Two sets of locks, over 1 ½ hours to get through them. The Serbs call the Danube, Dunot…I can't spell it. There was little traffic on the river, just a number of cruise ships and a hand full of small pleasure boats. After the two locks, there was more along the river banks both sides, besides cliffs and trees, typical two-story houses some even clustering into small villages.

In one conversation I learned that after a cruise, many suffer from "CD" Cruise deficit, when you actually have to do something for yourself, like cook and clean! 😊

Today was Tea Time, at 3 P.M.; Very similar to cruise ship tea Times, scones, cakes, ice cream, fruits and a chocolate fountain; At 5:45 Mexican cocktail hour, 25% discount on select Mexican themed cocktails...Just before supper, the port talk and at 9; growing up and living under communist rule by our cruise director.

She was born in 1979, and she is Hungarian. At that time there was no unemployment, everyone had a job, everyone had money; then the communists came, shortages in food, materials, supplies ...the average working wage was 340 EU/month, the well-paying jobs only available to those who were members of the party; when supplies including food was available everyone was notified and stood in line for their portion, including flour, sugar, and occasionally fresh fruit. Most had cars, but you received vouchers for gas, and you could only drive on designated days controlled by the number of your license plate. Only news was provided by the government, and it was only local, and information was filtered. If anyone had an outside source or information it was not shared, if it was shared with the wrong person, the police would become involved; "don't trust your neighbors, they will turn you in" .... Travel was restricted, needed papers to leave, needed papers to return, then came the NATO bombing...for a long time many were always afraid that something would happen...

It was a 20-minute talk, at times a bit emotional, we were all provided with typical snacks, puffed (like Cheetos w/o cheese) peanut flavored, bark like candy, chocolate white a white cream, a sweet liquor shot, a sour liquor shot was also provided.

Tuesday, June 21, 2022 Day 14, A Day on the river. Different time zone, all clocks set an hour forward. A 10 o'clock end of cruise/Transylvania extension talk, a Balkan BBQ, consisting of sausages cut in half, (TASTED LIKE A BREAKFAST SAUSAGE LINK, AND WAS THE SIZE OF A SMALL BRAT) paprika dressing, mustards and onions, with bread slices and beer served up on the top deck to look forward to, and just moving' down the river on another warm sunny day!

We docked at 3 P.M. and went ashore on a walking tour in the city of Ruse, Bulgaria, the city is referred to as "Free Spring", 160,000 population, and the fifth largest town in Bulgaria, largest on the river. half way through, Lynn pooped out, and we meandered back stopping at a souvenir shop, getting those needed things for those back home, and found my rocks for others.

At 5 P.M. We were treated to an icon painter and a priest. He is an orthodox priest married with 3 kids, travels for the church and provides social and educational guidance to various parishes, we asked about celibacy and he said in this orthodox church he found a perfect mate it was a choice, and he found a perfect mate.

Mass is to know GOD; no greater teacher than love, in mass all are equal, men and women.

The artist explained that the icons were an expression of the orthodox catholic church, The legion is that a man had an incurable disease, he washed his face in a fountain, dried it with a cloth, and when dry, showed the face of Christ, and he was cured the dyed cloth has since disappeared, and the icons represent this, a very nice one sold at the presentation to one of our groups for $140.00US…

Captain's farewell party followed, where captain presented the entire crew, and drinks and appetizers were served.,

After dinner we had folk dancers, complete with music, and to wrap up the evening we stayed for the DJ; I had asked him to play Sweet Caroline, which he did, and I led the refrain, along with another woman who was part of the 16 total people left!

I finished up with a dance with Lynn, we were the only one's dancing, and I called it a night, Lynn stayed another ½ hour and she said she was only one of less than ten left…at 10:30 P.M.!!! OLD PEOPLE!!!!

Wednesday, June 22, 2022; Day 15 a full day in Veliko-Tarnovo, a 12th century Bulgarian capitol. The two-hour bus trip there, gave our guide time to fill us in on Bulgaria. The Bulgarian mountains divides North and South, we ae about 200 miles from the Black Sea the main crops are wheat, sunflowers, flour, and barley, plus a lot of fruit including pears, plums, peaches, persimmons, apricots chestnuts, and almonds. As we traveled it was mostly farm land with an occasional small town, they do have four seasons here, most of the roads are to and from…
The population before communism was nine million, after only seven million, trees and shrubs line the roads so only glimpses of the extensive farm fields, and only an occasional horse of small gathering of cows, since they do have four seasons, we were delayed twice by road crews repaving and fixing pot holes, and what seems to be universal, one guy working and three watching…

We stopped at the hotel for a potty break, a shot tour of the local castle and grounds, then back to the hotel for a great lunch, salad, and then a beef stew, served in a bowl with a fork to eat, and a small tart dessert; all excellent!

Off to the 16th-century village of Arbanassi; tour a quaint church, to witness a four-monk choir that resonated the main chamber, a short drive to a local museum of the same age, and back to the ship, a full day, eight and a half hours!

Dinner and goodbyes to those not taking the extension, packed our bags for leaving on the extension in the morning, caution taped the cruise director's door, and finished up the packing and note taking, Lynn went up to the lounge for final goodbyes.

Thursday, June 22, 2022; day 16; we leave the ship by bus to start our extension.

Everyone was on time and we left with our new day guide for our trip that basically is an eight-hour drive across Romania to Transylvania, an all-day bus ride.

Ruda, our guide actually learned most of his English and impression of the U.S.A. by watching Dallas, the TV series. His first language was German…As we entered Romania the line of trucks crossing the border was 2-3 MILES long, he told us he asked a friend, and it can be over 30 hours just to show papers and permits waiting in line.

Romania is the third largest producer of wheat in the E.U., the country is mountainous, and yes, we then saw another line of tractor trailers a ½ miles long pre-waiting line…The gas price posted was 8.74 LE; 4.5 LE equals $1, and that is per liter… (about $8.00/gallon) In the back someone said "that's not bad, about the same as California" …I guess not, but the wages here are far less than in California!!!

Back to life of the guide, Transylvania means the country beyond the forest, and Baclava, the desert pastry, actually originated in Lebanon. When the communists ruled the country, there was propaganda on TV at least two hours on how great life was under communism, there was no power after 9 P.M.

In the education system, two major languages must be learned, he took German and Russian; after eighth grade you are tested and given the options of the further schooling you are eligible for. He stated that

Noah

the standards are high, and of the 57 grads in his class, only 14 stayed in Romania, the rest recruited outside the country,

He limited his talk about the communist society by just stating it is sick, and had no good example of where it was good for the people. We asked about the farms here, and he told us they are family owned, not the State; the corn grown here is for corn oil.

Bucharest is actually the 5th largest city in the European Union, with four million people. Many major U.S. Corporations have E.U. headquarters here, one we saw a lot was Coca Cola! It also has the largest subway system in Europe, and entrances are designated with "M" (from the French) There has been three major re-constructions, WWI, WWII, and three major earthquakes! The average wage in Romania is around $1000/month equivalent in LE (pronounced lay)

Gypsies actually came from Egypt, they were brought as slaves and actually sold with the land, and the term Gypsy is no longer correct, "ROMA" now is the correct form. Hindus were brought by the Mongols to repair and fix their weapons.

Lunch in Sinai a, a former Royal summer retreat, was at an expansive hotel, and options were plentiful, it seems all meals must have soup, and of course bread.

The towns in Romania are quite safe, there is a lot of graffiti, the German influence is quite nice, the communist building plain, a good number of houses observed between the large towns and smaller villages are run down, in disrepair or abandoned. The saying here is the politicians are like diapers, they need to be changed often…sound familiar? The cities all have airports, the nuclear plants here were Western designed, so much safer, the country also has oil and its own refineries.

The fairy tale Peles Castle, was elegant, over the top and a very interesting tour, the pictures I took turned out well, the rooms are expansive, decor beautiful, and the grounds well kept. The quarter mile hike was all downhill to the place, the walk back a bit challenging, no railings for steps or steep declines, Lynn stayed on the bus for the 1 ½ hours, and yes it was a good decision.

As we passed over the mountains, Transylvania started to emerge the trees all green and plentiful, the mountain scenery gorgeous, and we are told that Transylvania was the model for the King of thrones series on Television. Transylvania is the plateau between the mountain ranges.

The bears are a threat in the mountains, and do enter the area below on occasion, other animals in the wild are wild boars, lynx, goats (the rams will go above you, and push rocks on you from above) and rodents.

Brasov is the main town we will be staying in, it has its German section, soviet/communist section and others, there are some remaining walls and arches, and entrances from the 9th century still standing.

Just before stopping we had a bus tour of two squares to see a bit of the town, finally at the hotel by 5:30; collected our keys and found our rooms.

Dinner was at a restaurant around the corner and down a staircase again with only a partial railing, and consisted of fried pork belly, vegetable soup, polenta, stuffed cabbage, sauerkraut, with apple strudel for dessert.

Another day done, tomorrow is Bran Castle Dracula's home and a city walk.

June 24, 2022 Friday, Day 17. We slept well, but getting tired of traveling. European breakfasts are fantastic, always plenty to choose from and this was no exception. The walking tour was described as an hour and a half of walking on cobblestone, so Lynn opted out.

Our walking tour started out on the Saxon side of town, we passed a graphic on a church, and it was explained that the priest didn't want to lose the young by not permitting them to paint the mural…so much for sanctity of the church…graffiti is graffiti, and yes, lots all over town…respect is redefined? SAD

The streets are narrow for protection in the event of invasion, the only problem was when there was a fire. When the communists and Stalin invaded, they took everything, everything was the property of the state, they even changed the names of everything…the joke was after the communists were defeated that a butcher had a new salami, and he wanted to name it, his wife smelled it, wrinkled up her nose, coughed, and said "It stinks like Stalin, call it Stalin salami"

The phrases "Saved by the bell" comes from everyone buried with a bell, this was also for the reason of a wake in other cultures, many diseases put people in comas, others the people were so sick, they pretended to die, this was for those that rethought, or came out of the coma.

The Saxon vs Roman Catholic was just another segregation, plus taxes for those who wished to sell but not support the community. The Black Church is black, tainted due to fire…one of the statues shows Mary with baby Jesus standing on the crown…religion over state?

We asked about the holes in the cement blocks, they were put there to help erect the heavy blocks, not bullet holes.

A Statue of Martin Luther, here they believed the Lutherans were a good idea in that the Roman Catholic church masses were always in Latin, and the locals could not relate, it was also a concern that the Roman Catholics always demanded more money and was too rich and powerful. It was stated that the Lutherans, or protestants relayed more to the people in services provided in native languages.

We walked the 5th narrowest street in Europe; The difference between a bastion and a tower? Tower is square, bastion is round; the Saxons did not have a formal army...

The tour lasted the full 1 ½ hours, lots of pictures, we picked up Lynn, paid for the optional tour the next day, and off to the Bran Castle, home of Dracula!

The castle is on the Slovakia border, the creator of the legion was a man who was very rich, and he had a blood disease. His blood was very thick and if he went outside in the sun, his skin blistered. In Romanian, Vlad sounds like "devil"; there was also legions about people turning into animals at night, and Vlad's father was actually a Knight, and his shield /family symbol was a dragon and "dragon" is just another Romanian name for devil…

The path to the castle is about 500 meters, and a good 40-degree incline, the stairs inside, and there are many, have no railings, so both Lynn and I opted just to stay in the garden and merchant areas.

We sat and watched for a while, then went into the extensive food and gift shops, had ice cream cones, a pizza, soda, beer, and bought those final "must have" souvenirs.

Met up with the group, took the freeway back to our hotel, and the night was on our own. Tomorrow was to see another more medieval town and the home of Dracula's birth.

June 24, 2022 Saturday day 18; we took the optional tour to Sighisoara a UNESCO site, this is the longest continually inhabited medieval city in Europe, and the supposed birth place of Dracula!

It took almost 2 hours to drive to the city, an hour and a half back, the landscape is very green, rolling hills, we went through a number of small towns, most houses face the highway, have sheds and garages behind with nice sized fruit and vegetable gardens, and flowers planted in many flower boxes under windows. There were 10-15% in decay, roofs caving and property seemingly abandoned.

On the way our guide filled us in on gypsies, so compare what was said before to this version:

They came from northwest India, the name gypsy in Romania means a person one should stay away from; every other country in Europe has other names for these folks. Gypsies resist adapting to others laws, conforming only to gypsy law, girls are sold by the families at 13, but it may be an agreement between families just after birth, so it is not uncommon for 14,15, 16-year-old to be pregnant, boys are exploited early on as workers, the girls not sent to public school, the boys may go, but are not social, or rule followers.

Gypsies are good with instruments and physical labor, have a connection with the earth, tents, outside living is common, colorful clothing, many layers with many pockets, be careful around them they are accomplished thieves. If they have housed the dwelling is only 3-4 square meters, there is TV reception, and our guide stated, "They are not Romanians".

We entered "the Rich Forest" acres and acres of trees in a mountain terrain, 30-40 minutes up and down hills and valley was very fresh, thick and very green!

Romania started as Batchia, then the Roman invasion, then it morphed into Romania.

The flag, top RED, represents the blood of soldiers defending the country, Yellow represents the grain, and bottom Blue, for the sky.

Sighisoara, 300–400-meter 30-degree road or old grown over stairs to get there, the guide got cars/cabs for those needing them to go up to the gate. Inside brightly colored houses, all two story, cobblestone or worse streets and if a sidewalk very narrow. We waited for the clock tower to chime and change figurines. A place indicating Dracula's birth place on the second floor, touring the walls with a look over the city below. This was also the residence of the Bloody Sailor, who was aware of where the vital organs were and stabbed around them to prolong death of his adversaries, yup have a picture of his bust.

We toured around, had lunch with another couple and back to the hotel by 6.

There was a row of venders across the street, so Lynn and I visited them, and Lynn also wanted to return to a shop a block away from the hotel that had cork purses in the window. It was open, and yup, Lynn got another "perfect" purse!

That was all for the day, Tomorrow is the Premier Peasant Fortress, another UNESCO site. The weather has been sunny and clear the entire time we have been on this journey; the drivers here in Romania seem to have a suicide wish, the bus has been cut off several times by drivers braking into turns just ahead…impatience seems to be a world-wide problem. I also asked about the war between Russia and the Ukraine, our guide said they were 600 KM away, and the census here is that it is finally winding down, at the beginning, her husband was nervous that he would be enlisted to fight, and many families had alternative countries to go to in the event the war expanded.

June 26, 2022 Sunday day 19; we have the fortress excursion planned, it will only be about 3 hours with the bus ride, the balance of the afternoon, lunch and supper on us.

The fortress was constructed in the 13th century by the Teutonic knights and later with a fortified wall by German colonists in the 15th century. (I got a picture of the date on the wall) Three hundred storage rooms for supplies and people for potential sieges; in all, the fortress protected the church from fifty attacks in the course of its history.

It is on the western border of Transylvania part of the buffer zone from other countries.

We were shown a stone at the right side of the main church entrance door, this was for those caught sinning, a shaming stone as people passed through; men usually for stealing or fighting, women for indiscretion.

There are four major areas in the church, the uncomfortable benched made it hard for women in that they had to sit straight while men could lean back.

We also found three stork nests, I did get another picture actually one with two small ones and a parent.

As promised, we did return early afternoon and within a half hour there was a hard down pore of rain. We were to meet another traveler, and given the rain, we ate at the hotel. Nice long lunch, then the afternoon was just a lazy one, getting ready to check out tomorrow for our final bus ride to Bucharest.

June 26, 2022, Monday day 20, luggage out by 7:30. Last day before our flight back. The bus ride to our lunch stop was 4 hours, and then an hour and a half to Bucharest, Romania's largest city; over two million inhabitants.

On the way, our local tour guide gave inside account of her family as they grew up in the Communist regime after World War II. Her grandfather was arrested and taken away because he owned a business, everything owned was confiscated, and her grandmother was shamed because she was married to a business owner.

Romanians are loud, they claim Latin descent, use touch and have strong family ties. Church attendance is down, and nationalism is gaining power. The older people are very generous, and eat everything on your plate is expected. Low self-esteem prevalent do to 40 years of communist rule.

We passed through the mountains and were close to the snowy topped highest mountain and ski towns. The highest mountain here is 2507 meters! It reminded Lynn and Ime of the Swiss Alps.

Gas here 8.69 RON/liter.

After WWII; the communists took charge with secret police. You were not to say or do anything against the party or be arrested. Many of the opposing parties were executed, along with a number of priests, the communists did not want people to gather together...various prison camps were formed, labor camps, and house arrest used to enforce the communist policies.

Noah

The you men were sent to re-education camps correcting and indoctrination, torture, psychological experimentation and brainwashing was implemented to anyone infracting the rules.

Her grandmother was saved by a Russian doctor and stated that it was not the people but the government that was to blame.

It was common to have electricity turned off a few hours at night, children were not a word to be used, they were hawks of the motherland. Many people listened to Free Europe in secret and discussed only with trusted others. The communists readily burned books, many churches hid them, and conducted secret classes in the church to help educate the children.

A Hungarian priest actually lead the revolution with help from outside the country…they were finally free of the communists in 1989.

"i.e.," here is pronounced Chee; Bucharest is called the Paris of the west due to their own Arch of Triumph; The huge apartment buildings by the parliament house, had 5 rooms per apartment vs the usual 1 or two rooms for the people here, these were communist rich leaders and sympathizers

We viewed the buildings, some toured the parliament, others took a walk through the old section, we went to the hotel, got our room, crashed for an hour or so, had a great final meal, and called it a day.

Tuesday, June 28, 2022 final day; attempted to pre-board but no printer, and no euro-phone to confirm, so again had to do everything over again on a hotel computer.

We flew from Bucharest to Munich, Bucharest was a relatively smaller airport than Munich and Chicago, and Lynn told the ticket agent she would walk…. oops, they cancelled the wheelchair assist for the remainder of the flights! We checked into the flight in Munich, and no assist, finally after three "discussions" we were the last to board the plane, a bit aggravating, and of course Lufthansa, required masks on all the time while flying, it was bad enough the 2 1/2-hour flight to Munich, but the 10-hour flight to Chicago was trying! Lynn insists on flying business, and I felt sorry for those in economy since my seat wouldn't adjust right the screen was not always interactive, and of course flying west, it was always bright the entire trip.

In Chicago, it took the outside crew over a half hour to line up the tunnel to the terminal, a wheel chair with person was ready, lucky because it was quite a walk to border control, having Global Entry now, all we need is facial recognition and we skipped a good hour of waiting in line, picked up our luggage and out for the last bus home. Oh, I forgot to take my passport out of the machine, went all the way back, and WOW, it was on top!!

Bus ride home went well, a lot of lane closures on the way, we ended up being ten minutes more than thought, our friends Art and Pat picked us up and we were home by 10:30…another adventure done!

Noah

Dracula's summer castle

Just a few extra notes:

My name (Noah) in Romanian …HOAX; Lynn's …JTNHH (ACTUALLY THE N IS REVERSED AND THE FIST LETTER IS LIKE THE SYMBOL FOR PY) Both kind of fit!!

We saw no pickup trucks in Romania, no used car lots, no repair shops other than car dealerships, most Romanians can only afford used cars given the average salary/wages are about 1000EU (equivalent) per month and gas now being 7-8 Eu per gallon!

It took two full days to put together the Shutterfly picture album, 3-4 hours to proof and assemble the log, and 5 days since the return, we are both trying to recover, this old stuff is getting old!!

We are agreeing that the last trip overseas will probably be the Greenland trip planned for next year. Our next adventure is the Great Lakes Cruise, after that the Mississippi Road trip the end of August.

The cost of gas keeps going up, I desperately hope the politics soon changes; the biden (I refuse to capitol this fools name) administration hopefully shows how poor liberal policies work for ordinary people…not to say I am ordinary!!

Just four weeks between cruises, it took a good week to recover from the last one, distributed the pens, rocks, shot glasses, and checked on post card deliveries, delivered three people for the ERS program, finally had the flooring damaged by the leaking dishwasher replaced along with a section in the bedroom that had a wear pattern, and the dishwasher replaced, it was 20 years old and repairing it would be almost the cost of replacing , now Franklin requires electrical and plumbing permits to replace them? WOW

Educating Noah…Travelin'

Great Lakes Cruise
07/29/22-08/09/22

We met our friends, Pat and Art Kunsler, at an estate sale they were running for his sister. As we toured the house (everything left was ½ price) we found a couple boxes of Christmas cards and escaped for under $5.00!

Pat asked when our next adventure was, and we told her it was Friday, less than a week away. She asked how we were going to get to the start, and we told her we needed to arrange a ride from home to the dock in Milwaukee. She quickly volunteered to pick us up with Art, for the ride down! WOW, another worry gone!

The days before will be busier than usual, a fire inspection by the condo association, our annual air conditioning check-up, one ERS ride set for Wednesday, and hopefully the installation of the new dishwasher that actually came in last Thursday, and was to be installed on Friday, but no call from the installer, Thursday, or Friday… (We even went to the store again on Tuesday, after waiting 20 minutes the manager finally came, and she then checked, the hold-up was the permits? From Franklin? as of the time we left for the ship, no word from the installer on the when he would actually show up… covid?? Or just a continuation of poor service??) besides the usual clothes wash, camera and computer charges and packing!

I got an urgent message Wednesday, stating we needed a ArriveCAN, entry document to enter Canada, once I found the actual application, one site even wanted to charge me $65.00 each, I attempted a number of times to scan our passports and vaccination cards, but nope, my printer refused to scan…print yes, copy, yes, scan no; After attempting and researching for literally hours, I went to the phones. Started everything again, then the phone would not transfer pictures to the application, and even trying to fill in the rest, I had to wait till Friday morning since the application must not be submitted more than three days before we entered Canada. I left a message with the ship line since the help line was closed after 5 on Thursday…. Friday morning everything seemed to work, transferred pictures, and even entered Lynn's information. When everything was done, it was submitted, and approved…but only me ☹ So I went on Lynn's phone

Noah

and did everything else backwards with me as additional traveler, …same result, only her, but by 10 A.M both approved 😊 …harder to get into Canada than Europe…WOW!!

Our ride with good friends Pat and Art picked us up early, we arrived without any problem, the we had to be tested for covid. of course, we were told this was not necessary before but now, yes it was, we both passed, and let on to the ship. The luggage was already in the room, there are only a little under 200 passengers on this cruise.

We unpacked, safety drill, went over excursions options briefing, went down to sign up for a few that required deposit and even though I was in the first 12-15, one of the excursions we wanted was already filled… (only 10-person slot) I asked if they would start a standby list and they complied, the guy behind me thanked me for that.

The lecture was on the great lakes and was fascinating, here are the notes;

The great lakes are the oldest part of the Canadian Shroud 2 1/2-3 BILLION years ago! Our continent rotated /rotates counter clockwise and the lakes were formed 1.1 billion years ago, documented by gravity maps and well digging documentation.

Lake Superior, the deepest of the great lakes at 1330 feet deep, the shores are actually defined by coral, which can only exist within 30 degrees of the equator, there are huge salt mines below Lake Huron, and lake Michigan… Door County in Wisconsin is actually part of a coral reef!

The great lakes all flow east and north, the age of Niagara Falls is 12,000 years and it recedes about 3 feet per year.

Michigan used to be below the equator, and under water, it progressed to be an island, and now a state!

The reason for the Wisconsin, Michigan, Illinois farmland is that at one time it was all swamp land. Lake Michigan was an old river bed; The southern Mississippi river was one of the oldest North America rivers and was 200 miles wide; Vicksburg has the most dunes from the ice ages or glaciers, the Missouri river and Ohio river were the edges of the glaciers.

The water flows UP, the land is moving north.

Both lunch and dinner we were able to sit at tables of six, nice folks, only formal dining on this ship. No buffet. Casual clothes allowed, even shorts...since there is no pool.

Happy hour was included with an open bar, sat and chatted, dinner with two other couples was excellent, and the option of ½ portions was welcomed!

The entertainment was a guy and gal, played a variety of oldies, and yes, a few Fred Astaire trained odd couples dance to some of the tunes, I danced one slow one with Lynn so that we could retire back to our room...yea, we have joined the old fogies off to our room before ten!

One thing we learned from the guitarist; all Johnny Cash's songs have a railroad train beat in the background...so listen next time to see if he was right!

Saturday, we both slept well, we docked last evening at 10, small port area in Muskegon, Michigan. Sunny, light breeze, and upper 80's!

Free trolly rides starting at 9, two trolleys in the morning, one in the afternoon, making continuous loops of about 30 minutes each.

We did the entire loop to get the info and locations of the stops we wanted to make, the actual town went from boom to bust, coming back since the 1990's.

The second round we got off for the Muskegon Heritage Museum, across the street from an Amazon factory...this factory was not the internet Amazon, but actually a knitting mill in the 1920's that made socks and undergarments!

The museum was three floors, a volunteer demonstrated a player piano, there was a twelve-cylinder tank engine displayed, a Brunswick pin setter for a bowling alley exposed, Michigan is one of the largest pickle producers in the U.S. (November 14th is National Pickle Day), there was also a penny candy display, and they gave one piece away no charge!

Back on the trolly, two blocks, walked along a short stretch of little shops, then to the Saturday Farmer's Market, one of the largest we have seen! The veggies all looked so good, mushrooms were magnificent, it was a bit crowded, so Lynn did have some difficulty navigating between strollers, kids, and just stupid people only out for themselves... (seems more now a days than ever!).

We were picked up with perfect timing to be taken back to the ship, I did get some pictures of some of the classic gorgeous homes from the early 1900's.

Lazy afternoon, both of us even took naps, another lecture on Beaver Island, the largest island in Lake Michigan ...just another thing close to where we lived most of our lives and didn't know about!

I will also spatter in additional information on other American and probably Canadian subjects as they were conveyed during question-and-answer period, like the Great Lakes holds 10% of the WORLDS fresh water...

Beaver island is located off the coast of Shalala, north of Travers city in northern Michigan.

This is mainly the story of one man, James Jesse Strang, (1813-1856) who crowned himself King of Beaver Island, the only King in America after the revolution; he coronated himself July 8th, 1850.

King Strang was brought up a Baptist, but was converted to Mormonism and baptized by Joseph Smith the creator of Mormonism, and supposedly named James Strang his successor, with King Strang producing a letter and claiming an angel also ordained the transfer; he also claimed he owned the Vorge plates, and claimed if these plates were exposed or seen by any other human, they would vanish for all mankind.

Bingham Young, another successor, led his followers, about 50,000 to Salt Lake City, James Strang with a following of about 12,000, to Beaver Island.

Of the 12-year reign, 6 years was on Beaver Island; the King, having that many followers, was also a representative in the Michigan government.

King Strang was murdered by a jealous husband, and at that time the community of Mormons was accused of stealing fish, blocking various fishing areas from outsiders, and conflicting with mainland residents.

After the King was killed the remained of his followers, approximately 2600, moved down to Voree, Wisconsin, just above the Wisconsin, Illinois border.

Educating Noah…Travelin'

Holland Michigan was also started by a religious group, Calvinist separative, who were actually starving when they landed, actually stole food from the local Ottawa Indian tribes and actually drove them out. At this time there are 170 churches in Holland Michigan.

The relation with local tribes with the French, were mostly friendly and reciprocal, the British…no, Brits were bullies…

Of the Great Lakes, Lake Michigan is the deadliest (most ship wrecks), one of the major battles in the war of 1812, was fought at Mackinac Island.

Happy hour brought just about everyone into an area, (60-75 of the guests on board) dinner was excellent, the briefing on our next port of Mackinac Island was extensive, and the band played 50's music to end the day.

Sunday, Mackinac Island Day, forecast was 76 degrees F, and sunny. We didn't sign up for any tours since we have been here before, no motorized vehicles allowed on the island, mostly bicycles and horse drawn carriages. We crossed under the Mackinac bridge a bit after 7A.M., it is five miles long and as with the Golden Gate, one of the longest bridges in the U.S.A.;

We waited for most of the ship to empty, since we were only going to walk the main streets and visit the various shops. We docked only about 2 blocks from Main Street, and it being Sunday morning, ½ of the shops did not open till 10 A.M.

Another perfect day, upper 70's light breeze and clear blue sky.

We explored main street, lots of bikes, but pedestrians had the right of way on the crosswalks and sidewalks, watched bikes passing the carriages on the right and from behind…DUH… we spent the whole two plus hours of walking, exploring shops, contributing to the economy and actually finding the post office was great! I asked directions to the post office and after 3 times actually found it…and on the island, there is no delivery service…. (Service??)

After our exploration, and documentation of the beautiful flowers displayed, we fought upstream to get back to the ship for lunch and another lecture. Oh, lunch at the Grand Hotel is $75 each, downtown a sandwich is (only) $17.00……Room at the grand hotel, high season, $700-$800 PER PERSON!

Noah

The presentation was by Moria Croghan; a descendent from the family that constructed and owned the Grand Hotel and other properties.

Mackinac island is 9 miles in circumference and its' base is limestone rock, from marine saltwater 500 million years ago, and current form is from the last 10 Glaciations; the first human inhabitants date back 7000 years; the importance of this island is that it is located in the largest fresh water system and high elevation.

Then the Antisnobbish Tribes came from the west seeking the "Great Turtle" joining the Algonquin, Odawa, Chippawa, and Potawatomi.

When the Europeans came, they brought two major things, written language, and disease! Both biased toward the Europeans so treaties negotiated numerous times always favored the Europeans…plus the concept where in native culture, no one owns the land, water, or the wind; all was owned privately or by government. The U.S. Government instituted the 1836 Indian removal act displacing much of the tribes.

From the mid 1800's on, this island was considered a summer gathering place for Indians, missionaries, and fur traders, in the 1800's fur was very fashionable in Europe, and that is where most of the pelts were shipped. After fur trade faded, lumber was the next best business here.

Although Michigan has the most ship wrecks, there are plenty here, between Lake Michigan and Lake Huron, more than 114 ship wrecks known, the average lifetime of a ship, was no more than 10 years, due to lack of good maps, poor weather predictions, and ever-changing currents.

Mackinac island is 20% urbanized, and 80% State Park since 1875; the second state park established after Yellowstone national Park.

Here in the summer, the water temperature can get as warm as 68-69 degrees, and "back in the day", porch sitting was considered a cure for a number of diseases.

I did the calculations and confirmed with the ship's pilot, we passed Beaver Island about 4 A.M.; and the cruising speed of the Pearl Princess is 17 knots/hour; no chance of a photo.

Educating Noah...Travelin'

First brief on Sault Saint Marie:

We never really get to Lake Superior, just travel up the St. Marie River, Lake Michigan and Lake Huron are the same height, below superior; we were warned, "if you don't want the "look", it is SUE St. Marie, not Sault St. Marie...

Father Marquette was one of the most famous missionaries, all traders were required to have a missionary with them, if not, their pelts were confiscated; here also the Indians were crowded out, this was accomplished by three treaties, all initiated by the U.S. government and all biased against the tribes, very similar to the Trail of Tears in the south.

In Canada, the Indians are referred to as the First Nation. Every nation of Indians had their own religion and language; The name INDIAN was imposed by Christopher Columbus assuming the discovered land was India.

Missionaries were the biggest influence due to the schools, and taught behavior;

The international bridge here is 2.8 miles long.

Happy hour was on the top deck, open bar and entertainment, in the fresh air was great! Dinner was great, a short second brief on the next day activities, and then the duo played 60's music.

The dance floor got crowded, I and a couple other men got called up to do a Temptation Routine, the interesting thing besides the music, is that the guitarist provides back round on many of the songs and artists. We stayed for the last song, had the best time yet, everyone called it a night....10 P.M. yup old fogies!

Monday, August 1st, Canada! Sault Ste. Marie, Ontario Canada, established by Jesuit Missionaries in the 17th century. The rapids here connect Lake Superior to Lake Huron, a combination of Native Ojibwe, French and English settled here to form this town.

We arrived ½ hour later than projected, we all stayed in our rooms or lounges till customs officials performed the face-to-face verifications.... there are 197 passengers and 65 crew...after a half hour we were all cleared....do the math!! (I guess face to face has been re-defined also...)

We were off the ship with light rain, and took the shuttle to see

Noah

what is offered, 10:15 A.M. this is a ghost town, in the entire loop, we saw 5 cars actually moving, and it looked like only the museums were open just for us! We decided to just return to the ship, the rain was getting heavier...I located stones for the last collector and we were back on ship by 11, next activity is a 1 P.M. lecture on Lake Superior. By the way, we were docked just across the river from the Edward Fitzgerald Museum, about the ore boat that sunk, and actually a song written about by a Canadian, Gordon Lightfoot, that was very popular.

Light lunch, the lecture was about the lecturers walk around Lake Superior with his wife, so the few facts I got were: Lake Superior has the largest circumference of any fresh water lake in the world, there are thousands of ship wrecks beneath its surface, also.

Tobacco is a traditional gift offered to the Great Spirit, and can be tossed into the lake as an offering.

Several hours to kill, nothing organized, a few rooms with card tables and jig saw puzzles; tried to nap, raining on and off and cool, asked about the one excursion we tried to get on, and the event director said they asked and were rejected three times, 10 people were all that was offered and no more...He suggested the other excursion offered but it was only $5 dollars less and no lunch included...To date we have not heard from the captain, besides being ½ hour late at this port, nothing...

At least happy hour starts exactly at 5:30, hopefully the day will get a bit better!

Dinner was, as usual, excellent, the table conversation was engaging, and when I noticed that it was almost 8, we adjourned for the presentation by Kenny, the resident entertainer on "Rock Stars and Actors-Canadian or not?

This was the hit of the day, great presentation, and knowledgeable; here are the notes:

Canada has 9 providences (With this trip, we now have been to them all!)

Guy Lombardo the guy that wrote New Year's Eve song "Blue Skies Smiling at Me"

The yacht in the bay close to our ship in Mackinac Island was Paul Anka, singer "Put Your Head O

On My Shoulder" and writer know for the song he wrote for Frank Sinatra…" I Did It My Way".

As mentioned before, Gordon Lightfoot, another song of his was "Rainy Day People".

Anne Murry. Her song "Snowbird" was about her life when she left her husband for her road manager, and then returned to him after 10 years….

Guess Who band…" American Woman" …a song about an American woman fan that was obsessed with the lead singer…

Bachman Turner Overdrive… "Taking care of Business", sold the rights to the song for 30K every time it was used …it has been played in at least 10 commercials!

Lynyrd Skynyrd…" Sweet Home Alabama".

Celine Dion…" Titanic", and her most popular song "I'm Your Lady" (sold 385 million)

Kenny Loggins… "Footloose" he also wrote "Taking care of Business" for Elvis

Neil Young, David Bowie, William Shatner (Star Trek), William Burr (Perry Mason), Mike Meyers, Keanna Reeves, Michal Bublé, Joanie Mitchel (Clouds), Shania Twain, Michael J. Fox, Donald Sutherland, Kiefer Sutherland, John Candy, Dan Ackroyd, Christopher Plumber…. All Canadians!

This won't mean much to many under 50, but the back ground and information given was priceless!

And it was really refreshing to see how proud he was to be born in Canada, although he became an American citizen…when so many ignorant, stupid, spoiled Americans believe America is so bad….

Tuesday August 2, 2022; light rain is forecast, but it is clear, bright, and low 70's. We dock in Little Current, on Manitoulin the world's largest freshwater island, and known for its swinging bridge, we didn't dock until 1 P.M...

We are in Georgian Bay, above Lake Huron, and completely Canadian. What lake is completely American? Lake Michigan!

The bay is very large, 120 X 50 MILES!

Noah

People started moving here as the glaciers receded, the effect of the glaciers was to push land down into the mantle. There is evidence of both whales and seals in the Great Lakes and this bay.

Lake Superior, above, is only 3200 years old; and in this bay there are 30,000 islands.

The native's belief was that the God of the bay had a bad temper, when a wife was arranged for him, she backed out, his temper showed when he slammed his fist into the ground and formed the bay, then grabbed a fist full of earth and threw it into the bay forming the multiple islands.

In Canada, The Hudson Bay Department /general merchandize stores were replaced by the Canadian Tire company just in case you're looking.

Meteors bring in nickel and copper; in the war of 1812, the battle of New Orleans was actually a year after the war was over...communication was that bad!

The Bad Lands are Holy sites for the Native cultures, tribal nations are divided by language, each nation has subsets of clans and totems. Trading crosses cultural lines (money talks?) there were over 500 Nations when the Europeans came.

We had signed up for the History experience Anishinaabe Aadziwin (The Anishinaabe Way of Life) excursion, and when the time came, we were told both the history and art excursions had been combined, along with the drum presentation at no extra charge so we loaded onto two busses and off!

It was almost an hour ride to the site of a burned down school, on the way there we were given background of the nation, the guide seemed new, had to refer to his phone notes often... At the site which was about three stories of an old shell we were told his life, his troubled teens, his addiction for ten years and that in his mid-30's he was clean. He inferred that parent no longer knew how to bring up children, that the "old ways" were not encouraged by the government, the difference between territories, and how the natives respected women (even though kidnapping young girls of other tribes was common) On and on about the suppression of the culture and way of life... After the lecture, we reboarded the bus, drove to an Indigenous art gallery where we viewed a number of paintings with price tags ranging from a couple hundred to a couple thousands and even millions of dollars…The single lock door, wood construction of the 1500-2000 square foot building seemed to indicate any need for security??

Back on the bus, to a Lacrosse playing field, where we were told of the drum tradition, had three sets of drum and chanting sessions, including two with a woman dance in a traditional native jingle dress. The first dance was hands on hips, and a light two step, the second had arms waving and a bit smaller stepping.

We got off the bus at 5:30 All Aboard; so, we could not explore the town; but I did see the price of gas…$184.9/liter (about $7.36/gallon…comparable to Europe…ours at the time we left was $3.85/gallon)

As we left, I took picture of the swing bridge both open and closed it is a one-way bridge, I also took a picture of the extensive car back-up on the highway.

The evening entertainment was Country Western, Lynn tried to line dance with the group, but too many of the women were confused and a lot of bumping and misdirection. Kenny, the musician, stated that he was surprised that so many were still on the dance floor or even in the room after 9:30…everything wrapped up just a bit after 10; thirty people at the most….

Wednesday August 3, 2022; forecast is rain and temperature in the low 70'sF;

Parry Sound, Ontario, Canada, located on the eastern shore of Georgian bay, the is the world's deepest freshwater port, and named after the Arctic explorer Sir William Edward Perry. We opted for a town walk-through, after a short ride on the shuttle, and yes, it was raining…

We explored a few stores. They do take U.S. dollars but do not convert, so in reality the stores gain twenty-two cents on a dollar…and most of the people on this cruse will have no idea what a bonus is to them!

This is the location of the CPR train trestle,1695 foot, built in 1908, got pics, even with a train on it!

Took a picture of the waterfalls, two train murals downtown and some very nice flowers! On the way back...we walked the four blocks, I took a picture of the sea plane place with planes and moose (statue), due to rain, the flights were cancelled as an optional excursion.

Lunch with picture, had fun with the waiter and his buddy, by reporting them to the officer in charge, the officer worked with me and we all had a bit of fun. Rain keeps fallin' but the fiddlers promised still showed up!

Four fiddlers played on the dock next to the ship, yes, it was raining, and the limited room on ship rear decks was even more limited by lack of cover and the noise from the air conditioning blowers.

We gathered in the 4th deck lounge for a presentation by a local brewery with tastings of their beers. After the presentation, everyone was offered a can of their favorite! I wanted to know what made porter beer a porter, he told me coco beans...chocolate...no wonder I like it!!

The program after dinner was "name that tune", and of course there were a couple that shouted out the name, and half way through the bay got a bit rough...so the event director actually passed out Dramamine for those that wanted. Of the 15 points on the first game, three teams had 13, two others 11, we only had 7; the second half way through Lynn was not feeling good, my memory stinks, and I didn't come close; they started a third session, and I just gave up; the obnoxious teams were getting even more so.

Thursday, August 4, 2022; Midland Ontario. At the dock, we were greeted by a bag pipe ensemble; as we worked our way to the bus, there was a welcoming tourist area that provided BUTTER TARTS, a Canadian specialty, and I capitalized because that's how GOOD they are!

We had a complimentary "Discovery Harbor Exploration" a bus provided and lasting 2 ½ hours, decks 201-330 at 9:45; Staterooms 331-518 at 2 P.M. I thought we had signed up, we got to the bus...oops; however, there were cancellations and they got us on. This was a recreation of a British Naval and military base. Buildings, workshops, officer and crew quarters along with two ships; I actually showed a couple kids how to swab the deck using a mop...why was the deck swabbed? Sailors were usually barefooted, dry decks produce slivers.... The tiny black flies were a nuance, kept biting me, Lynn, no problem...I must be sweeter?

In the afternoon we walked the town, took pictures of the wall murals, and a goose sculpture, the musician Kenny saw me on the way out and pointes to a coffee shop that has the "best coffee in Canada", so Lynn and I walked over there, you could smell the coffee before entering, and bought two pounds, had them ground, and when we returned, gave him one, the other for our buddy back home!

When I gave him his coffee, he was practicing in his room with his partner Cheryl "that Blonde", I asked if she had tried one of the butter tarts offered, she said 'no" so I gave her the last one I got before returning to the ship. I did ask how many tarts the two girls that were giving them out had brought...100...that's how many that lasted 5 ½ hours, by a ship with 173 passengers and 65 crew??

Guest presentation about water, snow, and winter in North Country; First, water: One of the most magical things on earth, when freezing it expands and magically changes, it holds heat longer than solids, in this shallow lakes and bays, as the ice melts in spring it sinks to the bottom and bring oxygen to the plant and animals for the following seasons. This happens at 4 degrees centigrade, of 39.4 degrees F. Ice is considered a mineral, that magical 4 degrees centigrade, it turns into lattices.

We were warned that when we are out in the very cold and work up a sweat, if it is also windy, the water/sweat is taken, called "wind chill" and will dehydrate the body, thereby we need more hydration, and coverings to prevent the effects.

In the spring, looking over the melting ice on the lakes, it will look like the water is boiling, due to the evaporation, water being warmer than land, and with the right wind, the evaporation has this visual affect.

Snowflakes are formed by dust and humidity forming crystals, when snow melts, it absorbs its own water.

Turpentine (Ethylene Glycol) comes from pine trees similar to maple syrup from maples.

Wood Frogs sound like they quack, and actually freeze themselves solid each year, Box turtles hibernate, and painted turtles change their breathing to osmosis to survive the winters.

Noah

The guest lecturer joined us for supper, everyone got involved, and it was a very interesting meal!

The evening entertainment was Funky and 70's; only to be interrupted by an announcement that three passengers had tested positive for covid…a handful of passengers ran out to get masks, only to wear them under their chin, or put them on the cocktail tables when singing along with the band? One guy was actually crying…

Since the initial screening, passengers and crew check in and out of the ship w/o any screening; since day 4 there has been no TV for messaging or programming, and no music channels on the TV ever. Our phones, with Verizon, do not work in Canada, and internet in ports is weak if at all, and intermittent when available, on water, no internet period!

Friday, August 5, 2022; a day on the lake! Woke up to a bright sky, beautiful blue waters and smooth sailing.

Since it was a day cruising, everything is set back for those who want to sleep in, about ½ of those in the hallways and functions are wearing the masks now, breakfast saw only ½ the crowd. We tried out the yoga stretching, a nice ½ hour, the instructor, and one other passenger besides us.

Trivia…here is some examples:

Who were the creators of Motown Records: Smokey Robinson and Barry Gordee?

True or false:

Russia and Japan signed peace treaty after WWII? False (Technically still at war)

Was Kate Smith the first woman to sing God Bless America? True

Was Napoleon of Average height? True he was actually 5'4", at that time 5'2" ave.

Smokey Robinsons eye color was green. True His eyes from his French mom

Great lake lecture: Oceans, lakes or seas?

What is beneath the surface, currents, and underwater structures. The straits of Mackinac under the Mackinac bridge at channel that was a river connecting Lake Michigan to Lake Heron, Lake Heron was dry

Educating Noah...Travelin'

land 7,000-8000 years ago. All the great lakes were a combination of smaller lakes. The ridges below, called "pop-ups"1-3 meters high and 4-5 meters wide extending for kilometers are the result of seismic activity.

Great Lakes (this may be repeat) 84% of North American fresh water, 35,000 islands, the currents based on the spin of the earth and Lake Ontario is an east west lake. Lake Michigan current north to south, and the lower half is shallow, thereby the waves are higher.

Waves:

Ripples...capillary waves, disturbances in the water

Tides... are a type of wave

Seiche...slosh waves, little structure

Fetch...Distance over open water, thereby higher waves, built by wind

Rough...a wave that rides on top of another wave, one example in 2011, lake Michigan 23 feet high!

Tsunamis... in the oceans created by earthquakes, in the Great Lakes, created by weather.

The highest recorded waves in the great lakes 8-9 meters high, fresh water waves are closer together.

Lakes or Seas? 100,000 square miles of coast, 6000 vessels have sunk, Lake Huron has the highest traffic, Lake Erie is second in ship wrecks due to being shallow.

There is a legend about the Great Lakes Triangle; The Sargasso Sea is in the middle of the Atlantic with no shore line...This is also a major eel breeding ground; there is the Caspian Sea, a salt water sea called the Dead Sea; and the Gulf of Mexico and Hudson Bay are also referenced as "seas".

We missed our naps, played bingo, and we both won loser bingo, where we were the last standing without one number being called!

Motown Hit Songs and history, presented by Kenny the musician:

Motown records was started in 1959 by Smokey Robinson and Barry Gordy. Smokey sang in most of the demo's' One of the first acts signed was Diana Ross and the Supremes who had 12 #1 songs in 1962, most successful 3 girl group ever. If you have 3 hits songs you have a singing career!

Spinners with Smokey Robinson from 1964-65; broke up, and Smokey was the only survivor.

Marvin Gay had temperament and drug problems; he was shot dead by his father.

Mary Wells was 17 when she was discovered, her first hit was "My Guy" in 1965.

The O Jays refused to wear suits and were known as "tough guys".

Temptations were a crossover band, #1 selling group of all time in records, lasted 10 years.

4 Tops of "Sugar Pie Honey Bunch" fame, it was the original name of a failed group consisting of three girls and a guy all white.

Stieve Wonder, when born he was so small, they put him in an incubator, He had R.O.P which made him blind, his actual name was Steveland Harvey Morris. He was the recipient of 25 Grammy Awards, and the United Nations named him the "Messenger of Peace".

Smokey Robinson, chairman of Motown, actual name was William Robinson Jr., was with the group Miracles, and had green eyes, from his mother.

The songs he wrote totaled five pages!

Last entertainer, Michael Jackson; awarded "Most Significant Entertainer" with the most recorded performer, at 300 million records world-wide.

There was a military get together, 8 vets on the ship, we talked for ½ hour, I was the only one who took the honor flight, then a program honoring us, opening up the bar an hour early.

Entertainment was centered on Motown.

Saturday, August 6, 2022; partially cloudy, high of 90F.

Our first excursion was the Henry Ford Museum, we had to take our passports to cross back into the U.S. It took a bit over ½ hour to get there, the Border guard were unhappy that we took the bridge rather than the tunnel, even though the bus driver told them the truck

Educating Noah...Travelin'

was too high and had scraped previously, but it worked out...

We had free reign when we arrived, told to report back at this particular entrance at 12:30, and off we went!

We had been here before...like about 35 or so years with the kids, we didn't recognize anything! Amazing museum, presidential limousines (called the Beast), locomotives, airplanes including the Write Brother's Kitty Hawk, tractors and implements and a car and tractor cut open to see the inner workings and how they were engineered. I drove a race car simulator, best speed was 2 minutes, mine 3.BUT, I did not hit the wall, I actually felt a little queasy during and after, that never happened before!

The ride back was not good, it was in the 90's and the bus air was not working well at all; again, we went over the bridge and were stuck at the Canadian Border...for ONE AND A HALF HOURS! Finally put on the side and had to go into the building, show our passports and ArriveCAN stickers...lots of grumbling, and unhappy people...finally Kenny the entertainer and escort approached a group of agents and got them to assist the driver through the rest of the complex and back on the road!

We were to return by One P.M.; We returned for lunch at THREE! The dining hall was open for us.

Bonkers for Bonco, only one passenger with Lynn and I showed up, we played three dice games, each of us won one set, and we all got hats as prizes!

The entertainment, was the British Evasion; cut short to give the crew a break and ended everything at 9:35; of course, the usual crowd after one cocktail was down to a total of 35-45 passengers.... you know.... oldsters! However, Cheryl the entertainer, came over to me just before the band started playing and kissed me on the cheek, exclaiming "Thank you for the butter tart" ...yup she loved them too!!

Sunday, August 7, 2022; Sailing Lake Erie; partly cloudy. Mid 80'sF, a day at sea.

Erie, is the southernmost, shallowest, and smallest by volume of the Great Lakes, and named after the Erie tribe of Native Americans.

Lynn slept in so we missed the Yoga for a late breakfast.

Four games of trivia, Lynn actually won with another person one of them, but it is hard to believe two of those playing actually knew 38 of the forty questions!! No, the answers were not checked!

Lake Erie presentation; Only 65 meters deep at its deepest spot, built, as the other great Lakes by the glaciers. One of the features of this lake is the extensive sand island named Long Point entirely of sand.

Under Lake Erie is the most extensive salt mine in the U.S. and is still in operation, manned by 160 men and women miners working 8-hour shifts, 24/7, and no, this is not open to the public.

The Cuyago River Fire was discussed, the 1952 was the largest caused mostly by oil slicks, then due to pollution, the river no longer sustained live, no oxygen; finally, the 1969 environmental act was enacted to bring the lakes and rivers back to sustaining life.

More dread, Zebra mussels, other salt water mussels, and sea lampreys ...and efforts to control all of these.

After lunch, Dance, Dance, Dance; Lessons on line dancing, I went for a while as support for Lynn, all old women, 12 at the most and they actually did pretty well!

Kenny, the entertainer did a music presentation on Hit songs with cars";

Bruce Springsteen "Born to Run" after visiting the Ford Museum, John Lennon was also inspired after seeing the JFK 1961 Lincoln President limo, he was assassinated in; Stephen Wolfe "Hot Rod Lincoln"; "Mustang Sally"; Rod Stewart "Forever Young"; Prince with his "Red Corvette", Beach Boys, "Fun, Fun, Fun, till her Daddy takes her T-Bird away, and Celine Dione. With each mention, the Duo played the songs!

Followed by another lecture on the Welland canal connecting the Great lakes to the St. Lawrence Seaway. 1824-1829 was the first, 43 kilometers long and 40 locks, after three rebuilds the locks have decreased from 16 to 8, and can now accommodate much larger ships, and is two lanes. There was an attempt to in 1900 to blow it up, but failed. At present, the canal is owned by the Canadian government, can accommodate ships as long as 1000 feet, and 40 million tons of cargo pass through per year.

Majority Rules; again, less than 18 players, and again a very few seemed to win knowing most of the answers, even though the Green Bay Packers was the best Football team, Favorite car BMW, handsomest man in the world; George Clooney....

Brief of Niagara Fall on Monday, and included Tuesday morning disembarkation instructions.

Happy Hour, supper, 50's and 60's songs.

Monday August 8, 2022 partly cloudy, high in the mid 80's. port Colborne, Ontario. Today we explored the Canadian side of the three falls in the Niagara compiles, the Horseshoe falls, American falls, and the Bridal Veil Falls; with the grandest, Niagara being 165 feet tall!

95 percent of the passengers will be participating, we are told to wait in our cabins till called one deck at a time starting with deck 5.

It was a 45-minute bus ride to the falls, there are actually three falls, and we saw all three. Due to the extensive walking down to the boats, Lynn opted to stay above and check out the town. I joined the group, we all had to walk down a third of the way through a complex of tunnels and ramps, to an elevator, and then a few more ramps, where we were all given a rain coat with hood. Each ferry easily takes a couple hundred tourists, with most opting the open top deck. Once loaded, the ferry progresses up the river, passes all three falls and returns, a good dosing of mist from the falls is an under-statement! The entire cruise last only 15-20 minutes, everyone then is left off to shed the rain gear and go through the ramps to the elevators and then through the gift shop. The bus was parked two blocks away, there were two people "late" so we left 15 minutes later than we should have, which cut the other observation point and gift shop visit to only 20 minutes, and with this group, it took almost ten to exit the bus...luckily ½ of the group stayed on the bus!

We arrived ten minutes late for "all Aboard"; but the locks were also delayed by two hours, so we actually did not leave port till 4 P.M.

Lunch with three other couples, another looser session of Bingo, the other talk was just reminisced of his travels around the great lakes and the threats of human effects on climate. I mentioned that the water level had increased a hole millimeter more than projected the last decade, but he references more of his data.

I tried to review our flight plan but again the internet did not work, and since we are in Canadian waters the phones are also out....

Noah

Last dinner with our group, transfer instructions regarding buses and times, and open bar and entertainment till about 9;45 with only 6 people left…

Luggage out of room by 10 P.M.

Tuesday August 9, 2022 going home…

Breakfast was 6-8; our bus out at 7:15…everyone was to wait in their rooms till called…7:20 our bus was called… the elevator was too full twice so we negotiated the steps; checked out of the ship and walked a block to the bus, identified our luggage and it seemed all the compartments were full…Got on the bus, and that two was full, Lynn and found two seats by seat hogs, but there were still 6 standing in the aisle.

The program director then got on the bus, informed everyone that two buses were for our group…surprise! The extra luggage was loaded onto the other bus, along with 8-10 stragglers, and we were off at 7:45.

The airport is on the other side of Toronto…55 minute drive; no one knew which bus their luggage was on, and of course stood in everyone else's' way…15 minutes later we were looking in the terminal for Delta…Tried express check-in, nope, only info, no tickets (no internet on board for the last 4-5 days)..asked for help…she said she would return as soon as finished with the other couple, then I saw her helping people in the luggage line…after seeing her help THREE people there, I went over, confronted her, and was told I needed now to get in line behind 4 other couples. When we finally got to her, she just said that we were in the right line…everything would be taken care of at the desk… FOURTY FIVE MINUTES LATER, AT THE CHECKIN, WE ARE TOLD WE WERE 15 MINUTES LATE to check bags for our flight…but she was able to reschedule us now flying out of Toronto to LaGuardia, New York; and from there to Milwaukee, only 1 1/2 hours between flights; and starting now at 5:15 P.M.… now getting home at 10:10, instead of 6:30… The chutes to put your luggage in refused our luggage, had to get assistance and told she has had to help everyone else before us the last 20 minutes; T.S.A. The kiosk machines did not work and had to be manually processed…by the time we were settled in by the Delta gates it was 10 A.M. Oh, masks required in Canadian airports, and planes flying out! grrrrrrrr

Educating Noah…Travelin'

That 4:30 flight turned into 5:10; then 5:30, then 6:30…after loading, we taxied for a bit, then stopped, told LaGuardia shut down for incoming flights, waited 50 minutes, then got O.K. and proceeded for the 50-Minute flight to New York, LaGuardia airport.

When we landed, we found our connecting flight was also held back and to hurry to catch! It was on the other end of the terminal; leafing at 11:35. The plane arrived at the gate at 11:50, the passengers let off and then the announcement the crew would not continue on, and that we would have to be rescheduled.

Next available flight…7:30 A.M…too bad, so sorry, we were given 2 vouchers for food each and sent on our way…We stayed in the airport, all the chairs had arms so no laying across, most slept on chairs or on the floor, every hour or so all the phones were updated on the next flight, with both gates and times changed, finally at 6 we used two vouchers to eat, they would only take vouchers at one side and only when food was ordered on the phone. We complied, then went bac to the last gate which now had depart time at 9:30. When it was time, the screen changed again, the gate person phoned in that the flight crew and plane was ready to load, screen changed back, we loaded, arrived 2 hours later in Milwaukee, we retrieved our luggage, and our ride with art was waiting outside! Back home finally a bit after 12 noon, Wednesday the 10th, luggage upstairs, into bed!

Noah

Mississippi River Road Trip August 21, 2022 to August 25, 2022

Since we finally made it home on the 10th from the Great lakes Cruise, both of us had severe colds, hacking and low energy, we worked with our daughter to get another car, to get Lynn's car back, brought our indoor plants back to life, had the VW oil changed tires rotated and checked and ready for this road trip.

I had gathered quite a bit of information from all the States we would be passing through, and we found the first two days, at the head waters may be a bit dull, however, you never know!

Sunday morning, smoothies, and off by 8:03 A.M. Mileage 32,375. Partly cloudy, looked great, a perfect day to start.

We drove and drove, two stops on the way, both gas and restroom stop, Lynn also packed a lunch, so we ate that at one of the Kwik Trip's and I am keeping all the gas receipts for gallons used and prices paid.

We arrived at the Mississippi River Headwaters at 5:10 P.M.; Itasca State Park, Park Rapids, Minnesota; Mileage starts: 32,958;

Walked over took pictures, had a bite to eat, took an eight-mile one-way scenic road, and headed down river to our first stop, a motel in Grand Rapids. Upper Minnesota has a ton of lakes and seems all the towns in north country are one or two horse towns, and lots of miles apart!

Everything is green, lots of trees a beautiful drive! Got to the motel after 8 P.M., a long day!

Monday, August 22,2022. The motel Lynn found on the internet was not what we expected, no air conditioning, odd room set up, and no included breakfast…neighbors kept TV loud into the night, plus rather loud talk to very late. We were up and out by 7:30…nothing in town was open yet?? But we did find a local diner and sat at the counter with the regulars!

The food was excellent, the company was very good, and it was a good start for the day. As we progressed south, we followed the trail, which incorporated crossing the Mississippi several times, there are a lot more islands than thought, we saw 4 dams and locks, a number of times the river split. The land, mostly farm and park was lush with trees and green. The weather was warm, partly cloudy and in the low eighties, beautiful for traveling!

The only problem, as with all upper Midwest states is road construction! We were re-routed, dead ended, and one laned…if we saw 1000 orange cones it would definitely be an understatement! We made it to Iowa.

We visited an eagle center, went to an offered lecture about eagles, oops, the eagles would not cooperate so they substituted a film on a red-tailed hawk…More disappointments to follow, the chocolate factory was closed for remodeling when we arrived, and sensing a cloud, we called the fish hatchery we were to visit, and yup, they would be closing 15 minutes before we would get there.

The rerouting in Iowa showed us fields upon fields of corn still in the field and fully tussled, lots of fields still not harvested, except for hay, plenty of bails, but none wrapped.

We wanted to be down the road from Minnesota and Wisconsin, and yes, we made it, to Dubuque, at a very nice inn, with Appleby's next door. Ate, found our room, comfortable and a full shower, done for the day!

Tuesday, August 23, 2022 Off by 8:10, not much in the morning, a doe crossed the road a 100 ft. in front of us, we slowed to see if she was with another, but no…it is very confusing following this scenic road; along with road construction, and closed roads. The fields full of soy beans, sorghum and corn, the small towns quaint and nice. We needed to stop for lunch, tried one in town and after two closed restaurants we drove to the next town and as we pulled up, the owner pulled her flag and flipped her sign to closed. Across the street was a bar advertising food, walked in, greeted by a tiny dog barking, called out and heard A voice in the back room saying "come in". I asked if they were open and served food, and she said "yes".

I went out, got Lynn, and we went to the back room where three guys were playing pool. The owner said they were having a party for her son who just came back from Marine Boot camp. She asked what we wanted to drink, took our order and said we were welcome to the "fixins" for the party for her son on the house. We agreed, had our drinks, helped ourselves to the shredded pork, beans, potato salad, beets and coleslaw, and of course two cupcakes. We watched the pool game as we ate, talked to them and her and congratulated her son... I said welcome to the 1%, and he told me it is now down to .4%; wished him luck, thanked her again, AND PAID OUR BILL OF $3.75 with a $10, and told her to keep the change! That woman was so proud of her son, her voice, how she talked about him, and the mile wide smile was refreshing! This young man found his way out of a dumpy, little town by joining the Marines.

We hit St. Louis at rush hour, crawled through downtown, got a picture of the Arch and the Budweiser plant; jockey-ed through not only rush hour but yup, lane closures.... It was past 5:30...and we started to find a motel, Lynn saw a dead armadillo on the road side, lunch was so generous, we stopped at an Arby's had two small dream shakes, filled up the car (cheapest gas yet!) $3.39/gal, and checked into the motel, Perryville Mo.

As with last night if the motel was 1/3 full, I'd be surprised.

Wednesday, August 24th, 2022. Off again for more adventure...first half of the day was sunny, partly cloudy and mid 76's F; the directions for the route combine highways and roads, maps, GPS and phones still confusing, crossed the river a couple times, the distillery was only open Friday, Saturday and Sundays? Located downtown Helena, Mo. that was mostly closed, and dead. So off we went to the Delta Blues Museum, they required masks yet, or would charge for one, so I got two out of the car... it was interesting but was strictly Blues. Clarksdale also has a department store as a base and we stopped at a bakery and café run by Mennonites. The waitress was fantastic, along with the food. We ordered two specials which included a sandwich, drink, and piece of pie...we took home half for supper, and wow!

The rest of the afternoon we progressed down the east side of the river, glancing when we got close, lots of white egrets!

Off the road in Vicksburg, Miss. La Quinta, and it was ¾ full!

Thursday, August 25, 2022, we both went to bed early, and were up at 6, so after packing up, and breakfast we were on the road by 7:15! Breakfast at La Quinta is one of the most varieties, and the ham was outstanding!

Educating Noah...Travelin'

If you look at a map, the Mississippi is very "squiggly" along the border, only a few glimpses of it, but many shallow ponds full of lilies, deltas, and a lot of white egrets. We saw a lot of very poor houses, many collapsed buildings, closed shops and gas stations, and yet some very large and palatial estates with gates at the entrances. As we approached Louisiana, the buildings and trailer homes multiplied, we crossed miles of elevated highway over Lake Pointchartain, and went downtown to the visitors center to get the facts.

We arrived at 11:35 A.M., milage, 34,751. The person we talked to was a retired teacher, who has lived here all of her life. Kathleen Medina told us the Mississippi actually ends in Venice Miss., but the 2-hour drive has nothing to see, in that "both sides of the highway have concrete walls, and completely boring!"

Thus, our trip ended there at the center, we bought some souvenirs, toured through the French Quarter and started back home.

The drive back was interrupted quite a few times with downpours of rain so hard, the windshield wipers had difficulty keeping up, and traffic slowed to 30 miles per hour on the highway 5 – 6 times for periods of 15-20 minutes.

A little after 5 we pulled off in Grenada, Miss. Checked into a motel, found an interesting place for dinner, actually took the dessert in a doggie bag for tomorrows lunch...neither of us can eat a full dinner any longer... We have noticed the entire trip, "help wanted" signs everywhere, in cities, in the country, and the places we stopped, we could tell those there were new, servers, cooks, and cashiers...where did everyone go? We also noticed that both new and used car lots and dealerships all seemed to have plenty of used cars...in all the states we went through and we are to believe a used car shortage.... where???

August 25, 2022 Friday! On our way home! We are going to stop for gas and food, but both of us want this to be the last day. It started out wrong, no breakfast...Baymont; It said on line that they all offer breakfast from 6 A.M.-9 A.M. but when we checked out, we were told nope...Lynn asked for a partial refund...nope...the manager stated "not since covid" ...how convenient, especially since the others except for the first had a very good assortment...Lynn told him they were just cheap and lazy!!!!! We have traveled through this planned demic and every motel had a breakfast for us.

Noah

Snacks for breakfast and off we go; 7:30 A.M.; the rest of Mississippi, 8:30, Tennessee, 10:45, and Kentucky 11:50 were easily maneuverable and the stops for relief and gas went fine, however not the cleanest, and two bathrooms had to be shared due to one or the other broken. Lynn actually had to be rescued since she couldn't get the door unlocked and opened.

When we hit Illinois, the number of detours and construction increased logarithmically, it seemed that ever ½ hour another back-up, and when we were outside the large cities, the drivers were much more aggressive!

As we progressed up Illinois, I suggested that since we missed Lynn's restaurant due to them being closed, we should make reservations at Bob Chin's Crab House; a restaurant we have wanted to try for years but just didn't get there. The GPS at 11:55 stated we would arrive there by 5:15; given the delays, and passing Chicago during rush hour and Friday, we made the reservation for 5:45.

The traffic around Chicago along with construction, took some concentrated maneuvering, and Lynn getting anxious a number of times, even when she attempted to close her eyes, but we made it to Chin's at 5:50.

The food was outstanding, the waitress exceptional, and even though we had herd horror stories of people waiting in lines, we were shown to our table quickly. However, when we left, there was a short line waiting.

The ride home was uneventful, arrived at 7:55 P.M. Unpacked the car, showered and in bed by 9…. another goal taken care of!

Final Mileage: 35,783, total mileage: 3408

Arrived at Park in New Orleans Mileage: 34,751

Great River Road Mileage 1793

Gas prices ranged from 3.29/gal to 3.99/gal (Ill)

Total gallons 107.4

Total gas cost: $383.12

Lodging: $554.00

Food: $488.45

Educating Noah...Travelin'

Souvenirs and snacks: $87.35

We decided this will be our last road trip, both of us have lost a lot of patience, plus our arthritis combined aches and pains, and we have done all the major rivers in the world now!

Noah

2-FER; MAIN STREETS and AMAZING APOSTLE ISLANDS Sept. 26-29th; Oct.2-5th

This is a bit different; we are both getting' older, and it took us both a full week to recover from the Mississippi road trip!

We meet in Elm Grove, a suburb of Milwaukee, where parking spaces have been arranged, both are bus trips.

It has been a warm September, in the eighty 's; it is mid-term season, so political ads are prolific, seems all the ads on TV now are lawyers, insurance companies or political B.S., it gets tiring! We thought this would be perfect for finishing off the great lakes in that we had explored the other great lakes earlier this year on the cruise, Lake Superior needed to be addressed, and what better way!

We arrived at 6:15, and a person from the agency showed up at 6:20 to tell everyone to move our cars farther back, and wait in our cars for the bus, it was in the 50's and a bit windy….very few waited in their cars, still no bus at 7:45, so one of the employees stayed with the luggage, while we were led across the parking lot, across main street and into a restaurant, we were hampered with the stroller, so we sat on the other side of the main divider at the elevated tables with the last people. Full breakfast scrambled eggs, potatoes, fresh fruit, two full strips of bacon, toast, and coffee or juice…very good, and included with the tour!

The bus showed up a bit before 9 loaded and off we went. Our first stop was Congdon gardens in Delevan Wisconsin. A guided tour, large spaces, few flowers still blooming, back on the nice warm bus and off to Monroe Wisconsin, through Illinois, and then back into south west Wisconsin. Lunch included with tour, lasagna or Salaberry steak, both very good and generous portions. The mayor of Monroe joined us to the Cheesemaking Center, where we were filled in on the art of making cheese. Here is some info I remember, 10#s of milk to make 1# of cheese, traces of morphine actually stimulate our taste buds; Lemberger cheese is wiped with a bacterium a number of times daily to cure it and ad that pungent taste. If any antibodies are found in a truck load of milk, the farmer is charged for the whole tanker and the milk cannot be used in cheese making, and finally Wisconsin is fifth in the world in cheese production only following four COUNTRIES, those being Switzerland, Germany, France, and Italy!!

We toured the rest of the city with the mayor as a guide, him pointing out various structures, only 7 major traffic intersections and how the town has grown; we dropped him off at an old age facility and continued on our way.

We were taken down a country road (U), outside a little town of Shulsburg, WI. and the guide indicated a sign on the side of the road, Gravity Hill, indicated an anti-gravity zone…The driver put the bus in neutral and the bus started rolling up hill…. The driver put the bus back in gear, we went back down a …. bit past, and did it again…same results, it is referred to an optical illusion, and actually cars have gone up to 20mph in neutral, and what seemed to be up-hill!!

We arrive in Dubuque after 5, got our room, went out for an ice-cream cone, walked around getting some wall art and headed back. it was Monday night, downtown, only things open after 6 were bars and hotels, and it was very dead!

Tuesday, September 27, 2022; breakfast at the hotel (we are staying here two nights) and off on the bus by 8 A.M. Full breakfast, and off to LeClair, Iowa; first stop was the Buffalo Bill Museum; actually pretty interesting, had a wooden steam boat tug that actually lasted 75 years on the river, the draft was only 3 feet, crew with captain was 4, plus cook, usually the captains wife…ne horn tube and three bells to communicate between the bridge and engineer, very basic, very rough, usually 12 hour day 6 days a week, with most of the time trans versing up and down the river.

Next stop was Antique Archeology, where American Pickers Show on History channel is based. When we visited the original base, with the motorcycle club, it was closed and only one building, now there are two, the second as in Pawn Stars, filled with self-promoting badges, t shirts, and tourist junk, we did get to go into the regular shop this time, and being only the size of a 3 car garage, had some stuff, but the 35-40 minutes we had to explore was way too much…the bus driver did have difficulty on the back streets, and actually got hung up trying to exit the alley…one of the passengers in the front went into the dentist office and had the owner of the car next to the curb move it so we could maneuver out....

Lunch was catered at a distillery, The Mississippi Distilling Company where we had a full lunch and a history lesson on the distillery and insights of alcohol production, yup, bought two bottles one honey bourbon, and the other a cream liqueur. The last stop was The National Mississippi river Museum; containing both fresh water tanks and salt water tanks, with an extensive variety of fish and animals, the otters were very active, and the turtles, alligator, and gars acted as if they were frozen.

Two buses back to the hotel, we took the earliest, my back was killing me, and Lynn was tired. this was a more modern bus, I guess designed by an expert...seats were tall, so all you saw ahead was the back of a seat, the seats were not comfortable, and the overhead bins paired down to 4 bins for each 12 seats...

Took a nap, then off to dinner. Dinner was fantastic! A place called Pepper Sprout, we had two appetizers, Lynn a hot crab spread, and I had Avocado cheese cake; as usual we couldn't finish either one but BOTH were excellent plus the pineapple Mexican pepper margaritas were outstanding. The waiter was exceptional, I over tipped, told the manager, that Gabriel was outstanding for attitude, up selling, and efficiency, he told us he would also pass it on to the owner.

A short walk back to the hotel, tomorrow breakfast is at 8, luggage out at 8:30.

Wednesday, 09/28/2022; another sunny day, in the 50's! Our first stop was Galena Illinois; We have been here before, quite a while ago, and enjoyed the town and vowed to come back.

The first stop was the Ulysses S. Grant Home, Lynn couldn't go in, too many stairs, and she says she was there before...I took pictures, the stair cases were narrow and small!

We then were dropped off by main Street for 2 ½ hours to take in the town and have lunch on our own. Spread money around town chocolates, chocolate covered bacon, lunch with two other couples and a couple of Christmas gifts for Lynn.

Back to the bus, for a short trip to a farm to walk with the goats. The family farm has 26 goats and when ready, we started walking a path, they were let out of their pen and walked with us...sometimes they were behind us, sometime with us, and sometimes ahead of us. They eat everything, about 1/3 of their weight every day, have a lifespan about the same as a dog, about 13-17 years. They were easy to feed, we were given carrot slices and they gently took them from our palms. The trek lasted about 35-40 minutes and covered about a mile…there were two guides with us and three pointed out the names and traits of individual goats, as the group walked, many were brushed as the goats went back and forth, and yes, half way, pictures even in the country, were taken feeding them snacks. Everyone found this small adventure to be both unique and interesting; back on the bus to Dodgeville, our final motel, then to meet up with John McGivern and his crew, for a dinner and performance both highly entertaining, plentiful and fun, John recognized us from his cruise, after the show and dinner, we had a question-and-answer period, and photos. Wrapped it up for the night, we will be the back-drop audience for his shoot at the House on the Rock tomorrow, our final day of this trip.

Thursday, September 29th, our final day of the first of the two-fer.… even in the country, short staffing, no coffee after ½ hour of the self-serve breakfast was open, no decaf for those that wanted, garbage bins over-flowing. We met the McGivern crew at the house on the Rock for their shoot. We were part of the audience, we know it will be aired next April, I don't know if and how much we will be edited out, but just another couple seconds of fame!

The House on the Rock has been expanded considerably, lots of walking, and much of it not easily accessible with a roller assist. It has more gardens, more displays, but the map provided is confusing, staircases and entrances blocked for the upcoming Halloween adventure. The three hours there went fast, back on the bus, lunch at a local restaurant, then off to the Cave of the Mounds. Again, we were here before, nothing has really changed except there are now two gift shops, and a beer garden, and no, the beer garden was closed …. offered water…. but just not the same!

The next stop was Mt. Horeb, we had a person from the common counsel step on and show us about 10 of the 26 trolls in the city, the problem was the other side of the bus saw 7 or 8 our side 3-4. We dropped him off, bathroom break, and headed back home, we arrived a bit after 6, home before 7.

Noah

Friday and Saturday at home, then off on another 4-day trip…. rest, wash, restock, recharge, and repack……

Sunday October 2, 2022 another adventure,

The last for the year, Apostille Islands; our pick-up time at the college northeast park and ride is 6:30 A.M.

We arrived at the park and ride at 6:10 and watched the bus pull in. Parked the car and unloaded rollie and our one suitcase and were the first on the bus! The rest of the folks showed up on time, and we were off just a bit before 6:30. Our three other pick-up spots were Watertown plank road, Johnson Creek, and the American center park and ride in Madison.

Total with the driver and guide 34 people in the group.

Our first stop heading North was a quick trip for potty break, the second, Minocqua on our own for lunch and walk around. We did both, ½ the stores were closed being Sunday, the others tourist prices... we had a lunch, the soup Lynn ordered was over seasoned, so the waitress did not charge for it, the ice cream cones we had at another place were one scoop cheap cones $0.50 for both, yeah, I'm cheap...but the cones were good... (mine was better!)

Walked the town, visited some shops and were first back to the bus with 45 minutes to spare...finally everyone showed up, and we were off on time.

The colors are turning, beautiful shrubs, trees, lakes and forests. The next stop was a half hour at the Northern great lakes Visitor center for a ½ hour, to learn about the area and what to look for... Finally, an hour drive to end up in Bayfield, Wisconsin, at a local restaurant for dinner, included choice of fish, chicken, or prime rib...all generous portions, all well prepared. a short drive to the motel where we were to spend all three nights, we had requested 1st floor since no elevators, we got 2nd floor, one of the other guests generously traded rooms, and we were in our room a bit after 7; a long travel day, about 340 miles, even with a much better bus, we were both tired.

Monday, October 3, 2022, up at alarm 6:30; included breakfast started at 7. We joined the group, most if not all in the dining room for scrambled eggs, hash-browns, fresh fruits and coffee or juice...no one went away hungry! Met at the bus for a short ride to the ferry for the 25-minute ride to Madeline Island.

Madeline island or Mooningwanekaaning the Ojibwe name, the largest of the Apostle islands, 14 miles long, 3 miles wide, with 45 miles of paved and unpaved roads, the French claimed it in 1693, (evidence of the Ojibwa since the 1300's), it has an annual population of about 300 -350 residents; it was the first of the islands to be clear cut for its lumber for building Chicago, silk had replaced fur in Europe, so brown stone, sand, fish and lumber were taken. This is the only island of the Apostle islands that is not designated as a state park.

Tourism was the next product which waned from the 1890's until about the late 1980's when tourism made a come-back. the ice caves are about 2 miles from this island, the apostle islands were named for the twelve apostles in the bible by the missionaries with the French.

We picked up a local guide for a bus and walking tour of the island, she was very informative and she has lived on the island 40 years. Our first stop was a park where we got up close and personal to the inland waters, then a tour of local homes and roads, the Christian church and craft store, then another included generous lunch at a local restaurant, finishing with a walk around the Main Street (about 2 blocks) to explore a number of shops…all tourist priced. Since there is a lake affect, the colors are not as bright since the warmth of the water slows the turning of the trees and foliage.

We met back on the bus, ferry back to the mainland, and short trip to the motel where we had the rest of the day to ourselves.

Down time was appreciated, nappy time, then journalizing, then we met with a small group for dinner. The restaurant was packed, and we found out why, the food was excellent, plentiful, and reasonable at today's rates. After we walked back to the motel, Lynn wanted to watch her Dancing with the Stars show now on Disney Plus, but even the expanded choices on the motel TV, not available, seems everything is getting way out of line!

Tuesday, October 2, 2022, the breakfast is pancakes! The weather all four days was in the 60's-low 70's, sunny and light winds. Monday, we woke to a spectacular sunrise, Tuesday a light cloud cover. After our pancake breakfast, we left for a tour of Apfelhaus Cidery, featuring hard and non-alcohol ciders, a historic (last of 5 remaining in the country) 1928 SEARS and Roebuck barn…#2061…. $895.00…I'm not sure if that was the delivered price… After sampling all different ciders, I liked the apple pie flavored the best, walked up to the hay mound story for a vista of the bay, and toured the souvenir shop, next we went to another orchard with a bakery, recommended apple cookies, and apple stick. I bought one each, we agreed the stick was best, the cookie was less apple taste and more gingerbread. Both filling and good, we then toured the town of Bayfield.

A two-hour sit-down lunch at the Old Rittenhouse mansion…four course meal…then off to the dock for a Grand Tour Cruise. This was a 55-mile cruise on a motored catamaran, showing most of the Apostle Islands, the two light houses, and the soon to be ice caves. The boat had 141 of us, the tour, narrated the entire time…most of the islands had no buildings…I did get pictures of anything more than forested islands.

We were on our own for the rest of the afternoon and night, luggage out at 7:30…Wednesday is the last, returning day.

Wednesday October 5, 2023 Our last day. We left promptly at 8:30 A.M. everyone was on time, the same last people…but they were always on board at the specified times. The foliage back seemed to have turned more than on the way up, the colors were more vibrant, reds, oranges, yellows accented by the greens.

We had a scheduled stop at the Bonnie and Clyde gangster park, but that was cancelled and substituted with the Wisconsin Concrete Park. No reason given, but the concrete park was interesting, we got to stretch, and walk around. The weather was perfect for the entire 4 days of the trip, one of the groups suggested a tavern for lunch, called ahead, and they agreed to having 40 folks for lunch! The staff was excellent, food great, and they were able to turn the whole group in an hour…wow pre covid service and work ethic!!

We had four drop off points, we were the first at the beginning and last to drop off…6:15 we were dropped off, bus gone before we were loaded, and home by 6;45…. that is enough for a while!!

Lynn had her right hip replaced on the 18th of October, four days later she was transferred to a nursing facility, where she stayed till November 3rd. Communication with me was non-existent as far as progress, and minimal with Lynn, quality has been redefined to marginal at best. For the transition, I bought a walker, a recliner, and extended shoe horns, rearranged the living room and everything was set when we arrived home. Spending the two weeks alone, I watched a variety of TV shows, and watched a Wisconsin special featuring a farmer that raised a Japanese breed of cow, called Wagyu; claimed to be the best beef in the world! Found a local small butcher shop and bought a bit more than three quarter pound, for, wait for it…$98.53…It sells for about $125/pound!! Looking on line, I actually got a bargain!! So, for supper, I grilled that steak, baked potatoes, and my sweet corn…she loved it! Yea, it was very good, could almost cut with a fork!!

I also attended a mandatory meeting for my stint at the Franklin voting event on the 8th. 1 1/2 hours of computer orientation for six senecios…. I was the first to show up at the Sports Center for voting, waited for others, punched in at 6:15 A.M. worked till 8:30 P.M. no food or water provided, but there was rest rooms and a water fountain in the hall way sitting that long and low my back gave out, checked out and came home too long, just a doughnut and water fountain water all day, probably the last time, especially since she waited till a week before, asked me to submit application at the event, and then told to take to city hall after, very little concern for those hired and volunteering, the flow was basically constant, and my districts were actually less than the other five also at the center.

Lynn finally had her right hip replaced. (October 18th) The surgeon told me everything went perfectly…here is the rest of the story, everything was healing well, on the 6 week anniversary we went out to the movies, getting up from the movie seat, Lynn started to experience lot of pain in her right leg, after two days, pain did not go away, the surgeon was on vacation, and without a back-up, we asked and confirmed a trip to emergency… the x-rays showed a fracture, prescribed pain pills and told not to walk on that leg; one day short of SEVEN WEEKS, since the operation. (December 5, 2022) x-rays were reviewed, found a fracture just below the rod inserted, "oh, sorry, let's get another x-ray next week to see how the fracture is healing…have a better day" …. hopefully better news to follow….

Educating Noah…Travelin'

2023

January, week 12 the quack allows Lynn to go to physical therapy, fracture healing well…three weeks to our Caribbean get away and looking for the bottom of the Bermuda Triangle.

A week from today we will be getting on the ship! Lynn is doing better, using the cane more and actually making a few meals and helping with the wash. I have been going with her to walking club, and getting in some steps and renewing old friendships. Had another severe gout attack, three quarts of tart cherry juice and a lot of Ibuprophen I am doing much better!

Last cruise to Carib?

Feb.3-13, 2023

It is 8 days before, having trouble with the portable computer I take along for day-to-day diaries, the last one got axed after many attempts to work with it, only to find that later, it was our wonderful internet connection, we must be in an odd zone, in that we had problems with Time Warner, and satellite also.

We are finally getting snow, 1-2 inches at a time, then a day goes by, then another few inches.

Everything packed, now cruise lines require you to fill out an application on your phone, and answer health questions the day before the cruise.

Thursday, February 2, starting the count down. Suitcases in the car, answered all the health questions for the cruise (Required now and has to be on a phone) on the application checked bus schedule to make sure the time is still good, yep, 4:25 A.M. scheduled to leave the house at 3:50…parking is still free if less than 2 weeks at the bus terminal, just now the terminal is no longer attended since covid, so no bathrooms or warm waiting room.

Spent over 4 hours trying to get the TSA pre-screen on or tickets, 6 phone calls 2 e-mails, finally found out that the 6-digit code on the back of the ID card was the one in front of the 6-digit code on the back of the card on the left!!

Noah

Straightened out Celebrity and had them add both to the United air tickets and American tickets coming back, and re-printed the United tickets. Contacted On Line Vacations to have them correct any further trips, and checked Delta for our final cruise in July.

Oh, by the way, TSA confirmed the wrong number by e-mail...duh!!!

3 A.M. we were both up and getting ready, out of the house by 3:51!

Arrived at the bus station, at 4:15, bus showed up on time, and we are off! No slip needed to park car for less than two weeks!

Arrived at ORD, Chicago O'Hare a bit before 6, checked in luggage, waited 15 minutes for Lynn's wheel chair, but it was worth it, there was a 20-minute wait at TSA, but since we had a wheel chair assist, we bypassed the line, and made it to the gate with 20 minutes to spare!

Flight on time, loaded quickly, and everything went well, found the luggage and the representative from the cruise line.

OOPs, the ship encountered heavy fog, would not be docking until after 1 this afternoon. We were corralled with 50 some other cruisers, on a bus, then 40 minutes to the cruise terminal, off the bus, identified luggage, made sure cabin numbers on them, then primary check in and wrist bands, then on the bus to a shopping mall to await the ship being unloaded, cleaned and take on the new cruise folks (us).

Off to the shopping mall, waited from 12:30 to 6:30 and only got on the return bus due to Lynns wheelchair request and Rollie, the walker...two busses after us....

Back to the port, ½ hour, back in another line, more security checks and finally back on board, fighting for an elevator with the most people on walkers and wheel chares we have seen on a cruise!

Found our cabin, requested they separate the bed, and went to supper, it is now after 8:30...Had a nice supper in the cafeteria, found our Muster station, checked in with them, had a martini and back in the room, no luggage yet!!

Napped and waited for our luggage. Oh, and now, it seems that the programs are now on the stupid phones, must have the Celebrity app.!!!

Educating Noah...Travelin'

10:00 P.M., luggage finally arrived, we partially unpacked and went to bed...no hot water either....

Saturday, up at 7:45, traded times in the bathroom, unpacked some more, actually found a bit more storage, this is the smallest room we have ever had on a ship, rivaling even the closet we had in Norway.

Still no hot water, reminded room attendant to separate beds, (had to remind her again at noon) Buffet breakfast, OK lots of walkers and unsteady people, and some seem to always have the right of way!

Trivia, met the couple we hung out with yesterday, lost the first game, Lynn and I tried the bow and arrow game, my shoulder too far gone, Lynn missed too!

Lunch in the café, nice selection, again too many seem to have forgotten cueing and manners, Lynn stayed for the delayed game, I checked out shore excursions, spa for Lynn, stores...they wanted $155.00 for a shirt?? And a big watch sale...no one under 30 wears them!!

Two more trivia's, tried to go to dinner...one flyer said open at 6, another said 5:30. When we got there the 5th floor was for reserved and special guests?? Went down to the 4th floor, lines to another room, then we were told no openings, but given a pager...peak times per brochure was 7:30-8:30???? We waited for ten minutes, lines grew longer, turned in the pager and went to the cafe for supper.

After dinner at the café, we walked the ship, took in the last of the early song and dance show then, two more Trivia with our friends, the last one we had all 15 questions right and won more tickets for the final day prizes.

First full day at sea, we were tired, moved ahead the clocks one hour and now in bed by 11:30...yeah, actually 10:30 but we didn't want to be Geezers the first full day at sea!!

Sunday, alarm set for 7:30; day is planned, meeting times for Lynn and me, Lynn's Valentines Spa-day is at 9, I have to clear up charge questions, book excursions, and sign us up for egg drop. After breakfast we went our separate ways, it is a bit warmer today, another sea day, traveling at 18 knots against a 40-knot wind, walking on deck was difficult pushing against a rather relentless wind.

We were the first to sign up for the egg drop, I also asked the game

Noah

host for a copy of the questions asked at the last trivia, he said he would try....(he never came through)

Program on Mayan Secrets and sacrifices, diving in wells in the Yucatan, caves created with a meteorite hit 1000 's of years ago, eyeless eels, fish and blind fish, 2000year-old pottery... On land, all the cattle are covered with ticks, they are the size of poppy seeds, and yup, if not pulled out without the\head...infection!

In the caves below, a lot of bat guano (poop), very slippery, and if in a cut or cavity very infectious... along with the pottery skulls were found...over 100, NO BODIES...

Beheading, beliefs were that there would be "no eternal rest" for the enemy beheaded!

There is also evidence that some were cooked...the sacrifices killed or cooked, these were identified at birth by placing a branch on the forehead to flatten the top, and give the special identification, it was an honor to be one of the chosen.

To eat a person, they were first covered in mud, then leaves and tied to a spit, turned slowly and a tube inserted in the mouth to keep them alive as long as possible.... does this make you hungry??

Straightened out some billing problems, seems the martini bar charges are outside the standard package and must be paid for separately, booked three excursions, and started scrounging around for materials for the egg drop, much harder now with much less paper, cardboard, and plastic; we will see...met up with Lynn, had lunch, was brushed by a runner on deck, and went back to the room for Lynn to nap, and meet with the attendant for some supplies for the drop.

This afternoon, three gameshows in a row, celebrity heads, Smudge (upper head of one lower head of another), Top of Oprah's face over Michelle Obama lower half, guess the celebrity by audience giving clues to volunteer, and finally a general knowledge trivia, Black swans come from Australia.

Kept looking for egg drop supplies! Cardboard coffee cups no longer out... only in the morning, got some scotch tape from the main guest Relations desk, string from the hobby activity, and some small bags from the cookie folk. Also helped Lynn a bit with ribbon, and some extra small bags.

Educating Noah...Travelin'

Dress up night, we will be eating in the formal dining room, the desk called and told us they apologized and made reservations for us!

We got seated right away, 10 minutes later, bread sticks and the wine guy showed up, declined the wine, and asked for the drink guy to order a drink under $10.00 which would be included with our drink package; 20 minutes, waiter took our orders, 45 minutes we got appetizers ordered, one hour ten minutes from arrival, the meal, one and a half hours from entering we finished our deserts and left. Oh, and the drink guy never showed up....

Two more Trivia's, our team won one of them, with 15/20; What is the 15th wedding anniversary gift supposed to be? Crystal...

Watched the last half of the Neil Diamond show, and wrapped things up. Tomorrow our excursion starts at 7:45. Oh, and again, hottest water in the cabin is barely, Luke warm....

Monday, early rise. Puerto Plata, Dominican Republic; Up at 6:15; breakfast, then down to deck one. We were warned that the pier was lengthy, so we grabbed a shuttle cart to the shore. We found our group, about 30 people, and we were off to the bus which was the farthest away

The excursion was "small group: The Best of Puerto Plata" and yes it was, at least 6 stops, two distilleries with samples, two chocolate companies with samples and a cigar factory, all with demonstrations, and informational presentations. We toured the town, about 300,000 residents, the average salary is about $300.00/month, the teachers got bumped up to $800/month, uber motorcycles are everywhere, $1.00/ride, and yes, we saw two sometimes three on a bike, most were 200-250 CC; gas here is around $5.00 US / gallon; 60% of the population is tourism.

Included with the tour also was a local meal, rice and beans, chicken and rice, pork and rice, potato salad, plantains, fruit, water and or soda; served buffet style, all hot and all delicious.

This also included a tour of a garden with a variety of spices, fruits, orchids, and even a coy pond.

The tour was to last only 4 hours, we returned in 6 ½ hours; traffic was somewhat regulated, but many motorcycles did not obey signals, and there are special police here, Tourist Police...

Noah

When we got back to the pier, shared the cab back, and only two of the four elevators were working causing another backup. I did finish Lynn's birthday shopping; she now has another ring!

A couple trivia, then supper in the café, watched a very good show, "Uptown", very nice, Lynn and I were both called up to play Friendly Feud, (we were on opposite teams) and both tied; Finished up with another Pub Quiz, we enjoyed, but did not win.... both of us tired...In the room by 10:30, journaled, charged batteries for the camera, and restocked the wallet for tomorrow, St. Thomas. Oh, and we finally have hot water in the shower and sink!

Tuesday, February 7th, we docked a bit past 10:30, got a picture of the islands coming in, and the pilot boat that joined us just outside the harbor.

Went to the front desk, told them that new seating assignment was good and that we would be checking it out tonight, got some more paper and tape for Lynn; and checked with future as to the list of hotels recommended and utilized by celebrity, also found that this boat is 21 years old.

Trivia 10;30, Our usual teammates didn't show, so we invited two we worked with the day before...ONLY 11/17 POINTS ☹ "What is a lithosphere" Ans. "Earth's crust"

Lunch on deck, hamburgers and fries...Stella Artos beer not included in package, but Corona was...

Scheduled excursion at 1:15, so we went to the cabin, used bathroom, got out money and tickets and off to meet at the windmill on shore, as directed.

18 people loaded into an open-air canopied pick-up truck conversion designed for 20 small, thin people, four rows, where most of us old and packing a few more pounds, yes, we were in the back, 5 across! (We were snug, to say the least!)

This was a tour of the island, going to the very top, and three lookouts on the way, one up, and two down. It did rain in spurts, a few downpours, and the people on the outside rows got wet, it was also raining when we got to the top, soaking everyone while we negotiated down three staircases and into the pavilion where you passed through a store with every type of souvenir you can imagine.

Educating Noah...Travelin'

Lynn could not negotiate the steps, I did, looked around, and took a few pictures and went back, it was a 20-minute stop, and I was the second last back. The other stops were shorter, brief periods with no rain, then we toured the town, let off ½ the passengers and returned to the harbor. Got some great pictures including 6 iguanas!

This 1 1/2-hour tour lasted 2 ½ hours, constant narration as to life on the island and history of the island, everything on this island is imported, no exports, all the houses have cisterns and septic systems, and the cost of diesel generated island power is very high; there are many beaches but most are private, the one main beach has a day charge of $5.00 per person for maintenance. This a USA owned island, bought from the Dutch. The weather is constant 65-75 degrees, warm water Caribbean on one side, cold water Atlantic on the other side, as with the last island tourism is big here and employes most.

We did notice a lack of motorcycles and bicycles here, streets are all one way in town, and they drive on the left, out of town the roads that were once donkey paths are narrow, and have hairpin turns, and no shoulders, or sidewalks...

Back to the ship for lunch on the deck, three trivia in the afternoon, ate at the regular restaurant, we now have an assigned table for two.

Went to the one woman "Diva Show", finished up the night three trivia and a game of majority Rules...no prizes, joined with a few more people, and finished up at 11.

Wednesday, St, Kitts; our tour today starts at 9:45 and we meet in the theatre. Wind today at 17 knots. Today was the Caribbean Scenic Railway Tour! I arrived at the theatre ½ hour early to scout out how to facilitate Rollie and Lynn to find out when checking in, that the slower and handicapped folks signed up were to leave early...got our tags.

Waited for Lynn and we took off to the end of the pier. The end of the was farthest I have seen, at least THREE FOOTBALL FIELDS ...good guess, ½ mile, and a larger Royal Caribbean Seven Seas cruise ship parked right next to us, and emptied at the same time...masses of people, only three 7-person shuttle carts slowly going to and from for $1/person...nope, we didn't get one either way...lines too long. At the end of the pier, we waited ½ hour to leave in a small ten passenger bus for a 45-minute tour of the island before loading on to the narrow-gauge double deck railroad train that circled the island.

We opted for the lower airconditioned compartment, and many others chose the upper open-air accommodations. There were a lot of small old houses boarded up, the estates own them and many no longer live on the island, the island has cisterns and running water, there is also a common septic system.

There is a veterinary school and medical school for nurses and doctors, people come from all over the world to study here. Oh, I asked, gas is $5-6/gallon, and power comes from Diesel generators, no real industry, wind and sun most if not all the time…solar? wind? The driver states electricity costs hundreds a month…

The train ride included rum drinks, water, and soda, brief entertainment by two costumed men dancing, the rest was just rocking back and forth and at times noisy…no narration, most of the modern buildings seen were Eco organizations, Government buildings, or mansions, along the tracks were many stripped out cars, herds of cattle and goats; we saw quite a few egrets, but not one monkey, we were told there were many in the forests. It again was windy and it did sprinkle, but in all it was a pleasant trip. Our bus was waiting for us at the end, 15 minutes back to the pier, walked 4-5 blocks through the many tourist stores, and then the hike back to the ship.

A couple trivia and games, dinner in the dining room…again too slow, no desserts…watch a production show, played a few more participation games, and finished up the night on the deck with the activity team celebrating the full moon. (I was warned not to howl!)

The production staff did a bit of a show, many of us were given light batons to wave with the music, Lynn and I gave ours to some late commers.

Thursday Phillipsburg, St. Maarten; It is less windy, but starting our it was quite warm, only to be mid 90's by noon.

We wanted to return to the new Amsterdam Cheese and Liquor store, so we looked for a cab. Oh, this morning FOUR CRUISE SHIPS ARE DOCKED, ours was the smallest, and furthest from the dock…the very end of the pier.

The cab station was very crowded, every cab taking 8 passengers, we asked which one to take to go to the store and directed to a loading cab. We were taken as everyone else downtown for $3/person, when we told the cabbie, he told us he didn't know, that we had passed it outside the gate, and said it would cost $3/ person to ride back with him and drop us off before the port.

He dropped us off, offered to charge only $5, but I insisted on the whole $6!

We shopped, got the cheese Lynn wanted and walked back the five blocks to the port!

Our beach tour was to leave at 12:30 and meet at the pier… on the way out before we looked for signs… none, at the end of the pier we looked for representatives…nope, nothing;

Lynn was tired and said she would try to get one of the three shuttles running the piers. I walked back to the ship; found an officer and he indicated an area next to the water tent with four chairs as the waiting area. It was 11:45, I sat and waited; 12:45 a representative came out, I confirmed where, and told him Lynn was at the dock, he gave me the shirt stickers and told me to look for our group as they walked to shore. As I walked the pier again, I met Lynn half way, explained, and we turned around to find some shade and bench to wait…the shuttle never showed…probably working another ship…

We joined the group as they left the pier at 1:50, walked with them to the buses, and there we were informed that the beaches were high water today, and limited access to walkers, offered a refund, we took it and walked back to the ship, sunburned and tired.

We tried eating in the dining room again, our assigned table for two…we have never had a table for 2, always requesting large tables to meet and greet…Appetizers in ½ hour, wine offer ¾ hour in, drink guy a no show; main course just after an hour, finished dessert in 1 ½ hours…last time here!

Two trivia, and done for the night

Friday, 02/10/2023 San Juan, Puerto Rico. Yesterday afternoon, the gout in my left elbow returned with a flair, took what I had for pain, half way through the night, pulled out my stash of needs, and wrapped the upper and lower arm with an elastic bandage which seemed to help a bit. In the morning, I went ashore and as I got off the pier, spotted a Walgreens. Looked for tart cherry juice…nope, asked where the pharmacy was, and told "Walgreens in Puerto Rico don't have pharmacists". Down the block CVS; pharmacist just recommended Advil; but told me there was a cannabis store about five blocks away, and gave me directions…

Bought two postcards, headed back to the ship, and asked about the doctor on board. Since we were at Port, $360.00 for consultation, but if I waited until we cast off, I could make an appointment for only $280.00… NOPE

Had lunch with Lynn, played corn hole, Lynn on one team of four, and me on the other, our team won, then took a nap with more of the meds…

Trivia's, went up to the top deck to watch Black Adam, had a bit of problems with the lift, watched about 15 minutes, and it started to rain (it is an outside theatre on top of the ship) tried to use the lift, stalled a number of times on the way down, but a crew member was nice enough to work it with us to finally get down to the next deck.

Dinner at the café, a nice production show, officers vs. guest show, Pub quiz, and finished up the night with a very god Liars club!

Saturday, February 11, 2023 A Day at sea. Last night clocks set back an hour, received our luggage tags for Monday, and worked on our egg drop projects, scheduled for 11:15 A.M.

Egg drop was a success! Lynn won first prize, actually the only prize, there were 10 contestants, mine placed and the eggs did not break, but Lynn's was right on target and eggs were good! She won a T-shirt!

Lynn and I went to a paper folding class, origami, and made two birds…fold here, there, pull out this, a lot more complicated than we thought!

I didn't participate in the ship building this time, there were only three contestants, a kid whose ship was too small for the six-pack required to haul. And a life preserver? Wrapped in a bag, and a bottle ship that actually qualified and floated with the 6 pack.

Trivia's, everyone prepared for fancy night. Other opportunities for the photo people to take pictures, and others to show off…The dining room is offering lobster, and the show doesn't impress so we are going for dinner again in the dining room. Games and trivia finished up the night. Today it was very hot, in the 90's and little wind, my gout is a bit better but the low chairs and sitting creating back

Educating Noah...Travelin'

problems for both Lynn and me.

What animal can clean its ear with its tongue...Giraffe

What animal has the most teeth? Lion, Crocodile or snail? Snail, over 2000

What do you call a nose that is 12 inches long? A Foot

What was the animal Walt Disney afraid of? ... Mice

What do you call a group of Unicorns? Blessing

If Bob's peacock lays 3 eggs in the neighbor's yard, who gets to keep? only peahens lay eggs

Sunday, our last day at sea.

The wind is at 17 knots, the temperature is low 60's... a bit of sun early, I counted over 40 lounges with clips, towels, or personal belongings on them and no one in the pools or whirlpools; And a majority are over 50-60...We joined or friends for the morning Trivia, the I went down in the paper airplane competition, and lost again, although I would have won 2nd with the sleek plane I made, but the bird only made it to the first flight. Lynn went down to make paper fish, as with yesterday, we can't do it by ourselves!

After lunch, I went down to the desk again to enable my phone to use the on board WIFI, Lynn got her's to work with the help of friends, but couldn't remember how it was done, the laptop also refused, but if I got the phone to work, I can clear the mail!

I took the phone down, asked the service person to put on the internet, she took the phone, hit a number of buttons, and handed it back letting me know the internet was installed, I thanked her and left...I have no idea what she did, but it works and only a few hours left on the ship...

I deleted over 100 e-mails, then went to the production show, an adult matinee show "Elysia" the show had a few sexual inferences, a lot of prancing and acrobats utilizing hanging straps.

Met for another Trivia, and then cashed in the 90 tickets we had acquired for 2 pens and a fanny pack.

Tonight, is the Superbowl game at 6:30, all the screens and theatre will be showing the game.

Noah

We ate at the regular restaurant, surprising how many eating during the game. We wished our waiter a happy life, gave him a bit more for tip (Tips were included on this cruise) and played one more trivia, a group "Yes or No" where members of the audience are interviewed for 3 minutes and asked various things to say either "Yes" or "No" only one out of seven lasted 3 minutes without saying either yes or no...lots of fun!

A bar quiz ended the entertainment...did you know that a museum in the U.S. has a display of Abraham Lincoln's poop?? Yup, we didn't know either and now you do!

Luggage out by 10 P.M.

Monday departure; Gathered in the theatre, when our group was called, we checked out, well kinda, my card did not work at two stations, but finally did, caught up to Lynn, TSA was fairly quick and out the door.

I had signed us out for transfers and paid, no directions outside, we were told by one attendant that all departures were to the right. We stood with a big group of people, then I watched as others were boarding another bus on the left; I held our place and had Lynn check...that was the transfer's line! We joined the group, loaded on to the bus, and took the 30-minute ride to the airport, where they dropped us and luggage off at the baggage area.

I asked around, found the elevators to the third floor, Found the American ticket area, and got our tickets. It was 10:00 A.M., our flight to Chicago was moved from 3 to 4 P.M.

Had to go through TSA again, although I had informed Celebrity (they made the flight reservations) of the pre-check number and the need of a wheel chair for Lynn, nothing on the ticket, so we were sent into the regular lines, I asked if I still had to remove my shoes in that it was only a month till I was 75, he told me "Not over 75 needs to remove shoes" so complied, this time the metal detector did not catch any replacement of my six...GREAT SECURITY!

Found our gate, all was in comfortable walking distance so not having the additional wheelchair wasn't really necessary, but it seems that since and during covid, quality has been redefined!

Only 4 ½ hours to wait... Bought some lunch, did some walking, found some Dayquil for my pounding sinus headache, and settled in for the wait.

Until 3:30 everything going well, and then the announcement that the flight will be delayed 20 minutes…So we actually got in the air just before five.

Everything else went fine, the car was still waiting for us, quick drive, Home at 10:45; in bed by 11:15!

It took almost two weeks to recover, traveling laptop died; my computer had problems, another flair on the gout in my left elbow…took the walker down to the basement, Lynn will use for a while at walking club.

Noah

July 29-August 18, 2023

This may be our last cruise, the airlines are worse, cruise ships also becoming disappointing. It is a back-to-back, I need to be at all three points of the Bermuda Triangle, and actually set my foot on Greenland.

It is two weeks out, it seems service is dead, and too many accept this. This cruise is again with Celebrity, and now we are asked to put the Celebrity application on our phones, with all the information including our pictures. It only took a few hours and a couple of phone calls to get it done, yeah, getting past the robots was also a chore, but mission accomplished!

The O'Hare airport now does not allow buses to pick-up passengers at the terminals, you must use the Multi-Modal-Terminal, and after 3 e-mails to Coach USA, and the O'Hare airport, all I know to date is that there are some bathrooms in that facility, but that is all….no one seems to know or care…if you can actually talk to someone!

I also confirmed that the shuttle to the hotel the first night is included, times and where it is, and that the cab ride to the port is only about 20 minutes and reserved a 1-1:30 time slot for check-in at the port.

I only booked one excursion for the entire back-to-back and that is the second day on the Bermuda Island. It is a half-day tour, and I booked it on the second day, because the first day was too close to arrive, and given our luck, and with our speed, we didn't need the stress. Delta hasn't changed the flights to New Jersey again, so we should be good to go; Lynn still using Rolli; it is getting evident that international travel will soon no longer be an option for us.

We had a one-day tour with Happy Times Tours to Amish countries, and our friends Art and Pat Kuenstler joined us. We were picked up at 7:30 A:M at the College exit, where we joined Art and Pat; then another pickup point by the fairgrounds, another at a park and ride and final pickup in Madison. Our first real stop after a rest stop was at a restaurant for included lunch, it was 12:15 already!

The food was outstanding, including the desert, then off to pick up our guide and visit her shops, then to a tour of the countryside, the

Educating Noah...Travelin'

Amish came to Wisconsin in the 60's because our land was available and very similar to Ohio, a farm stop to look at quilts, another, to buy some bakery, and finally, a cheese store stop, where everyone got off and bought! We finally went home, after dropping off everyone else we were back to the college park and ride by 8:30 PM a fun but long day!

The week before we were to leave, our condominium manager up and quit. The owner of the company contacted me that she was terminating our agreement the following Friday late afternoon and we had 30 days to find a new management company.

The manager of our condo association abruptly quit, the owner contacted the board the Friday after, the board annual walk- thru was not attended by the management firm either...I was told in January that management did not want managers to be on site, but we had an agreement with our manager (second one in 3 years) that she would walk thru and attend annual meeting ...so much for service. Our three-page list of observations was forwarded, hopefully we will have another dedicated manager before the end of the month...we will be looking into options for new management...again!

We met up with Lynn's brother and sister-in-law at the lavender fest in Menomonee Falls, Milwaukee and the surrounding areas have festivals all summer from Summer Fest, Italian Fest, Mexican Fest, German Fest, and the state fair, not counting the church festivals that many are still around! This weekend is Harley motorcycles 120th anniversary, thousands of motorcycles here for the weekend including Bastille days downtown! In that the population doubled with the riders, we skipped Bastille days for just a walk in the Whitnall Park Botanical Gardens, two acres of annuals and perennials.!

Did some hectic research, called several management firms, got several bids and several "misunderstandings" from real estate firms that just wanted to manage renters...Coordinated with the board, and settled with a firm that was recommended three times to different board members, got a partial financial

extension, signed all the papers and hopefully a smooth transition the next two months.

Saturday, Day 1, September 29, 2023; at 7:50, Camille picked us up and took us to the Milwaukee airport. We had to wait twenty minutes for the wheelchair assist, and TSA went slow but well even with our known traveler documentation…short-handed, understaffed used as an excuse, but we were ready at the gate.

The flight was only a bit over 2 ½ hours, and we arrived in Georgia at 1:30; upon arriving we found our connecting flight was cancelled…we were given priority standby on a flight leaving at 5:30 and sent to gate F1…had to take the crowded train to the farthest section and then the farthest gate, luckily, they left us there with the wheelchair.

We sat and waited and did not see the flight come up on the board, so I hiked it to a Delta help station, and was told that the gate had been moved to E1…hoofed it back to Lynn, back to the elevators, back to the train, for the ride to E-terminal and then to the very end E-1 Gate.

It was then 4:15, nothing on the board, no crowd, so again found a Delta desk…oops, now the gate was E27! The opposite side of the terminal.

Checking in with the attendant, he told us the flight was fully booked, and we would have to wait till the last booked passenger boarded to see if there were any seats available. At 5:25 we were given the "go"; and, had two adjoining seats toward the back of the plane.

We started to taxi, then stalled, Newark was closed…after a bit over an hour, we took off, an hour into the 2 ½ hour flight we were diverted again to Virginia Beach for fuel and had to wait again for Newark to reopen…1 ½ hours; we were told that the terminal was basically closed, but could exit the plane with all carry-ons for an hour or so to stretch our legs…about half the plane de-planed. A bit over an hour, some seats were empty when the doors were closed, even with stewards and stewardesses were sent out to bring everyone back!

The final hour of flight went well, we arrived in Newark a bit after midnight; went to pick up luggage, and no Rollie the walker! Made a claim at the baggage office, took the train to the shuttle pickup area, oh, and yeah, the door closed right after Lynn, and I had to take the next one to join her…the shuttle bus came and took us to the hotel, we were in our room at 1:20 A.M. Long day!! Oh, and yes, a party was still going on, we were on the 6th floor and the music and crowd were still quite loud…. until well after 2…or so Lynn says!!

Day 2, Sunday, September 31, 2023…up at 7:30, Lynn called about breakfast, they told her there was a charge, so I went down to

Educating Noah...Travelin'

the desk, got directions as to where the dining room was and the eat free tickets along with arranging for a cab at 11.

Our check-in time slot for the ship was 1-1:30, we are told to bring our phone app. And original information with health screen sent last night filled out.

Went down at 10:15 had breakfast, and checked out, the cab driver was there early and took our luggage and off we went!

It was 17 minutes, he knew the route, the ship was docked next to the 911 Memorial.

With the wheelchair assist we arranged we were escorted around most of the people, the scanner did not have any indication of metal with Lynn or Me, we showed our passes that were actually easier to read than the phone passes we were required to show, then we were on the ship a bit after 12!

Went to our room (cabin) and no luggage, so off to the pool deck to get /share a hamburger and fries, and we were actually surprised to see so many already on and eating. Lynn loves cruise ship burgers!

We separated, Lynn to explore the ship, and I went down to take better pictures of the memorial. It was past 2:30, and only a few left in line to get on board, I had my pass and hoofed it to the memorial, too the pictures and then came back, had my pass but still had to go through the metal detector...this time it went off, and on inspection all 6 joints beeped....so much for accuracy.

We thought to go a bit early for supper to miss the lines, nope the ship is full, we were waved to the side, and we asked for a big table to join other couples. Nope, we were told too many families booked and we were assigned a table for two close to a couple other tables for two, The menu was great, got my escargot and also a delicious mushroom soup, Lynn had her favorite, Bolognese, it wasn't as good as she liked but... The dessert was cheesecake...

Went back to the cabin to start unpacking, attended the comedian show, played true or false, and both of us too tired to carry on, so back to the cabin, finish unpacking, showered (not very hot) and in bed by 9...we are getting really old!

Day 3 Monday, August 1,2023 a day at sea, up at 8...time zone moved our clocks ahead 1-hour last night.

Noah

We tried to eat breakfast on the rear deck of the cafeteria but did find a table at the door, very crowded, lots of kids, people, and teenagers vying for food, this may be our last breakfast at the café, we will check out the dining room for breakfast…or that's the plan!

The Internet was not working on Lynn's phone, and only one daily program, so we let the steward know we wanted two every night.

Down to the help desk and were helped with the phone, then it didn't work on my computer, so back down with that, but since I didn't bring my passwords Facebook and messenger did not work.

Back down to the desk to follow-up on Rollie…they called, Rollie should arrive in Bermuda on one of the days we are there, the desk person said she will monitor for us!

Lunch in the cafeteria, the two upper decks have a lot more chairs, all lounges, low, and actually crowd the walking/jogging track now, we attended Pictionary, and found the families hogged the presentation and allowed kids under ten to draw…small pictures, and they stood in front of the drawing board which was only about 24X24 inches, so ½ of the team was left out, and no comments by the family!

After that exposure, and, no more point rewards at the games, no more winning souvenirs, beds no longer turned down, and no more small chocolates on the pillow at night!

We then did a trivia on 50's and 60's music, we didn't even come close, some had 17 out 20 questions…but like dining, only families sat together, and no real groups even attempted to form.

Supper, we thought we had a table assigned, but no, they accommodated us, but told us we had to stand in line every night to be assigned a table we will talk to the other dining room tomorrow morning!

Production show, mostly singing, three guys and three gals, saw a beautiful sunset, we are 1/2 way to Bermuda, the total milage is 758 miles from New Jersey, and the ocean depth ranges from 150 to 500 ft., water is dark blue and no land in sight!

Finished up the evening with a pub quiz, and a sing along with Abba, where most were on the dance floor or up and singing along with ABBA songs with lyrics on the screen: everyone dancin' and sigin' and smilin'. FUN!

Educating Noah...Travelin'

Eleven thirty, hot shower, and off to bed...you know, 60% of cruisers are in bed by NINE! 75% by TEN! We are not that old yet!

Day 4, August 2, 2023 another day at sea We now have two programs, planning what we want to do and meeting time for lunch. I opted for the lecture on Bermuda, Lynn went to the game of Crew vs guests.

The weather in Bermuda changes quickly, they have four seasons and in winter, just some occasional hail. There are 62-65,000 permanent residents.

The island is shaped like a "curved between the teeth cleaner", English is the official language. The island is 21 miles long and 2.5 miles wide.

Royal Navy Yard on one end, (West)Hamilton in the middle, and St. George on the other. (East) The closest land is America over 600 miles away!

The island is governed by the United Kingdom.

Rum is the drink of Bermuda, most popular drinks are Rum Swizzle, and Dark and Stormy; foods are codfish and potatoes boiled together and just codfish.

They still have a town crier, he is one of 200 left in the world.

He highly recommended the Crystal cave over the Fantasy cave, but with our leg and back problems we will probably skip (over 80 steps just to get down to them) ...but who knows!

Met up with Lynn for a light lunch, we promised to meet at the pool for interactive Music Trivia, but at one, it stated to rain. I tried to work with this diary, and having to use the mandated chrome service, I had to go down, find the expert, and after 35 minutes of instruction, I was able to get the modifications in and able to get to this program.

Phone message: Delta is shipping Rollie back to Atlanta, and flying Rollie out to the Bermuda by 2:35 tomorrow...with the forecast in Bermuda tomorrow of rain, this should be interesting!

Just as we finish lunch it started to rain again, and continued the rest of the day, so all poolside activities cancelled, most of the guests moved inside and many to the bars... I did a bit of research, the galley makes 40,000 meals a day, there are 2393 passengers on board and 941 crew members.

Noah

I had remembered from the past about tales of the Sargasso Sea, a mass of free-floating seaweed that entangled ships …. Bermuda is the only land mass in it! And it is a bit northeast of the center! This is extensive, covering areas in a 700-mile wide, 2000-mile-long area! The other closest land mass is the New Jersey area!

"Experts" claim it wasn't the seaweed but the lack of wind that isolated the sail ships, there are four major wind currents that lend to the ever-changing weather in the Bermuda area and conflict at times creating dead air or no wind currents for days.

However, the seaweed makes the salt water brackish, and open wounds are subject to infection.

Oh, and of course , Bermuda is at the top of the Bermuda Triangle that extends from Bermuda to Miami to Perto Rico and back, a total of ½ million miles…coincidence??

Trivia, then had to wait in line for supper, we were told to be there promptly at 5 to get our assigned seat, but we still had a half hour stand to get in?!? The couple we met the night before sat next to us, had a nice conversation throughout the meal…felt good to connect again during meals.

The show was a one woman show, she was very talented and a great voice, Pub quiz, officers vs. guest games…we just watched and were not picked, wrapping up with a Motown interactive Dance Party with the band and entertainers leading the show, the balance invited on the floor to dance with the entertainers as they slowly left the floor.

Another nice ending, 11 bedtimes, we beat the 75% in bed by 10!!

Day 5 Wednesday, August 3, 2023. First day in Bermuda! At first look, it is still raining but the clouds are lightening up, low 70's

We dock at 8:30; we will just go ashore and check out the area of this side of the island, we are told Rollie should be here this afternoon, but they expect an $80 charge to bring Rollie to the ship!

Up at 7:15; went out to the elevator and checked outside…we are in port…but it is raining and overcast!

Back to room (we have an inside room, Lynn needs dark and all we do there is sleep, shower, and note take!)

Breakfast in the café, seems many slept in, and we were fed and out in less than 40 minutes. Went back to the room, got our ID's and cash and off to the wharf!

The rain was down to drizzle, mid 70's and clouds are lighting up. I took the excursion paperwork along to see if they would move the tour back to today since tomorrow and Friday are holidays here, and the roads will be crowded with tourists and all the locals!

I identified one of the people we were looking for and he agreed to take us and another couple right away!

His name was Sydney, he is 76, and native to the island. This is a 4 ½ hour tour of the complete island, and as we drove, he agreed to make it complete rather than drop us off at a ferry with tickets included to finish the tour, both couples agreed.

We drove past an old arsenal and fortress built in the 1700's, drove across the smallest draw bridge over the Atlantic Ocean called the Somerset Bridge, and it's 18-inch opening.

Drove the south shore, stopped briefly at Gibbs lighthouse, mid 1800's, 117 ft tall, drove along the two-lane road, some pink sand beaches the weren't, although he tried to find one, some were light orange, others light tan…

Drove through the botanical gardens, nice but not spectacular, my battery in the camera died so that was the end of the pictures.

Tucker town where Ross Perot, Michael Bloomberg, and Abby Rockefeller have/ had mansions…according to Sydney most of the mansions are empty except for a few weeks a year.

Everything is expensive, a small two-bedroom condo $500,000; and up, $9.00 for a gallon of gas, only 6-8 beaches open to the public and one main beach where all the pictures are taken, the rest are private or hotel beaches.

The roofs of the houses are coral cotta, flat cut coral 14X12 tiles, that do not wear. This is a United Kingdom owned island, you drive on the left side of the road and the Bermuda dollar is even with the American dollar and interchangeable here.

There is a two-year college the kids go to, to learn a trade or to get a foundation for a profession, all religions have representation here, lots of immigrants, and due to the high cost of living, the minimum wage is set at $21.00; but he states there are a lot of under the table jobs paying much less, he goes to the USA for clothes, everything is imported here and marked up even for locals. The island is powered by diesel engines, not a windmill or solar panel in sight, except on a jewelry warehouse on the wharf.

Sydney said the Island is very safe and women have no problems being out at night, with or without an escort.

We were dropped off by the ship after 4 and a half hours, wished him well and tipped him properly.

Lunch back on the ship, three trivia, and we actually won one! But we missed working with a group the same as dining, we are traveling to learn, to talk with others, and expand our knowledge…very disappointing!

After dinner we attended the production show, and I went back to check on Rollie. There was a phone message that Rollie was delivered, I picked him up, returned the other walker to the medical department, (It was closed) but I left it locked in the hall… Got a smaller pillow for Lynn from the attendant, and I called it a night, Lynn will be at least going to the activities including guess it, and our favorite Majority Rules!

Day 5, August 3, 2023, the second day at Bermuda, it is NOT raining, but it is hot, and Humid 85 degrees and 80 % humidity!

Since we have seen the entire island, this is a holiday, and so we had a brief breakfast, and headed onto the wharf to do a bit of shopping.

I found a few stones for the collectors; we found a few trinkets and a minimum of souvenirs. Both of were tired and headed back to the ship, we wanted to spend some of the ship money so both of us made appointments for pedicures…one should know, like on the islands everything is expensive on ship, my pedicure…basic…with tip…$91.42.

Massages started a bit over $200 plus tip, you get the idea…

In looking back, there is a lot of similarity of the islands, they are all only have a few usable beaches, a very rich class that own most of the land and a working class that must pay a lot due to most of the products to live are imported, and the power is provided by diesel engines from the early 1900's!

Yesterday we were told there was a delivery charge of $80.00 for

Educating Noah…Travelin'

bringing Rollie from the airport to the ship, and I went up to the desk, protested, and left them $80.00 in cash…This afternoon, he desk left a message that Celebrity would absorb the cost and to pick up the money I deposited…I did, and didn't ask questions…wonder who was going to charge who…anyway, we now have Rollie back, and all I will ask for is the difference between business class and coach from Delta and never flying Delta again!

Nothing special in the afternoon, kept to air-conditioned areas on the ship, supper was now reserved for Celebrity!

The show was half acrobatic, one woman was extremely flexible and athletic, wow, we then went to the Yes/No show, we had our names in the bucket but didn't get picked…three minutes of questions with the host trying to get the guest to say either yes or no…or a variation, 2 people actually were able to win the celebrity T shirt!

We ended up the day at the 10:00 Full Moon Party at poolside; we lasted 40 minutes on the dance floor!

Day 6, Friday August 4th, 2023. Old habits hard to break, up at 7, Lynn has been sleeping through the nights, a rare thing since the quack replaced her hip last September!

We filled our calendars last night, after breakfast I went out and took a small tour of the docks…almost…then went back to the cabin for my ID, then off again. Returned for a SUDO challenge, then a trivia competition, Lynn complained she had nothing from Bermuda and sent me out again…I picked up a Bermuda T shirt from a vendor on the wharf …she liked it until trying it on…it was XL youth…Arghhhhhhh… I will have to put it in my stretcher at home to size it properly!

It is mid 90's and very humid, and lots of people are very red! Lunch on the deck, nappy time; Lynn Music Trivia, me a seminar on Chinese and traditional medicine.

Anchors up at 3:30 at the same time as another trivia. We are on our way back to New Jersey. I was the only one who attended the seminar, from the whole ship! The meeting place was not on any of the areas, it was mostly a sales pitch for acupuncture and herbal medicines, we agreed that if I wanted more information to arrange for a meet after five…I told him I would consult my wife…

Noah

Joined Lynn for two very hard trivia's, Marco Polo came from what country...(Venice) Where is the "coat hanger" bridge? (Sydney, Australia) ...What does "M" stand for in the 007 series? (Head of secret intelligence service M16)

Dinner included lobster tail, so we both had that! The show was a tribute to "Buble" three guys, and they did very well! I wanted to get the sun set over the water, but I was five minutes late, maybe tomorrow...it was a bit cloudy and those on the deck said it wasn't great!

We attended another game show, then had a lull before the 80's music challenge...we got there early because even at 10:15 the lounge was crowded...our side guest leader could not answer any of the questions, and had difficulty hearing the answers from the side, but it was fun...VERY HIGH VOLUME, and lots of action everyone jumping up and down and getting into the encouraged action.

Day 7, Saturday August 5, 2023. Clocks back one hour; our final day at sea on this cruise...both to and from Bermuda the seas have been very smooth, little if any rocking of the ship. With the exception of the first day in Bermuda the weather was hot, sunny and lightly clouded both the sea and sky beautifully blue!

Or that's how it started, after breakfast it started to rain, then it would stop, then start again, all day long!

So, our last sea day was mostly inside, another two trivia's, bought a card for the Deal no Deal game, after the two pedicures we still had $20 balance on our account and one card was $25.00, two cards $30, four cards $50,00...with my luck one card bought me participation.

Afternoon, the theatre was full of people playing the game, the two contestants walked away with over $200 each, with what was shown most everyone lost, 40-50 won $10.00 casino play money and down from there, total of 10-15 won over $20 casino play money...No big winners, except the two picked to play.

Another trivia, we arrived late, I volunteered for a game of Heads up, I really didn't know what they wanted me to do, but we got through it, with 9 points in the allotted time, lost to a team that had 16 points before we even got to the room.

Dinner the final one with our new friends on the table next to us Scott and Tracy, they are only an hour and a half drive from the port, and they made the dining besides the excellent food a pleasure!

An excellent show and another "Say It" participation game. Not too many kids wanted to play, fun to watch, and we called it a night.

Day 8 Sunday August 6, 2023.

Change over day, most getting off, we must get new pass cards, new photos and submit new health questionnaires…and told to meet at 9:15 at the lounge on deck 4.

We stayed in the cabin till 8, hoping to avoid the crowds…Nope, a large number of folks just took their carry-ons up to the cafeteria and camped…

Had breakfast, found an area to sit while most of the ship was called to exit.

I turn in the health questionnaire at the desk, had them re-enter my credit card, , joined Lynn for our new photos and new passes, and we walked up to the pool deck, then found by an officer who told us we needed to leave the ship completely, then at the very end show our face at a screen and then walk back, it was then what we thought was done, but upon reaching our cabin, no internet, and I could not open WORD.

In a 20-person line, after a bit over ½ hour and having the "expert" check accounts, I refused to pay $274 for 9 days of internet…he "found" the free internet we were supposed to have and guided us into Lynn's phone and this computer, funny how my pin changed to 2140… BUT it worked! Only 15 minutes wasted after 20 plus in line just for a "free" or "included" service.

Nice lunch, nothing scheduled for the afternoon, we napped, Lynn caught up on internet and Facebook, and I brought notes current.

Anchor up at 3:30; before that happened about 6 couples were paged twice to report for the safety briefing; I was brushed by a cow who just ignored me when I excused myself in an aisle, and we checked about reservations for the evening…and that too is still "iffy".

Supper we were actually seated at one larger table , then moved to a round 6-person table with our favorite waitress Indri! An older couple joined us, and two women traveling together. Good conversation, and hopefully this will be the group throughout the cruise!

The show was a stand-up comedian, he was funny, but did talk a bit fast for me, the theatre was very full!

We wrapped up the day with a True or False game…we lost…again… And a Pub Quiz where out of the twenty questions we only got 4…we did meet someone in the hall on the way out and agreed to have her join us the next games!

Tomorrow is a day at sea, thunderstorms forecast…should be interesting!

Day 9 Monday, August 7, 2023. Today was cool. Lower 70's, foggy, like cruising in a cloud, but the waters are calm, waves less than a meter high, no lad in sight.

Attended destination highlights, pointing out what to see In Halifax, Nova Scotia, our next port tomorrow and the other ports. I Listed the highlights and we will probably find a cabbie to work with us…we will see.

Next was a presentation on "How to Increase your Metabolism"; seems only 15% controlled by exercise, 35 % by food, the balance by alkaline and acidic balance, not very much information except for "sign up for my class"… and pay to find out…Need to look into natural liver cleanse and alkaline foods…

Officers' vs guest bean bag toss…guests won, Lynn and I both sunk four bean bags! Again, no prizes; Champaign ring toss, out of the 30 or so participants one woman actually got the rope ring around the bottle of Champaign…finally a real reward!

We participated in beginners' origami, it was the same as the first one, a piano and a hat. Then the old farts went back to the cabin for a nap, there was a phone message that we actually have a reservation…let's see what happens!

We actually got past the two lines that extended into the lounge, we have never had this much BS until now…We were seated with the retired pediatrician and his wife, they are quiet, especially him he has Parkinsons and talks very little. The new couple were from Pennsylvania and the table was live with talk and I do admit, the food was outstanding…everything!

Educating Noah...Travelin'

The show was a three-man show featuring the 60's Frankie Valie songs and the songs from Grease. The entire theatre was full, maybe 15-20 seats up front empty, otherwise full!

The movie outside was the only option we were going to do, but it was down in the 60's so we passed. I did get a sunset...kinda...there was a low cloud bank that the sun disappeared behind before the sea. Tried to get hot water out of the shower...nope! Not even Luke-warm tonight!

Day 10, Tuesday, August 8, 2023. Halifax, Nova Scotia. This morning it started out in the low 60's but by the time we ate our breakfast and put some different clothes on, it was low 70's, partly cloudy and a light breeze. The ship docked at 7, we were of the early few to get off after 9.

Here we needed a government ID with picture and our sea pass, the new driver's licenses are good enough!

Not much this early in the terminal, and then we walked by the double decker buses, inquired, they said we could charge it on our ship account and so we took it!

We sat up by the driver, so we got information from him and the tour person in the back. The tour was a good 1 ½ hours covered a good section of the city, including the graveyard of the titanic...the ship is about 300 miles east in the ocean. The driver asked about Biden and Trump, their reaction to Trudeau is about the same as ours to Biden...

Gas is $1.84...PER LITER...we asked about homeless and the driver pointed out the government housing and a few tent camps...Back on the pier, found a few stones for my collectors, the two local shops we HAD to go through, collected some American dollars, the pier shops were then also opened so our walk back to the ship entrance was much slower, and my wallet got a bit lighter.

Lunch on the ship, took a few more pictures of the harbor, not too many on deck... Trivia at 2:45; talked to a few people, had one take a picture of my "Being cremated is the last chance I have of a smoking hot body" T-shirt, and a number of thumbs up...

Half the ship off yet so it is a lazy afternoon, a game of Pictionary, another trivia, supper was with the same folks six of us at the same table, and we all agreed to keep it!

Production show, a game of Guess it; one member of the team draws symbols representing any number of things without words of using your expressions…we /our team WON!

Pub quiz and at 10:15 ABBA NIGHT…everyone up and singing along and dancing to ABBA ; very loud, a good 40-50 people dancing and singin' …we only lasted three songs, but it was a lot of fun!

Day 11, Wednesday, August 9, 2023; A day at sea, it is 62degrees F, windy the ship rockin' 1-1/2-meter waves, no weather forecasts or radar on the on-board TV, no forecast anywhere… Our first inside activity, was a trivia at 10:15 and I wanted to enter and name our egg drop creation…oops, last night we were supposed to move our clocks ahead by ½ hour… the notice was in the middle of the daily notices and not reinforced this morning.

I did get the name added to our egg drop entry, and did get the device started, but actually showed up 15 minutes late to the trivia, the guests did beat the officers, but our team was at only 8 out of 20, the officers 7, and the winning team 17…

Attended a lecture on Puffins, the theatre was full, basically no outside activities and a lot of people sit on the ends of the aisles…

There are three main types of Puffins, Horned, with a population of about 1 million, Tufted with a population of 4 million and the largest of the three, and last the Atlantic Puffin, the smallest and 12-14 million.

Puffins spend most of their life at sea, body is 11-12 ", wingspan 21-23 inches weight 1 lb.2can fly 48-55 MPH, wings beat 400/minute, due to body shape and weight, they run to take off.

When breeding time comes, feet turn vibrant red, they return to the same place every year, same partner, finds partner via acoustics, particular grunts, offering pebble after several attempts and finally she gives in and they click bills together.

Every flight they return to nest with up to 10 fish or eels, they can spend up to 20-30mseconds underwater, and in 45 days bring in about 2000 fish!

Most years most females are taken, an open beak and standing tall with chest out means too close!

When they swoop…they poop!

Life span of 25-30 years.

Norway trains dogs to find puffin nests they eat puffins! (Norwegians)

I finished to make the drop device for the egg drop, a couple trivia after lunch, lots of people in casino…lt looks like an early night, rain, fog, and wind, nasty outside on the decks.

We now are able to skip the line to get into the dining room, one couple did also, and we informed the last couple to do the same…the meal and conversation was great, one couple a retired pediatrician and his nurse, wife, the other worked for a bearing company, and his wife.

After dinner, an officer vs guest gameshow, we just watched, and a pub quiz, we had another couple join with us and a single woman, we scored 14/20!

Day 12, Thursday August 9, 2023. St. John's Newfoundland. It is starting out at 14 degrees C, 61 degrees F; it is in the upper hemisphere and mid-summer…It's raining pretty hard, had breakfast, then checked the front desk for the forecast and dock conditions…no terminal. Umbrellas are in the rooms, this is the only place to get today's forecast on ship, not in daily program, or on information screen in room…oh, and satellite poor if at also only some channels beside internal available…notice CNBC and BBC seemed to have only very limited, but FOX is currently unavailable…

Back to the cabin, put wallet and camera away and will meet Lynn up for trivia at 10.

Looks like a long day, and just more food!

Trivia…here are some examples:

1. What country has the shortest national anthem? Japan
2. When did the European Union accept the Euro as common currency? 1999
3. European world considered this fruit as poisonous until the early 1800's? Tomatoes (Pewter plates were used, the juice leeched the lead)
4. In 1952 Albert Einstein was offered the presidency of what country? Israel

Noah

5. Most populated city in the world as of 2023? Tokyo
6. National animal of Singapore? Lion

That was your lesson for the day!

Light lunch, and we split up, it was down to a light drizzle, so yup, had to put my foot on Newfoundland, and had to get those rock s for those folks back home!

The only things mentioned to look at here by the briefing at the beginning of the cruise was a forest, a museum, and multicolored row houses….The walk to get out the gates was only about a block and a half, I walked about four blocks around downtown…it was like a ghost town except for traffic and people from the ship; approached by a bum (now called homeless), walked through two of the three souvenir shops, found a couple of for rent store front like back in the US, prices here are high also, walked past 7 or 8 pubs but I guess it is too early…back to the ship, the entrance sign indicated a close gate, so I assumed it was another gate down the sidewalk…nope after two blocks , I returned and just unlatched the gate and let myself in…a guy comes running over, I showed my card, and told the folks behind me to follow…I asked why the gate was latched, but no answer…Back on the ship, washed the stones, went up to join Lynn, we were the only participants in the bean bag toss...Lynn won, got the prize, and she will be gloating about this till …FOREVER!

Not much in the afternoon, two more trivia…on one of the elevator rides picked up an older teen, wearing headphones, no words, and rode two floors, still no words, no expressions, as we traveled through various decks, many on their cell phones and it didn't look like books, just entertainment web sites, also watched quite a few looking at phones during presentations and entertainment. Walking the corridors by the rooms there were quite a few "DEEP SLEEP" magnets on the cabin doors, telling the cabin attendant to skip this one…

One of the couples at our table never showed up, we will see if tomorrow he recovers. (He had a stroke awhile back and is suffering from Parkinsons).

We heard an announcement that as we left the seas were getting a bit more aggressive 3–4-meter waves and wind picking up…we will be at sea two days before reaching Greenland, hopefully that "Global

Warming" will kick in, this 60's low 70's in August is not what was bargained for!!

The show was a very good magician by the name of Jason Bird; a one man show, engaged the audience, and fun.

Watched a game of "SAY IT" six games were played and in 90 seconds one team of two strangers got 10 correct! They are now giving out medallions and phone buttons to winners.

Lynn wanted to check out the shops, even on sales, very expensive and limited sizes.

Both of us tired for some reason so we called it a night…the hot water worked again!!…oh, and the clocks were moved forward that night.

Day 13, Friday August 13, 2023, A Day at Sea Starting out in fog, 50's F, waves about 2-3 meters and a 15-mph wind, stabilizers are all deployed, 50% chance of rain, on and off…not friendly on deck.

Morning Trivia, started to get to a lecture named: The stuff they don't teach you on TV…turned out to be about football and coaching…not being into professional sports, I lasted 15 minutes, tried to attend a fat sculpting session…that was cancelled before it was started…but since I was the only one there, they made me a special appointment for 12:30…

Joined Lynn and another couple in the second trivia…we won again with input mainly by the other couple… (It's not what you know but who…)

We went to a seminar on whales, got there 10 minutes before it started, but the whole theatre was full to capacity and then some…we stood in the back, got most of the lecture and the upper ½ of the screen, we hope it will be on the internal TV.

Whales are identified by small differences besides size, some a white ban chevron on the pectoral fin, and most by the flukes.

Whales hold their breath up to twenty minutes, when they exhale the blow hole emits exhaust up to 200 mph! The furthest whales from Iceland and Greenland travel is the Dominican Republic…estimated at 16,000 a year; the world population of whales is estimated at 135,000…grown since the calves have learned to go under the nets! Mom stays with the calve 10 years, life span is up to 90 years.

Noah

How do you know how long they live? The ear wax changes every year, when a carcass is found, the rings of ear wax is counted to reveal the age.

The bumps on the heads of the whales have 1 hair, and these bumps are sensors of magnetic fields, called vibrissa. Whales feed all day and night, and when they flap their tail, it is a warning to STAY AWAY!

Just one note for now, The Blue whale is the largest creature on earth…ever! They are attracted to little kid voices…

Lunch in the spa area, small portions and it worked out well!

Attended my cool sculpting session, he was 5 minutes late to that, some information given, it does kill fat cells, results in 2-4 weeks, and then he gave me the price…four 8X3 areas for a 35-minute session…$800/area, total of $3200.00…I told hm I would have to discuss with my wife and left…

The progressive trivia filled the entire lounge, we got 9/20…

Dinner we are still missing the same couple, they are now threatening to move us to a table for four.

The show was Take 3; a three-person women ensemble one piano, one singer and fiddle player, and the third a base player, they combined classics with Broadway, they were very good, and yup, the theatre was packed again!

Our last event was the game yes or no, it was fun, had two winners!

That was it, we are both tired….old…farts, back in the cabin at 9:30. We are in the Labrador Sea, it never got above 55 degrees and never left the fog bank…foghorn sounding all day, we are promised good weather in Greenland, tomorrow is another sea day…quite a few DEEP SLEEP magnets on cabin doors.

Day 14, August 12, 2023. Another sea day; 51 degrees F, medium clouds, 5-10 mph winds, and calm. Lecture after trivia, we had 15/20…How to pronounce the name of the village in Greenland? "Crack-a-duck" with a slur on the end…Prediction for tomorrow 4 degrees C, or 31 degrees F light clouds…Seals of the North Atlantic was the title, the auditorium again was jammed packed.

There are our dominant seal species in the north Atlantic:

Educating Noah...Travelin'

Ringed, Grey, Bearded, and Harbor.

Every seal has a special spot match coat. When threatened they form a U with their body to warn the threat off; February is pupping season gestation 10-11 months, females pregnant yearly and blood on the ice indicates a baby birth, seal milk is 46% fat, babies gain on average 2# per day.

Every seal has a special location to match their coat, their toenails are razor sharp, they can dive 1500feetand stay under water for 20 minutes, at the base of the dive, their heart slows to 13 beats per minute. Seals have fur covered flippers and steer with the front flippers.

They eat cod, herring, sprat, and various plankton.

Grey Seals...Hok Nose, sea pig..." Hooked nose sea pig", 50% of day in water; males are bigger but females rule; she chooses mate

Ringed Seals...White circles on body, each distinctive in pattern, they can dig 2 ½ feet of ice to surface; pups are white fluffy fur, these seals are world-wide and prefer harbors.

Bearded Seals are the largest, 575-800#s colors are from brown, gold, grey to black, they have a distinctive breeding song, the whiskers are used to sense crabs and crayfish on the bottom.

Threateners are polar bears, humans (they are hunted) and climate change...

Sea Lions are the opposite, steering with rear flippers, and propel with the front flippers and flippers are naked. Sea lions also bark, have grippers on their flippers, and can rise upon all four. There are no sea lions in the North Atlantic.

Lunch at the spa, small portions, tried a shake I had to pay for, and I tried a few thinks including the shake but were too healthy for Lynn (lacked taste like a lot of vegetarian stuff (my opinion) ...

One game of ladder ball. I placed in the final three, One of the women responded to my request at the beginning for a luck hug, she gave me one then two others when I asked later, lots of fun, we tried to encourage this kind of interaction, which seems to be lost and not encouraged since covid.

Not much except for Deal or no deal, I tried before, nothing yesterday I tried three slot machines...the $10.00 turned into .25 in

Noah

less than 7 minutes…lesson learned!

Interactive music trivia, and then to progressive trivia, again the lounge was packed, found wo members of our team, got a bit snubbed in that they invited another person and he contributed more than we did…

Dinner was uninspiring selections just OK, and the waitress will see if the missing couple will ever return; we may have to go to a table for four…

The show was very good, then we watched a game show called Whisper challenge…two teams of 6 all have headphones on, and the first is given a phrase to pass to the next member by reading lips…seems both teams had one person that didn't have a clue…

10:00 Disco never dies…listened for two songs, then danced to one, then off to LaLa land…she had enough!

Day 15, August 13, 2023, Sunday…Qaqortoq, Greenland. Lynn decided not to go, ramps very steep and no accommodations for Rollie so I got my tender the lounge and the ticket, proceeded to foyer, five minutes later we were called to go own to deck 1 to the tender. The capacity top and bottom of the tender was about 100. The trip to shore, about 15 minutes.

Being Sunday, many places were closed, but I did find a souvenir shop open, along with some small local vendors…the t shirt I bought for Lynn and a postcard basically wiped out the 350 DDK I brought with me, I then found a grocery store and asked for "Hardfiskur" she pointed to a 1-2 Lb. package, I told her it was only for a taste, so she found me a small ¼ lb. package for about $2.50 US I gave them a $5, they gave back 15 DKK change.

Toured the town, a couple kids posed for me on some rocks in a river, nesting duck on the riverbed, very few residents, took picture of the icebergs that weren't too far away, and a glacier. Found some rocks, and headed back to the tender, then back to the ship. It has warmed up a bit, in the low 40's F, partly cloudy skies.

Searched out Lynn for lunch, found her favorite Lamb Sharama in the cafeteria, but after 45 minutes, ate lunch and down to the cabin to clean the rocks, and put everything else away.

Afternoon, Lynn went to dance class, met up for Scattergories, we shared our table with another couple and two single travelers, good, interesting conversations.

The show was outstanding, Karen Grainger; a one woman show with a voice that changed with the wig she put on...sounded very much like the singers she imitated, she was very engaging and entertaining.

A game of challenge, and ending up the evening with majority Rules, lots of fun...bedtime, after 11 plus we must move our clocks ahead an hour tonight.

Day 16, Monday August 14, 2023. Last night clocks ahead one hour. Prince Christian Sound (cruise) this was supposed to be the most scenic view of Greenland; entering at 7 A.M, It is a bit warmer...mid 40's...BUT solid fog...thick fog, cannot see the water from the decks, much less scenery...This viewing is supposed to at least last till 1 P.M....It is a fjord that separates the southernmost islands from the rest of Greenland where Norse history intersects with the small modern communities. The mountains reach to 4000 feet, with a number of glaciers.

As the morning went on the fog lowly lifted, and by noon, we could see mountain tops, glaciers snow in valleys, and yes, I went from side to side, floor to floor to document for the photo album. With a population of only 30,000 people, Greenland is unspoiled by humans, there was various commentary over the loudspeaker, and yes global warming was mentioned often though the number of ice ages wasn't and the relatively new 300–400-year-old icebergs only cursory, or that we are actually at the end of an ice age...

A Documentary movie on Iceland was offered in the theatre, and it was very interesting, here is a small taste...Iceland is the most volcanic place in the world, 20% of Iceland is covered by glacier, ½ the population of the razorbill birds breed here, and Iceland is one of the best fishing grounds in the world.

Back to the room (it is now low 50's) I had been outside a good portion of late morning and early afternoon getting those must-see pictures, I was asked by a couple people how I could be out there in just a T-shirt and pants...I told them I was actually a shaved polar bear... so a brief nap, and I had to try that Hardfiskur I bought in Qaqortoq...not bad! I guess you could call it a light fish tasting jerky, I promised one of our tablemates a taste and put that sample in an envelope for dinner and put the rest back in the refrigerator. As throughout both cruises the internet is slower than dial-up, and very intermittent. I have asked the Guest relation three times now if we actually due cross the arctic circle during this cruise in that he maps I have seen show us really close…as of now still no answer…

The stage show was the three-woman team again and outstanding…their name…Take 3!

Yes or No game, Pub quiz, and Totally 80's game show ended the evening, bed just after midnight.

Day 17, Tuesday August 15, 2023; Clocks moved ahead last night again one hour. It is in the low 50's F, light clouds, 1–2-foot waves, calm and blue!!

First thing we went down to desk relations, but, since the service was not good, went to the concierge desk to find out about the arctic circle! I stated this was the fourth time I was asking and they agreed to give me an answer. Phone calls were made, computers checked and according to the bridge, we will come within 1km of the arctic circle in our journey…

After breakfast morning trivia, then "Beyond the podium with Brent Nixon: Orca of Iceland". Here are some notes:

Orca- the killer whale; A family or group is called a POD.

Orcas have a language, and it is global, they can communicate with orcas from other oceans, a global language, and some sounds can be heard up to 5 miles under the water.

Orcas can be found worldwide, but Iceland is the core of orca density, especially between Iceland and Norway.

Springtime when the ice breaks up is puppy time, the same as when the herring are running and plentiful, and they have only one calf. Coincidence or planned?)

Pregnancy lasts 14-16 months, birth when one of the group dies, a baby orca is about 400 lbs., borne tail first, and can swim immediately. Boys have straight dorsal fins and what looks like a pitchfork marking on the bottom, the middle tine is extended; babies stay close to mom 4-5 years.

Each of the four different types of Orcas has its own characteristics, depending on size, color and diet. The Bigg's Orca have a limit of 6 per family, others have pods greater than 50. They all hunt one area for only 6 hours, and then move on.

What do they eat? They all love salmon, some go after seals, proposes, dolphins, other whales and other fish, some types, sharks, fish and mammals…

Last notes: In Orcas, mom is boss, some dorsal fins can be up to 1.8 meters; life span usually 50-60 years; babies in some pods never leave mom; You identify them by the saddle patch of white.

Dolphins: crest shaped dorsal fins, bulbus nose, bigger jump vs porpoises: sloped forehead, triangular dorsal fin, and never jump.

Picked up our two fresh eggs for the egg drop and joined Lynn in the cabin to add the eggs and put the finishing touches on "unscrambled" my rig.

Six contestants showed up, all but mine had some sort of parachute; We dropped on cue and our partners had to remove the eggs in 60 seconds. Our drift a bit on target only half in. but the eggs were unbroken. We won 2nd place, first place given toa woman who used a Celebrity umbrella hooked to a purse…

Lunch and trivia's followed; I was upset and thought I would protest and play with the Manuel, the cruise director by writing a note that since Lynn won the last egg drop in February, I have heard here brags daily, and that using Celebrity items and not recyclable items, actually broke the rules. I gave the note to Laura, one of the activity people and told her to act it up that I was really upset…let's see what happens.

Dinner with a new person at our table, he was very pleasant and was a good fit…The show was another Karen Grainger one woman show…excellent; a game of true or false, and we were both too tired, so we called it a night.

In the cabin, was a certificate for crossing the Arctic Circle…Tomorrow 11 o'clock; agents will be on ship early to stamp passports, our assigned time in 8:00…more to come!

Day 18, Wednesday, August 15, 2023. Low 50's and partly cloudy, what a great day to visit Akureyri, Iceland. The second largest city in Iceland, known as the capitol of the North Iceland, and gateway to Iceland's greatest wonders, including waterfalls, lava fields, and warm natural waters. Since we have been here before and seen these wonders, it was hard to justify the $110-200/person 2–3-hour tours.

Last night was a phone call from Manuel agreeing with me but he will still check the book!

We had passports in hand and ID's after breakfast, went up to the lounge and no one there but a number of other guests...I volunteered to go back down to the help desk and yes, the notice was for the 17th, not today, I reported the confusion, and that too didn't seem to bother the staff in that they pointed out the date...I asked why are all the people on the ship allowed in Iceland a day before without the passport check and they just ignored me...

I returned to the lounge and told the people there that the date was right, tomorrow, and no problem leaving the ship...

A little after noon we left the ship, we are in a fjord and the scenery is breathtaking, but no seals, whales or puffins.

After looking around, trying to get past the small tour companies and asking the security guard about the two hop on op off buses that were gone now...He didn't know anything and directed me to a tour company rep who could care less about other options, we flagged down a cab that just entered the parking area and asked to go to the Botanical Gardens. The short drive was about $25.00, and I agreed, It was shorter than we thought, but then again everything is high here. When we go out, I asked about a return cab and he said the people in the park would call one for us....

The plants were plentiful, and I did get a lot of pictures plus the stones for the people back home, and after a bit over an hour Lynn was getting tired so we started looking for someone to call a cab...no one around!

I walked across the parking area and into the hospital and asked the receptionist if she would call...She did, and I thanked her. The cab arrived in just a few minutes, we asked him to take us close to the port where there would be some shopping, he said there was a shopping area relatively close, and when we told him we were from Wisconsin, he told us he was a big Packers fan!

Dropped us off and gave directions to the ship, found a store for the post card folks, (Stamp to USA was 2 Eu) asked where I could find that fermented shark and they directed me to a grocery store 3 blocks away.

Walked the street, visited another few shops, took a pict e with a troll, bought some must have souvenirs, but passed on a puffin hat ...We did find a small food truck offering the fermented shark! Three pebble sized pieces for 650 Kr...about $4.50 US...little taste actually soft, light salt and a bit sour, I offered a small piece to Lynn, she declined, so I ate all three...no problems!!

On the walk back to the ship, I took a picture of the Sargasso Weeds, and talked to a number of the crew who seemed to acknowledge us.

On the ship, rested up, dinner, the dining room was very sparce, no one other than us at the table; we went to the magician show, retired to the room for a brief nap, then to watch the Liar's Club at 10:15. Lots of fun, The stories were funny and imaginable.

Day 19, Thursday, August 17th, 2023. Partly cloudy, 53 degrees F; Today we have the passport check, we are also visiting Isafjordur, Iceland. We are here from 8-5. Lynn has another pedicure at 9, so I will try to catch up on paperwork and prepare for the day and our departure on Friday. Since Lynn has the walker, we bypassed the long line and were in and out in 5 minutes, looks like we will be tendered in, Lynn may not go ashore. It took a bit over 4 hours to check and stamp everyone's passport.

We both went ashore, I pointed out two oyster beds to the crew, as we waited for the tender...Only about 10 minutes to the dock, this like the other Icelandic port, was industrial. Walk a block to the parking lot, only private and celebrity tours offered, few cabs.

This port had no cabs, the walk to town about 6 blocks, the guards were no help, we wondered in, took a picture of gas prices, they are by liter, also a three masted sail ship. The one store we did find was a liquor store, another was a resale shop...no effort to sell, not much to see, seems like this stop was just for immigration and security to check all passports and stamp them before leaving tomorrow to stamp them again. The weather is clear, light clouds, a little sprinkle now and then but nothing really to worry about. Temperature in the low 60's F.

Tendered back to the ship, had lunch, then participated in whatever was offered, mini golf, trivia, and guessing games. Dinner was shared with two other new people, and the other couple we had shared the cruise together, passed out the tips, went to the show, then returned to the room to finish packing and charge devices.

The internet still very slow, dial up slow, and like the TV very intermittent, long periods of time "no signal"…

Luggage out before 8, we are to meet in the lounge at 9 A.M. tomorrow morning for debarkation and transit to the airport In Reykjavik, Iceland… our flight out Icelandic Air at 4:45 PM.

Day 20, Friday, August 18, 2023, checked and rechecked all the drawer, closet and bathroom, off for our final on ship breakfast.

A bit before 9, off we went, our luggage was in a different tent? Numbers went 15,16,17, 19….18 was in a different tent along with another 19???

Off to find our transfer bus, asked two different people, found it, tried to get Rolli by our other luggage but was ignored, after assuring he was in bus, I joined Lynn, these buses do not lower, so both of us had difficulty getting in the rear door.

Everyone seated and seat belts on and wait, the bus engine started and stopped four times after lower doors opened and reopened multiple times…oops, transfer luggage and everyone to another bus. I went around, found rollie in the corner of the luggage department, and transferred him myself to assure he was with us!

It was a bit over 50 minutes to the airport, lots of barren land, moss covered wasteland, and at least 8 roundabouts, gas price on sign…285.7Kr/liter. (About $8.35/gal. U.S.)

I self-checked in both us and luggage, not too difficult if you have passports and flight numbers; located the self-baggage deposit, followed the prompts and the luggage was gone. Just a preview of what is to come…ROBOT WORLD!!

Got tired of waiting around, bought a doughnut to share for 500 Kr, asked around about gates and told me I could go through security but that our 4:45 flight to Chicago gate would not be announced till 3:30.

Security here, shoes off no matter, all metal out, computer in separate bin, carry on in separate bin, shoes in separate bin, then both of us wanded and felt, arms, legs, waste bands, ankles…most thorough ever, even more than China!

After security, walk through the shops and stores, a huge selection of alcohol! and yes, we had to buy a puffin souvenir each! A couple self-checkouts here also, with cameras all over the stores.

Check-in was orderly, flight off on time, best in-flight meal ever, shrimp and scallops appetizer, duck confit salad or a fish stew, with warm buns lemon curd for dessert; 6 3/4-hour flight. Landed at O'Hare at 6:20. Wheelchair assist was waiting; Rolli was to be at the oversize luggage... We bypassed most if not all the immigration lines with our Known Traveler ID, now you just look into screen, no passport needed and you're in! Collected our luggage, picked up Rollie, then ff to find the intermodal train on the second floor; you take the one heading east, to the bus terminal, and that is where we waited for the last bus to Milwaukee at 8:45.

Arrived at the bus station at 10:10, Tiffany drove up right behind the bus, upstairs with luggage by 10:55!

That is the end of that adventure!

Noah

Final cruise

This, regrettably will be the last for us. January 14th through the 24th, 2024. 10 days in the Caribbean. It is on our favorite cruise line, Norwegian and with our deteriorating bodies and the deterioration of the airlines and airports, the wars in the Ukraine and Israel and it is another election year, the rest of at least this year will be all political, and hate!

The first two snow storms of this winter just happened the week before flying down to Miami from Milwaukee, the first Tuesday wet, and heavy, the second all day Friday and Saturday morning with our flight scheduled to take off at 6:30 AM…

Friday afternoon at 4P.M., cancelled; "We will get back to you shortly on replacing this flight"…6:35 P.M., power to condo out.

6:15 A.M. email from American rerouted to Sunday at 6 AM, or take an alternative…selected a 1:15 P.M. Saturday to D.C., and ending up in Miami at 8:30 P.M. , we were not sitting together, but not that long of flights… Oh, and power came back on at 6:30 AM house temperature was down to 63 degrees F.

Called Camille, our ride and she will be picking us up at 10:30. She wasn't sure about the pixel picture we were to photo, hopefully the desk at the airport can help and provide the requested wheelchair for Lynn as originally asked for.

We did take the option, Cammie was on time, we arrived early, confirmed everything at the American Airlines desk, confirmed wheelchair assist that of course was not transferred.

MKE to DC 1:30 FINALLY LEFT at 4:50 P.M., D.C. to Miami was to leave 5:28 (was originally 4:50) was changed to 8:55! We arrived in Miami at 11:45 P.M. called for the shuttle promised by La Quinta hotel where we had reservations and told the shuttle service stopped at 9 P.M. (this was not in the original information) took a cab, asked which La Quinta, we said "airport north" he made a phone call and took us to the correct one….

Checked in, done, asked about cab or transfer to dock in the morning and told they have a service for $15/person plus tip; which I opted for at 10 A.M.

Educating Noah...Travelin'

Sunday, First day of cruise, the transfer was cheaper than the cab and 4-5 times farther, the baggage handler at the pier said it was customary to give a tip for tagging and delivering the two bags to the cabin, so already it started...I tipped so we would actually get our bags!

Norwegian Encore has 17 decks, we checked in, our cabin was on the 10th deck and the last aft inside cabin 10603, located after the 10900 series(??) the smallest cabin we have ever had!

This cruise 4008 passengers, 1800 crew; the steward said last cruise was 4600!

First day at sea, played games, sunned, ate, familiarized ourselves to the ship, tried to install internet on phones, after a number attempts settled for partial...everyone wants everyone to use /live by the phone!!

We were contestants in the not so newlywed game with three other couples, we didn't win...but throughout the cruise we were recognized and congratulated on being the most interesting of the couples!

Day three Puerto Plata, Dominican Republic; walked the area at the end of the pier, extensive shops, both of had fish pedicures, $20 each, for 10 minutes in little tanks of water and small fish nibbling...during the sessions we hand danced with the attendants, and after, both of us felt great!

Back on the ship, played trivia's, contests, and origami, and of course got a bit of sun.

Day four, San Juan, Puerto Rico; tour at 7:30 'El Yunque Rain Forest Drive" We have been to this island before but never the rain forests so this was the only excursion I signed us up for on the cruise do to Lynn's severe limited mobility.

Nice views of the island, four stops and we learned a lot of interesting facts. Christmas is celebrated from Nov.1-3rd week in January, no evergreens grown on the island, most trees imported from the southern hemisphere, never colder than 55 degrees F, more humid than Florida, frequent power outages, rain comes and goes quickly, flowers bloom in summer, and they are U.S. citizens. Back to the ship, sunned, participated in on ship activities, the cheapest beer was $8, plus 20% service and then a tip was also asked for ....

Noah

Day five, Tortola, British Virgin Islands; Lynn not feeling well and tired, I walked the area around the end of the pier and bought her a hoody since the air on the ship was cooler that most liked including the crew! Found the stones I needed to bring back for friends, spent the balance of the day on board, sunning and participating in events.

I stopped at customer relations, asked if any informative lectures, nope, asked if anything more than one show time musical played three times though out the cruise with reservations required, and nope, three comedians had several shows, and that was it for entertainment… I asked for a supervisor, and explained that Lynn was having increasing problems with the eight-inch threshold to enter our bathroom and if there was a handicap room available in that we had tried a month before the cruise and told the ship was full, but that there were now 600 less passengers, any accommodation?... PLEASE.

She asked me to wait , disappeared for about ten minutes , then told me one handicap cabin was not taken; and she would enable us to switch cabins; I asked if there would be a charge, she said "no" and would send an attendant to our room to facilitate the change!

I got Lynn, we repacked, and we moved to 13627; a cabin on the 13th deck midship! WOW!!

Day six, St. John's, Antigua; Lynn not up to walking, light rain, most of day, I did explore town area, same, same, high-end jewelry, watches and souvenir shops along with a few taverns and restaurants; specialty restaurants actually requiring collared shirts and long pants! We had a complimentary invite for one and it was very nice. I had also complained about the new cabin had no hot water in the shower, our new attendant Su; ran the water extensively and solved the problem.

Day seven, St. Maarten, Phillipsburg… 33 sq. mile island, smallest landmass in the world governed by two nations, the Netherlands and France. 99 nationalities inhabit this island, blending European and Caribbean cultures and known for the culinary capital of the Caribbean. Lynn opted to stay aboard it is lightly raining again off and on, I did do some exploring on the island, not much different than the other islands, and returned to the ship to keep Lynn company and work the games and events.

Day eight, St. Thomas, Virgin Islands; the only place in the USA where you drive on the left side of the road; St. Thomas known as rock city due to hilly terrain. "Discovered" in 1493 by Columbus, the

Educating Noah...Travelin'

English, Dutch, French, Spanish, Knights of Malta, and Danes have ruled this island; the U.S. bought from Denmark for $25 million in gold.

Lynn stayed on ship, we were the third ship back on the extensive pier, which meant the walk to shore was extinctive with no rides offered, it was a ½ mile to town via cab, I walked around the area explored some shops, and yes, a bit of rain on and off, we were only docked here from 6A.M to 2P.M. so I returned to the ship to get a little sun and join Lynn in activities. We did attend an adult comedy show in the theatre; a woman in the front row would not stop talking and heckling for ½ the show, we all booed her and someone finally went down to talk to her, but you could see a phone she was holding so I guess she was recording her encounter; everyone felt bad about the comedian who was treated so badly!

Day nine, day at sea, most chairs on deck hogged, we did secure two and did get some sun.

Day ten, was to be Bahamas; the sea was very calm, but they claimed too rough for the tenders, so landing was cancelled and we continued to sail..."so sorry, too bad" no apologies and when talking in the elevators, I agreed with others something other than high seas cancelled the tenders...I suspect too many cruise ships at this port....but no consequence's, so everyone stays on board, casino and all bars open...money for the cruise line!!

Oh, and since it was a nice sunny, calm day, there were no chairs available on deck.

Day eleven return home, disembarkation went relatively smoothly, TSA is facial and just a show of passports, luggage was found easily and the transfer bus was waiting for us.

At the airport we checked in , got our wheelchair, the gate was at the other end of the airport, and we had a 3 ½ hour wait, the plane was on time, loading went well and no events when we flew. Arrived a bit early in Chicago, the gate was far from the baggage area and we were lucky to have the wheelchair, after luggage pickup we were dropped off at the shuttle train to take us to the transportation hub.

We saw our bus outside, and rushed to it, the driver said we were too late, at 4:33 and would not open the luggage door or let us in...then stayed at that spot till 4:46??? We complained to the attendant and he

Noah

agreed with us that she was just lazy…we did call Coach USA to complain, and did catch the next bus at 5:30. Home and picked up by Tiffany

Notes: NCL like Celebrity have declined in quality, this ship is more like Carnival, with service charges for everything except basics including a mandatory $25/guest per person gratuity, there was also a special area called the Haven which access was only for member to the tune of $25/person /day if you wanted.

Don't get me wrong, the cruise lines have become more corporate where money is more than anything else, the service people are as friendly and helpful as ever along with the lower workers and staff, and they are less staffed and work harder, but as the rank goes up the more corporate takes over.

Trivia:

What % of plants require pollination? 80%

What country has the largest bowling alley in the world? Japan

How many National parks in the U.S.? 63

What is the periodic symbol for lead? PB

What country has the most vending machines per capita? Japan

Where did bagels originate? Poland

THIS IS THE END OF OUR WORLD TOURING.

We have seen enough of the world, we will continue on short USA trips, but no more extensive week or more trips by planes, trains or automobiles. Lynn is having her second hip replaced soon, I am starting to have balance problems and my replacements are beginning to fail along with memory and thought loss for both of us. We are both eating half portions, and I only have one goal left and that is to live longer than my father. We will be moving into an apartment within the next two years and we realize we have done more than most getting the best education in the world by experiencing it in travel and experience!

Educating Noah...Travelin'

www.ingramcontent.com/pod-product-compliance
Lightning Source LLC
Chambersburg PA
CBHW041315110526
44591CB00021B/2792